Integration of Customary and Modern Legal Systems in Africa

UNIVERSITY OF IFE

INSTITUTE OF AFRICAN STUDIES

A Conference held at Ibadan

on 24th - 29th August 1964

AFRICANA PUBLISHING CORPORATION · NEW YORK
and
UNIVERSITY OF IFE PRESS · ILE-IFE, NIGERIA

Published in the United States of America 1971
by Africana Publishing Corporation
101 Fifth Avenue, New York, N.Y. 10003

Great Britain: Meier & Holmes Ltd.
18-22 Inverness Street, London N.W. 1

Germany: Internationaler Universitaets-Buchhandel
Muenchen 15, Landwehrstr 37

Library of Congress Catalog Card No. 71-151214
ISBN-0-8419-0068-x

Printed in Nigeria by
The Caxton Press (West Africa) Limited, Ibadan

DIRECTOR OF THE CONFERENCE

PROFESSOR ANTONY ALLOTT

WORKING COMMITTEE

Dr. S. O. Biobaku, C.M.G. (*Chairman*)

Dr. F. A. Ajayi

Prof. O. R. Marshall

Mr. R. L. Marshall

Mr. E. B. Craig

Mr. A. B. Kasunmu

Mr. D. D. Abasiekong

Mrs. Frances Ademola

Edited by The Law Faculty, University of Ifẹ

CONTENTS

Introduction ix
Abbreviations and Modes of Citation xvii
Table of Cases xix

PART I

GENERAL

1. A Note on Previous Conferences on African Law 4
   by Professor A. N. Allott.

2. A Background Paper on Restatement of Laws in Africa 18
   by Professor A. N. Allott and Eugene Cotran

3. Critical Observations regarding the Potentialities and 44
   the Limitations of Legislation in the Independent
   African States *by Rene David.*

4. Some Remarks on Law and Courts in Africa 58
   by J. Keuning.

5. The role of justice in the application of the law in the 74
   francophone states of Africa, *by Michel Alliot*
   (translated).

6. Discussing African Law *by Professor A. N. Allott.* 86

7. Integration of Legal Systems in the Somali Republic 94
   by Dr. Paolo Contini.

8. The Judicial Development of Customary Law in 116
   Nigeria *by Dr. F. A. Ajayi.*

PART II

LAW OF CONTRACTS AND CIVIL WRONGS

9. Integration of the Law of Contracts 136
   by B. O. Nwabueze.

v

10. The Law of Contract and of Civil Wrongs in French—   160
Speaking Africa *by Rene David.*

11. The Codification of the Law of Civil Wrongs in   170
Common Law African Countries
by Professor A. N. Allott.

PART III

LAND LAW

12. Integration in the Field of Land Law   200
by Chief F. R. A. Williams

13. Problems of Harmonisation of Traditional and   216
Modern Concepts in the Land by Law of French-
speaking Africa and Madagascar
by Xavier Blanc-Jouvan

PART IV

LAW OF SUCCESSION

14. Integration of the Customary and the General   242
(English) Laws of Succession in Eastern Nigeria
by Dr. N. Okoro

15. Integration in the Field of the Law of Succession in   260
the Mid-Western Region of Nigeria *by M. Odje.*

16. The Law of Succession in Ghana *by N. Ollennu*   294

17. Law of Succession in Uganda *by H. F. Morris*   312

PART V

MARRIAGE AND DIVORCE

18. Integration of the Law of Husband and Wife in   330
Western Nigeria *by A. B. Kasunmu*

19. Towards the Integration of the Laws Relating to   352
Husband and Wife in Ghana
by W. C. Ekow Daniels

20. The Law of Husband and Wife in East Africa 396
by James Read.

21. Integration of the Laws of Marriage and Divorce in 412
Kenya *by Eugene Cotran.*

22. Birth, Death and the Marriage Acts: Some Problems 438
in Conflict of Laws *by J. W. Salacuse.*

Names of participants in the Conference 459

INTRODUCTION

I The Conference

The 1964 Conference on the Integration of Customary and Modern Legal Systems in Africa held at the University of Ife was not the first conference to discuss the problems of integration or harmonization or unification of "laws and courts" in Africa. Indeed as shown in one of the background papers presented—Professor Allott's paper on Discussing African Law—, the Ife Conference was the fourth of a series of conferences first called since 1960 to discuss the problems attended to above.

The Ife Conference was in a sense, a follow-up to the London, Dar es Salaam and Venice conferences. The organisers of the Ife Conference accepted some of the general conclusions reached at these past conferences, that is, the desirability of having an integrated system of "laws and courts" in certain fields within a given legal order in Africa. How should this integration, particularly in the field of the applicable laws, be carried through? Is it something which should be done solely by the courts or through legislation? These then were some of the immediate concerns of the Ife Conference. In the words of the organisers, the conference was intended "to demonstrate how practical legal draughtsmen, judges and jurists can reconcile and harmonise co-existing systems of traditional and non-traditional law."

Background papers were invited from some participants and these were circulated beforehand to those who presented papers on the integration of laws on certain specified topics chosen by the organisers. Land law, Succession, Husband and Wife (including marriage, custody, divorce, etc.) Civil wrong and Contracts were chosen as areas of concentrated study.

This volume brings together all the papers presented at this conference. The records of the daily proceedings are however, not included. All the papers published in this volume were submitted in English except Professor Alliot's paper on "The Role of Justice on the Application of law in the Francophone States of Africa" which was submitted in French but was translated into English by Mr. Peter Flynn formerly of the Faculty of Law, University of Ife. A striking feature of some of the papers published is the recurring themes emerging from the different papers, indicating that the problems posed in many of the jurisdictions considered are fairly common. This is not surprising since most of the countries discussed were formerly British controlled, and the received laws in these territories are invariably the same. The solutions however suggested and advocated by many of the participants are in some instances different.

II. The Background Papers

The essays contained in the first part of this book are the background papers and essays on the integration and administration of justice read at the Conference. In a joint paper by Professor Allott and Mr. Cotran, the problems of restatement of laws in Africa are reconsidered, particular attention being given to the Restatement of Customary Law project of the School of Oriental and African Studies, University of London, under the directorship of Professor Allott.

No one who is familiar with the African scene will dispute the importance of a restatement either of the various customary laws or of the received laws applicable on the African countries. In the traditional or native courts, the judges who invariably are elders in the locality are presumed to know the customary laws of their area even though these are unwritten. One only has to read reports of these native courts and also the conflicting testimonies of chiefs on customary law in the superior courts to see the appalling ignorance of what the law is. The value of a restatement of customary law is also obvious if one looks at the reforms of native court personnel now taking place in many African countries. No longer are these courts presided over by laymen, but by trained lawyers. If what happens in Nigeria is anything to go by, there is the tendency for these lawyer-presidents of native courts to apply English law in the guise of customary law.

The various approaches to the problem of restatement are fully discussed in this joint paper. The University of London restatement project has already resulted in the publication of a volume by Mr. Cotran and published by Sweet and Maxwell on the restatement of the law of marriage on Kenya. One problem which arises in connection with a restatement project is the method adopted in ascertaining the law in a given area prior to restatement. Professor Twining has, in a 1963 lecture delivered at the University of Chicago Law School, expressed concern on the methods used in both the Kenya and Tanzanian Projects[1] in that "the standard research tool of anthropologists in the investigation of so-called 'primitive law' has not

---

1.   The Tanzania project has resulted in the enactment of the Local Customary law (Declaration) Order 1963.

been employed."[2] He was referring to what he called the detailed reporting and analysis of actual trouble cases as opposed to questioning of either individual informants or a panel of experts. Mr. Cotran has, in the paper on the Restatement of laws in Africa, defended the method used in Kenya. Analysing "trouble cases" from the case files of the African courts he says would be worthless since only some 5 % of these cases would be of any assistance.

One of the problems hotly debated at the conference was whether any change in the law should be brought about by legislation or through the judicial process. The Blackstonian theory of judges discovering but not making the law did not find much support in Professor Keuning's paper on "Law and Courts in Africa" nor in Dr. Ajayi's contribution on "Judicial development of Customary law in Nigeria". In fact, they both advocated a more vigorous creative role on the part of judges. Keuning would like the judges to re-interpret the traditional law for their own times, extend it, and where necessary, supplement it in new situations, bearing in mind that " their legal creation [must] remain in harmony with the framework of the customary legal system, so that an optimal amount of certainty is achieved and the mutual cohesion of the rules continues to exist in the law on the move."

Dr. Ajayi's paper is of further interest in that he discusses some of the judicial techniques—historical, analogy and evolution— used by the courts in the development of customary law. He adverts to some of the problems of judicial lawmaking especially on how the doctrine of judicial precedent could lead to a premature crystallization of customary law. One can also refer here to the dangers inherent in the use of analogy as a tool of development, particularly to the confused thinking this has brought on the West African scene in the attempt to explain the position of a family head via the concept of a trust, and also explaining family property in terms of co-ownership under English law.

There is no doubt that the judicial process takes a longer time as opposed to legislative measures in effecting a change. Many of the African countries cannot afford the time to wait for a judicial change in the face of the many urgent problems which have to be solved. Furthermore, the nature of the judicial process itself limits the scope of judicial lawmaking. The legislature is not bound by any doctrine of precedent, and has at its disposal wider investigatory powers and procedure than the courts. However, the legislature must avoid

2.   Twining, *The place of customary law in the national legal systems of East Africa*, The Law School, University of Chicago, 1963 at p. 47 See also, Tanner, "The codification of Customary law in Tanzania", (1966) vol. 2, E. A. L. J., 105.

passing what Professor Michel Alliot in his paper calls 'revolutionary legislations' which appear in statutes only but are seldom observed and enforced. An example of such an ill-fated legislation was the introduction of the Swiss Civil Code into Turkey in 1926, a point referred to in Professor Keuning's paper. In a critical paper on the 'Potentialities and Limitations of Legislation', Professor Réné David attempts to isolate those areas where the legislator must act with caution. He provides ample justification for the introduction of a European (French) civil code of contract into Ethiopia. Not many people however will share Professor David's inhibition of legislative inaction in areas predominantly governed by custom. In fact, it would seem that it is in these areas—land, marriage and divorce, succession—that urgent legislative action is needed.

The problem of integration often faced by many African countries is either in integrating customary law with the received law, or in integrating the traditional courts with the Western type of courts. However, the integration problem in the Somali Republic is a bit more complicated. The republic arose as a result of a merger of the former British Protectorate of Somaliland (where English law applies) and the Italian trust administered territory of Somalia, where Italian law applies. The attempts made at integration are sketched out in Dr. Contini's paper and this should be of interest to those connected with the administration of justice in the Cameroons Republic where a similar attempt is going on in a triangular marriage of French, customary, and English laws.

III. Land Law

The inclusion of problems relating to land as a specialised area of concentration at the Conference is not at all surprising. After all, despite the urge to industrialise, agriculture is, and will for some time still be the mainstay of the economy of most of the Sub-Saharan African countries. The problems facing agricultural development in many of the African countries are intimately connected with the traditional system of land holding. Land originally cannot be alienated, and even when this is allowed, the machinery and conditions governing alienation are so cumbersome and unreliable that one invariably buys a law suit. This at least, is the position in southern Nigeria. Furthermore, but for recent developments, the use of documents to evidence title was not known under customary law, and no creditor will risk giving out a loan secured only by an oral title. The right to hold land was not strictly tied down to the ability to use land. One can go on *ad infinitum* listing the many impediments customary land tenure has on agricultural development.

But does one have to jettison customary law completely in the field of land law in favour of a Western type of land tenure? Should the land tenure structure be individualistic or communal in nature in order to support rapid growth in agriculture? President Nyerere in his famous exposition of African socialism has rejected the "capitalist system" of individual ownership of land. "To us in Africa, land was always recognised as belonging to the community." There is also the question of whether interest in land should be freehold or something short of this, either in the form of a leasehold or a right of user like the certificate of occupancy allowed in Northern Nigeria and Tanzania.

The above then are some of the policy decisions which many African countries will have to make in formulating land tenure policies. Professor Blanc-Jouvan alludes to some of these problems in his paper on the harmonization of traditional and modern concepts in the land law of French-speaking Africa and Madagascar. He discusses the land policies of Senegal, Guinea and Madagascar, and relates the differences in land policies to the ideological leanings of the countries concerned. Although Blanc-Jouvan writes specifically on French-speaking Africa, there is no doubt that many African countries will be influenced by the political ideology of the particular state in shaping its future land policy. Kenya and Tanzania in the English-speaking African countries are clear examples of this. The move in Kenya is towards an individualistic type of registered landholding as outlined in Kenya's brand of African Socialism contained in Kenya Sessional Paper No. 10: "African Socialism and its Application to Planning in Kenya." On the other hand, Tanzania is moving towards a communal system of landholding, with the abolition of all freehold interests in land.

Chief Williams in his paper on the integration of land law in Nigeria, focuses attention on the attempts of the court to integrate some aspects of the law. The nagging question of whether a sale of land is void or voidable for want of consent is also discussed. Although Chief Williams will favour the rule that a majority should be able to sell, and that a sale with or without the consent of the family head should be voidable, the decided cases don't support his views. Legislative intervention in the field of land has been negligible. Judging from the newspaper reports and from the many commissions of inquiry into communal land in Nigeria, it would appear that the Communal Rights (Vesting in Trustees) Law of Western Nigeria has not solved the problem for which it was designed—that is, to ensure that communal land is not arbitrarily disposed of by the chiefs or natural rulers.

IV. Husband and Wife, and the law of Succession

Two separate sessions were devoted to the problems of integration of the law of husband and wife, and the law of succession. It will be convenient to deal with these two broad areas together in an introductory essay since the problems relating to both areas are closely interwoven. Nine papers were read in these two areas and the countries covered are: Nigeria, Ghana, Kenya, Uganda and a general paper on East Africa by Mr. Read. The problems posed in many of these papers are identical. This is understandable, since the received laws applicable in the countries covered are similar.

The defects in the existing laws in relation to both statutory and customary marriages were fully discussed and suggestions made as to how to remedy these defects. Starting first with customary law in relation to husband and wife, the vagueness of the law in relation to age of marriage, the precise time at which a marriage comes into existence, prohibited marriages, and the proving of the existence of a marriage are among the problems tackled. There was a unanimous agreement that it is desirable to introduce a system of registration as a means of proving customary marriage, but that non-registration should not affect the validity of the marriage. The informality of proceedings for divorce under customary law, and the attempts at effecting a reconciliation which is of prime importance in divorce proceedings under customary law came in for special mention. The reforms being proposed by the Governments of Ghana, Uganda and Kenya have also given prominence to the reconciliatory and informal approach to divorce under customary law.

In the application of the received English law relating to marriage, there was again a general criticism of the technique of incorporating English law by reference, in that it leads to uncertainties as to the time limit for applying English law, since the law of marriage in England is not static. Which English law, for example, governs age or prohibited degrees to statutory marriages in the countries under consideration?

Family law is a fertile field for internal (or what Kollewijn calls "interpersonal") conflict of laws problem, and Mr. Read discusses the problem posed by double marriages or "double-decker marriages" as he calls it in East Africa. Mr. Salacuse analyses the Nigerian cases involving conflict between customary law and the received law in an attempt to chose the applicable law in a given transaction. The choice of law process extends beyond the act of marriage itself and covers areas like legitimacy and succession. While many people might not agree with Mr. Salacuse's elusive "manner of life test" in choosing the applicable law, the suggestion will yield better results when compared with the inflexible approach of the courts.

The projected legislative attempts at integration in Ghana and Uganda are featured in Dr. Ekow-Daniel's paper and also in Mr. Read's paper. Whether polygamy or monogamy should be abolished was regarded by Mr. Read as a policy decision which has to be taken by politicians and not lawyers. In fact rather than abolish polygamy, the Ghana White Paper on Marriage, Divorce and Inheritance retained the two forms of marriages although the position of a second wife was made less attractive for purposes of inheritance. Mr. Cotran's paper on Kenya deserves special mention in that since writing the paper, he has acted as Secretary to the Commission set up by the Government of Kenya to reform the law of Marriage and Divorce. The report of the Commission published in 1968 reflects some of the points and solutions suggested in Mr. Cotran's paper.

The search for a fair scheme of distributing the property, (both real and personal), of a person who dies intestate dominates both Dr. Okoro and Dr. Odje's papers. They are both critical of the law which automatically applies English law to the distribution of the estate of an African who contracts a statutory or Christian marriage. They both will want to see the extended family being given a share in the distribution of the estate of a deceased person. The different systems of inheritance operating in some of the countries discussed were thought to present a difficult problem for any legislator to integrate. How can one reconcile the matrilineal and the patrilineal schemes described in Justice Ollennu's paper without causing disruption in the social order?

V. Civil wrongs and contract

By including "civil wrongs and contracts" as one of the topics for discussion, the organisers of the Ife Conference could proudly claim to be pioneers in the attempt to focus attention on this aspect of law in Africa. This area has often been neglected in past conferences on African law, and also in many writings on African law. The reason for the exclusion is that it was felt by many that customary law has little or nothing to offer in those fields and one might as well substitute the received law in its entirety.

There are those who argue that there is no law of contract under customary law since one cannot enforce an obligation which is to be performed in the future—that is, an executory contract. Mr. Nwabueze in his paper on "Integrating the law of contract in Nigeria" brings out clearly the basic differences between the conception of a contract under both English and customary laws. He refers to the divergence between customary and English laws on the question of contractual capacity, formal requirements, limitation of action and the doctrine of consideration.

Professor David writes on the codification of the law of civil wrongs in French-speaking African countries while Professor Allott writing on codification in common-law African Countries, provides an organisational framework for structuring a code on civil wrongs. He emphasises the importance of avoiding the use of technical English words like "malice" and antiquated terms like "detinue" and "trespass to the person".

In conclusion, we would like to thank the Ford Foundation whose generous grant for Conferences made to the Institute of African Studies of the University of Ife made the holding of this conference possible. We should also like to thank the Institute of African Studies, whose staff organised this Conference in conjunction with the Faculty of Law, whose members assisted in the editing of these papers for press. Finally we commend the patience and the forebearance of the contributors despite the long delay in the publication of the proceedings of the conference.

A. B. KASUNMU
Acting Dean, Faculty of Law,
University of Ife, 1968/69 Session

ABBREVIATIONS AND MODES OF CITATION

(Only law reports other than those of the United Kingdom are referred to below.)

All N.L.R.	—	All Nigeria Law Reports.
D.Ct.	—	Divisional Court.
D.Ct. '21-25 D.Ct. '26-29 D.Ct. '29-31 D.Ct. '31-37	—	Selected judgments of the D.Cts of the Gold Coast Colony.
E.A.	—	Eastern African Law Reports.
E.A.L.R.	—	East Africa Protectorate Law Reports.
E.A.C.A.	—	Court of Appeal for East Africa.
E.N.L.R.	—	Eastern Nigeria Law Reports.
F.Ct.	—	Full Court.
F.Ct. '20-'21 F.Ct. '22 F.Ct. '23-'25 F.Ct. '26-'29	—	Judgments of the F.Ct. of the Gold Coast Colony.
F.S.C.	—	Federal Supreme Court of Nigeria.
G.L.R.	—	Ghana Law Reports.
K.L.R.	—	Kenya Law Reports.
L.L.R.	—	Lagos High Court Law Reports.
N.L.R. N.R.L.R.	—	Nigerian Law Reports.
N.R.N.L.R.	—	Northern Region (Nigeria) Law Reports.
R. & N.	—	Rhodesia and Nyasaland Law Reports.
Red.	—	Redwar Reports, Gold Coast
Ren.	—	Renner Reports Gold Goast.
Sar. F.L.R.	—	Sarbah, Fanti Customary Laws.
T.L.R.	—	Tanganyika Law Reports.
U.L.R.	—	Uganda Law Reports.
W.A.C.A.	—	West Africa Court of Appeal.
W.A.L.R.	—	West African Law Reports.
W.N.L.R. W.R.N.L.R.	—	Western (Region) Nigeria Law Reports.
Z.L.R.	—	Zanzibar Law Reports.

TABLE OF CASES

A. G. *v.* Egbuna (1945) 18 N.L.R. 1

Abbapesiwa *v.* Krakue (1943) 9 W.A.C.A. 161

Abdi *v.* Abdulla (unreported)

Abdulrahman bin Mohamed & ano *v.* R [1963] E.A. 188

Abiodun Re Soluade & Beckley (1943) 17 N.L.R. 59

Ackah *v.* Arinta (1893) Sar. F.L.R. 79

Ackworth *v.* Ackworth [1943] P. 21

Adedubu *v.* Makanjuola (1944) 10 W.A.C.A. 33

Adegbola *v.* Folaranmi (1921) 3 N.L.R. 81

Adeline Subulade Williams Re, (1941) 7 W.A.C.A. 156

Adeoye *v.* Adeoye (1961) All N.L.R. 792

Adewonyin *v.* Ishola (1958) W.N.L.R. 110

Adjei *v.* Ripley (1956) 1 W.A.L.R. 62

Agbo *v.* Udo (1947) 18 N.L.R. 152

Agboruja, Estate of (1949) 19 N.L.R. 38

Aggryba *v.* Aban (1845) Sar. F.C.L. 118

Aileru *v.* Anibi (1951) 20 N.L.R. 46

Aiyede *v.* Norman Williams (1960) L.L.R. 253

Ajayi *v.* White (1940) 18 N.L.R. 41

Ajibabi *v.* Jura (1948) 19 N.L.R. 27

Akwapim *v.* Budu Div. Ct. 1931-37, 89

Akwei *v.* Deodei (Ed) 3 W.A.L.R. 132

Alake *v.* Awawu (1932) 11 N.L.R. 39

Alake *v.* Pratt (1955) 15 W.A.C.A. 20

Alayo *v.* Tunwase (1946) 18 N.L.R. 88

Alhaji Amodu & John Holt *v.* Idah (1956) N.R.N.L.R. 81

Amachree *v.* Goodhcad (1924) 4 N.L.R. 99

Amarfio *v.* Ayorkor (1954) 14 W.A.C.A. 554

Ammetifi, Isaac Re (1889) Red. 157

Angu *v.* Attah [1916] P.C. 74-28, 43

Aoko *v.* Fagbemi (1961) W.N.L.R. 147

Apatira *v.* Akanke (1944) 17 N.L.R. 149

Aralawon *v.* Aromire (1940) 15 N.L.R. 90

Ashogbon *v.* Oduntan (1935) 12 N.L.R. 7

Ashon *v.* Snyper (1869) Sar. F.C.L. 136

Ashong *v.* Ashong (unreported)

Asiata *u.* Goncallo (1900) 1 N.L.R. 41

Asiedu *v.* Ofori (unreported)

Asumah *v.* Khair (1959) G.L.R. 353
Ata *v.* Henshaw (1930) 10 N.L.R. 65
Awo *v.* Gam (1913) 2 N.L.R. 100
Ayoola *v.* Folawiyo (1942) 8 W.A.C.A. 39
Bachoo *v.* Bolia (1946) 13 E.A.C.A. 50
Baindail *v.* Baindail [1940] P. 122
Bajulaiye *v.* Akapo (1938) 14 N.L.R. 10
Bakare *v.* Coker (1935) 12 N.L.R. 31
Balogun *v.* Balogun (1943) 9 W.A.C.A. 78
Balogun *v.* Balogun (1934) 2 W.A.C.A. 290
Balogun *v.* Oshodi (1929) 10 N.L.R. 36
Bamgbose *v.* Daniel (1952) 14 W.A.C.A. 111; [1955] A.C. 107
Barnes *v.* Mayan (1871) Sar. F.C.L. 180
Bassey *v.* Cobham (1924) 5 N.L.R. 90
Baxter *v.* Baxter [1949] A.C. 277
Becker *v.* Becker (unreported)
Bethel Re, (1887) 38 Ch.D. 220
Binba *v.* Mensah (1897) Sar. F.C.L. 137
Boham *v.* Marshall (1892) Sar. F.C.L. 193
Bolajoko *v.* Layeni (1949) 19 N.L.R. 99
Brimah *v.* Asana (unreported)
Buraimo *v.* Bamigboye (1940) 15 N.L.R. 139
Captain *v.* Ankrah (1951) 13 W.A.C.A. 151
Carboo *v.* Carboo (unreported)
Caulcrick *v.* Harding (1926) 7 N.L.R. 48
Chaware *v.* Johnson (1935) 12 N.L.R. 4
Cheni *v.* Cheni [1963] 2 W.L.R. 17
Chiba *v.* Agoowah (1873) Sar. F.C.L. 128
Coker *v.* Coker (1943) 17 N.L.R. 55
Coker *v.* Coker (1938) 14 N.L.R. 83
Cole *v.* Akinyele (1960) 5 F.S.C. 84
Cole *v.* Cole (1898) 1 N.L.R. 15
Coleman *v.* Shang (1959) G.L.R. 390; [1961] 2 All E.R. 406;
    [1961] A.C. 481
Comm. Eastern Provinces *v.* Ononye (1944) 17 N.L.R. 142
Comm. of Police *v.* Ewiah (1956) 1 W.A.L.R. 69
Cowern *v.* Nield [1912] 2. K.B. 419
Currie *v.* Misa (1875) L.R. 10 Ex. 153
Davies *v.* Randall (unreported)
Davy-Hayford *v.* Davy-Hayford (unreported)
DeGraftt *v.* Mensah (1871) Sar. F.C.L. 125
Din, Estate of, (unreported)
Dolling *v.* Dolling (unreported)
Dolphyne *v.* Ansah (1885) Ren. 60

Duncan v. Robertson (1891) Sar. F.C.L. 134
Dunlop v. Selfridge [1915] A.C. 79
Edet v. Essien (1932) 11 N.L.R. 47
Eferekuman Aro v. Jaja (1925) 6 N.L.R. 24
Egebor v. Agberegbe (unreported)
Ehigie v. Ehigie (1961) W.N.L.R. 307; (1961) All N.L.R. 842
Ekpendu v. Erika (1959) 4 F.S.C. 79
Eleko v. Officer Administering the Govt. of Nigeria [1931] A.C. 662
Engman v. Engman (unreported)
Ero v. Ero (unreported)
Esan v. Faro (1947) 12 W.A.C.A. 135
Fagawa v. Kano N. A. (1958) N.R.N.L.R. 64
Ferguson v. Duncan (1953) 14 W.A.C.A. 316
Fonesca v. Passman (1958) W.N.L.R. 41
Fowler v. Martins (1924) 5 N.L.R. 45
Gall v. Gall (unreported)
Giwa v. Ottun (1932) 11 N.L.R. 160
Godwin v. Crowther (1934) 2 W.A.C.A. 109
Golightly v. Ashrifi (1955) 14 W.A.C.A. 676
Gooding v. Martins (1942) 8 W.A.C.A. 108
Griffin v. Talabi (1948) 12 W.A.C.A. 371
Haastrup v. Coker (1927) 8 N.L.R. 68
Half Jack v. John (1911-1916) D&F 60
Halmond v. Daniel (1871) Sar. F.C.L. 182
Hawkes v. Saunders (1782) 1 Cowper 289
Hogan, In the Matter of (1886) Sar. F.L.R. 92
Hotonu, Re (unreported)
Hughes v. Davies (1909) Ren. 550
Husi v. Ali (unreported)
Hussen v. Min. of Interior (unreported)
Hyde v. Hyde (1866) L.R. 1 P&D. 130
Idowu v. Adisa (1957) W.N.L.R. 167
Inasa v. Oshodi (1930) 11 N.L.R. 10
Inyang v. Ita (1929) 9 N.L.R. 84
Jacobs v. Oladunni (1935) 12 N.L.R. 1
Jirigho v. Anamali (1958) W.N.L.R. 195
Jones v. Mends (1872) F.C.L. 128
Jordan's case (1528) Y.B. 19 Hen. VIII F. 24
Kabui v. R. (1954) 21 E.A.C.A. 260
Kajubi v. Kabali (1944) 11 E.A.C.A. 34
Kallin v. Kallin (1944) S.A.S.R. 73
Kassim v. Kassim [1962] 3 W.L.R. 865
Khoo Leong v. Kwee [1926] A.C. 525
King v. Williams (1824) 2 B&C. 538

Koney *v.* U.T.C. (1934) 2 W.A.C.A. 185
Konobi *v.* Le Mantse (1946) 12 W.A.C.A. 102
Kosi *v.* Nimo (unreported)
Kosoko *v.* Nakoji (1959) N.N.L.R. 15
Kugbuyi *v.* Odunjo (1926) 7 N.L.R. 51
Kwakye *v.* Tubah (unreported)
Kwesi-Johnson *v.* Effie (1953) 14 W.A.C.A. 254
Labinjoh *v.* Abake (1924) 5 N.L.R. 33
Lamb *v.* Threshie 29 Sc. L.R. 727
Lawal *v.* Younan (1961) All N.L.R. 245
Lewis *v.* Bankole (1908) 1 N.L.R. 105
Lintott Bros *v.* Solomon (1888) Sar. F.L.R. 87
Machi *v.* Machi (1960) L.L.R. 103
Majiyagbe *v.* A. G. (1957) N.N.L.R. 158
Malek Sultan *v.* Jeraj (1954) 22 E.A.C.A. 142
Malomo *v.* Olushola (1954) 21 N.L.R. 1
Mankata *v.* Anorli (Ed:) 1 W.A.L.R. 169
Many *v.* Kumah (unreported)
Martins *v.* Fowler [1926] A.C. 740
Mawji *v.* R. 23 E.A.C.A. 609; [1957] A.C. 126
Mensah *v.* Krakue (1894) Sar. F.L.R. 87
Mensah *v.* Lomoh (1935) Div. Ct. (1931-37) 119
Mercantile Union Guarantee Corp. *v.* Ball [1937] 2 K.B. 498
Miller Bros. *v.* Ayeni (1924) 5 N.L.R. 42
Mogaji *v.* Nuga (1960) 5 F.S.C. 107
Mphumeya *v.* R. (1956) R&N. 240
Mwakio Nwanguku *v.* R. (1930) 1 T.L.R. 602
Neizer *v.* Donton (1874) Sar. F.C.L. 129
Nelson *v.* Akorifanmi (1959) L.L.R. 143
Nelson *v.* Nelson (1951) 13 W.A.C.A. 248
Nelson *v.* Tackie (unreported)
Neva *v.* R. (1961) R&N 538
Newton *v.* Holm (1913) D&F (1911-1916)
Nimo *v.* Donkor (unreported)
Ntiashagwo *v.* Amodu (1959) W.R.N.L.R. 273
Nwokedi *v.* Nwokedi (1958) L.L.R. 94
Nwugoge *v.* Adigwe (1934) 11 N.L.R. 134
Nyali Ltd. *v.* A. G. [1955] 1 All E.R. 646
Odunjoh *v.* Odunjoh (unreported)
Ohochuku *v.* Ohochuku [1960] 1 All E.R. 253; [1960] 1 W.L.R. 183
Okiji *v.* Adejobi (1960) 5 F.S.C. 44
Okoe *v.* Ankrah (unreported)
Okolie *v.* Ibo (1958) N.R.N.L.R. 89
Okonkwo *v.* Eze (1960) N.R.N.L.R. 80

Okpaku v. Okpaku (1947) 12 W.A.C.A. 137
Okua v. Yankah (1894) Ren. 109
Oloko v. Giwa (1939) 15 N.L.R. 31
Omodion v. Fasoro (1960) W.R.N.L.R. 27
Onwudinjo v. Onwudinjo (1957) 2 E.R.L.R. 1
Oshodi v. Balogun (1936) 4 W.A.C.A. 1
Oshodi v. Dakolo (1928) 9 N.L.R. 13
Oshodi v. Imoru (1936) 3 W.A.C.A. 83
Otoo Re. (1926-29) Div. Ct. 84
P. Z. & Co. v. Gusau (1961) N.R.N.L.R. 1
Pappoe v. Wingrove (1921-25) Div. Ct. 2
Pearce v. Aderoku (1936) 13 N.L.R. 9
Penin v. Duncan (1869) Sar. F.C.L 118
Phillip v. Phillip (1946) 18 N.L.R. 102
Pillans v. Van Mierop (1765) 3 Burr. 1663
Quassua v. Ward (1845) Sar. F.C.L. 117
Quaye v. Kuevi (1931-7) Div. Ct. 69
Queen v. President & Members of Akugbene Grade 'C' Court, Ex.
    p. Chief Carter (1960) W.N.L.R. 146
R. v. Amkeyo (1917) 7 E.A.L.R. 14
R. v. Bassey Mba (1939) 15 N.L.R. 53
R. v. Ebong (1947) 12 W.A.C.A. 139
R. v. Menans (1922) F. Ct. 61
R. v. Obongo (1920) 3 U.L.R. 31
R. v. Odongo (1926) 10 K.L.R. 49
R. v. Oumu (1915) 2 U.L.R. 152
R. v. Robin (1929) 12 K.L.R. 134
R. v. Sarwan Singh [1962] 3 All E.R. 612
R. v. Toya (1930) 14 K.L.R. 145
Risk v. Risk [1951] P. 50
Rotibi v. Savage (1944) 17 N.L.R. 77
S. C. O. A. Zaria v. Okon (1960) N.R.N.L.R. 273
Sackey v. Okantah (1911-16) D&F 88
Sackeyfio v. Tagoe (1945) 11 W.A.C.A. 73
Sackie v. Agawa (1873) Sar. F.C.L. 126
Sapara, Re (1911) Ren. 605
Sarah Adadevoh, Re (1951) 13 W.A.C.A. 304
Savage v. Macfoy (1909) Ren. 504
Sec. of State v. Rukhminibai A.I.R. [1937] Nag. 354
Setse v. Setse [1959] G.L.R. 155
Shorunke v. R [1936] A.C. 316
Sinha Peerage Claim [1946] 1 All E.R. 348
Smith v. Smith (1924) 5 N.L.R. 105
Sogunro Davies v. Sogunro (1929) 7 N.L.R. 79

Soluade & Beckley, Re (1943) 17 N.L.R. 50
Somefun, Re (1941) 7 W.A.C.A. 156
Sowa v. Sowa [1961] 1 All E.R. 687
Suberu v. Sumonu (1957) 2 F.S.C. 33
Sulemon v. Johnson (1951) 13 W.A.C.A. 213
Swapim v. Ackuwa (1888) Sar. F.Ct. L. 191
Tamakloe v. Attipoe & ano (unreported)
Thomas v. Thomas [1842] 2 G.B. 851
Thynne v. Thynne [1955] P. 272
Tijani v. Sec. Southern Provinces (1921) 3 N.L.R. 21
U. A. C. Nigeira v. Edems & Ajayi (1958) N.R.N.L.R. 33
Ugbona v. Morah (1940) 15 N.L.R. 78
Uso v. Iketubosun (1957) W.N.L.R. 187
Uwani v. Nwosu Akom (1928) 8 N.L.R. 19
Vasila v. Worsta (1920) 3 U.L.R. 26
Welbeck v. Brown (1882) Sar. F.C.L. 185
Wilkinson v. Rogers (1864) 12 W.R. 119
Williams v. Williams (unreported)
Wilson v. Glossop (1888) 20 Q.B.D. 354
Wobill v. Kra & ano. (1947)12 W.A.C.A. 181
Wobo v. A. G. for Federation (unreported)
Yaotey's case (unreported)
Young v. Young (unreported)

PART I

GENERAL

A NOTE ON PREVIOUS CONFERENCES ON AFRICAN LAW

by

A. N. ALLOTT

PROFESSOR OF AFRICAN LAW, UNIVERSITY OF LONDON;
DIRECTOR, RESTATEMENT OF AFRICAN LAW PROJECT

A NOTE ON PREVIOUS CONFERENCES ON AFRICAN LAW

Judicial Advisers' Conferences, 1953 and 1956

These conferences, which were convened by the British Secretary of State for the Colonies and presided over by his Legal Adviser, were small, technical conferences of lawyers and administrators principally concerned with the functions of native or customary courts in the then British African territories. The conferences, which were stated in their title to be concerned with "native courts and native customary law", in fact devoted practically all their time to the problems of the native courts. There was some discussion on the policy of integrating native courts into the main judicial system of each territory, the general opinion being in favour of such integration. There was practically no discussion of the legal problems that might arise as a consequence of such judicial integration. Reports have been published of both conferences by H.M.S.O. in London as supplements to the Journal of African Administration.

London Conference on the Future of Law in Africa, 1959-1960

This conference, which was convened under the auspices of the Commonwealth Relations Office and the Colonial Office, met in London from 28th December, 1959 to 8th January, 1960. It was specifically designed to remedy the gap noted in the work of the Judicial Advisers' Conferences by examining the possibilities of a reconciliation between the imported English type of laws and the indigenous, customary and religious laws in common-law Africa.

Participants included representatives (judicial, legal and administrative) of Commonwealth countries and British territories in Africa. Membership was strengthened by representation of the Sudan and Liberia at the conference as well as by the presence of distinguished academic and legal experts from Britain and the U.S.A. It should be noted that there was no representative from the non-common law world in Africa or outside.

The conference discussed the contemporary definition and ambit of customary law in Africa; the place of Islamic law in African legal systems; the policy that should be adopted regarding uniformity of customary law in any particular country; the problems of the ascertainment and recording of customary law; the nature of the conflicts which currently arise between statutory, common, local

4

customary and religious laws in the fields of crime, marriage, family law, land law, contract and tort, evidence and procedure; and the fundamental question of the ultimate objective to be pursued by African countries, whether there should be a unified or a plural type of legal system in each country and what should be the place of customary law in such a unified or plural system as the case may be. The conference also examined in detail the role of the judiciary and the legislature in adapting customary law to changing social circumstances.

The conclusions of the conference were as follows:[1] "The general conclusion of the conference was that uniformity of the law would undoubtedly make a valuable contribution to the administration of the law, and is therefore desirable in principle. While on a territorial basis, complete uniformity of law, and in particular of personal law and land law, may be impracticable and, indeed, undesirable for some time to come, it is generally true to say that between communities and areas there are many variations— especially in native law and custom—which could and should be eliminated, thereby creating a greater degree of uniformity than at present exists. Laws concerning trade and commerce should, in any event, be uniform throughout a territory.

"It is desirable that there should be for each territory a record or digest of the native law and custom in relation to family relations, marriage, divorce, succession and land tenure. A useful precedent is the Digest of Customary Law in the Punjab by Sir William Rattigan and his successors. The record should be prepared in consultation with the 'elders' of each community, so as to ensure that it reflects their common opinion. It should be under the direction of a central advisory authority, which should be able to collate the native law and custom of different areas with a view to co-ordinating them, where possible, to ensure that the number of local variations was restricted to the minimum. The central advisory authority might well include a sociologist, an administrative officer and a lawyer. The record should not as a rule be given statutory form, lest it become too rigid. It should be available for guidance only so as to ensure flexibility. It should be receivable in the courts as a public document admissible without formal proof, and carry the same sort of weight as a received text-book. It should be revised as frequently as necessary so as to ensure that it keeps pace

1.   Proceedings of the Conference were published in A.N. Allott (e.d.), *The Future of Law in Africa* (Butterworths, 1960), from which these extracts are taken.
2.   Some of the information which follows is taken from the *Journal of African Law*, (1963) J.A.L. 133, by permission of the Editor.

with changing conditions. In the compilation of it much assistance will no doubt be derived from research now being organised by the School of Oriental and African Studies. It is realised that in many territories field officers are so fully occupied with administrative matters that they will not have time to do much recording themselves; but it is hoped that in these cases all facilities will be given to enable the research workers to organise a system of recording by whatever African bodies are considered appropriate."

A unified or dual system of law? "In answering the fundamental question whether there should be a single system of law—including English and other law—in African territories, it was said that it is necessary to ask another fundamental question first, namely: what is the nature of governmental policy generally in the African territories? It was submitted that the policy everywhere in the African territories independent and colonial, is to foster the development of peoples in every way; and that the basis of such development must be economic development. Economic development may be retarded by a piecemeal system of law, and it may be fostered if there is one unified system of law which enables all persons in the territory to enter freely into commercial transactions. The ideal may be to have one single system of law, and that based on English law; but this may be a theoretical and not a practical objective.

"Further efforts should however be made to stabilize customary laws and steps to this end could include: (i) local research into and recording of customary law; (ii) codification of accepted or generally recognised rules, production of legal text-books and law reports; and (iii) attempts by judges and magistrates to stabilize the rules of customary law as far as possible, especially those rules which are accepted as general or universal principles. In deciding which rules of customary law are worthy of such judicial recognition the following requirements should be met: (i) the custom should have been in existence for some time; (ii) it should be of general and not merely of local application; and (iii) it should be capable of enforcement in a court of law.

"What limits should one set to flexibility in the administration of customary law? First, it was suggested that there should be no replacement of customary law by English or other foreign law in the fields of personal law, marriage, divorce and succession. Secondly, it was suggested that the judges and magistrates should, as far as possible, attempt the task of reconciling the old and new systems, and in particular should try to adapt general principles of customary law from time to time to accord with changing social conditions. Thirdly, it was suggested that odious and incompatible rules of customary law might have to be abolished by legislation."

Criminal law. "The general criminal law (whether *mala in se* such as murder or theft or *mala prohibita* such as traffic offences) should be written and not unwritten; and should be uniformly applicable to persons of all communities within a territory or area having its own separate judicial system. But this general criminal law might be supplemented (where local circumstances render it desirable) by particular local criminal laws applicable in defined localities (provided that these are not held to be discriminatory in their application to particular communities)."

Evidence. "The improvement and co-ordination of evidence and procedure are generally more urgent than the reform of the substantive law."

Torts. "The general law of torts or wrongs, and of restitution for money had and received, should be uniformly applicable to persons of all communities. In spheres in which native law and custom has evolved rules of its own (e.g. regarding trespass to land) and these rules are uniformly applicable over a wide area (e.g. a Region in Nigeria), the general law should incorporate the principles common to native law and custom and English law, with such additions (either derived from one of the systems or representing a compromise between them) as might seem appropriate. Where native law and custom has evolved no rules, or its rules are manifestly inadequate in the conditions of today, the general law should, as a rule, follow the principles of English law on the matter, but without the refinements or technicalities peculiar to it. But there should be no hesitation in supplementing or varying the principles of English law (when the customs or law of the people render it desirable) by new principles, so as to render compensation or restitution recoverable in appropriate circumstances."

Contract. "There should be a general law of contract (that is to say, the law regulating agreements not covered by legislation nor concerned with land tenure, nor with marriage, divorce or succession) uniformly applicable to persons of all communities, races or creeds, which should follow the general principles of the English law of contract, but without some of the refinements and technicalities peculiar to it, and with such modifications or additions as would incorporate those rules of native law and custom which it was desirable to recognise as part of the general law. But this general law of contract is not to be applied when the parties expressly or implicitly agree to their contract being governed by the law in use among the members of a particular community, race or creed, or the circumstances are such as to show that both parties must be taken to have reached agreement by reference to it, and in certain circumstances the courts might appropriately recognise a rebuttable assumption that the parties intended that the law governing the contract should be some law other than the general law."

Commercial law. "The objective in regard to commercial law is that the law should be written and should, if possible, be made uniformly applicable by legislation."

Land law. "It is important that the land law should be so developed as to meet the rapidly changing conditions in every territory. In some areas (e.g. certain towns in West Africa) title to land is so uncertain that it is said with truth that 'when you buy a piece of land you buy a law suit.' In some areas (e.g. Kenya) traditional African land tenure impedes the progress of the people; so that there is a desire for a change to a system of individual ownership. But in considering any modification of customary law it is essential to examine the possible repercussions in the sphere of personal relations or social organisation of the proposed changes. The ultimate objective may be said to be that in any geographical area within a territory (the area not necessarily being co-terminous with the boundaries of the territory as a whole) there should be a single, uniform system of land law which, while encouraging the exploitation of the land and its resources, would also have full regard to the traditions, family and personal law and human needs of the population. On the unified land law should be based a system of registration of title which would use predominantly English terms to describe customary interests in land, and which should not only enable land to be dealt with in ways such as lease and mortgage which derive from English law, but should make provision for any incidents and practices of the customary law, which it is desired to conserve, e.g. the possessory mortgage."

Family Law. "Questions of family relations, marriage, divorce, wills and succession are so essentially personal that they must in large part continue to be governed by the customary law of the community to which the person belongs. It follows that a marriage or divorce which is valid by the customary law of the parties will continue to be recognised as valid by the general law of the territory. Succession on death (so far as Africans are concerned) should, as a general rule, follow the customary law. But it is often difficult to have adequate proof of the validity of a customary marriage (e.g. evidence that all the necessary formalities have been fulfilled) and indeed to know whether it has been performed or not. Consideration should be given to the possibility of introducing or extending the registration of marriages, and also of births and deaths, with provision for issue of appropriate certificates. Many difficulties are arising where a person desires to place himself outside the operation of his customary law, either generally (as by becoming detribalised and adopting Western ways) or specially (as by entering into a monogamous marriage or by making a will in English form). Thus in almost all territories, the option of marrying according to the general law (i.e. of contracting a legally binding monogamous marriage) is open to all persons including Africans living as members of a community subject to native law and custom. Such a marriage may be solemnised in a church with Christian rites; in most territories, the alternative of a civil ceremony before a registrar is also available. While such a marriage entails the application of the general law to such matters as the personal relations of the spouses, the possibility of divorce, etc., there are certain matters (e.g. property and succession) which may still, in some measure, at any rate, be governed by native law and custom. In this sphere it is important that every effort should be made, by legislation or by judicial decision, to harmonise the English law with customary law. Moreover, quite apart from the question of marriage, a man should be enabled to dispose by will of property which he has acquired himself, (i.e. property to which he has not succeeded in customary law). If he does dispose by will of self-acquired property, the court should be enabled to secure that proper provision is made for his family; and in considering whether proper provision has been made, it should have regard to the customary law.

"As regards legislative provisions for the formal renunciation by individual Africans of their personal law in favour of English law, comparable provision has been made in French, Belgian and Portuguese territories, but the conference thought this undesirable as it tends to create a privileged class. But it may well be desirable to recognise the changed legal status of a person who has become detribalised or has moved from one community to another so long as it is proved to the satisfaction of the court that he has by his whole way of life, renounced his allegiance to customary law and taken as his own the general law of the land, or the law of another community. Every person also has the fundamental right to adopt a, or change his, religion; such an act would involve, in the case of religions such as Islam or Hinduism, a consequential change in the personal law."

Colloquium of French-speaking Law Faculties on Economic Development and Legal Change (held at Dakar, May 1962)
A report of this meeting is given in *Annales Africaines* for 1962.

Conference on Local Courts and Customary Law in Africa (9th-19th September 1963)

The Conference on Local Courts and Customary Law in Africa, held in Dar es Salaam, Tanganyika, was intended to be both a follow-up of the very successful and useful conferences of judicial advisers held under the United Kingdom auspices in 1953 and 1956, and an opportunity for independent African states to compare progress in the development of their judicial and legal systems. The conference was held under the auspices of the Faculty of Law at the University College, Dar es Salaam and the Ministry of Justice in Tanganyika, and it attracted a distinguished participation from a large number of African countries and from overseas. Among those taking part were judges and magistrates, law teachers, administrators and politicians; this diversity of backgrounds and interests undoubtedly contributed greatly to the value of the conference discussions. The two main questions which the conference was called upon to consider were: (i) the future of the local (including customary and African) courts, and (ii) the place of customary law in modern African legal systems. The former question involved a scrutiny of present achievements in the reform of the local court systems, and in training their members for the new tasks which they are being required to perform. All African countries, apparently, have already integrated or will shortly integrate their local court systems with the superior and general law courts; but progress in such integration is uneven, and the process cannot be considered as complete until, for instance, legal practitioners are entitled to appear in local courts on the same terms as they currently appear before courts constituted by professional magistrates or judges. This question of legal representation was one of the more controversial matters before the conference; although majority opinion appeared to be in favour of extending the right to representation as universally and as speedily as possible, the view that one must proceed with caution when doing so was also heard.

Another question which provoked considerable discussion was in regard to which authority should exercise ultimate control of the local courts both in judicial and other matters. The independence of the judiciary in general terms was strongly re-emphasised by the conference; but it was recognised by some of the participants that in the present transitional period, whilst the local courts were being developed, it might be necessary for administrative reasons to leave control of the non-judicial aspects of the local courts' work to a ministry of justice (or its equivalent) and its team of expert local courts' inspectors.

Among the conclusions from the conference were:[3]

Local Courts. "The conference was not concerned with formal arbitration proceedings of the kind usually provided for in Arbitration Acts or Ordinances, but only with informal methods of settling disputes commonly known to customary law. It was recognised that these informal proceedings would inevitably continue and that they had an extremely valuable function to perform in providing speedy and harmonious settlements and in relieving the congestion of the courts, especially in petty matters. The general view was that detailed legislation governing these kinds of proceedings was undesirable, but no recognition of any sort should be given to proceedings which did not satisfy the principles of natural justice.

"In accordance with this principle and with the recommendation that the local courts should become an integral part of the independent judiciary of the State, it was agreed that control of local courts should be invested in the Judiciary, an independent department of the State."

Customary law: the ultimate objective. "The issue was complicated by the fact that in several of the countries represented at the conference, Islamic law formed yet a third element, in addition to the indigenous law and the law of European origin which had been adopted or enacted as part of the law of the particular African state. Islamic law had often become fused with customary law. Sometimes it was regarded as a distinct and separate system of law, and sometimes a law which was chiefly or partly Islamic in origin was administered as customary law of a particular community.

"The variation in circumstances and policies among the various countries made prediction of the likely lines of legal development in the different African countries difficult. Nevertheless, broad trends did emerge and it was with these that the conference was concerned.

"There was wide agreement that there was no question of the disappearance of customary law in the foreseeable future as a significant part of African legal systems. There were, however, certain fields in which customary law had never been applicable (e.g. company law, bankruptcy, banking laws, etc.) or where modern conditions demanded its replacement (e.g. customary criminal law as such may be eliminated and retrograde features in family law, law of succession or land law may be suppressed). In many other fields, it was clear that customary law would survive but would do

3. These conclusions are *verbatim* quotations from the Conference Report, published by the Ministry of Justice, Dar es Salaam, 1964.

so in a different form and would be applied on a different juristic basis. The movement towards recording or restating customary law in a written form had developed in a growing number of African States, even though different countries might have varying ideas about the use of these recordings. This reduction of customary law to writing could not fail to have a very important effect on the administration of the law. Furthermore, in so far as integration is successfully achieved between the legal rules of European origin and those of indigenous origin, the incorporated rules of indigenous law will apply in a quite different way and upon a different juristic basis. If the recorded customary law is 'codified' (i.e. is officially made into an authoritative code) the law will apply thereafter as statute and not as customary law in the ordinary sense.

"The conference recognised the terminological problem created by change in the juristic form of customary law. The term 'customary law' was not accurate to designate a law whose authority was directly dependent on statute, which was the case where customary law was incorporated by statute or was contained in an order or schedule made under a particular statute. On the other hand, it was convenient in some instances to distinguish between rules of different origins. The term 'law or rule of customary origin' was suggested as an alternative.

"Considerable difference of opinion existed as to whether the customary law should be maintained as a separate entity or whether an attempt should be made to integrate the customary law with the general law of the land, from whatever source this law may be derived. The customary law was itself highly diversified in almost every country and it was clear that the more the different systems could be unified the better for national progress. The conference considered the question of how far this could be accomplished without attempting to impose a law so alien to the norms of a community as to be unacceptable. It was also considered to what extent unification of customary law could be combined with reforms in such matters as marriage, e.g. age and consent of parties, and in other matters which are vital to the social welfare.

"It seemed clear that it was only in the sphere of the law of family, of succession and of land tenure that the customary law could survive as a separate system. Here some countries were content for this to continue indefinitely and for the customary law to be administered by a distinct system of courts. Others felt strongly that the jurisdiction of the court should not be defined by reference to the type of law applicable to a case. They also wanted to integrate even the laws of marriage, divorce and succession in a single national system. Most countries seemed to be of the opinion that this was not feasible in the foreseeable future and that it was inevitable that a monogamous form of marriage, the Islamic form of marriage, and customary marriages should continue to co-exist."

Criminal law. "Every country accepted the principle that the penal law should be written and that the present position in some countries, whereby unwritten criminal offences existed side by side with a written Penal Code, must be altered, but the remedies varied."

Marriage. "In the present state of African society it was difficult, if not impossible, to devise a single system of marriage law replacing the different kinds of marriage, but the conference strongly recommended that a general regulatory enactment in regard to specific aspects of marriage should be passed in each country. The legislation should:-

(a) Unify, so far as possible, the procedural requirements for different forms of marriages and state minimum requirements (e.g. in regard to age, consents, registration) for all marriages.

(b) Ensure that the different types of marriages enjoy social and legal parity of status.

(c) Eliminate, so far as possible, the variable consequences at present attaching to different kinds of marriages (e.g. in regard to the evidence of wives married by different forms), more particularly in regard to those who are not themselves parties to the marriage (e.g. children of the marriage). It is recognised that some of the essential features of different types of marriage (e.g. monogamy or polygamy) are at present incapable of being integrated into a single system, but other aspects (e.g. maintenance of wife and children, matrimonial property rights) may be capable of being unified.

(d) Bring the law of marriage more closely into line with the people's requirements. Certain parts of the existing statute law (e.g. concerning bigamy) are presently rarely enforced. The law, once it has been revised, should be more strictly enforced but arrangements should be made (e.g. at the marriage ceremony or during registration) to ensure that the parties clearly understand the legal consequences attaching to the particular form of marriage they have chosen."

Divorce. "The conference recognised that the increasing divorce rate was a grave social problem in several African countries. The main question was whether, and if so how far, extra-judicial divorces or other proceedings for the settlement of matrimonial disputes should be recognised, encouraged or suppressed. There were strong arguments in favour of making all divorces judicial; at the same time there was considerable value in the conciliation machinery (through family arbitrations and other similar forms) afforded by customary law. Such conciliation might be made an essential preliminary to any judicial proceedings for dissolution, or made a condition precedent to registration of a divorce. As a minimum objective, all divorces should be registered."

Succession. "It was generally felt that the unification of the statute and personal law relating to succession was premature, in view of the diversities of existing systems of customary and religious laws; but there was scope for an outline law. This law would prescribe the choice of law in succession cases, regulate and, as far as possible, unify the procedures for administration of estates, create a general power of testamentary disposition (where this was desired) available to African and non-African alike, and incorporate family protection provisions (such as are found in many national laws outside Africa) limiting the amount of property which could be disposed of by will and ensuring that those who were dependent on the deceased during his lifetime are adequately provided for, notwithstanding any change of will or change of personal law which may have been made by the deceased."

Land law. "The nature of the problems encountered by different countries varied. In some the diversity of applicable laws, notably the possibility of transferring and holding land either under the general or customary law, leads to conflictual problems. Elsewhere, as in Tanganyika, this problem does not arise. All countries, however, are concerned to promote the full economic exploitation of their natural resources; and in some instances, customary systems of land tenure may stand in the way of such exploitation.

"There are a number of different ways of dealing with this problem, e.g. by registration of title; introduction of individual titles; imposition of conditions on the use of land by land-holders; etc. But the conference recognised that there was no one way of achieving the necessary development and that social as well as economic factors were important in choosing which land tenure system to adopt. The unification of the customary and general laws relating to land was not an essential prerequisite for such development, though it might be advisable to promote integration, or at least harmonisation, so as to eliminate conflicts. The unified or harmonised land law need not necessarily imply the supersession of customary law in this field."

Commercial law. "There is little scope for the application of customary law principles in this field (even though many customary laws have elementary forms of associations and corporations the structures of which might be taken into account in modern law)."

Contract and civil wrongs. "In any unified law of contract, consideration might be given to the incorporation of some of the features of the customary laws of contract. In any event special and simple forms of contract under customary law (e.g. contracts of marriage, loan, service) were likely to be retained in the foreseeable future, and the principle should prevail, wherever possible, that the court should enforce the system chosen by the parties as the proper law of their contract.

"As for civil wrongs, a code of civil wrongs, replacing the present general law and comprising the best features of the existing general and local laws of torts, might be introduced. There is no reason why this should be a slavish imitation, for example, of the present English law, which has a number of illogicalities and anachronisms."

Responsibility for development of customary law. "There were good grounds for maintaining that whether customary law was incorporated in a single body of law or merely authoritatively restated, the usual 'repugnancy clause', to which the applicability of the indigenous law was always subject in the past, should be discarded.

"One view was that customary law is in a special category and, as such, its future development should, wherever possible, proceed from below (i.e. through the agency of the persons subjected to it) rather than by imposition from above (i.e. by the Central Government); but this view was without prejudice to the power of the Central Government to intervene directly in the development of customary laws where this was unavoidable.

"The other view is that the government does have a direct responsibility for the development of law in force in the society, and there is no compelling reason for placing customary law in a class by itself because its function and purpose is that of the law in general, i.e. normative rules of conduct regulating affairs in society. Where conscious effort at development is made by Central Government there is no justification for implying that it will necessarily constitute an imposition from above.

"The conference considered the various ways of modification of customary law. These included:-

(a) Recommendations by the actual recording authority to the Local Government Authority or to the Central Government or to a specially set up central authority. These authorities can modify the customary law on the basis of the recommendations of the recording authority.

(b) Modification by the local authority through bye-laws either on its own initiative or in response to a recommendation under (a) above, or from other authorised bodies.

(c) Modification by the Central Government either through substantive or subsidiary legislation either on its own initiative or in response to recommendations under (a) above, or from other authorised bodies e.g. District Councils.

(d) Modification by development through case law."

Internal conflict of laws. "The conference considered the various views on the best method of dealing with these internal conflict problems and noted that the conflictual problems may be determined in a number of ways by:-

(a) laying down detailed statutory rules, e.g. Ghana;

(b) laying down a general statutory provision that the most appropriate law should be applied;

(c) having no statutory rules and leaving it to the courts to work out their own rules.

The conference believed the first method was preferable and recommended that detailed legislative rules should be introduced to decide the choice of law."

Conference: "From a Traditional to a Modern Law in Africa", Venice, October 1963

"One disappointment at the Dar es Salaam conference was the paucity of representation from the civil law world—only the Ivory Coast and Ethiopia were able to send delegates. Now that more and more African legal problems can be considered on a continental basis, and one country can learn from the experiences and difficulties of another, whatever the origins of their legal systems, this was unfortunate. The meeting at Venice convened by the Fondazione Giorgio Cini and Présence Africaine with the co-operation of UNESCO from 3rd to 6th October, 1963, helped to supply this deficiency. The general theme of the conference was the movement "from a traditional to a modern law" in Africa and the presence of experts from French-speaking African states (such as Senegal, Mali, Cameroun, Mauretania) and from France and Switzerland meant that the special problems and the special solutions of the civil law and 'code' countries were fully brought to notice."[4]

4.   Taken from the *Journal of African Law*, "Notes and News", (1963) J.A.L. 134-5.

A BACKGROUND PAPER ON RESTATEMENT
OF LAWS IN AFRICA:

The need, value and methods of such restatement

by

A. N. ALLOTT

PROFESSOR OF AFRICAN LAW, UNIVERSITY OF LONDON;
DIRECTOR, RESTATEMENT OF AFRICAN LAW PROJECT

and

E. COTRAN

LECTURER IN AFRICAN LAW, SCHOOL OF ORIENTAL AND
AFRICAN STUDIES; FORMERLY RESEARCH OFFICER,
RESTATEMENT OF AFRICAN LAW PROJECT

RESTATEMENT OF LAWS IN AFRICA

This brief report examines in a general way the questions:-

(i) What is a "restatement"?

(ii) How far is such a restatement necessary in any African country, whether of the indigenous or the received statutory or common laws?

(iii) What would be the value of such a restatement for the achievement of the integration or greater harmonisation of the constituent elements, customary, common and statutory, in an African legal system?

(iv) What methods ought to be adopted in order to produce such a restatement or set of restatements, bearing in mind the primary objectives of such a work?

A. RESTATEMENT AND THE GENERAL LAW

I. The meaning of "Restatement"

It is interesting that some of the standard English dictionaries, such as the Shorter Oxford and Chambers, contain no separate article defining or explaining "restatement", which merely comes in a list of other words beginning with "re-", the import of which is mere repetition. The fact that this term, now so important for legal purposes, merits no separate entry, is illuminating. In legal dictionaries there is either no entry or a very restricted one.

The Oxford English Dictionary, though giving no special legal sense to the word, at least reveals that *"Restate*—To state or express over again or in a new way" has an ancestry stretching back to 1713. The term is now acquiring a special legal meaning, initially thanks to the American Restatement, and now including the restatement of customary laws in Africa, thanks to the establishment in London of the Restatement of African Law Project.

What, then are the main implications behind the legal use of the term "restatement"?

(i) "Restatement" implies prior statement, but it is very much more than mere reiteration of what has been said before. The implication of the term, as sharpened by its use in the American Restatements, is firstly that the new statement—of the law, in this instance—somehow brings together, clarifies, connects, rearranges in a more logical and comprehensive way, previous expressions of the law on a particular topic. Previous statements of the law, however imperfect, must be in existence, otherwise what we have is not a restatement, but a novel exegesis of the law, which may be the fruit of original research, or even of legislation of one kind or another.

(ii) The second main implication which now lies behind the word "restatement" in legal contexts is that the re-presentation of the law is an authoritative and learned one. The compilation of the American restatements was so designed as to guarantee as much authority for them as possible. All the resources of American legal science were engaged on the task, and the processes of verification and criticism were such that no loose or unsupported statement could survive to the final version.

(iii) The third implication of the use of the term "restatement" is that the work is done with a practical purpose in view, that is, to put into the hands of users a more precise and comprehensive statement of the applicable law, upon which they can rely in execution of their daily tasks. Who are these users, and what are the tasks that they perform and in which restatements might be of assistance? In the United States, the primary users are legal practitioners and the courts, but law teachers, and to a less extent law reformers or law makers, also rely on them as expository of the existing law. There is no reason why the emphasis should be the same in other countries which desire to resort to restatement for the ascertainment or improvement of their laws.

(iv) A fourth implication is that the new statement of the laws, though authoritative, has no binding force; it is specifically not a code of laws. Whatever force it has depends on the intrinsic value of the work produced, and on the reputation of those who prepare it.

(v) A fifth implication, at least in the United States, is that a restatement of the laws is necessary because of some unnecessary complexity in the existing laws and the existing statements of them. The complexity—as far as the United States is concerned—is in the multiplicity of co-ordinate jurisdictions within a single national territory, each semi-independently administering what was in its origin basically the same law, but which has now fragmented, thanks to diverging judicial decisions, into as many laws as there are jurisdictions applying them. There is no reason, if we accept complexity or divergence of existing laws as a motive for restatement, why such complexity or divergence should be confined to that found with the common law and equity in the United States. Africa knows other kinds of legal complexity and other reasons for legal divergence which are equally relevant here.

We may summarise the implications of "restatement of laws" as follows:-

(i)   Restatement implies a re-arrangement, in improved from, of statements of the existing law.

(ii)   The restatement is authoritative, prepared by persons or bodies whose reputation and methods guarantee the authenticity of the restatements they produce.

(iii)   The restatement is prepared for practical use. There may be more than one category of interested users.

(iv)   The restatement is not a legislated code. To codify the restatement would entirely alter its nature and value.

(v)   The method of restatement is especially useful where the laws restated have been the subject of divergent expression, or where they are complex in character.

The answer to all these questions is emphatically in the affirmative. Before demonstrating this point, let us briefly recall what is meant by "an African legal system" here. Two different kinds of legal systems are involved: (a) the first is the territorial legal system of Western type or origin; e.g. the respective legal systems of Senegal, of Nigeria, of Kenya; (b) the second comprises the local customary and religious laws, which prior to colonisation existed autonomously and in their own right, but which now survive as component parts— sometimes fragmented, sometimes integrated, sometimes semi- autonomously—of legal systems of the first type. Our enquiry must be directed to both types of legal systems, especially as the specific object of this study is to explore means by which the integration or harmonisation of the different elements in African legal systems may be promoted.

(i)   *Dissatisfaction with the existing legal systems.* There is widespread dissatisfaction with existing African legal systems. The reasons for this are:-

(a)   In so far as the territorial legal systems were evolved during the colonial era, especially by wholesale borrowing of the metro- politan law, they may be felt by independent African countries to be not wholly in tune with current political and economic imperatives.

(b)   As far as the former British territories are concerned, their territorial legal systems are an uneasy and uncertain amalgamation of rules derived from the law of England, and rules elaborated on the spot by legislation or judicial manipulation.

(c)   In so far as the territorial legal systems are dualistic or multiple in character—thanks to the parallel recognition of Western and indigenous laws and institutions—the uncertainties of the present legal system are increased, owing to the poverty of rules regulating internal conflicts of laws.

(d)   The achievement of personal integration, psychological and social, by the individual requires that he should not be confronted with a choice between irreconcilable legal alternatives (e.g. monogamous or polygamous marriage) or between two incompatible modes of life (one based on Western notions, and one based on traditional practices or values). The achievement of national integration may imply that divergencies between Western and indigenous components of the legal system, or between a variety of local or personal laws, should be reduced or eliminated by integration of the laws.

(ii) *Paucity of information on existing legal systems.* What is said below relates specifically to the former British territories, but is probably equally applicable in the civil law countries, especially those which have changed their legal systems recently from the colonial pattern.

One of the major obstacles to legal research, to the proper Administration of justice, and to law reform in Africa is the absence or inadequacy of legal texts setting out the laws currently in force which clearly indicate how they diverge from their parent models and how apparent inconsistencies between different components of the legal system are resolved.

Information on customary laws is just as unsatisfactory. The position here is complicated by the fact that most research into customary law in the past has been carried out by anthropologists or sociologists and not by lawyers; their results may well be unusable by a lawyer, or require qualification or interpretation into legal terms. Many customary laws have never been studied, or studies of them were made many years ago, or were confined to one aspect of the law or one section of an ethnic group.

Almost everywhere in common law Africa the reports of judicial decisions, which are the expression and most authoritative source of the common law, either do not exist, or provide inadequate local coverage of all the different aspects of the law. This is a special problem where the law received from outside the country is involved; there may well be no recorded evaluation of how far an English rule, or an English decision, is of authority in an African country which has taken over the English law. Since in many places the received English law only applies so far as local circumstances permit, and subject to such qualifications as are necessary to render it applicable to local conditions, authoritative pronouncements on how far the English law applies and with what modifications are urgently needed.

There is equal difficulty with the received statutory law in the former British territories. Most of them took over the English "statutes of general application" that were in force in England on a certain date. Only a handful of the statutes in force in England at such a date (e.g. 1st January, 1900 in the case of most of Nigeria) have ever been involved in decided local African cases, and the question of whether they are of general application and received into the country or not answered authoritatively.

Legal textbooks of any kind dealing with the law in force in African countries are few in number; most have been produced in the last two or three years, and by no means exhaustively cover the different branches of the law.

(iii)   *The complexity of African legal systems.* African legal systems are complex in several different ways:-

(a) The territorial legal systems are complex because they contain rules of law drawn from different sources. In common-law East Africa, to give an illustration, the general legal system of, say, Tanganyika was originally based on the codified law of British India; in so far as such law did not apply, then the law of England (statute and common law) as in force in 1920 was resorted to. Both sorts of law could be changed by Tanganyikan legislation, and have been progressively modernised or replaced in this way over the years. The reconciliation of these divergent elements—sometimes the same, sometimes considerably different—may prove a problem. There are thus uncertainties as to the content of the land law and the law of contract, each of multiple origin. Reconciliation of these divergent elements depends on legislative initiative through the enactment of codes entirely replacing the prior law on a particular topic, or through judicial pronouncement, which is inevitably limited to the special circumstances of the case before the court.

(b) The territorial legal systems are complex because they usually provide for the recognition and simultaneous application of various laws of non-Western, mainly African origin, notably of local African customary laws, and of religious personal laws (Islamic law in both East and West Africa; Hindu and other Asian laws in East Africa; Christian marriage law in several states, e.g. Sudan, Ethiopia).

(c) In several African states federations have been created. There are two types of such federation: those where the legal systems of each partner or component territory or region belong to the same legal family (e.g. the Federation of Nigeria); and those where the partners have had different colonial experiences and have acquired different kinds of legal systems (e.g. Cameroun, with a French and an English component; Somali Republic, with an Italian and a British component). The former type is analogous to the United States, though one should remember that the United States is juridically mixed through the recognition of the civil law in Louisiana.

(iv) *Families of legal systems in Africa.* There are several different levels of such family relationship between African legal systems. At the inter-state level, one has the families created by previous subjection to the same colonial power. Thus there is the civil law legal family (including former or present French, Belgian, Italian, Portuguese and Spanish possessions). Muslim North Africa generally adheres to the civil law system too. Then there is the common law family, comprising former British West, East and Central Africa north of the Zambezi, and including Liberia and the Sudan. A third cluster of legal systems comprises the so-called Roman-Dutch systems of southern Africa below the Zambezi: the Republic of South Africa, Southern Rhodesia and the former High Commission Territories; because of the powerful, and in some instances obliterating, influence of the English legal system on Roman-Dutch law in southern Africa, it would be more precise to describe the legal systems currently practised there as "Anglo-Roman-Dutch law"; these systems provide a very real bridge between the civil and the common-law worlds in Africa.

Intraterritorially, Nigeria provides a unique example of a set of related legal systems created by the subdivision of a formerly unitary legal system; on the establishment of the federation in Nigeria, the component Regions took over the law of Nigeria as the foundation of their regional legal systems. Although these systems are now beginning to diverge, they all share in essence a common ancestry.

Another kind of relationship between legal systems is found within the domain of the African customary law. African customary law is, of course, not a single legal system with variations, but a set of systems which developed for the most part independently of each other. There is, however, sufficient connexion between these systems generally, a connection emphasised by their common administration by the same system of superior courts and by the common exposure of those subject to them to the same historical and socio-economic environment, for one to be able to talk in a meaningful way of such systems as a "family". Such an emerging uniformity is especially noticeable at the territorial or national level (note, e.g., the emergence of a Ghana common customary law).

The fact that all the customary legal systems are African, or that some of them are now associated in a territorial legal framework, is not the only possible link between them. On examination one finds that the different systems of customary law may be allocated to different families, usually thanks to coherence of the societies in which they occur in a particular linguistic-cultural grouping. Legal similarities within such a customary law family are usually attributable to common ancestry, but in a few instances culture-contact may have been at work. Examples of such ethnic groups possessing similar laws are, from West Africa, the Yoruba and the Ibo of Nigeria, the Akan of Ghana; from East Africa the Kikuyu of Kenya, and some of the lacustrine peoples around Lake Victoria; and from southern Africa the Tswana people of Bechuanaland. The term "homeonomic" has been coined to designate such groups possessing similar laws. It is vital, for our present purpose, to emphasise that common membership of a homeonomic group does not imply identity of laws between the members; on the contrary, local variations, sometimes of considerable importance, may be found.

(v) *The divergence of legal systems.* The risk of divergence between the laws belonging to one of these law families is a very real one in contemporary Africa, and examples of such recent divergence are multiplying.

At the inter-state level, each African state is tending to assert its own identity, in the legal as in other spheres. Legal changes are rarely co-ordinated between states. Even those states which started off with basically the same law may now be losing this connexion through reforming legislation or through varying judicial interpretations.

Divergence between the legal systems is also at work in Nigeria, where each region has a wide latitude to modify the laws which it inherited. There are thus important divergencies newly created between the land law of the Western and Mid-West Regions and the rest of Nigeria, and between the criminal law and procedure of the Northern Region and the rest of Nigeria.

The customary law as practised in different parts of a homeonomic area or group may also diverge, thanks to differing interpretations or developments of the law by local courts in different places, or to varying local legislation by local legislative bodies competent to change the customary law. Such divergence was, for instance, observed between the customary criminal laws as currently practised in different parts of Kikuyuland.

II.   The value of restatements in African legal development

The reasons for attempting a cure of these ills, so far as they are recognised as such, are therefore clear. The question remains whether restatement is a possible method, or even the best method of effecting a cure.

The uses, methods and results of restatement in the sphere of customary law are discussed in a separate section of this paper,[1] and

1. See *post*, Part B.

will not be further discussed at this point. Two different kinds of restatement are possible in regard to the law that remains:-

First, there is a simple restatement of the existing general law, jurisdiction by jurisdiction. Such a restatement would attempt to combine the various elements in the general legal system, choose between alternative interpretations, and re-present the law in modern, consistent, terms.

Secondly, one might attempt to go further, and so to restate the general law that its harmonisation or even integration with the customary and other personal laws would be promoted or achieved.

The former is a much simpler proposition, though even this is a more complicated undertaking than that which was set in motion in the United States. The penumbra of uncertainty touching the extent of application and adaptation of the received laws, as well as the need to reconcile legislation and common law, aggravate the difficulty of the task. The need for such a restatement could be denied by no-one, except those who would argue either that is unnecessary to know what the law is in order to change it, or that it is unnecessary or even risky to clarify what the law is except in relation to a particular problem before a court. Opponents of the first kind would tend to favour codification without prior investigation, in other words codification with one's eyes shut, as the appropriate means of developing the law. Opponents of the second kind, who can be expected to be more numerous in the countries influenced by the casuistic methods of the common law, would favour piecemeal judicial interpretation and development as the most appropriate method of advancing African law. Neither position, at least in its least compromising form, would appear to be tenable. It is our firm contention that (i) those administering the law should know precisely what it is, and (ii) those wishing to change the law, especially in the direction of harmonisation or integration, must know what it is that they are trying to harmonise or integrate. If such a task had been undertaken years ago under the colonial regime, many of the present legal difficulties facing African countries might have been avoided.

As regards restatement with the second kind of objective in view, it is submitted that many of the differences or barriers between legal systems, whether between the law of England and the law of France, or between the law of England and the customary law of an African people, are more apparent than real, that they are created or aggravated by the different legal training and background of those who write about or administer them, and by differences of legal terminology. It has often been remarked that when a French lawyer writes about customary law, he naturally attempts to fit it into

French legal categories, and the English lawyer into English categories. If the same authority or set of authorities is responsible for preparing or restating the laws of different kinds, the tendency will be to accentuate their natural similarities; the assimilationist tendency will be even more pronounced if he (or they) has gone to the trouble of working out a set of terms, an analysis, and a structure of presentation which are adaptable to the one kind of law and to the other.

Restatement of the customary law with this occidentalizing tendency has been going on for many years in Africa, but unsystematically. One has only to look at the reported decisions of superior courts in English-speaking West Africa interpreting the customary laws applied by those courts to see that the vocabulary of description of the customary law tends to be drawn from legal English, and that the judge is naturally tempted to accommodate African conceptions in English legal categories. Thus the institution of family property may be described by an English or English-trained judge in terms of joint tenancy, of corporations, of trustee-beneficiaries, or of agency— all conceptions of the English law which have to be adapted or stretched to fit the African institution.

The reverse sort of restatement, the stretching of legal terms to fit another legal system, has not been so conspicuous, but it has been going on subliminally. Whenever a native court, or an African speaking an African language, has tried to apply the concepts or rules of English law to a legal situation before it or him, it is possible that such reverse restatement may take place, and the English law will be "africanised" in consequence.

What we would submit here is that a more conscious and systematic, indeed a more scholarly, attempt might be made at such interlegal translation, and that the method of restatement, provided the terminology is worked out by someone with an understanding of linguistics and its application to legal statement, is probably the most suitable for this purpose.[2]

III. Methods of Restatement

The methods to be adopted in restating the laws depend

(a) on the types of laws being restated, and

(b) on the purpose for which the restatement is intended. Discussion of restatement methods will therefore be given separately in respect (i) of the general, Western-type, law and (ii) of the customary laws. Some of the remarks made in respect of the former will obviously apply to the latter, though the methodological

---

2. See *post*, part C.

problems and some of the practical difficulties facing such restatements differ somewhat.

Our users, it is worth recalling, will comprise the courts, both superior and inferior (including the local or customary courts); the practising profession; law teachers and law students; law reformers and legislators, including those who wish to promote unification as well as technical improvement of the law; and legal researchers, in so far as they do not fall within the preceding categories. The general public, those affected by the laws, should not be forgotten; simple, precise statements of the law should be of the greatest utility for them, not least in common law countries where the task of ascertaining the relevant law in a given situation may often be a challenging task for a trained lawyer, and an impossible one for the layman.

All the restatements must meet certain general requirements and follow, so far as possible, a uniform presentation. These requirements include:-

(i) Inconsistencies and doubts in the existing law should be removed as far as possible.

(ii) Local divergencies or discrepancies should be resolved, or at least noted and compared.

(iii) The applicable law should be stated in as precise, but not necessarily heavily technical, language as possible. A code form is the most suitable for making such statements, and the discursive style of treatment appropriate to law textbooks will be avoided.

(iv) Restatements of one kind of law must employ a uniform terminology, even if prepared by different hands. New terms may have to be devised, or old ones re-defined, to achieve this. Where possible, there should be uniformity of terminology between restatements of different kinds of law (e.g. customary and statutory).

(v) The restatements must have as much authority as scientific scholarship can give.

(vi) There must be arrangments for periodic revision to conform to new interpretations and the changing society in which the law operates.

IV. Restatement of the general law

Certain branches of the law lend themselves to restatement on an inter-state or inter-territorial basis. In common law West Africa, for example, restatement of the law of obligations (contract, etc.) might well be on a West African, and not a national basis. Differing national interpretations or applications of the law could be noted in the same way as the State Annotations of the American Restatement. Such inter-state restatement would promote harmonisation of laws, and would make the results of scholarship available to all.

At the national level, federations such as Nigeria would obviously prefer to restate their laws nationally and not regionally so far as possible, except where legislation has caused a sharp divergence between them.

Apart from these examples, it is assumed that the unit of restatement will be the state—or, where it is multi-jurisdictional, each several jurisdiction.

The United States, as a land of private enterprise and initiative, naturally approached the task of restatement from the point of view of legal scholarship, and without governmental inspiration or control. Is a similar approach possible in Africa?

One notes, first of all, that legal scholarship in Africa is generally at a less advanced stage than in Europe or North America. The financial resources of scholarship are also much less. Governments in Africa tend to be more interventionist in many spheres, and this tendency is not absent in the law, which after all has to be legislated by parliaments and administered by courts which are public organs. But the room or need for private scholarship is not for these reasons substantially diminished. Even government schemes must call on private scholars for assistance; and the best answer would appear to be some form of collaboration between government and scholarship. Where there are bodies or individuals competent and willing to take the initiative at the academic level, they would appear to be the best agencies to undertake the restatement of the laws; but they should receive governmental support and financial backing, and might in turn, without compromising their scholarship, bear the needs of the makers and appliers of laws in mind and consult with them regularly.

Where such scholastic initiative is for some reason impossible, then governments should not hesitate to get things moving, as the need is urgent. The best method of proceeding in such instances might be to set up a semi-autonomous body, an institute or a commission, charged with the task of restating the laws, and competent to decide in detail on its staff, its working procedures, etc.

The American Restatements were the main product of an American Law Institute specifically set up for this and related purposes:

> "to promote the clarification and simplification of the law and its better adaptation to social needs, to secure the better administration of justice, and to encourage and carry on scholarly and scientific legal work."

A similar Law Institute might be established in each country or group of countries. Ideally it should be linked with a university or other academic body.

One of the difficulties that has to be faced is the shortage of trained scholars. As far as the general law is concerned (the customary law position is somewhat different), this difficulty can readily be overcome by appealing to scholars from other countries of the same legal tradition to assist. Some form of institutionalized co-operation in the legal sphere between richer (in jurists) and less fortunate countries might be advisable. (The existence of an International African Law Association, linking lawyers interested in African legal problems wherever they may be, is relevant here, and the Association should be a suitable channel for procuring legal co-operation of this kind between scholars of different countries. The national or local sections of the Association could also provide a local focus for this work.)

The main tasks will be to allocate the work to responsible scholars (sub-division of labour will be essential in a job of this kind); to arrange for some sort of centralised direction of the activity so as to promote uniformity of arrangement and treatment; to determine what should be the language and arrangement of the sections of the restatements.

The original American method of having a sole Reporter for each topic, advised sporadically by a Committee of Advisers, modified itself spontaneously into a system of small expert committees, with the "Advisers" now taking a hand in the actual drafting of the restatements. Some form of consultation between scholars is quite essential in preparing restatements, as the sole reporter, however well qualified, may well overlook matters which are of importance. (In the preparation of customary law restatements in the Restatement of African Law Project in London, we rely on the criticism by colleagues of draft statements prepared by one member of the Project to ensure that there are no substantial omissions, that nothing is improperly included, that the terminology is precise, and conforms to the general pattern laid down, and that the expression is clear and consistent.)

It is difficult to overstress the importance of choice of arrangement and terminology. If one of our primary objectives is to promote the assimilation or harmonisation of the general and customary laws, the best avenue for such assimilation is undoubtedly through the adoption of a uniform vocabulary. One has only to contrast the vocabulary and arrangement of the law of civil wrongs in England (split between the law of torts, breach of contract, breach of trust, matrimonial offences, quasi-contract, etc., and burdened with historical survivals both of language and classification) with the comparable customary law of an African society to see that many of the apparent contradictions or lack of them between Western and African laws are accidental and not of the essence. A new or improved vocabulary can only be produced by careful comparison of the substantive laws involved, and the systematic re-arrangement of them according to a new and more logical classification.

A. N. Allott

B. RESTATEMENT OF THE CUSTOMARY LAW

This part will deal with the need, methods, and value of the restatement of the customary laws in Africa, with special reference to the Restatement of African Law Project of London University (hereinafter referred to as RALP).

I The necesity for the restatement of customary law in Africa

Perhaps more important and urgent than the restatement of the general law in African countries, is the vital necessity for the restatement of the customary laws. The reason for this is quite obvious. Whereas in the case of the general law, the lawyer has at present the assistance of the local codes and legislation, the text-books, commentaries, and law reports, both local and English, in the case of customary law the lawyer can find no assistance whatever in the form of writing. Customary laws remain to a very large extent unwritten, and their ascertainment remains, so far as the courts are concerned, a matter of evidence, proved through the assistance of experts (or rather so-called experts) on the customary law, whether witnesses or assessors. In more specific terms, one can enumerate at least four reasons which make it necessary, indeed essential, to restate customary law in African countries.

(a) *Lack of knowledge.* In many parts of Africa, the customary laws of the various ethnic groups within a territory have never been investigated. Hence large gaps remain in our knowledge. It is senseless to speak of reform, change, maintenance or abolition of the customary law when we do not even know what it is.

(b) *Inadequacy of existing records.* Existing written records on customary law may be classified under three heads:-

(i) *Writings by individual researchers.* Many individual works on customary law, mainly by anthropologists and administrators (though a few by lawyers), have been written from time to time.

Although a few works are of outstanding value (e.g. Schapera's *Tswana Law and Custom;* Gluckman's work on the peoples of Central Africa; Rattray and Danquah on the customary laws of Ghana; and more recently Obi on *Ibo Law of Property*) most of them are of little or no use because (a) they were written by persons of anthropological, rather than legal, background, and do not bring out the matters of interest to a lawyer; (b) most of them were written a very long time ago, and though of historical interest, do not represent the customary law of today; (c) many of them deal with only one or two ethnic groups within a country, and others deal only with one subject, e.g. land law, or the law of marriage.

(ii) *Provision of ad hoc machinery for recording customary law.* The legislation of many Commonwealth African territories provides machinery by which native authorities, e.g. chiefs and elders, local government bodies, or specially set up local panels, can declare their customary law in writing, and some of them have power to recommend or effect changes in the customary law. For example, in Kenya, before the Law Panels were reorganised (for which see below), a Law Panel had power to record the customary law in its area, and recommend changes to the African District Council, which had the power to effect the change by resolution of the Council. These Panels, however, in common with other similar *ad hoc* bodies in other parts of Africa, functioned very sporadically, and one can derive little assistance from their declarations. They failed to make a systematic recording of the customary law in a way that would be useful to a lawyer.

(iii) *Records of African/Local/Native Courts.* In certain parts of Africa, proper records in these courts were only started recently. But even where they exist, they are often of little value in discovering the customary law. Reasoned judgments are very rarely given, the judgment often consisting of a few lines giving the facts and the result. My experience in East Africa has shown that only about 5 per cent of African Courts judgments may usefully serve in recording customary law. Law reports of cases decided in the African Courts or on appeal there-from are non-existent (except for small digests here and there). Although in West Africa the general law reports from the superior courts contain many decided cases on customary law, in East and Central Africa, mainly due to the dual system of courts, a handful of cases only may be found involving decisions on customary law.

(c) *Uncertainty as to what the customary law is.* The lack of adequate written records of the customary law as shown above has led the superior courts in Africa to treat it as a question of fact to be proved by evidence.[3] Although this is gradually being rectified (see, e.g., Ghana Courts Act, 1960) this remains true of most parts of Africa. As and when customary law ceases to become a matter of evidence, the need for its restatement becomes more essential. As regards the African/Local/Native Courts, it was assumed in the past that the judges of these courts knew the customary law, and need have no written record of it. This is ceasing to be true today, firstly because the tendency is to appoint legally trained judges who may be posted to an area where their own customary law is not applicable, and secondly because the mixing of African populations and urbanisation has resulted in the existence of various customary laws within one area.

(d) *"Inferiority" of customary law.* The existence of an unwritten customary law side by side with a written imported law has brought about an unfortunate trend of treating the customary law as an inferior system. This trend was not only apparent in the colonial era, but can be clearly observed among the African elite in the independent African countries today. It is submitted that in order to enhance the status of customary law, it is necessary that it should be accorded the same treatment as the imported law, and its restatement and recognition will certainly have that effect.

Enough has been said above to show that there is a definite need to restate customary law, but, before leaving the subject, I must deal briefly with the view—still unfortunately held in some quarters —that the restatement of customary law at this stage of development in Africa is undesirable. The objections to restatement may be grouped under three heads:-

(i) First, there is the extreme view that customary law does not exist; that in fact if one attempted to find out what it is, one would receive a different answer from each informant on the same matter. This of course is nonsense, and it is submitted that the holders of the view are either absolutely ignorant, or lack the knowledge of how to set about investigating customary law. The results achieved by RALP, which are set out below, clearly show that there are clearly defined rules of customary law in every African society. Provided the proper machinery is employed, those rules can be discovered and recorded accurately.

(ii) The second view, less extreme than the first, is that there are so many variations in the customary law within one tribe or one ethnic group, that it will take a lifetime even to complete the recording of the law of one tribe. Even then, they say, the recording

3. For details, see Allott, *Essays in African Law*, Chapter 4: Judicial Ascertainment of Customary Law.

will have so many exceptions as to be of little use. It is submitted that the variations existing in the customary law are often exaggerated, and are more apparent than real. From personal experience in Kenya I have found that there are certainly more similarities than dissimilarities in customary law, and this even applies amongst groups that are completely divergent in ethnic origins and mode of life. One would not have expected for example to find that some of the rules of customary law amongst the Masai (a Nilo-Hamitic tribe traditionally nomadic) should be almost identical to the same rules amongst the Kamba or Kikuyu (Bantu people traditionally agriculturalists) or amongst the Digo (traditionally matrilineal), but the fact remains that they are.

(iii) The last objection to restatement of the customary law, and perhaps the best one, is that customary law is in a fluid state, and changes in the African states. To restate customary law, it is argued, would mean freezing it at a premature stage and hindering its future development. Whilst recognising this danger, it is submitted that this would only happen if the restatement of customary law was codified in the form of a statute. If, however, the restatements are only used as a *guide* to the customary law, just as text-books are used, and provision is made for their regular revision, the danger of rigidity would disappear. It is certainly not true to say that once a law is written, its development is in any way hindered. One only has to look at the African legislation to see how many amendment slips are introduced each year, and also at the English legal text-books to observe how new editions are brought out regularly to keep pace with the law, which, it is submitted, is changed not because it was previously written or unwritten, but because the people whose life it regulates desire a change.

II. Methods of restatement of customary law

The inadequacy of the existing sources on customary law, coupled with the need for its restatement, led the School of Oriental and African Studies, University of London, to initiate in 1959 a comprehensive research scheme whose eventual aim is to facilitate, and where feasible undertake or assist, the restatement of customary law in the Commonwealth African countries. The methods employed by this scheme, known as RALP, have been outlined by its Director, Dr A. N. Allott, elsewhere,[4] but it may be useful to summarise them in one African country—Kenya.

At the outset it must be said that the methods employed by

---

4. Allott: "The Recording of Customary Law in British Africa and the Restatement of African Law Project" in *La rédaction des coutumes dans le passé et dans le présent*, Brussels, 1962.

34 A. N. ALLOTT & EUGENE COTRAN

RALP were so designed as to remedy the defects at previous attempts of recording customary law. Hence the methods included the following important points:-

(a) Its staff is composed wholly of lawyers, and not anthropologists or sociologists. At present (1964) the staff include the Director, two Lecturers in African Law, four Research Officers, all of whom have an English legal training with a special training in African customary law, and one Bibliographical Assistant. Each Research Officer is in charge of one region of Africa, divided for purposes of the Project into three Regions—West Africa, East Africa, and Central and Southern Africa.

(b) The restatements will be comprehensive and include all the fields where customary law still plays a major part, viz. The Law of Persons and Family Relations; The Law of Marriage; The Law of Property; and The Law of Succession.

(c) The restatements will include all the ethnic groups within a territory. Groups with similar laws (termed homoenomic) will be treated together for purposes of the restatement.

(d) The Project is a self-sufficient body, commenced as an academic initiative. However, where African Governments desire collaboration, RALP will give all the assistance it can, as has been done in Kenya and Malawi.

(e) The final restatements produced will be no more than guides to the customary law. No codification is intended.

The work of RALP, which started in 1960, is divided into two stages:-

1. *Preparation of Bibliographies.* Complete bibliographies of all known published and unpublished materials on customary law have already been completed, and will be published shortly. These bibliographies, arranged by ethnic groups, have revealed our present state of knowledge of the customary law.

2. *Restatement.* If the Bibliography revealed that a certain customary law was well investigated, a draft statement of it would be compiled on the basis of the available materials. This draft statement, which is no more than provisional, is then referred to a body of experts on the customary law in the relevant territory. The composition and selection of this body would vary from territory to territory according to whether government collaboration is forthcoming. In Kenya and Malawi, where RALP and the Governments are working together, Law Panels were selected for each ethnic group, and the Panels consisted of African Court judges, chiefs, elders, with the widest representation of local opinion possible. In other territories, the selection would have to be left to RALP, whose staff will invariably consult the same type of person as those

who sat on the Law Panels in Kenya and Malawi, but in an unofficial capacity. The essence of this procedure is to put a text, however provisional and inaccurate, before the local body rather than start from scratch. The provisional text will be arranged according to a uniform plan devised by RALP, which will ensure that the material is organised in a proper fashion, and will reduce to a minimum unnecessary local variations.

The work undertaken by RALP in Kenya reveals how the above methods worked in practice. In 1961, the Government of Kenya requested RALP's assistance in the comprehensive recording of the customary law of the Kenya tribes. By that time, RALP had completed stage 1 of its work in relation to Kenya, i.e. a bibliography of all published and unpublished sources on the customary laws of the Kenya tribes had been compiled. RALP therefore suggested that one of the members of its staff should go out to Kenya and carry out stage 2, using as the local body of experts referred to above the Kenya Law Panels which had been operating for some time. These Law Panels were, however, reorganised, so as to consist of African Court judges, chiefs, local elders, one or two young educated members, and where possible one or two women. The Panels were also reconstituted on an ethnic, rather than a District, basis.

The Kenya investigation was divided into two distinct stages. The first stage consisted in the restatement of the surviving customary *criminal* offences, with a view to incorporating them into the written law of Kenya. The second stage consisted in the restatement of the customary *civil law*, principally the law of marriage, family relations and succession. The two stages differed in one material respect. Whereas the terms of reference as regards the customary criminal offences was to restate them and recommend how best they could be incorporated in the existing general criminal law of Kenya, with the civil law we were concerned with restatement and no more. This is important in showing how a restatement of customary law may be used (as was done in the case of the customary offences in Kenya) in bringing about a unification between different customary laws, and between the customary law and the general law (for which see below under III).

The discussions with the Law Panel, which normally consisted of about fifteen members sitting together, revolved around a consideration of the draft statement already prepared. The drafts were all according to a uniform plan with the same headings and sub-headings. The statements of every rule was discussed in detail until agreement was reached. The discussions were conducted in the vernacular language with the assistance of one or more interpreters.

A detailed restatement of the customary law was then drafted. This indicated the general rules with examples, local variations, wherever they occurred, and modern developments where it was clear that the traditional customary law on the subject has undergone a change. This detailed restatement was again considered by the Law Panel, and was also circulated to all those concerned with the administration of customarylaw —e.g. African Court judges who did not sit on the Panel, local administrators, District Councillors, etc. The purpose of this thorough procedure was to ensure that no errors appeared in the final restatements, and that the local population, whose law was being restated, should be duly associated with the Project.

One of the criticisms advanced of RALP, and in particular of the Panel system in Kenya, is that there is no way of ensuring that the members of the Panel are reliable informants on the customary law. The answer to this criticism is fourhold. Firstly, the members of the Panels are not selected at random. Great pains were taken to ensure that every single member of the Panel had proved his ability and was knowledgeable on the customary law. Secondly, the thorough system of checking and re-checking already referred to, which subjected the restatements to the independent eyes of persons who did not sit on the Panel, shows that the views of the Panel were not accepted without verification. Thirdly, the Panel members were duly warned at the beginning, and sometimes during the course of the meetings, that they should confine their discussions to what the law is, and not what it ought to be. Finally, the criticism assumes that the person conducting the investigation is ignorant of the customary law. This of course is far from being the case, for it must be remembered that he had spent a considerable time reading up all materials on that particular customary law before convening the meeting, and had often already seen the African Court records in the relevant area.

Furthermore, the only alternative to the Panel system is to try and record the customary law from the case files of African Courts. It has already been indicated that only some 5 per cent of these are of any assistance. Thus, to do the job thoroughly relying solely on these records, would take a few years to complete one tribe, let alone hundreds of tribes.

III. Value of restatement of customary law

The value of a restatement of customary law may be viewed from three different angles. First, it is valuable as a restatement as such, since it will greatly facilitate the administration of customary law. Secondly, it is of value in bringing about a unification or harmonisation between different customary laws. Finally, it is of great value for those African Governments who desire to effect a unification between customary law and the general imported law.

(a) *Value as a Restatement.* The value of a restatement of customary law, and hence certainty in this field, need hardly be stressed. So far as the judges administering the customary law are concerned, it has already been pointed out that it is no longer true to say that those judges know the customary law, and certainly the judges of the superior courts are in no better position. To them, therefore, a restatement of customary law will be invaluable. Practitioners are at present excluded from appearance in African Courts in most African countries. This state of affairs, however, is unlikely to continue for very long, and an advocate faced with a customary law problem, a matter in which he is, to say the least, a novice, will greatly welcome the existence of a systematic restatement which will provide the answer to his problem. Finally, law faculties are gradually springing up in most of the African countries, and all of them make provision for the teaching of African customary law. To the law teacher in these faculties, who again is a novice in the field of customary law, a restatement will be of considerable assistance.

(b) *Value of restatement in bringing about unification between different customary laws.* Certain African Governments (e.g. Tanzania, Malawi) take the view that the existence of a diversity of customary laws within their country is not consonant with their idea of building up one nation free from tribal and sectional interests. Tanzania, for example, has embarked upon a project which aims at the complete unification of the customary laws of the mainland Tanganyika tribes. It is submitted that the restatement of customary law can contribute greatly in achieving this end. It was pointed out earlier that the first stage of the Kenya Government Restatement Project consisted of recording the customary criminal offences in order to incorporate them in the general criminal law of the territory. This was in fact done in three stages:-

(i) First the customary criminal offences were restated with the assistance of the Law Panels.

(ii) It was found after stage (i) that in fact the offences recognised by the different tribal groups were very similar. Hence it was considered desirable to make an attempt at unification of the offences in each Province of Kenya, and the Law Panels sat together at Provincial level for this purpose. At each Provincial Meeting it was possible to produce a statement of offences acceptable to all the groups. Although certain compromises were necessary, it did not prove difficult to achieve complete agreement, acceptable to all. The final result was the production of a list of offences recognised by all Kenya customary laws, with very few local variations.[5]

(iii)   Finally, the whole of the written criminal law of Kenya was examined to see how best the offences could be incorporated into that written law.

But even if no active attempt at unification is initiated, it is submitted that the restatements of the different customary laws, without more, will eventually lead, through development by case-law, and its administration by the same personnel, to the emergence of a customary common law.

(c)   *Value of restatement in bringing about unification between the customary law and the general law.*   The eventual aim in African countries must be to bring about a complete integration between the general imported law and the customary law.   We can see signs of this already happening in certain African countries, exemplified by recent and proposed legislation in Ghana.   It has already been shown how this was achieved in the field of criminal law in Kenya.   In other fields of customary law, however, such as the law of marriage and divorce, it is much more difficult to bring about and, it is suggested, it must be *preceded* by a thorough knowledge (hence a *restatement*) of the customary law.   It is very important that a new unified law on a matter affecting personal status, such as marriage, should not bring about a disruption of the way of life of a particular people if these people are not yet ready for the change.   If this is done, it will simply result in having a law which merely exists on paper. Numerous examples of this type of law can be given, but suffice it here to point to the provision enjoining monogamy upon those Africans who marry under the provisions of a Marriage Act or Ordinance.   Needless to say, this provision is often ignored.   Again, the system of converting customary tenure of land in Kenya into land held under individual registered title has not worked very satisfactorily, because on the death of the registered holder the land, despite provisions to the contrary, still devolves in practice according to the customary rules of inheritance.

It is suggested that the principal reason for these anomalies is that the new law is passed in ignorance of what the customary law on the subject is.   If, on the other hand, the draftsman or legislator has a complete restatement of the customary laws which he is attempting

---

5.   See Cotran, *Report on Customary Criminal Offences in Kenya,* 1963. Government Printer, Nairobi.

to integrate with the general law, then he can see at a glance what aspects can and what aspects cannot possibly be unified.

E. Cotran

C. SYNTHETIC RESTATEMENTS

Instead of the separate restatements of customary law and statutory or common law respectively, therefore, the answer may be to attempt what may be termed synthetic restatements of all the applicable law, statutory, common, religious and customary, relating to a particular topic. One cannot possibly hope that there will be uniformity of rule as between all these types of law in respect of all matters; but a surprising measure of agreement on broad principles, and even on questions of detail, may emerge.

The first essential is to have adequate information about the different types of law in force in the country. For this purpose, the restatements already mentioned should provide the basis.

The next step is to state the rules of the applicable laws in a single text. Wherever possible, this text will show uniform rules applying to all systems. Where this is not possible, the differences will be recorded at appropriate points, not as local variations so much as variations between one system and another.

The preparation of a single, largely integrated, text implies the choice of a common arrangement and analysis, and a common vocabulary, applicable to all the different systems. Such common arrangement and vocabulary would in any event emerge in time as the result either of judicial decision or of codification; so that the restator is in a sense merely anticipating the natural lines of development. The devising of such a common vocabulary requires a major effort in applied comparative law; the many discussions which have been going on, mainly in academic circles, in recent years in regard for instance to the description of rights in land are relevant here.

Sometimes the law reformer, or person seeking to develop the law, may feel that the more appropriate way of producing such a synthetic law is by codification, implying the elimination of the variant systems and their replacement by a new unified law. This, for instance, would appear to have been the line of development in Ethiopia. On the other hand, many countries may not be ripe for such an extreme step at this time, and the restatement approach has the advantage of leaving the growing points of the law intact.

There may be those who feel that such a programme is too

ambitious in our present state of knowledge and development of comparative law. The reply to them is that codification is an even more ambitious and radical step to take, and that in any event some countries are endeavouring to do by statute what is recommended to be done by private scholarship. A notable example is Kenya, where laws which substantially unify the laws governing the control and registration of interests in land, and the rules of testate and intestate succession, have been or will be enacted.

Another indication of the possibilities is to be found in the work being done at the School of Oriental and African Studies. During the session 1963-64, for example, an advanced seminar was concerned with the codification of the law of torts or civil wrongs in Africa. The objective is to restate the English common law rules governing torts, breaches of contract, breaches of trust, etc., in such a fashion and in such language as to subsume within the new "code" the parallel rules of customary law. Sometimes an inescapable divergence is to be found, e.g. in the rules governing the liability of a parent for the torts of his offspring; in this event the "code" must choose between one policy and another. But in other instances there is surprising coincidence of rule, which is especially evident once one has stripped away the irrelevant disguise imposed on the English law by antique categories and terminology. In still other instances the English law, with its roots in a highly developed case-law, has detail which is lacking in the boarder sweep of the customary laws; the situation here is not one of incompatibility between the systems, but of rules present in one system paralleled by a gap in the other system(s).

The preparation of such synthetic restatements could, if necessary, be accelerated by telescoping the restatements of customary and statutory law referred to in the first parts of this paper. In any case, it is essential that as far as possible the same language and arrangement should be used in restatements of the different laws. This objective might readily be obtained by ensuring that for each topic the restating team, or at least the restator in chief, was the same for customary law and for statute/common law.

CONCLUSION

The objective set for the American Restatement when the American Law Institute was founded in 1923 was stated as follows:-
   "The purpose was to state rules representing the soundest and most consistent legal thinking, backed by the weight of judicial authority."

At first this objective, and the work of the Restatement, was—we are told—"received with skepticism both by the profession at large and by the courts"; but this scepticism has now entirely evaporated, and the restatements are recognised for what they are, not only the foundations of legal scholarship in the common law field in the United States, but an essential reference tool for the practitioner, the court, and the law reformer. Similar objectives, we may hope, may be achieved by the restatement method, adapted to the very different juridical condition of African countries; and one may also express the hope that doubt as to the value of the method (so far as it exists) may be equally dissipated by the same process as in the United States, by the indispensability of the results of its application. It rests with legal scholars everywhere to ensure that this hope is realised.

CRITICAL OBSERVATIONS REGARDING THE POTENTIALITIES AND THE LIMITATIONS OF LEGISLATION IN THE INDEPENDENT AFRICAN STATES

by

RENE DAVID

PROFESSEUR DE DROIT COMPARE A LA FACULTE DE DROIT
ET DES SCIENCES ECONOMIQUES DE PARIS

CRITICAL OBSERVATIONS REGARDING THE POTENTIALITIES AND THE LIMITATIONS OF LEGISLATION IN THE INDEPENDENT AFRICAN STATES

The political structure of African states has been completely revolutionized by the events which have so recently made these countries independent states. "Decolonization", however, is not an end in itself, and it becomes more and more evident that African states must render account accordingly. These new states are "underdeveloped" and their governments are required, first and foremost, to make up for lost time. New institutions must be created to exploit the economic resources which they possess and to turn them to profit in the shortest possible time; a true social revolution must be achieved if they wish to improve their very low standard of living. In addition to this task, for most of these countries, must be added the necessity to forge a national consciousness to replace a tribal organization or a particularism of local tradition which is incompatible with the notion of a modern state.

How should one go about modernizing these countries, and by which means can one assure their orderly development? Quite naturally, one turns in many instances to *legislation* as a means of achieving this. In the case of the French-speaking African states, a European of Europe, particularly France, had achieved their own revolution and had modernized their political and social structure, thereby opening the way for the formation of modern states, through the use of *codes;* the African states which are familiar with this technique for development are quite naturally inclined to use this example as a model. The tendency to reform through legislation is no less marked in the English-speaking territories. The tradition in the common law countries is, without doubt, one which assigns less importance to legislation than is the case in the continental countries of Europe. This tradition, however, has been abandoned to a large extent, since legislation in these countries during the nineteenth and twentieth centuries has been assigned the function of reforming society and building a new order. Legislation and regulation have since then become, in the common law countries, as abundant and complex, if not more so, than on the continent of Europe. At the other extreme, one can point to the Soviet Union and the "socialist" countries as examples of states where the law, conmpletely identified with the will of the government, recognizes legislation as its primary, if not its *sole*, source. In consequence the African countries see, no matter which way they turn, the same phenomenon—societies and states which aspire to develope and transform themselves by recourse, essentially, to the techniques of *legislation*, the latter being understood to include not only laws passed by the legislature but also administrative regulation.

Legislation and regulation are quite easily considered by governments and by citizens themselves in all countries—be they European or African—as a panacea, a remedy by which one can cure all maladies, a means by which one may obtain, through social planning, all that the society desires.

Experience unfortunately indicates, however, that the contrary is the case.

It is possible by wise legislation and appropriate regulation to effect certain reforms and contribute to the achievement of a certain amount of progress. The possible uses of legislation and regulation in this field are, however, limited. In the developing countries of Africa, in particular, well conceived laws and regulations, appropriate to the conditions of the countries and taking into consideration the circumstances of all the factors conditioning their application, are simply aids to the development of these countries. Poorly conceived laws and regulations run the risk not only of their own demise; they risk—and this is more serious—compromising and handicapping the development of the country, contrary to the intention of their authors. Such poorly conceived laws constitute a cause of friction in these countries, as they discourage the efforts of those, whether they be nationals or foreigners, who wish to co-operate in achieving the progress of the national economy.

Having noted the receptive attitude in all countries toward legislation as an appropriate means of stimulating and guiding the development of a country, we shall not elaborate further upon the merits of legislation. Our purpose will be simply to warn against too great expectations and against the abuses possible in legislation, while at the same time emphasizing the conditions which must be fulfilled if one wishes to obtain from laws and regulations the favourable results expected.

It seems to us that three points merit development in this field; first, a definition of the relations which can be successfully regulated through legislation; second, the formulation of laws and regulations; and third, the application of laws and regulations.

I. In which human relationships can the legislator or administrator act constructively through legislation?

This question is rarely posed in developing countries. In these countries, it is apparently assumed that legislation can be applied in the areas in which it is the will of the legislator to intervene. Accordingly it seems to be assumed that the legislator instinctively detects those areas of human activity where he should, or should not, intervene. Remembering, however, that the frontiers of the law have always been flexible, it is recognized that today those frontiers are still imprecisely defined. Thus on the continent of Europe "law" (droit) was traditionally, through the centuries, restricted to what was called "private law", covering only relationships between citizens, to the exclusion of relations between the State and its citizens; this distinction was not made in the same manner and with the same implications in common law countries. At the present moment, in contrast, the issue of relations between employers and labour, through the technique of collective bargaining is, in a country like France, considered an appropriate area for legislation and for law; while in England the conventions of collective bargaining are rather a kind of "gentleman's agreement," not strictly coming under the law.

In African countries this subject poses a particular problem according to the individual characteristics and complexity of a given country's structure. Side by side with "modern laws", more or less copied from a European model, there exists in the majority of African states a "traditional law" which is quite distinctive from "modern laws". Modern African states are, in effect, frequently composed of communities, more or less artificially joined together in a State wherein the communities continue to live, each following its own "custom". It is accordingly by the "customs" which prevail in each community that the individual rights of the inhabitants of a given community are regulated—that is to say, this is the substance of the private law which regulates the relationships of individuals.

Should an integrated legal system concern itself with regulating these matters which the colonial powers abandoned to the area of "customary law"? Should that system at least attempt to make customary law more precise, to systematize it, and if possible to reduce it either to some degree of unity, or to certain major regional systems of customary law? It appears that this view is gaining ground in different African states, and that an effort toward codification or even toward unification of "customs" has begun.

We may ask if the legislator, in embarking on this path, has not been led astray. It seems possible that he is venturing in this undertaking into a domain which is not appropriate to him, and where he may only create difficulties, friction and frustrations.

Legislation and law are made to regulate only those relationships between individuals in which conflicting interests are definable as well as clearly opposed. The law becomes arbitrary and destructive of established order as soon as it attempts to regulate relationships between individuals who feel that they have worked out a fairly successful *modus vivendi* for themselves. The legislator begins to err as soon as he attempts to legislate relationships between husband and wife, between parents and children, between a village community or tribe which has as its major preoccupation not the affirmation of individual rights for the benefit of individual members but, on the contrary, has the idea of maintaining the cohesion of the group which it forms and the solidarity of its members, because they cannot conceive of life outside their particular community.

"Customs" have neither the rigidity nor the "juridical" nature which jurists tend to attribute to them. The regulation of internal relationships between members of a family or, in Africa, of a village or a tribe is a matter of mores not of law. Resolution of the conflicts which arise in these relationships is a matter of conciliation and arbitration; it is not the function of jurists operating in the courts. In seeking to convert customary rules into legislative rules, no matter how faithfully one seeks to adhere to customs one strips them of their true nature; one gives them a fatal rigidity by seeing in them rights and by injecting into them a principle of individualism opposed to the notion of community solidarity and to the community of interests on which they are based. This deformation is magnified when legislators seek to create a regional or national customary law out of customs which, by tradition, are and must remain local and distinct. Unification of customary law is possible and will, no doubt, come about by spontaneous evolution; it cannot be accomplished by the brutal and artificial action of the legislator, who runs the risk of destroying the very principle on which the authority of custom is based.

Let us make our position clear: We do not for a moment think that African legislation must not concern itself with those matters concerning personal status or land ownership which are at present within the sphere of "traditional law". It is essential that significant transformations should be achieved in this area, or it will not be possible to maintain, side by side in harmonious coexistence, a modern state and communities which live according to the traditions of times gone by. In our opinion, the essential transformation of "custom" is a task which can only be accomplished through education, and which might be described as a gradual evolution; it cannot be achieved by the revolutionary process which promulgation of modern legislation represents.

The legislator has nothing to gain by exposing himself to the failure which must inevitably follow from a pretentious and premature intervention into customary law. If his ambitions require him to act in this field, it should be sufficient for him to establish appropriate regulations for those who are not subject to traditional law (for example, strangers or foreigners), or to facilitate relations between individuals belonging to different communities, or else to regulate the activity and the status of those citizens who have left their traditional society for a new type of life with new relationships.

Those citizens who move to urban areas, who become traders or civil servants, adopt a new way of life, and it is natural and appropriate that they should be subject to a new law and be freed from customary or traditional law. On the other hand, for those who continue to live, to think, and to react as in former times, traditional custom, with all the guarantees and safeguards that it brings with it, without doubt remains the best rule of life possible. One gains nothing in wishing to impose on these people, under the guise of "law", an individualism which causes the disappearance of the values of traditional solidarity without replacing those values by any positive new acquisition.

It seems to us that the most persuasive example here is that of Roman law, in which a "modern" *jus gentium*, ordained in the first place to regulate relations between people from different non-Roman communities, replaced the traditional Roman *jus civile*, because the modified *jus gentium* was demonstrably more effective as legislation. We can also mention the manner in which the more modern common law, as set forth by the Kings' Courts in England, gradually eliminated the "local" customs which were considered retrograde and undesirable. It is therefore clear—and the two examples cited above support this—that the new *jus gentium*, the national "common law" of African states, will have to take greater account of current customs, which it must modernize in the course of creating a new synthesis. This harmonization and adaptation to environment are the conditions of its expansion and eventual success.

It will serve no purpose, however, to seek to force the pace and rhythm of evolution. The African legislator must guard himself against the inevitable temptation to enact legislation that can only be an abuse of logic, and tend toward excessive centralization, contrary to the lessons of modern sociology. Nor is it necessary for a modern state to combat particularism in all its aspects in a totalitarian spirit, and it is probably undesirable for states which are under-administered to undertake tasks that traditional institutions can continue to execute, often in a manner much more in conformity with the habits and wishes of those concerned. The African states have a good example in the manner in which the institutions of trusteeship has been utilized, and continues to be utilized, in many spheres of life in England. English law ignores, *and consciously ignores*, that which takes place in very important institutions in England, such as the Catholic church or the Non-conformist churches, the universities, the Inns of Court, or the Stock Exchange; it only knows the trustees of these institutions and leaves those concerned to regulate their affairs among themselves as they see fit. The internal conflicts within these communities are actually resolved with the aid of techniques of arbitration; the law reports of the English courts contain hardly any decisions regarding the internal disputes of such institutions. In a similar manner, Muslim law, tied though it is to religion, takes no notice—apart from certain exceptional situations—of the continuation of traditional customs; it undoubtedly exercises an influence, often very considerable, over these situations by reason of its moral superiority, but it does not attempt to forbid the interested parties to have recourse to arbitration by authorities whom they recognize according to their tradition.

The legislator in African countries should, it seems to us, take heed of these examples, and accordingly limit to the greatest possible extent his direct intrusion in the area which is properly that of "traditional" law. We use the word "direct" intrusion consciously, for it is quite certain that the legislator cannot dissociate himself from the desire of the population which he governs and with which he must co-operate to achieve evolution of traditional law through education. It is clear, on the other hand that the authority of the state must intervene in forceful fashion in situations where it is essential to forbid and correct certain practices contrary to morality or to the dignity of man; the reserve which it seems appropriate to us to recommend to the legislator does not exclude completely the possibility and the duty, on his part, of exercising a *control* over the manner in which traditional institutions function, and of preventing possible abuses by these institutions.

II. Problems posed by the formulation of laws and of administrative regulations.

Making laws and regulations seems easy to the layman. Those who have had practical experience in this matter know, however, how difficult in reality this task can be. To decide what is best for the development of a country can only be done after a thorough investigation, and for those in a position of responsibility it often implies a very difficult choice. To express that which has been decided in a clear and pertinent fashion requires a technical skill not possessed by laymen.

This dual problem concerning the choice of the political methods which will be adopted and the translation of these methods into legislative or regulatory form is present in all countries. The problem is particularly acute, however, in underdeveloped countries, where one must contend, on the one hand, with the demand for immediate legislative action caused by the sense of urgency characteristic of these countries; and, on the other hand, with the scarcity of qualified personnel both to conduct the preliminary inquiries which are necessary and to draft the laws and regulations in a proper form. Laws and regulations are often enacted under pressure of circumstances with understandable haste, haste which is not conducive to careful draftsmanship. Loopholes in the texts give rise to abuses, to ambiguities, or to contradictions that render the task of those who must apply the laws more difficult.

How can one remedy this situation? There is no completely effective and perfect remedy; in the most developed countries, those most richly provided with specialists in political science and law, one often hears complaints—and not without reason—against badly drafted laws, against the chaos of regulatory issuances which are redundant and complex. These problems, of course, are to a certain extent inevitable from the moment that the State assumes the task of directing the economy and reforming society, in addition to executing its traditional function of police power. Quite obviously, there is no question, particularly in Africa, of the State's renouncing these tasks.

A certain degree of progress can and must, it seems to us, be achieved in this regard. The heads of African states are too often misled by the haste with which they must legislate, or through the relative case of modelling their laws and regulations on European examples which are poorly suited to their needs. A joint study of legislative problems which most frequently and particularly confront African states would allow the establishment in several fields of a series of *model laws*, which would not—except in the case of international conventions—be binding upon the states, but which would provide them with a set of examples, proposed by experts, which take special account of the particular circumstances of Africa and of the needs of underdeveloped countries.

From any point of view it is costly if not impossible for African states to proceed individually to pursue intensive studies which will support the promulgation of codes or other comprehensive laws destined to have permanent value. The legislation which must constitute the judicial skeleton and provide the foundation of law in different countries surely would gain strength by being drafted by experts. This is quite independent of the supplementary advantages, hardly negligible, which would derive (as we shall see later) from the contribution that such joint and expert action would make toward development of more or less completely uniform laws in African countries.

That which is true for domestic laws and regulations is no less true for international conventions. In a spirit of international co-operation, the African states quite often accept international conventions. Possibly this acceptance is not always to their advantage. It occurs most often in regard to texts which have been drafted without consideration of their own situations; these conventions can be amended so as to take account of their situations only after discussions in diplomatic conferences where the African states have the possibility of effective intervention and are adequately represented. The clear interest of African states is to be represented to have their viewpoint forcefully presented and taken into consideration, at an earlier stage when the projects are formulated which will thereafter be submitted to international conferences. The African Legislative Centre which should, in our opinion, be created, could provide assurance that the interests of African state would be presented at this stage in the formulation of projects for international conventions. Such a Centre could, in addition, act as a counsellor for the African delegations in international conferences, and then at a later stage in the formulation of the projects could examine whether or not it would be advantageous for African states to adhere to various conventions, to adhere with reservations, or to demand when necessary the revision of a particular convention.

The African Legislative Centre, which we consider might become an indispensable instrument of African juridical policy, could at the outset be an organization of modest dimensions. A Secretary-General, assisted by one or two deputies and some clerical personnel, could form the nucleus of the Centre. The mission of the Secretariat and of the Centre would neither be to formulate projects on its own nor, to counsel African governments itself. The Centre would confine itself, in each case, to recommending the most competent experts to governments, and it would serve as a liaison agency between these experts and African governments.

At present, Africa finds itself divided between countries of the Roman-Germanic tradition and those of the common law tradition. It is essential to take account of this state of affairs, even though efforts may be undertaken to change it. The *rapprochement* which, even in Europe, is now taking place between the legal systems of the Continent and of England augurs well for future *rapprochement* of the two systems elsewhere. For the present, however, it will be necessary in most cases in Africa to base plans for the future not on one but on two legal models, one for those countries of the French juridical tradition and the other for those countries of the English juridical tradition. In so far as international conventions are concerned, however, nothing prevents the study and adoption of a common position by all African countries, without regard to the difference between the two groups of countries. As for domestic laws and regulations, it would seem possible, even today, to arrive at some uniform models, or at least to harmonize the models in a certain number of areas of interest among all African states, notably in several areas relating to commercial law.

Finally, it seems to us that three distinct areas of possible action can be traced here. In certain areas one can undertake drafting of laws common to all African states. In other areas the duality between the countries of the French and the English traditions will have to be maintained, with the exception that certain possibilities for harmonization between the two systems can be pursued. In still other areas, the laws of the different states will continue to be different, taking account of the difference existing between the cultural and social situations, beliefs, and interests of the various states.

III. Problems relative to the application of laws and administrative regulations

To draft and enact laws and regulations is not an end in itself, even though certain legislators appear to act as if this were so. Laws and regulations are not useful until they are *known*, and then only to the extent that they are *applied*.

This verity poses a problem in all countries, for everywhere the legislature and the central authority have a tendency to concentrate on enactment of laws and regulations which they deem to be desirable, while simultaneously taking too little interest in the problems of applying them. Many laws and regulations, well conceived in the eyes of theoreticians or of their authors, are thus deprived of practical effect, for they remain unapplied if not completely unknown. Even in France there was recently the case of a school headmistress who, with refreshing candour, advised the Minister of Education that "my most essential working tool is my wastepaper basket."

This situation is critical in African countries, given the shortage of jurists and of administrative cadres which unfortunately prevails in the majority of these countries. The situation is even more grave, and therefore merits yet more attention, since these or failure of administration and of justice thus represents to them, more than to European countries of a liberal, or more or less liberal, tradition, a threat to the essential development of these countries. This threat cannot be offset to the same degree as in Europe by the initiative of individuals and the action of private groups. What measures can one propose for the amelioration of this situation?

As far as the law is concerned, it seems to us that the problem has been too exclusively regarded from the purely legislative angle. African states have adopted, or are inclined to adopt, codes and laws according to the models and the techniques which have prevailed so long in Europe. While this is helpful, it is not sufficient under the conditions which prevail in Africa. Codes and laws, no matter how hard one tries to make them easily comprehensible, are documents which, because of the technical requirements of legal draftsmanship, only people having a legal background can understand. The citizens of Africa who read a code can no more comprehend it than can French citizens, if they are not lawyers. The curriculum of schools for general education in Africa or elsewhere does not prepare students for correct understanding or interpretation of a code nor enable them to find their way through the maze of the law or of the existing judicial decisions.

This problem is not of great importance in European countries where there exist lawyers aplenty. One should not, however, make abstract laws in Africa, where outside the large centres there exists only a very small, usually insignificant, number of lawyers. Laws and regulations are condemned to remain ineffective under these conditions, if one is content with simply communicating the texts to those who are subject to the laws and regulations and to those who must undertake their implementation. The essential thing here is usually not so much the texts of the codes, laws, or judicial decisions, themselves being very complex documents. The application of laws is conditioned by the existence of *complementary documents*— elementary manuals, circulars, and instructions—drafted with a view to explaining the texts to a lay public, e.g. those authorities charged with application of the law at the local level, or even citizens in general.

The Emperor Justinian, in the sixth century A.D., complemented the codification of the law contained in the *corpus juris civilis*, or civil law, by a brief manual, entitled the *Institutes*, from which we still draw the principles of Roman law. The treatises known generally under the name of *coutumiers*, and in England as *books* of *authority* (particularly the *Institutes* of Bracton and Coke), played an analogous role in Europe in the period preceding codification. Even today the situation is the same; the law of the countries of Eastern

Europe, especially in the "socialist" countries, would only be a mass of theoretical rules which were quite inapplicable if there did not exist, alongside these codes and laws or regulations, manuals and other types of guides designed to facilitate the understanding of these laws by those concerned.

Even more perhaps than in Europe, it is important that such manuals and guide books be placed at the disposal of those affected by laws and regulations in African countries. There it is necessary to develop elementary manuals, on the one hand, to the end that all those who are affected, even if they are not lawyers, may understand the law of their country and co-operate toward achieving the political objectives of their governments. An example might be cited in this regard from the "socialist" countries, without implying agreement with Marxist-Leninist doctrine; the numerous brochures that one sees in these countries designed to popularize the law, to make comprehensible the essential regulations of the government, and to gain support for the political measures of the government, could fruitfully serve as models for African countries, where it is no less important to acquaint and educate the people with the rules under which one hopes to accomplish modernization of these countries and the growth of their economies. Another measure which appears essential is to make it easier within each central administrative agency or department to know and understand administrative regulations. It would be most helpful if, at regular intervals, the rules set forth in the regulations promulgated by a given ministry or department were laid out systematically in plain language, in a large manual for the employees of the ministry or department; the publication of such a manual would have the effect of weeding out all those regulatory measures which have not been implemented and which had not previously been expressly eliminated. One may complain perhaps that the editing of such manuals is an onerous task which the ministries could only accomplish with great difficulty. The reply to this objection is that if the ministries are incapable of understanding this task, the officers and employees of the ministry scattered over the countryside are, *a fortiori*, incapable of applying the unelucidated texts of these regulations which are sent out to them from headquarters. The requirement of annually revising all regulations could well have the effect of reducing the excessive proliferation of regulatory measures, a highly desirable objective in *all* countries. The work of editing and revising the central service manuals, undertaken annually, is on the other hand without doubt less difficult than might appear; the difficult thing is to establish the framework—and here aid could be very helpfully furnished by European countries—it would not be difficult, in so far as the regulations will have been published, to integrate new regulations into these basic manuals. As far as the basic manuals are concerned, as discussed above, it should be possible in many areas to establish them in common for the different African countries, especially if the desired efforts have already been undertaken to unify, or at least harmonize, the laws of these different countries.

In conclusion, particular attention should obviously be paid to the problem of the education and training of jurists and administrators for African countries. What we have said above amply demonstrates the urgency of this problem. A significantly important number of jurists and administrators must be trained, and that in the shortest possible time, if it is wished to create the necessary conditions for the effective application of programmes decreed from above for the progress of the country. The establishment of lower level schools of law and administration, furnishing their students the necessary tools for the exercise of their professions without cutting them off from the environment in which they will be called to exercise their profession, is of primary importance in the African states. One may well wonder if it is not from among these jurists and administrators who have acquired a degree of experience and have proved their zeal and their qualities as organizers, that it will be possible to recruit the personnel to whom, during the second stage, will ultimately be given the most advanced training, qualifying them for the highest posts in the administration; just as in France, among the students of the Ecole Nationale d'Administration, some are recruited by competition open to students and others by competition open to civil servants. If, in each country such schools of law and administration are established at the elementary level during the first stage, it would seem reasonable, in order to enlarge the horizons and widen the experience and wisdom of the students, to permit students to benefit further from foreign experience and to bring them together in sufficient numbers under the direction of instructors of a higher level. Thus there might be interest in founding a school or schools of advanced administration on an international or supranational level, possibly with part of the course being given in Africa and another part in a European country. It might be added that, at this higher level, it would be eminently desirable to subscribe to the principle of bilingualism, French and English, so that the African elites may understand each other and may make a reality of the current ideal of African unity, or at least of the solidarity of African states.

CONCLUSION

The conclusions to which we have come can be summarized as follows:

In the first place, in so far as the proper domain of law and regulation are concerned, it seems that the legislator must, as a general rule, respect the autonomy of the local communities which coexist within his national territory, while attempting on the one hand to exercise an influence on the development of these communities, and on the other hand exercising over them a degree of control required to eliminate the most flagrant abuses.

In the second place, in so far as the drafting of laws and regulations is concerned, it seems that a considerable improvement of the current situation and a possibility of rapid progress would be opened up if African states undertook to act in concert in a number of matters, through the creation of an African Legislative Centre. The task or duty of this Centre would be, on the one hand, to propose model laws as regards different matters, and on the other hand to make recommendations to African states at the time of drafting, discussion, and adoption of international conventions.

In the third place, there is a need to concentrate on the creation of better conditions for facilitating the effective application of laws and regulations promulgated in Africa. In this regard, stress must be placed on the one hand on the necessity for publishing manuals, general instruction books, and other informational documents for the use of those affected by the laws, and on the other hand on the necessity for training jurists and administrators as soon as possible and in as large numbers as possible.

The solutions which we have proposed certainly call for discussion, and do not pretend to be anything but an appeal for such discussion. The author of this report knows that his knowledge is limited to certain states, and that it is quite rudimentary as far as even these states are concerned. The author also takes account of the fact that, no matter how well intentioned, his viewpoint is conditioned by his status as a French citizen on the one hand, and his position as a university professor and a bourgeois (of recent vintage) on the other. Finally, this paper has had to be drafted under certain conditions of haste, little conductive to profound reflection on the problems that the author has had the termerity to evoke and consider. The author hopes, nevertheless, that the conclusions at which he has arrived (and which are *not* improvised) can furnish useful elements for this conference.

SOME REMARKS ON LAW AND COURTS IN AFRICA

by

J. KEUNING

PROFESSOR IN CUSTOMARY LAW AND THE DEVELOPMENT
OF LAW IN NON-WESTERN SOCIETIES,
UNIVERSITY OF LEYDEN

SOME REMARKS ON LAW AND
COURTS IN AFRICA

"Integration of customary and modern legal systems in Africa" is unquestionably a thorny problem. Integration is "to *make* or *grow into* a coherent whole", says my dictionary. It is the first of these, the active "to make", which the initiators of this conference evidently had in mind. The problem put before the participants is: "to demonstrate how practical legal draughtsmen, judges and jurists can reconcile and harmonize coexisting systems of traditional and non-traditional law", and papers are expected "on problems and techniques of harmonization or integration of traditional and non-traditional systems of law in a particular jurisdiction in the following fields: Land law; Husband and Wife (including marriage, custody, divorce, etc.); Succession; Civil Wrongs and Contracts".[1]

Coexisting systems of traditional and non-traditional law.
Before we can say anything about reconciliation and harmonization in this respect we must be aware of certain essential characteristics peculiar to each of these systems.

Traditional Law
Here we are immediately and unavoidably confronted with the (negative) view of Professor David[2] that, "the regulation of internal relationships between members of a family or, in Africa, of a village or tribe is a matter of *mores, not of law*. Resolution of the conflicts which arise in these relationships is a matter of *conciliation and arbitration;* it is not the function of jurists operating in the courts" (italics mine). This statement is, I submit, a misjudgement of the social and juridical reality of African society both in the past and in the present. In this view, *law* is only possible in a Western or westernized society, and the administration of law in courts would be possible only by individuals who have studied Western law (ignoring Islamic law for the moment).

I cannot agree with this. In my opinion it is wrong and an injustice to African socio-political systems to put traditional law or customary law between quotation marks as though it did not

1. The passages between quotation marks are taken from the brochure announcing the conference.
2. Critical observations regarding the potentialities and the limitations of legislation in the independent African States, page 47, *Supra.*

58

constitute law in the true sense. It is equally wrong to state that the
solution of conflicts in family, village and tribe is always a matter of
conciliation and arbitration. This too represents a misunderstanding
of African reality with its courts of chiefs and elders in the past and
its customary, African, local, etc., courts in the present. I think
I need refer here only to the investigations done by Gluckman,
Holleman, Schapera, Peter Lloyd[3] and many other social-anthro-
pologists, administrative officers, etc. In their works we often find
"cases" discussed: lawsuits which are conducted according to a less
formalized and less detailed procedure than is the case in Western
law, with a different concept of relevance than in a lawyer's process,
and the use of a different method by the judge or bench with respect
to interpretation and application of the law. Nonetheless, there is no
question whatever, I submit, that legal decisions are handed down,
that distinctions are made between social or moral norms on the
one hand and legal norms on the other (even when the latter are
not established in formal rules), and that arbitration and conciliation
(even though the latter may be the aim) are not essential to the
resolution of a conflict. In other words, verdicts were and are given.
I cannot resist the temptation to cite one example *in extenso* because
it seems to me to illustrate the point in question so clearly. It is
taken from Gluckman's "Judicial process among the Barotse of
Northern Rhodesia":[4]

> Case 45: *The case of the ungenerous husband.*
> "In this case the wife sued for divorce, alleging ill-treat-
> ment by her husband and that he infected her with syphilis
> acquired in fornication. The husband counterclaimed for
> damages on the ground that his wife had got syphilis in
> adultery and infected him, and, through him, her co-wife.[5]
> The *Kuta* (court of Chiefs, JK) held that the husband was
> responsible for the infection and granted a divorce.
> KALONGAR (R 15) (this number indicates his place
> in the hierarchy of chiefs, JK), giving the concluding
> judgment, stated: 'The woman is freed and she will take
> home with her half of the crops which she planted (this
> is the legal rule in such cases, JK). There has been so much
> ill-feeling in this case that we will send an induna (lower

3. Max Gluckman, *The judicial process among the Barotse of Northern
   Rhodesia* 1955.
   J. F. Holleman, *Shona customary law*, 1952.
   I. Schapera, *A handbook of Tswana law and custom*, 1959.
   Peter Lloyd, *Yoruba land law*, 1962.
4. at p. 172
5. We are thus concerned here with a conflict within a family, between
   members of a village or tribe.

chief, JK) to see that it is fairly done. Now what else (to the husband), my kinsman, will you give her of the goods of the marriage to take with her?' (As stated above, a woman who sues for divorce loses her right in all goods of the marriage which she has rejected, save in crops planted by her.)

Husband: 'I will give her nothing; she has made me diseased and bound me here with lies.'

KALONGA: 'Come, my kinsman, you cannot do this. When you married her, taking her from her parents, you all rejoiced together. You hoped that you would have a strong marriage, with children to bind you together. It has not worked out thus, but you cannot send a woman home to her parents, naked like a dog. We beg you, give her a blanket and a dress and some plates.'

Husband: 'I will give her nothing, not even a shawl.'

KALONGA: 'Very well. We have power (mata) to make you divide the crops, *for this is our law (mulao, and we will send someone to see this is done. But we have no power (mata) to make you behave like an upright man. Go.'* (Italics mine)

This was shortly before the kuta adjourned for its noon-day recess. As it was about to adjourn for the day at 4 p.m., the husband returned to the post and asked if he could speak to the kuta. He said that he had been reflecting on KALONGA'S words and saw that he was wrong (*nifoxize*). He would give his wife a dress, a shawl, a blanket, a pot, and a plate.

KALONGA thanked him: 'We thank you, my child. This is behaving like a decent upright man', and he and the other judges clapped their acknowledgements."

"Thus"—Gluckman comments—"the kuta has clearly in mind a distinction between obligations it can compel people to observe, and obligations it can only urge on them as right. This gives the Lozi a distinctive body of legal rules which does not cover all obligations which are approved as moral".

This case may raise the objection that it concerns an African kingdom with a clearly-defined political structure and an administration of justice that is to a certain extent institutionalized, of a kind also known for some of the peoples of East and West Africa (although this objection would be irrelevant to Prof. David's line of thought). Concerning the Ibo, who according to the classification of political systems in Africa provided by Fortes and Evans Pritchard must be assigned to those societies "which lack centralized authority, administrative machinery, and judicial institutions—in short which lack government..."[6], Miss M. M. Green states: "We shall see when we consider the judicial function that in this society law is distinguished from custom in the sense that it is *enforced* directly or indirectly *by the community and that this distinction is recognized by the people*"[7] (italics mine). It is this judicial function exercised by or in the name of the community which, in my opinion, should be taken as the criterion for the "quest for law".

We can, I believe, only consider and discuss reconciliation and harmonization of coexisting systems of traditional and non-traditional law if we assign traditional law the important value that it has in its own context, that is within African society, and for African men and women in their mutual relations. And this law ought not to be devaluated by equating it with *mores*.[8]

I cannot here go further into this point on which I am at variance with Prof. David's view: "theoretical considerations of the nature of customary law will be secondary," says the brochure outlining the objects of this conference.

There is one feature of autochthonous African law, which should be brought out with some emphasis, however. *Traditional* law is a dangerous term. Those who have had no direct experience with the nature of African law and custom and the procedures associated with them may easily be misled by this term: it does not do justice to the dynamics and flexibility of autochthonous African law, or to its inherent capacity to adjust to changed social and economic conditions. African law can only be called traditional law in the sense that there has been no sharp break with the past; but it has become law in a state of progressive development, especially in recent decades. It is law 'on the move', and in recent years an accelerating move.[9]

In my opinion it is not realistic to state, without qualification and differentiation of the large majority of Africans, that they "continue to live, to think, and to react as in former times..."[10]." This

6. M. Fortes and E. E. Evans; *African political systems*, 1st ed. 1940, 6th reprinting 1961, p. 5. See also John Middleton and David Tait; *Tribes without rulers* 1958.
7. M. M. Green; *Ibo village affairs*, 1948, quoted in T. Olawale Elias; *The nature of African law* 1956, p. 29. Comp. I. Schapera, *op. cit.*, Chapter II, The nature and sources of Tswana law. How this enforced directly and indirectly by the community" is effected, even when a "Conciliation" is finally achieved, is described in detail in J. F. Holleman; *Hera court procedure*, NADA (The Southern Rhodesia Native Affairs Department Annual), Vol. 29 (1952), pp. 26-42.
8. In agreement, I refer here to Mr. Contran's remarks on page 15 under (d) and (1) of *A background paper on restatement of laws in Africa*.
9. The requirements for the administration of justice will be discussed below.
10. David, *Supra*, at p. 48.

view ignores the development changes, material, intellectual and spiritual, which have resulted from the "impact of the West" even in rural societies, although by this I, of course, do not mean to say that traditional custom no longer has any importance.

It seems to me no longer possible in rural areas to leave the maintenance of social and legal order "between members of a family, of a village, or a tribe" to traditional institutions. These traditional institutions no longer have the same meaning and influence in the social system that they formerly had. The position—and even more the role—of chiefs and elders has changed now that they and their communities have become part of a larger political, social, and legal order. The solidarity felt by kinship groups, villagers, or members of a broader traditional community has also become less strong and there is less need of it, for one thing because peace and order are now maintained over a much larger area than formerly, which has led to far greater social mobility, more inter-group contacts, and increased individualism. The sanctions wielded by the traditional institutions—the chief's position of authority, the force of public opinion, the threat of social ostracism—have lost much of their power, albeit not to the same extent for everyone and perhaps most of all for the younger generations.

The State cannot avoid interfering in and taking the responsiblity for the course of justice at the village level in rural areas; and even less so can it let the law take its own course in urban areas. However, in my view it would defeat the object if the urban population were to be indiscriminately subjected "to a new law and be freed from customary or traditional law".[11] This presumes a gap between urban and rural societies which—with the possible exception of members of the small westernized elite—does not exist.[12]

Non-Traditional Law

(a) *Islamic Law.* Although in origin non-traditional, the reception of certain aspects of Islamic law (especially pertaining to marriage and inheritance, often taken over only partially) was (and is) for the most part a gradual process, which enabled the development of a symbiosis with the autochthonous law. I prefer to see Islamic law considered part of the prevailing law and custom, as is the case in Northern Nigeria, to take one example. This does not mean that no problems are encountered on this point in the practice of law and the administration of justice. But in my opinion these problems can (and must?) be entrusted to the insight and

11.   David, *Supra*, at p. 48.
12.   Comp. e.g. the publications of A. L. Epstein on the mining towns in the Copperbelt of Northern Rhodesia.

diligence of the courts, which in turn must take into consideration the directives of the highest Court of Appeal.

(b) *Modern legal systems*, or, in other words, imported Western legal systems. I must confine myself here to a few general remarks, if only because I know but little about these legal systems as such. This Western law was not intended for the Africans when it was originally imported. In spite of the British standpoint that "Common Law, Equity and the Statutes of General Application" formed the *general* law in the colonies and protectorates, roughly 90% of the legal actions in British Africa were dominated by the autochthonous law. In the French and Belgian territories an African was required to satisfy certain rather stringent requirements for assimilation before metropolitan law could be applied to him, and these *assimiles* formed only a small minority.

The modern legal systems were intended in the first place for the local European and for the legal aspects of economic activities with a Western pattern. As such they also became operative for Africans who participated directly in such economic activities. In the French and Belgian territories Western law grew out of their own law and custom if they could satisfy the demands stipulated by legislation; in the British territories only certain facets of English law were put at their disposal (for instance in the Marriage Ordinances). For the African population, autochthonous law remained the generally applicable law, and for them Western law remained subsidiary.

For the administration of this Western law, special courts were set up on the metropolitan pattern and these courts followed metropolitan procedures. The latter also held when these courts had to deal with suits according to customary law (usually issues of great importance on appeal), in which case substantive law and the rules of procedure and evidence did not belong to the same legal system even though there was a certain amount of adjustment. In the British territories these Courts of foreign origin treated the autochthonous law as a foreign law whose rules had to be proved as fact. Since independence, little has been changed basically, I believe. Notwithstanding the integration of the courts and notwithstanding the fact that the judges in these "English Courts" (in the West African States) are now almost exclusively Africans, customary law and the law of metropolitan origin exist side by side, and this is also the case in the actual situation for the large majority of the customary (local, African) courts on the one hand and the "general" courts on the other.

Are reconciliation and harmonization possible, and if so, how can they be realized?

The question, put in this way, assumes no replacement of the one by the other, no superseding of customary law by a modern legal system. And correctly so, in my opinion, I am in complete agreement with Professor David's warnings against an all-over legislation.[13] I have re-examined the reports of the introduction (in 1926) of the Swiss Civil Code into Turkey as given during a meeting of the International Committee of Comparative Law in Istanbul in September 1955.[14] If the principal law of a country should be a "living law", in other words must be consistent with the needs of (the large majority of) the population so that they can (and will!) align their behaviour to it, the Turkish experiment must be considered a failure, at least as far as such important aspects as matrimonial law, the law of inheritance and succession, and land law are concerned. The Swiss Code was only the law for a small urban elite and ... for the legal profession. It therefore was and remained a foreign, incomprehensible, and elusive law for 80% of the Turkish people, a law which could not be applied in the actual social reality. As a result, the internal relationships continued to be based on the rules of customary and Islamic law in their mutual connexion. 'But'—according to the social anthropologist P. Stirling who made a close study of life in a couple of Turkish villages over a period of a few years—"the next law has left the village informal system totally unsupported, with no means of plugging the gaps at its weak points. Hence the system which the new laws were intended to abolish continues, but in a less orderly form."[15]

"Legal engineering" must first of all take the social reality into account. It is too readily taken for granted, in my opinion, that customary law can have no importance with respect to modern industrial and commercial transactions. A good example of the application and recognition of customary law in modern relationships is the decision of the Ijebu Divisional Grade "A" Customary Court of 13 June 1961.[16] Some passages from the Judgment may be cited in clarification:

> "The Plaintiffs claim for themselves and on behalf of the Egbe Obagoroye of Isonyin the sum of £400, being the amount of loan free of interest given by the Plantiffs to the Defendant at the Defendant's request as by a Promisory

---

13. David, *op. cit.*, pp. 1-6. I am led to wonder whether the Ethiopian Civil Code is compatible with this point of view; see Journal of African Law, Vol. 7 (1963), No. 3, pp. 172 ff. (Krzeczunowicz).
14. UNESCO Int. Soc. Science Bul., Vol. IX, No. 1, 1957, pp. 7-85.
15. Ibid, page 32.
16. Suit No. J.D.G.A./12CL/60, Western Nigeria.

Note dated the 25th of January 1957 . . . "[17]

"Learned Counsel for the Defendant addressed the court, and submitted that the claim having been brought on behalf of an unincorporated Association, it is the principle of law that an unincorporated Association cannot sue or be sued unless it is registered. He cited the 21st. edition of Chitty on Contracts, page 673, in support of his submission."

"With respect to Learned Counsel for Defence, I do not agree that Egbe Obagoroye of Isonyin is an unincorporated Association such as is contemplated by the learned author of Chitty on Contracts. It is, as given in evidence, a traditional society, which is peculiar to Ijebu Community. It does not come under any Company Law or any Ordinance under the registration of Business Name. I agree with Learned Counsel for Plaintiffs on this point. The society comprises of individuals who from their boyhood formed it. Its aim, far from being commercial, is only to assist financially any of its members in need. As individuals, it is my view, that they can sue and be sued . . ."

"In the circumstances, and from the evidence before me, there will be judgment for the Plaintiffs against the Defendant in the sum of £400 and costs assessed at 40 guineas . . . "

We are concerned here with a mutual aid society of a traditional character (such as occurs in many different forms) which has retained its function in modern commercial and financial affairs. The judge did not allow himself—fortunately—to be misled by the defence Counsel's legal technicalities based on English law.

If—as is often advocated—commercial law, company law, etc., are to be regulated by written laws, then already existing institutions deriving from the past and having developed according to their own nature must not be deprived of legal protection. They must not be sacrificed to the constructions of the law. It should remain possible for simple transactions such as occur among the common people (petty traders, farmers, craftsmen) in both rural and urban societies, that, when disputes arise, they can be heard by a judge according to their own merits even when they do not fulfill the requirements established in the Code. This will serve legal and judicial certainty,

17. This sum was borrowed by the Defendant after he had gotten into financial difficulties as store-keeper and produce-buyer for the United Africa Company by buying up substandard cocoa.

as seen from the stand-point of the members of society. Such transactions and the disputes arising from them are of daily occurrence among the millions of African village and city dwellers.

In plain words: to my way of thinking, autochthonous African law (customary law) should wherever possible be recognized as being the best basis for the formal control of social and economic life and its development in the African milieu. It is the legal expression of African socio-cultural organizations. But we must be bold enough to see the law as a flexible legal system which can give expression to the dynamics of the present day. We must be prepared to give the courts of justice the responsibility to express socioeconomic, intellectual and spiritual changes in their decisions, striving for a true acceptance of a changing law that remains within its social context. This implies a judicial organization which has the confidence of all layers of the population, which is easily accessible, and whose actions are understood and accepted.

It also implies that written laws be enacted only for the regulation and stimulation of modern projects for the development of industry, commerce, agriculture and general welfare services. The primary consideration in such legislation should be that these projects must be realized in a society composed of people with their own ideas and who have their own particular ways of reacting to something new to them. Only marionettes can be made to act and move exactly according to another's will; in a human community the issue can only be forced to a certain extent; further pressure would lead to social unrest or even revolution. Experience has proved this more than once. One should, says a Dutch proverb, *niet verder willen springen dan zi in polsstok lang is:* one should not try to jump further than the length of one's jumping pole, which is perhaps best approximated by the English admonition to cut one's coat according to one's cloth!

Thus in my view, codified law only when necessary and African customary law the rule; and the latter applied and further developed by a sound judicial organization serving the needs of all social levels. In their interpretation of the law the judges dealing with the present must look back to the past and at the same time glance into the future. They must consistently consider the demands of the present against the background of the past. We must not recoil from judge-made law or, formulated more precisely, law developed by the intellectual activities of the judicial machinery. The judges must re-interpret the traditional law for their own times, extend it, and, where necessary, supplement it in new situations. But in doing so they will have to use extreme care that their interpretation and their "legal creation" remain in harmony with the framework of the customary legal system, so that an optimal amount of certainty is achieved and the mutual cohesion of the rules continues to exist in the law 'on the move'.

The administration of justice based on customary law should commence at the village level. To deal with the flood of small daily disputes there should be an official, supervised court with restricted competence and simple rules of procedure. The resolution of these internal disputes can no longer be left to a self-regulating arbitration and conciliation based on traditional institutions. (To do so would be to succumb to a romantic wish-dream.) As has already been said, the traditional sanctions no longer have their former force. The individual must be able to ask for and obtain the *protection of the law* regardless of whether he has the co-operation of his adversary. In addition, these petty courts must possess the means to apply coercion, for instance to summon a refractory defendant or witnesses and to provide for the carrying out of their decisions. The members of these courts at the lowest level could usually be recruited from among the chiefs and elders who as a rule have the best knowledge of local law and customs. They are also the ones who are accustomed to providing leadership in the social affairs of the small community. In such communities they are therefore the most appropriate judges to provide for the maintenance of those social norms which are also legal norms. These chiefs and elders must, however, be willing and capable of understanding social changes so that they can react adequately to them as judges. A chief who, as a traditional leader, cannot go along with his times cannot be a good judge and will have to step aside for someone with wider comprehension. Conciliation between plaintiff and defendant will often (but far from always) be achieved in these local courts, partly because of the totally public nature of the proceedings and the pressure of public opinion. Such completely open hearings also serve to discourage misuse of the power assigned to the judge. But it is not sufficient to prevent such misuse. To insure justice there must be supervision and review, and there must always be a possibility of appealing to higher courts.

Concerning these higher courts I will restrict myself to only a few points since detailed treatment would exceed the scope of this paper.

Because of practical consideration, only the highest courts can be staffed by legally qualified judges. For the foreseeable future the others will continue to be composed of lay-judges. I do not see any great or even fundamental objection to this. To be a good judge in customary law does not entail having completed the study of English or French law. Customary court judges must have, in the first place, a good knowledge of the customary law in their area of jurisdiction and they must also be mature, experienced people who as a consequence are capable of understanding social needs. They must have the confidence of those who are subject to their jurisdiction and who have to appear in their courts without counsel. It is the task and the responsibility of the lay judges to collect the facts of the case before them by making their own investigation. The argumentation cannot be left to the parties themselves who have very often had little or no formal education. The administration of justice by lay judges based on customary law must follow a procedure suited to it. For this, the adversary English court pro-cedure seems to me unsuited; it provides the rules for a lawyer's process in which counsels for plaintiff and defendant lead the examination, cross-examination, and re-examination while the judge is assigned a passive role in this part of the proceedings. The judge decides on the basis of the data put before him, taking as point of departure for his reasoning, precedents which he considers valid.

This seems to me impossible in customary law proceedings. The judge's task must have a wider foundation. He carries the direct responsiblity for the investigation at the sitting; he must assist both parties when they are unable to make their position sufficiently clear; he is required to be their trusted adviser. I have often seen this in actual practice at the customary court sessions I attended in Western Nigeria in 1961.

Conceived of in this way, the administration of justice by laymen should be placed in the hands of a team of at least three judges who supplement each other and who investigate a dispute and arrive at a decision together. This might, for example, take the form of a bench composed of a president with a secondary-school education and two members who are traditional chiefs. Besides his knowledge of law and society, the president can draw on his views on the exigencies of modern times as based on his education and experience of life in a wider field. The chiefs, as *members* of the court (as assessors they cannot function to full advantage) can join the discussions by imparting their knowledge and understanding of local conditions.[18] It seems to me that in customary law-cases the sole judge is too heavily burdened in Western Nigeria and elsewhere.

For the highest customary courts, lawyers can make an essential contribution as judge or counsel. These courts must effect the co-ordination of the decisions of the judges of the lower courts along the channel of appeal. These courts would also be the courts

18. For this point I may refer to my article, *Some aspects of the admini-stration of justice in Yoruba-land*, Nigerian Institute of Social and Economic Research, Conference Proceedings, March 1962, page 37.

of first instance in cases beyond the competence of the lower courts because of the large amounts of money or property involved in the dispute, the serious social implications connected with a claim, or as a kind of *forum privilegiatum* for those who occupy a prominent place in the community. Customary law is also a flexible legal system in the sense that its principles are also appropriate for those who have climbed high on the social ladder. There must be a willingness to employ a procedure proper to customary law in these higher courts, as well, and to avoid rules of procedure peculiar to an alien-European-legal system. This of course does not imply that fewer guarantees are required, and more than that the proceedings of the lower courts need not be surrounded by fewer guarantees. The legal procedures must be established by legislation based on the specific requirements belonging to a law-suit in customary law.

Another condition is that the judges (and lawyers) be well versed in customary law because they have made a thorough study of it. A university training should be accepted as a necessity for those who wish to fulfil a function—and it is a responsible function—in the higher levels of the administration of justice according to customary law (the "general law" in the process of gestation!). *The Restatement of Customary Law* will be of great use in this training. In fact, there is more literature on customary law than is generally thought. Jurists and judges can gainfully make use of sociological (socio-anthropological) studies, even though they will not find the *rules* already formulated in them. Moreover, in West Africa the High Court and Supreme Court judges are at present almost all individuals who have been familiar since childhood with the social environment in which the legal problems occur or who can, as Africans, familiarize themselves more easily with these problems than the members of the Bench in colonial times whose distance from the people was practically unbridgeable. I consider this an important point.

It has been rightly stressed that this Restatement is only to be used as a *guide* and is not intended as a code. The latter would perhaps be impossible in any case since the *Restatement* does not go into sufficient detail for that purpose.

One danger will always remain if this *Restatement* is given the appearance of a code. Human inertia must not be underestimated! It must, I submit, be clearly stipulated that notwithstanding the *Restatement* the judge remains responsible for establishing the rule in the case before him, if only to allow for changes in the law. When, in Java before the last war, the restatement of the rules of adat (customary) law was completed and published by Javanese adatjurists after some years of research, the bottom of each page bore the words, printed in bold type: THIS BOOK IS A DESCRIPTION, IT IS NOT A CODE![19]

The law must be prevented from becoming rigid. It is said that Hans Cory's Restatement of the customary law of Sukumaland, Tanganyika[20] in 634 clauses in 1948/1949 has led to such rigidity. This restatement was at the same time a unification and was "intended to be used in Native Courts and in European Appeal Courts in civil cases". In the *Journal of African Administration* IX (1957) I came across this passage on page 148: "If any attempt is made, at the present stage of development in Africa, to codify native law and custom there is a risk of crystallizing the law and custom of a particular moment in the development of a tribe, and of inhibiting future natural development and growth. *This has in fact happened in Tanganyika*" (Italics mine).

"He that believeth shall not make haste." We must, I submit, resist any urge we may feel to bring about a radical reformation of the law overnight. The national civil law of an African state should be *African* law. At the present stage this law is a law in diversity according to ethnic groups. Allott is correct in speaking of homeonomic ethnic groups, but he is equally right to speak of the local variations within such a group.[21] The smoothing-out of these variations is an objective worth striving for. Codification, in whatever form, is, in my opinion, not the right way to arrive at unification. This process must be allowed to take place gradually through the administration of justice. A deliberate but cautious operation of the appeal system will be effective here, but only fully so if important cases are published in law reports and widely distributed *in a language which is also understandable to the lower-court judges* (lay judges), in other words with as little legal jargon borrowed from European legal systems as possible. The problem of legal language (and of the language used in the courts) is indeed a chapter in itself which I cannot go into here.

19. Raden Mr. Soepomo: *Het adatprivaatrecht van West-Java* (*The civil customary law of Western Java*) 1933, 327 pages. Mas Mr. M. M. Djojodigoeno and Raden Mr. Tirtawinata; *Het Adatprivaatrecht van Middel-Java* (*The civil customary law of Central Java*) 1940, 724 pages.
20. Hans Cory; *Sukuma Law and Custom*, 1953, 194 pages.
21. *A background paper on restatement of laws in Africa*, page 7. Also in *The Unity of African Law* in Essays in African Law, 1960, p. 55 ff.

CONCLUSION

African Law is the general law for all members of the African community. This law is administered by a hierarchy of courts with their own appropriate procedure up to the highest level.[22] Practical educational opportunities for the lay judges and their personnel; a special university training for those who are to work in the higher levels of the hierarchy, with compulsory courses in customary law, sociology, jurisprudence in the Law Faculties and the Law Schools.

22. Tanganyika has, it seems to me, made a start in this direction. See, Journal of African Law, Vol. 7 (1963), No. 2, pp. 84-93.

THE ROLE OF JUSTICE IN THE APPLICATION OF THE LAW IN THE FRANCOPHONE STATES OF AFRICA

by

MICHEL ALLIOT

PROFESSEUR A LA FACULTE DE DROIT ET DES
SCIENCES ECONOMIQUES DE PARIS

[ENGLISH TRANSLATION FROM THE FRENCH ORIGINAL]

THE ROLE OF JUSTICE IN THE APPLICATION OF THE LAW

"What is the role of justice in the application of the law?" In some societies, the question would be meaningless; chief among these is french-speaking Black Africa, in which, prior to colonization, neither "law" nor "judges" existed at all.

It is difficult to compare customary law with our modern legal system, based on the idea of Law as a permanent, impersonal set of rules applying equally to all persons.

To begin with, nothing is less stable than customary law: one need only consider the upheaval brought about by religious changes. To some extent, the spread of Islam in northern Black Africa has even had a retroactive effect. In the north of Senegal, for instance, land is generally shared out among paternal lineages, descendants in the female line being excluded. But in Koranic law, all descendants are inheritors, whether they are male or female or descendants in the male or female line. In Western logic, then, if a lineage converts to Islam, its land should no longer be reserved for it alone; benefits should accrue not only to male descendants, but to all descendants of both male and female lines. Thus interests will run not only to descendants of the converts but to all descendants, as though the land had been subject to Koranic law from the beginning. One can see, therefore, the sense in which Islamic law can be said to have retroactive effect: the Islamic present projects itself into the Animist past and destroys it. Customary law, ignoring the notion of vested rights, does not conceive of the law as the foundation of a stable order.[1]

Moreover, there is no "judge" in customary law. Justice is the business of those in authority. In chiefless societies, such as the Kabre or the Diola, family heads endeavour to settle disputes by evolving a compromise acceptable to themselves, the "culprits", and their families. In chiefdoms, the powers of command, law-giving, and judgment are the chief's prerogatives: it was his duty to find, in the context of the various opinions and authorities prevalent in his group, an acceptable formula for the settlement of disputes. This judicial power was one with the power to legislate: if the latter

---

1. M. Alliot, "L'Acculturation en Ethnologie Juridique," in L'Ethnologie Coll. La Pleiade (Paris: Gallimard, 1964).

was delegated, the former went with it. Thus there was no one, properly speaking, who could be called a "judge."[2]

From this it follows that there could be no "application of the law" by a judge. Moreover, the African mind seems to have a horror of "judgment": failing an acceptable compromise, it is often preferred to let time solve problems rather than to force a decision. I recall participating in a *ngel* (the chief's traditional court) which was meeting for the third time over a single case concerning rape of a young woman. At the first session, the culprit had been ordered to marry the victim (which had been the couple's intent, despite opposition from the girl's family) after paying to her maternal uncle a sum equal to the value of a calf. Learning that the young man could not raise the money, the *ngel* met a second time to find an excuse for reducing the sum by half; the finding was that, since the culprit worked in town in the winter (and was thus considered somehow superior to a bush peasant), the law of the bushman could not be applied to the culprit. But on discovering that the young man could not pay even half the original sum, the court met for the third time, seeking to reduce the fine to one-fourth the price of the calf. It found the answer in the fact that the boy had been baptised, a Christian being absolutely superior to a pagan . . . This is more a search for compromise than it is the application of "equal justice for all" which we mean by "law".

Thus we find ourselves diametrically opposite the European concept. What will happen when that concept is introduced? How far will the effects of that concept survive independence in francophone Black Africa? Let us examine these questions in the contexts, first of colonization, and then of independence.

I. Colonization: The Judge as servant of the Law

Colonization brought with it the European idea of the supremacy of law. No more the chief, but the law, is the ultimate recourse and the means of defining the role of each individual. Law is imposed on administrator and judge alike; each must apply it in his own domain. Accordingly, it was essential to expound, in the form of rules, the new law which had become controlling.

Familiar with the technical advantages of laws—precision, fivity, amenability to modification through defined procedures—the European colonizers undertook to implant this new concept of law by making laws; and the domain of law was extended, to the detriment of custom, as far as possible. At first this involved the

---

2. The Nigerian situation is similar. See T. O. Elias, *The Nature of African Customary Law* (Manchester University Press, 1944).

public law, which from the beginning superseded the customary rules: the entire administrative organisation of the colonies was derived from quasi-legislative texts. The process moved forward rapidly. Some of the territories were subjected to completely new administrative regimes: systems of rule by administrative concession, control of property along the lines of the *Code Civil*, patterns of land registration modelled on the Real Property Act (Torrens Act) adopted by the Australian Parliament in 1858. Of the people themselves, some remained subject to the traditional law, either by legal mandate or through individual choice. Finally, certain branches of law were reserved in the French territories: these included the Penal Law (decree of 30 April 1946) and the Work Law (law of 15 December 1952).

Of course the new law met with resistance, and after having ignored customary law, the colonial legislators were in the end forced to allow it at least a provisional role. In the civil fields of capacity, marriage and divorce, inheritance, and lands not subject (under the *Code Civil* or as to registration) to the system of administrative concessions, and for some time in the field of criminal law, traditional law was applied to persons who had kept their original personal status. But it would go too far to hold that this amounted to recognition of "pure" customary law on the part of the legislators. For the very circumstances of recognition altered the nature of that law.

In the first place, traditional law was recognized only insofar as it did not conflict with the new law. But traditional law existed as a seamless whole: it was entirely artificial to try to separate rules controlling power from rules governing interpersonal relations, or to separate civil from criminal law. Traditional law was recognized, then, only at the cost of serious mutilation.

In the second place, recognized customary law was required not to be "contrary to public order". That fundamentally vague notion is the repository of an arsenal of European philosophical, moral, and legal ideas. In the name of public order, customs "contrary to the principles of civilization"[3] were abolished. These included slavery; mutilation and corporal punishment as penal sanctions (but not mutilation of an ethnic, esthetic, or religious nature); and trial by ordeal, when the judge based his decision on the result of the

---

3.   Art. 75 of the Decree of 10 November 1903 (reorganizing the administration of justice in A.O.F.): "La justice indigene appliquera en toute matiere les coutumes locales, en tout ce qu'elles ne sont pas de contraire aux principles de la civilization Francaise. Dans les cas ou les chatiments corporels seraient prevus, il leur sera substitue l'emprisonnement."

ordeal (though there is recourse to such methods when other types of proof are unavailable or result in contradictions). The same principles led to the imposition on customary law of European notions entirely foreign to it: vested rights, prescription, *resjudicata;* the right of each member of a family to claim his share of community property, and so forth. Here also, the recognition of customary law has resulted in grave deformations of it.

Finally, the recognized law was viewed in the usual legal way: as a set of rules the same everywhere and forever. It was for this reason that the cadi courts, which apply Moroccan Malekite law, were created for the Muslims of Senegal, whose customs were deeply rooted in the Sharia; the Court of Appeal of the A.O.F. eventually reached the stage of applying Koranic law to every African convert—even if he were the only Muslim in his kinship group.[4] Thus Koranic law was treated as a monolith, everywhere identical; the nuances of Islam were ignored. Similarly, the same court declined to recognize Christian customs: it insisted that custom was "immemorial", hence immutable over time, and that Christianity was too recent an importation into West Africa to have produced customs capable of meeting that test.[5] Such a refusal to recognize the subtleties of customary law—which results in treating rules devised for a particular time and place as if they were Western statutes—helped to force the islamization of West Africa and to prevent the spread of Christianity. This is still another fundamental distortion.

Thus, the customary law recognized by the colonial authorities differed on many grounds from the customary law practised by the people. Though unwritten, it had taken on the likeness of law, and had become fixed, like law, in the new juridical order; but it was, most of the time, far removed from the real customary law. Colonization had superimposed on the living law the fictive framework of "applicable law".

The primary role of the judge was to apply modern law or recognized customary law to the concrete cases submitted to him. This role, not functionally different from that of a judge in France or Belgium, was that of a technician. In France or Belgium, however, the technician becomes a creator when, generally through the passage of time, the law draws away from living realities. Then the courts, through the medium of new interpretations of the legislative text, play one of the most active roles in the growth of the law.

---

4.   Cour d'Appel de l'A.O.F., Ch. d'annulation 31 Jan. 1957, *Faton N'Dao* v. *Sassy N'Dao.*
5.   Cour d'appel de l'A.O.F., 1964.

In Africa this role was considerable. For there was a major dichotomy between "applicable law"—the State's law or law recognized by the State—and law as it was in the life of the people. The judge had therefore to conciliate, to arbitrate. It follows that his function could not merely be to ensure the consistent triumph of "applicable" over living law: the authority of the law was accordingly not always respected. But conversely, it was not always frustrated: it offered to the judge a variety of techniques for mediating between applicable and living law.

The first of these techniques was that of arbitration in civil matters. The European notion of justice—give every man his due— is so far removed from African concepts that it was necessary to establish, outside the state court systems, an arbitration system run by traditional chiefs. Decrees gave arbitration powers to tribal and village chiefs, village notables, and quarter heads, as well as heads of kin groups designated for that purpose by custom.[6] Failing that, arbitration took place before the president of the court, assisted by two assessors. Only if arbitration failed was there resort to litigation under normal rules. Although estimation of the number of arbitrations by traditional chiefs is impossible, in A.O.F. it definitely went beyond 100,000 per year. And in the last years of that territorial grouping, the number of conciliations before court presidents nearly equalled the number of ordinary litigations, in the neighbourhood of 10,000 per year.[7] Arbitration, allowing close links with the living law, but without seeming to (since it did not need to be pushed), has thus been a highly important institution.

The second legal technique for reconciling applicable with living Law is that of "extenuating circumstances" in criminal cases. In the French and Belgian systems, extenuating circumstances are matters for judicial discretion; thus in a case of conflict between custom and the Penal Law, such as one where traditional obligations conduce to the commission of a crime, the judge could soften the harshness of the repressive law by treating the influences of custom on the wrongdoer as extenuating circumstances.[8]

6. Art. 3 of the Decree of 31 July, 1927 for the Cameroons (East); Art. 5 of the Decree of 3 December 1961 for A.O.F.; Art. 5 of the Decree of 21 April 1933 for Togo; Art . . . of the Decree of 29 May 1936 for A.O.F.
7. In 1953, 11,354 arbitrations as against 10,151 judgments of first instance in the courts of A.O.F. and Togo (from) Poirier, 'L' Organization Judiciaire de L'A.O.F., "in *The Future of Customary Law in Africa* (London 1960) 1.
8. For Congo (Kinshasa): Elis. 6 Jan. 1924. Jnr. Col. 24 page 261; cited in Rivers, "Quelques Aspects du Droit Penal Congolais," *Annales de la Faculte de Droit de Toulouse*, XI, 183 (1963).

The judge was sometimes enabled to reconcile applicable and customary law by virtue of misleading translations. What meaning was he to give to legal rules forbidding testimony for or against a relative? The African definition of "relative" is of course, far removed from the French definition.

Finally, it must be noted that the most important juridical innovations have been made possible by the popular distaste for appealing, against judgments handed down by judges or tribunals near at hand, to courts both far away and expensive.

Traditional criminal law has also survived in the traditional courts. Eight years after its official suppression, the court of Fatick in Senegal ordered an adulterous wife and her lover to pay the outraged husband the traditional fine: a horse from the lover, a mare from the faithless wife, or rather the value, in Francs CFA, of a horse and a mare at the time of the judgment.[9] And has not traditional law also been preserved by the inaction of customary courts? Not to judge was part of the tradition; such failures to act often reflect the African horror of judgment more than the laziness of registrars.

Sometimes the judgment itself, though it should not, preserves customary law. We have seen that the judge may resort to the ordeal only when he cannot otherwise reach a decision. But some judges, who should have been able to decide according to evidence, relied on the traditional ordeal: they realized that another kind of decision would not settle the dispute, and they were certain that the judgment of God, at any rate, would not be contested.

These lower court judgments have also loosened the bonds imposed on customary law at the price of its recognition. In Black Africa, Malekite law has not always been integrally applied to recent converts: succession in particular is often left subject to traditional rules on the theory that the conversion of a single individual can have no effect on the distribution of communally-held property. So also have lower courts recognized with increasing frequency, despite contrary holdings of the A.O.F. Court of Appeal, Christian customs with special procedures (e.g. in the ordeal by oath), special marriage rules (nullification for impotence, monogamy, indissolubility), and a pattern of succession tending towards female equality.[10] The lack of appeals to higher courts has thus created a new jurisprudence, midway between applicable and living law.

Such was the role of the judge in colonial times. But it was not the primary role—that was reserved for the law (in the most general

9. Tribunal Contumier de Fatick, 1954, *Charles N'Dour v. Marie Faye.*
10. M. Alliot, "Christianisme et Droit Traditionnel au Senegal," in *Etudes Le Bras* (Paris: Sirey, 1964).

sense of the word, including all the applicable rules of customary law). The judge was a servant of this law, a technician charged with its application. Only when application was difficult, granted more often true here than elsewhere, was the judge properly a *creator*. Was independence to maintain this pre-eminence of the law?

II.   Independence: The primacy of the Executive

One would hardly have thought that independence in the franco-phone African countries would develop the rule of law and strengthen the position of the judge. But never has the primacy of of the Law been so strongly affirmed as in the constitutions of these countries and by their representatives in international assemblies, in colloquia[11] and in their writings.[12] From another standpoint, all the new states have announced their intent to pursue the legislative work of the colonizers, sometimes in the direction of reforms but always in the direction of extending it to the point of complete suppression of traditional law. Apart from numerous nationality codes,[13] most of the independent states have drafted codes of procedure,[14] penal codes, and work codes.[15] A number of civil codes are in the process of adoption;[16] Ethiopia, indeed, completely enacted its own civil code four years ago.[17]

At this conference, indeed, Rene David has sketched a theory of revolutionary law. One could say that in Europe any regularly promulgated and published law has an immediate effect on the legal order: if a law intervenes in matters of succession it acts on all estates opened after it takes effect. But in Africa the effects of a law are often slower in making themselves felt: the law acts as an ideal rather than as an instrument of immediate transformation, drawing customary law to it gradually rather than abolishing it; slowly shaping reality.[18] Thus we see that some African countries can, without apparent harm, tolerate side by side legislation so revolutionary that no European country would dare to enact it and peoples so passive that they seem entirely to ignore the legislative will. It

11.   Notably in Lagos.
12.   G. d'Arboussier, *La Justice an Senegal* (1961).
13.   All the Black African countries which gained independence from France except Dahomey.
14.   Congo (Brazzavile,) Ivory Coast, Gabon, Ethiopia, Mali, Mauritania, Malagasy Rep., Niger.
15.   Central Africa Rep., Congo (Brazzavile), Gabon, Guinea, Upper Volta, Malagasy Republic, Mali, Muritania, Niger, Senegal.
16.   Notably in Malagasy Republic and Senegal.
      1960.
17.   R. David, "La Refonte du Code Civil dans les Etats Africains," in
18.   *Annales Africaines* (1962) 160-170, and *Penant* (1962) 352-364.

may be bothersome that a custom contrary to new legislation is not in fact at once abolished by the law; but the problem is less serious if one realizes that the new law is actually an invitation to the old custom to disappear, that it will cause the custom, little by little, to fall into desuetude. This even allows the adoption of desired legislation at one stroke, rather than forcing the process of legislative evolution to proceed by degrees: the law seems able to be, textually, more revolutionary in Africa than in Europe, since its effects are less immediate. In this spirit Ethiopia has been able to adopt codes only doubtfully susceptible to immediate enforcement.

Who would deny that, in thus increasing the gulf between applicable and actual law, the role of the judge as arbiter between the two is augmented? Thus a good number of jurists maintain that the law and the judge are in fact the beneficiaries of independence.

In fact, the reverse is true in a great many countries. Legislative and judicial power are no more than appearances: neither the law nor the judge is considered an apt guardian of the State. It is the executive power which assumes total responsibility for that function.

The French-speaking African countries can be identified with a one-party presidential regime, where the functions of President of the Republic and secretary-general of the party are united in the same person Is this not a return to tradition? States in international affairs, these Republics are chiefdoms for internal purposes. And whatever may be the constitutional theory, the separation of powers has no place in fact.

Elected officials depend on the party. To it they owe their election; on it hangs their re-election: no personal charisma can prevail against the tyranny of election lists worked out at the national level.[19] The elected officials are equally dependent on the government, whose bureaux are the actual authors of most significant legislation. And party and government both mean in fact one man: the national leader, he is the master of legislative power. In truth constitutional words are so far devoid of meaning that the head of the executive branch assumes all legislative responsibility and the so-called legislative assemblies really perform a job of ratification.

This discrediting of law necessarily includes the judge. Responsible Africans no longer trust judges. With rare exceptions, the judges are left only routine and legal trivia; at that level, they fill, with less prestige, the role of their colonial predecessors.

But the governments do not support judicial independence in

19. The actual electoral system of all the Black African countries which gained independence from France, except for Cameroon (divided into six "circonscriptions.")

fields of law they consider especially important. The Ivory Coast, which is presently preparing a reform of its droit foncier intends to declare all unregistered lands (meaning nearly all rural areas) the property of the State, giving concessions to persons who will use the land productively. All judicial review of such concessions will be prohibited.

Similarly, the governments do not support judicial independence in particular matters which are deemed vital. The francophone African countries have not been immune to the wave of legislation in anglophone countries authorizing large-scale administrative detentions.[20] Most have not hesitated to set up exceptional, provisional tribunals to judge serious political matters. In 1961, Dahomey established for six months a Tribunal to judge the leaders of the opposition D.P.P., arrested without warrant in foreign countries. In 1962, less than three months after independence, the Mwami of Burundi created a Supreme Court with retroactive jurisdiction to quash an earlier order concerning the presumed assassins of his son and to retry the defendants. In the same year, leaders of the Union Soudanaise, the sole party in Mali, constituted themselves into a popular tribunal and condemned to death those of their opponents responsible for the Bamake riots. At that time the President of Mali told the judges what, *mutatis mutandis*, so many African heads of state might well have said: "The Mali magistrate must not, in the name of an independent judiciary and the separation of powers, lose sight of the fact that he is above all a fighter for the Union Soudanaise; for, with all such fighters, justice—a social institution of the State—is necessarily the servant of the regime which instituted it."

How could one say more directly that the African judge is no longer the servant of the law, but of power?

One could give contrary examples.[21] But they would not be many. And there is, in the subordination of justice to power, too obvious a return to the chieftaincy system in which judging is one of the chief's principal prerogatives for one to ignore the phenomenon or pass it off as exceptional or temporary. This subordination to power is rooted in African thought, and it is rather legislative and judicial independence which are exceptional.

---

20. Detention without trial for up to ten years is possible in Ghana (Law of 6 Nov. 1963). In Uganda, if a state of emergency is declared, the courts may no longer do more than make recommendations (Art. 20 of the Uganda Constitution).

21. Notably that of Senegal modifying the composition of the High Court of Justice, henceforth presided over by a magistrate in order better to establish its independence.

In the end, the judge's role in applying the law cannot be analysed, for francophone Black Africa, by examining in the European fashion the technicalities of applying general rules to particular cases. It rests too heavily on the concept of power which underlies the basic organisation of society. In the African tradition of chieftaincy, the power to judge, is an attribute of the chief or his representative. Properly speaking, there are no judges: to command and to judge are functions of the same man, in whom alone is vested the authority to choose among the interests, forces and ideals of the group.

The European idea is that the law performs this supreme function of arbitration, both justice and administration are subordinate to it. This was the idea of the colonial states. And the role of the judges, as of the administrators, was crucial to that process to the extent that the law—imported from Europe or developed from African traditions—departed from reality; there was then another problem of arbitration, between applicable and living law, and that was the role of the judge.

After independence, the law lost its pride of place and the judicial power tended to return to the chiefs. The judge remained a servant. But servants, of course, hold their authority at the pleasure of those they serve; to the European mind, it appears less honourable to serve power than to serve the law; it is unclear that the same is true of African thought.

Thus it would perhaps be more appropriate to study, not the role of justice in the application of the law (a typically European problem), but rather the role of justice in the actions of the political party: the question would better reflect reality.

DISCUSSING AFRICAN LAW

by

A. N. ALLOTT

PROFESSOR OF AFRICAN LAW, UNIVERSITY OF LONDON;
DIRECTOR, RESTATEMENT OF AFRICAN LAW PROJECT

DISCUSSING AFRICAN LAW

I

Less than twenty years ago cadets undergoing training in England for the Colonial Administrative Service, who were required to learn the elements of law as a preparation for their careers as magistrates in African territories, studied English criminal law and procedure. Students from West African countries (there were no African students from East and Central Africa) who wished to qualify themselves for legal practice in their own countries had to follow courses at the Council of Legal Education in London exclusively designed for future practitioners at the English Bar. Not one single work of scholarship in the field of African law had been submitted by an African candidate for a Ph.D. in a British University. In the whole of tropical Africa under British administration there was no local law school or faculty, save only for the training provided at the University of Khartoum. The suggestion that there should be a legal conference or a learned society exclusively devoted to the study and promotion of African law would probably have been greeted with derision; after all, African law (if it deserved to be called law at all) was something studied by anthropologists.

Today the picture has visibly altered. There are, of course, no more expatriate trainee administrative officers; locally recruited civil servants study in their own countries and study the law of their own countries. Today there are law faculties and schools dotted over the whole of former British Africa. An African student coming to Britain can now take papers in African law for the London University LL.M. degree, and for Part I of the English Bar examinations. If he is of sufficiently high standard, he may go on to write a Ph.D. thesis on an African law subject (many have). There is an International African Law Association with world-wide membership, and there have been a number of conferences on African law, both in Africa and elsewhere. It is now firmly established that the primary responsibility for investigating, as well as administering, the legal systems of Africa is in the hands of lawyers. The picture is much the same in the French-speaking areas of Africa.

Why has this revolution occurred? It would be a mistake to think that it is purely a product of the political revolution which has decolonised the major part of the African continent. The University of London, for instance, appointed its first lecturer in African law in 1948. Judicial Advisers' Conferences were held under United Kingdom auspices in 1953 and 1956 (at Makerere and Jos respectively); and the French at one period encouraged the production of "coutumiers" or written restatements of the customary laws in force in their territories. On the other hand, the psychological consequences of independence have been felt in the legal sphere just as elsewhere; and the coming of political self-government has undoubtedly provoked a radical re-examination of the colonial legal heritage.

It is primarily the politicians (today increasingly reinforced by the younger generation of African law lecturers) who have taken the lead in calling for fundamental changes in their laws. There is always a risk when law reform is sponsored by non-lawyers. Those who have not made a deep and sympathetic study of traditional African legal systems and their place in the modern world may not always appreciate what is legally practicable. But, equally, law is too important a subject to be left to the lawyers, and the professional lawyer may well be inhibited from making the sort of imaginative changes which the tempo of social development in Africa requires.

There are two main directions in which legal change in Africa has got to move. First, the apparently unconditional dependence of African legal systems on the laws of foreign countries has to be reduced. This dependence may be more apparent than real. Most of the British African territories, for instance, received the law of England as it stood at a certain date (1st January, 1900 for Nigeria; 24th July, 1874 for Ghana) as the basis of their general legal systems; but this received English law has only been applied (i) subject to such adaptations as are required by local circumstances, (ii) subject to African customary laws as far as disputes between Africans are concerned, and (iii) subject to local legislation, which in such matters as land law has wholly or substantially restricted the general application of English legal notions.

Secondly, the legal systems of Africa must be adapted so as to cope with the necessities of life in a modern and increasingly industrial society. The modernization of African law involves both an updating of the received statutory law of England so as to incorporate the most recent developments, and the development of a legal framework for states increasingly organised on "socialist", "welfare", or economically expansionist lines.

Cutting across but linked with the "decolonization" and modernization of the legal systems, there is the often-asserted desire to "re-Africanise" the African legal systems, by evolving or re-establishing institutions and ideas which have grown on African soil out of the practices and beliefs of African peoples. This desire expresses itself in two ways: by the citation of ancient African social practices as the justification for the introduction of new laws (as with the abolition of freehold tenure in Tanganyika); and by the enhanced status now accorded to African traditional customary laws.

The primary consequence of the introduction of British rule in Africa was the creation of a legal dualism, through the imposition on the one hand of territorial legal systems based on English (or British Indian) law, and through the recognition of customary and religious laws on the other. African governments are now looking for ways in which to reduce or eliminate this dualism, and to promote the evolution wherever possible of a unified national law. Their reasons for so doing are complex; among them are the simplification of the legal system, nation-building, and the search for a more "African" law.

II

It is this problem, that of integration of laws in Africa, that has been the particular concern of a number of recent conferences of various kinds and with various agendas. The first such meeting was a mainly British affair, held in London around New Year, 1960, under the chairmanship of Lord Denning. Official delegates (mainly judges, law officers, and native courts advisers) from Commonwealth countries and territories in Africa having the English common law as the basis of their legal systems discussed of "The Future of Law in Africa", with special reference to the place of customary law therein. The conference was very successful in many ways, but it is fair to say that the members of it mainly examined the problem of legal evolution in Africa from a "British" and a common law point of view. The question as put to the conference was whether any of the customary laws would remain in force in the Africa of the future, and the idea that future African legal systems would inevitably be largely based on the introduced Western laws was taken for granted. The legal problems posed by the political, social and economic transformation of Africa were almost entirely ignored (not surprisingly in view of the absence of African politicians).

The conference on local courts and customary law in Africa, held at Dar es Salaam in September of 1963, was originally intended to be a follow-up to the professional judicial advisers' conferences of those intimately concerned with the evolution and administration of the local courts (as the successors to the native courts are now generally called); but in practice the conference aimed rather higher and more widely. The general principles which should govern the development of the local courts systems and their integration into the national judicial systems were examined (e.g., in the context of the independence of the judiciary), rather than the administrative problems of supervision of local courts, their procedure, and the training of their members. At the same time, with the addition of delegates and observers from non-common-law countries inside and outside Africa, the close identity in legal background between the participants was removed. This inevitably reduced discussions to a more elementary level than would otherwise have been the case. The presence of some delegates intimately involved in politics in their own countries reminded the conference that law is an instrument of government and operates to achieve social ends. It would have been interesting to have had a fuller participation by political leaders, and to have elicited their views on, for example, the question of safeguarding the independence of the higher and lower judiciary. The Dar es Salaam conference also attempted a general survey of the future of customary law in Africa. This suffered, as did all the proceedings of this and of the London conference, from the over-ambitious attempt to predict in the course of a few days of discussion the future development of all the major branches of law in all the African countries. Nevertheless, the conclusions of the conference on this aspect of their work make interesting reading, and are a point of departure for further and more specialised conferences.

The attendance at the Dar es Salaam conference from French-speaking Africa was most disappointing (only one delegate from the Ivory Coast actually turned up). The balance was redressed at the much less ambitious conference convened by the Fondazione Giorgio Cini at Venice in October, 1963. This meeting, which took as its theme, "From a Traditional to a Modern Law in Africa", was attended predominantly by representatives of the civil law countries in Africa and Europe, the majority of whom possessed an academic background. The conference did provide a most useful opportunity, however, for a confrontation of common law and civil law attitudes to the whole question of the future of law in Africa and the place of the traditional customary laws in it.

The conference which is being convened by the University of Ife's Institute of African Studies at Ibadan, Western Nigeria, from 24th to 29th August, 1964, has as its theme "The Integration of Customary and Modern Legal Systems in Africa". The conference is designed to carry on and render more practically effective the work already started at preceding conferences, but the intention of the Working Committee (under the chairmanship of Dr. S. O. Biobaku, C.M.G., Pro-Vice-Chancellor of the University and

Director of the Institute of African Studies), is not to repeat the generalised discussions of previous conferences, but rather to explore the practical methods by which integration or harmonisation of the diverse laws coexisting within a single African country has been or can be achieved. To this end participants have been invited to submit background papers; some of these examine the potentialities in general terms of different methods of promoting integration of laws; and other papers each describe in detail the experience of selected African countries in integrating specific branches of their law. Among the papers of the former kind are ones by Professor R. David of the University of Paris on the uses and techniques of codification; by Mr. E. Cotran and myself of the Restatement of African Law Project in the School of Oriental and African Studies, London, on the uses and techniques of restatement; and by Dr. F. A. Ajayi, Solicitor-General and Permanent Secretary, Ministry of Justice, Western Nigeria, on judicial adaptation as a method of harmonising diverse laws.

The substantive papers will demonstrate how legal draftsmen, judges and jurists can reconcile and harmonise coexisting systems of traditional and non-traditional law, with due regard to the necessity for minimising the potentially explosive consequences of major changes in legal systems, and of maximising opportunities for harmonious and orderly development. Each paper will be a type of case study, examining how this objective has been attained in a particular field of law in a particular jurisdiction. Among the topics selected are land law; the law of marriage and divorce; succession; contracts; and civil wrongs. Criminal and constitutional law, both of which have been very frequently discussed in the past, will not be considered; in any event, the role of customary law in these fields is rapidly diminishing.

The emphasis of the conference will be firmly put on methods and techniques of guiding African legal development. Its results should therefore be of practical value to the legislator or draftsman in every African country, since all alike are faced with the necessity of modernising their laws. On the other hand, one must remember that conferences are not the most appropriate tools for the conduct of fundamental research into a subject; a great deal of work has already been done, in the universities and outside, to investigate this problem. The value of such a conference is first, that it publicly affirms the importance of the problem, and draws attention to its wider implications; second, that it provides an opportunity to take stock and to determine whether the current orientation, machinery and tempo of legal change meet the needs of African countries; and third, that it can provide a blue-print for the future for those who have continuing responsibility in this field: that is, those who make, administer, or study and analyse the law. These are the persons who have been invited to take part in the conference. But participation at the conference will not be restricted to delegates from the English-speaking and common-law part of the world: a number of experts in the law of French-speaking African states will also make their contribution. In this way not only will lawyers on each side of the legal iron curtain which divides Africa (between the common law and civil law systems) have a chance to learn more of each other's juridical objectives and techniques, but there is an opportunity for laying the foundations for a closer *rapprochement* between the respective legal systems. The "integration" or "harmonisation" of laws which is to be examined by the conference is that between the different components (customary and statutory, indigenous and imported) in a given national legal system; but one may hope that a by-product of the conference will be a coming together, or at least a harmonisation, of the different national legal systems in Africa in fields of mutual concern.

INTEGRATION OF LEGAL SYSTEMS IN THE SOMALI REPUBLIC

by

DR. PAOLO CONTINI

UNITED NATIONS LEGAL ADVISER TO THE SOMALI
GOVERNMENT AND CHAIRMAN OF THE CONSULTATIVE
COMMISSION FOR INTEGRATION

Note

The views expressed herein are those of the author presented in
1964 and are not to be taken as the views of the United Nations or
of the Somali Government.

INTEGRATION OF LEGAL SYSTEMS IN THE SOMALI REPUBLIC

The Somali Republic was born on July 1st, 1960. On that date the five days old independent State of Somaliland, formerly a British Protectorate, merged with the former United Nations Trust Territory of Somalia under Italian Administration, which achieved independence on the same day. The new State was defined "an independent, democratic and unitary Republic".[1]

In effect, however, in the beginning the only unitary elements were at the top of the State pyramid: there was a single President of the Republic; a National Assembly comprising the former Legislative Assemblies of Somaliland and Somalia; a Cabinet including Ministers from the two parts of the territory; and a Supreme Court with jurisdiction over the whole country. But most of the other elements were still separate: there were two different judicial systems; different currencies; different organization and conditions of service for the army, the police and the civil service; different taxation and customs; different governmental institutions, both at the central and local level; different educational systems. While Shari'a law was basically the same throughout the country, the general law applied in the two parts of the Republic was widely different. The Northern Regions followed the pattern of British dependencies in East Africa, and the law was a mixture of English common and statute law, Indian statutes and locally enacted ordinances; in the Southern Regions, it was a mixture of Italian law, colonial legislation and enactments issued during the ten-year Trust Administration.

The legal integration of the Northern and Southern Regions was a complex and challenging task.

It was decided, as a first step, that the legislation in force in the two parts of the Republic immediately before the Union would remain in effect until superseded by integrated laws.[2] This was necessary to avoid a legal vacuum and give the new State time to proceed to orderly unification.

In the first four years of life of the Somali Republic, considerable progress has been made in the integration of the laws and institutions, although much still remains to be done.

1. Law No. 5 of 31 January, 1961, Article 1 (1).
2. Ibid., Article 3.

It would be too taxing on the time and patience of this distinguished audience to describe in detail the major integrated laws enacted in the Somali Republic. Accordingly, I propose to confine this paper to a brief discussion of some concrete aspects of the integration process.

I. METHODOLOGY

Shortly after independence a Consultative Commission for Integration was established[3] to assist the Government in the preparation of draft laws for the integration of the legislation and institutions of the two parts of the country. The Commission includes lawyers and judges trained in Italian law, lawyers trained in the Anglo-Saxon legal system, and Somali officials and judges trained in Islamic and customary law.

Although most of the unified legislation in the last four years has been drafted by the Integration Commission, in some instances other procedures have been followed. For example, the National Assembly delegated to the Government the power to enact the penal code and the code of criminal procedure, and created a Special Commission for the purpose of preparing them.[4] A peculiar aspect of this procedure is that the recommendations of the Special Commission—whose membership was about evenly divided between deputies (members of the National Assembly) and legal experts— were made binding on the Government. Thus, in effect, the Assembly delegated legislative powers to a mixed body of deputies and legal technicians, a solution which did not prove wholly satisfactory.

In another case—the preparation of foreign trade and foreign exchange legislation—the work was done by an *ad hoc* commission with the participation of experts from the International Monetary Fund.

Occasionally, an individual legal expert would be requested by the Government to prepare a draft law, and in a very few cases bills originated within the Assembly.

It was realized from the beginning that the group of lawyers in the Integration Commission must not settle in a legal ivory tower,

3. Decree of the President of the Republic No. 19 of 11 October, 1960.
4. Law No. 5 of 30 January, 1962. The Special Commission was also charged with the preparation of a law on the Judiciary and a Traffic Code. However, a draft law on the Judiciary had already been prepared by the Integration Commission, and a draft Traffic Code by an *ad hoc* commission. Accordingly most, of the substantive work on these two laws was not done by the Speical Commission.

or impart advice distilled from pure legal theory. Had they remained aloof from the mainstream of a developing society, their effectiveness would have been sharply reduced.

Accordingly, the Commission has made it a constant practice to prepare draft laws in close collaboration with representatives of the Ministries concerned. Thus the finished product is usually accepted by the responsible Minister who presents it to the Council of Ministers for approval and then to the National Assembly.

In Somalia, one of the most difficult problems in legislative drafting is language. This is because there are, not one, but three written languages, none of which is Somali. All Somalis speak the same tongue, with minor differences in dialect, but no decision has yet been made on the official script.

The absence of an official written language creates serious complications. In the National Assembly deputies make speeches in Somali, which are interpreted into Italian, the language used in the Assembly's *verbatim records*. Draft laws have to be submitted to the Assembly in three languages, Italian for the Southern deputies, English for the Northern deputies and Arabic for those not sufficiently familiar with either. All legislation is published in the Official Bulletin in Italian and English, which have equal status even though neither has ever been formally recognized as "official".

The laws drafted by the Integration Commission are always prepared in English and Italian. When a draft law has been completed, the work is only half done, as the translation into the other language is a long, complex operation.

Translating a legislative text is a very difficult art. Reading English versions of Italian Codes or laws done before the independence of Somalia by highly qualified translators, we have often found expressions and concepts either meaningless or misleading in English legal terminology. This is because even the best translator normally is not a lawyer, and therefore unfamiliar with technical legal expressions.

At the same time, we found that the use of two languages in legislative drafting has some advantages. In the Integration Commission, all translations are reviewed, word by word, by two lawyers familiar with both languages. In the process, the revisers often find obscurities and imperfections in the original version, and the final draft is then improved.

Bilingual legislation also tends to liberate the draftsman from unnecessary and sometimes unintelligible legalistic jargon. Legislative texts are often burdened with verbiage accepted and perpetuated uncritically because of long usage. We soon discovered that those expressions were untranslatable or sounded awkward in the other language. Thus they were eliminated, to the benefit of clarity.

Immediately after the union of the two territories it was necessary to decide on the order of priority to be followed in the process of legislative integration. A work programme was approved by the Government and was generally adhered to.

Since all legislation and institutions had to be integrated, the programme had to be conceived almost as if a new State were being built *ab initio*.

One of the first things to do was to define who are "the people" under the Constitution, i.e. who is a Somali citizen.[5]

The two major areas in which laws were needed as early as possible, were the State structure and the economic life of the country.

In the first four years, the basic elements of a unified State have been established.

The two fundamental enactments relating to the executive branch are the law on the organization of the Government[6] and the law on Local Administrations.[7] The civil service law lays down the rules governing the conditions of service of those who keep the government machinery running.[8] The financial and accounting procedures of the State have been unified.[9] The public order law[10] establishes the powers of the police and other authorities in the protection of public order and security, and defines the limits of such powers. The Somaliland Scouts of the former Protectorate and the Army of the former Trust Territory have been merged into a National Army, and the police forces have also been unified.[11]

As to the legislative branch, the procedures for electing the representatives of the people in the National Assembly have been fixed by the political elections law.[12]

The integration of the judicial branch has been effected by the law on the organization of the Judiciary[13] and the establishment of a

---

5. Law No. 28 of 22 December, 1962.
6. Law No. 14 of 3 June, 1962.
7. Law No. 19 of 14 August, 1963.
8. Law No. 7 of 15 March 1962. As this law does not deal with pensions for civil servants, a unified pension law is being prepared. Pending its adoption the Northern Regions' officials are entitled to pension under pre-independence legislation, whilst the Southern Regions' officials do not have that benefit.
9. Legislative Decree No. 2 of 29 December, 1961.
10. Law No. 21 of 26 August, 1963.
11. Law No. 5 of 31 January 1961
12. Law No. 4 of 22 January, 1964.
13. Legislative Decree No. 3 of 12 June, 1962.

military tribunal.[14] In the field of criminal law the integration process has been completed by the new penal code,[15] code of criminal procedure,[16] military penal code and military criminal procedure code.[17]

In the economic sphere, a unified currency[18] and banking system[19] have been established, and a uniform regulation of foreign trade and foreign exchange transactions[20] has been instituted.

In the fiscal area the income tax, which was in force only in the Southern Regions, has been extended to the whole Republic.[21] For almost three years after independence the custom duties in the Northern Regions continued to be substantially lower than those in the Southern Regions. Despite some resistance, they have now been unified.[22] The integration of other central and local taxes is in progress.

There are some vital aspects of the economy which are still to be integrated, such as contracts, negotiable instruments, companies, copyright, patents and trademarks.

There has been the least amount of codification in the area governed primarily by customary law. For example, no attempt has been made to codify the law of personal status. Studies are currently being made of local customs regarding land tenure and the use of water. Any attempt to legislate in those matters should be made only with full awareness of the social aspects of the problem.

Dr. Keuning, in his interesting paper on law and courts in Africa, has rightly warned against the tendency of some "legal engineers" to extend unduly the area of statutory law, often disregarding the realities of deeply rooted traditions. Although on some occasions unrealistic deadlines have been set,[23] the Somali legislator seems to have generally escaped the temptation to overcodify.

14. In course of publication in the Official Bulletin.
15. Legislative Decree No. 5 of 16 December, 1962.
16. In course of publication in the Official Bulletin.
17. In course of publication in the Official Bulletin.
18. Law No. 13 of 23 May, 1961. (19) Law No. 18 of 14 August, 1963.
20. Decree-Law No. 9 of 8 August, 1964.
21. Law No. 3 of 19 January, 1963.
22. Law No. 7 of 10 June, 1963.
23. For example, the law delegating to the Government the authority to prepare a penal code, a code of criminal procedure, a judiciary law and a traffic code, directed that all this legislation, to be drafted in two languages, must be enacted in six months! (Law No. 5 of 30.1. 1962).

II. INTERACTION OF DIFFERENT LEGAL SYSTEMS IN SOMALI LEGISLATION

Somalia presents the legal draftsman with an unusual laboratory of applied comparative law. In a country where three legal systems coexist, the "integrator" should first, make an objective analysis of a given legal concept under English, Italian and, where necessary, Islamic law; second, choose the solution most suitable to local conditions, without any preconceived notion as to the superiority of one or the other jurisprudence.

I shall try to illustrate with some examples the interaction of different legal systems in the Somali legislation.

The form of legislative acts follows the Italian pattern, as precribed in the Constitution.[24] Thus there are no ordinances, statutes, acts or orders, but laws, legislative decrees, decree-law, decrees and regulations.

The reception of Italian legal concepts is especially noticeable in the Somali Penal Code. For example, Chapter IV, entitled "The Circumstances of the Offence" lists the aggravating and extenuating circumstances applicable to any criminal offence. In each case the judge must determine whether a particular aggravating circumstance (such as having acted for abject or futile motives) or extenuating circumstance (such as having acted for motives having a particular moral or social value) is applicable to the crime committed. This is different from the Indian Penal Code (which was in force in the Northern Regions), where the aggravating or extenuating circumstances applicable to an offence are specified in the section devoted to it; thus the provisions relating to each crime are self-contained, which makes it somewhat easier for the judge to apply the proper sanction.

As in the Italian Penal Code, the Somali Penal Code frequently prescribes the maximum and minimum punishment for a given offence. Thus the judge is given a narrower discretion than in the Indian Penal Code, where no minimum punishment is specified.

The Code of Criminal Procedure has been substantially influenced by English or Indian Law. For example, the rules of evidence were taken, with a few changes, from the Indian Evidence Act. The writ

---

24. The Constitution was prepared in Mogadiscio during the Italian Trust Administration and was originally intended to apply only to the Southern Regions at the end of the trusteeship. The technical work was done mostly by Italian jurists; as a result, the Constitution is largely influenced by the Italian Constitution. The Union was formed on the day of the entry into force of the Constitution, which was simply extended to the whole territory of the Republic without change.

of *Habeas Corpus*, unknown in the former Italian territory, has been introduced in the unified criminal procedure.

On the other hand, certain provisions of the Code of Criminal Procedure derive from Italian law. For instance, in the course of a criminal proceeding, the injured party ("parte civile" in Italian, or "partie civile" in French law) may petition the Court for the recovery of civil damages arising from the offence committed. If the accused is found guilty, the Court, in addition to pronouncing sentence, must decide upon the civil claim brought by the injured party. This joinder of criminal and civil proceedings, unknown in Anglo-Saxon law, makes it unnecessary for the injured party to bring a separate civil action and speeds up the judicial settlement of the civil as well as the penal consequences of a criminal offence.

Some provisions of the Somali Penal Code are influenced by Islamic customary law. An example is the prohibition to drink alcoholic beverages, applicable to all Somali citizens and foreign Muslims.[25] Another relates to the crime of murder, which is punished with death,[26] except that, where the crime is committed by a parent and the victim is subject to his parental authority, the punishment is reduced from death to imprisonment from ten to fifteen years.[27]

This provision supersedes a similar clause contained in a short-lived homicide law[28] which provided that where murder is committed by an ascendant, the punishment is reduced from death to imprisonment from ten to fifteen years. This reduction of the punishment benefited not only a parent, but any ascendant, and applied to any descendant, regardless of age or social status. Such a concept, deriving from Islamic law, was at variance with the rule of Somali customary law that neither parricide nor the murder of a child by his father are punishable. The reason for this rule is that the right of vengeance does not apply between members of the same group.[29]

During the preparation of the Penal Code the view prevailed that, although the reduction in punishment could not be eliminated, it should be restricted to cases where the victim is a child subject to the offender's parental authority. The result appears to be a combination

---

25. Penal Code, Arts. 411, 412—Prohibitionism is applicable to all alcoholic beverages, "of a strength exceeding 3 per centum of proof spirit" Art. 417).
26. Ibid., Art. 434.
27. Ibid., Art. 442
28. Law No. 6 of 10 February 1962. This law was abrogated on 1 April, 1964, the day of entry into force of the Somali Penal Code.
29. Santiapichi, 11 prezzo del sangue e l'omocidio nel diritto somalo, 1963, p. 49.

of the Roman law *jus vitae necisque* and the Islamic law principle that the law of talion is not applicable to premeditated homicide of a descendant committed by an ascendant on the ground that the offender's social status is higher than the victim's. [30]

The Somali legislation contains also provisions alien to the Italian as well as the English legal systems, and reflecting the conditions of an essentially tribal and nomadic society. It occurs not infrequently, especially among nomads, that the wounding or killing of a member of an ethnic group may cause reprisals by the injured group against the offender's, leading to tribal warfare. Payment of the 'dia' or blood-money is the normal device for avoiding clashes and bloodshed. The amount of the 'dia'—100 camels for the life of a man, 50 for the life of a woman, and a scale in proportion to the seriousness of the injury—may be agreed upon between the two ethnic groups or fixed as compensation by the court.

Occasionally, however, the group to which the offender belongs removes its livestock to distant places so as to avoid paying 'dia'. This is bound to bring about reprisals and bloodshed. To prevent the disappearance of the animals and its consequences, the public order law of 1963 provides[31] that where, following the commission of a crime against the life or safety of a person, there is reason to believe that acts of retaliation or vengeance will be committed by a person or group of persons, or that a serious breach of the peace will occur, the police or other public order authority may order the sequestration of animals or other property belonging to the persons who are presumably liable to pay compensation. Being reassured that the animals are in safe hands, the injured group is less likely to resort to violence.

III. INTEGRATION OF THE JUDICIAL SYSTEM

Unification of shariatic and Non-shariatic Courts
    Until the integration of the Judiciary,[32] there were separate Shariatic and non-Shariatic courts both in the Northern and

---

30. Minhadj At-Talibin, Manuel de Jurisprudence Musulmane selon le Rite Chafi'i, Batavia, 1884, Vol. III, pp. 117-118.
31. Law No. 21 of 26 August, 1963, Art. 69. A similar provision had been in force in the former Protectorate under the Political Cases (Attachment of Livestock) Ordinance, 1937, s. 6, and was extended to the Southern Regions during the British Military Administration (1941-1950).
32. Legislative Decree No. 3 of 12 June, 1962.

Southern Regions.[33] Perhaps the major problem in the integration of the Judiciary was whether the dual system should be abolished.

Those in favour of preserving the dichotomy argued that only Kadis, who had the necessary specialized knowledge, should sit as judges on Shariatic matters. They also resisted unification on the ground that for some years in Somalia there will still be foreign non-Muslim judges who should not decide on Shariatic affairs.

The supporters of unification, on the other hand, stressed that the abolition of the dual system would contribute to the development of a national consciousness; furthermore, the merger of the two types of courts would require the Kadis to learn State law and the lay judges to learn the Shari'a; a class of judges familiar with both types of law would then be formed.

In the end, the unitary trend prevailed and the Kadis' Courts were abolished. The integrated law on the organization of the Judiciary provides that justice is administered by District Courts, Regional Courts, Courts of Appeal and Supreme Court.

Organization of the Judiciary

The District Court has a Civil Section and a Criminal Section. The Civil Section has jurisdiction "over controversies where the cause of action has arisen under the Shari'a law or customary law and any other civil controversy where the value of the subject matter does not exceed 3,000 Somali Shillings."[34] The Criminal Section has jurisdiction with respect to offences punishable with imprisonment not exceeding three years or fine not exceeding 3,000 shillings, or both.

33.   In the Northern Regions the separation between the two jurisdictions was complete. The Kadis' Courts were courts of first instance: the Court of the Chief Kadi had appellate jurisdiction, and its decisions were final. The ordinary courts comprised the Subordinate Courts, District Courts and the High Court in Hargeisa. Until 26 June 1960, the day after the independence of Somaliland, appeals against decisions of the High Court were heard by the Court of Appeal for Eastern Africa in Nairobi, and thence by the Judicial Committee of the Privy Council. After the union between Somaliland and Somalia the Supreme Court in Mogadiscia was given appellate jurisdiction over decisions of the High Court (Law No. 18 of 24 May, 1961). In the Southern Regions, the Kadis had original jurisdiction in Shariatic matters; the Tribunal of the Kadis heard appeals from the Kadis; the Shariatic Section of the Supreme Court, consisting of the Courts' President and two Gadis, had appellate jurisdiction over the Tribunal of the Gadis. In view of the participation of the President of the Court (an Italian judge), the separation between Shariatic and non-Shariatic courts was not altogether complete. The non-Shariatic jurisdiction was exercised by the District Judges, the Regional Judges, the Judge of Appeal, the Assize Court, the Assize Court of Appeal and the Supreme Court.

34.   Legislative Decree No. 3 of 12 June, 1962, Art, 2.

The abolition of the Kadis' Courts was a bold move. It was made even bolder by the abolition of the system previously prevailing in both parts of the Republic, whereby District Commissioners, in addition to their executive powers, had been given judicial powers as District Judges.[35] Under the new law, only members of the Judiciary are allowed to exercise judicial functions.

The goal of these innovations is to create a class of judges qualified in all aspects of the law, Shariatic and customary law, as well as statutory civil and criminal law. Although a concerted training effort is currently being made, there is still a serious shortage of qualified judges. For the present, most of the former Kadis have become District Judges and serve in the Civil Section of the District Courts, dealing primarily with Shariatic and customary law matters. Lay judges have also been appointed as District Judges, and deal mostly with "other civil controversies" and criminal cases. In order to avoid burdening District Judges with excessively complicated matters, the law authorizes the President of the Court of Appeal to transfer a civil case to the Regional Court, where the judges are better qualified.

The Regional Court has no appellate jurisdiction, and consists of a General Section and an Assize Section.[36] In the General Section, as in the District Court, cases are heard by a single judge. In civil matters, the General Section has jurisdiction over controversies where the value exceeds 3,000 shillings, except those governed by Shariatic or customary law. In criminal matters, it has jurisdiction with respect to offences more serious than those dealt with by the District Court but less than those within the jurisdiction of the Assize Section. The Assize Section deals with crimes punishable with death or imprisonment for not less than ten years.

The question of the role of the assessors in assize proceedings gave rise to an interesting debate during the preparation of the law. Although assessors existed in both parts of the Republic, their role was basically different. In the Northern Regions, in conformity with the British system, assessors were generally persons familiar with local customs who assisted the judge in an advisory capacity.[37]

35. In the Italian Trust Territory District Commissioners were empowered to act as District Judges under the terms of Decree No. 7 of 22 March, 1958. In the British Protectorate the Judicial Districts and Appointment of Judges Ordinance, 1939, provided that District Officers shall be Judges of the District Courts.
36. The law provided also for the establishment of a Military Penal Section in the Regional Courts of Mogadiscio and Hargeisa and a Military Penal Appellate Section in the Courts of Appeal of the same places. These Sections, however, are in the process of being replaced by Military Tribunals.
37. Subordinate Courts Ordinance, 1944, S. 4(1)

In the South, on the other hand, the assessors were part of the Bench, similar to the "popular judges" in Italy who participate in the decision on both questions of fact and law.

The Assize Court in the former Trust Territory consisted of the Regional Judge as President and six assessors; the Assize Court of Appeal had the same number of assessors and was presided over by the Judge of Appeal.[38]

The advantages and disadvantages of the two systems were discussed at length. Those accustomed to the Northern system argued that while assessors might have performed a useful function in the past as native advisers to foreign judges on local customs, the gradual somalization of the judiciary greatly reduced their role. Furthermore, it was said, the experience with assessors in the former Protectorate was not very satisfactory: it frequently happened that the assessors, being motivated by personal or group loyalty, would recommend the acquittal of the accused, and the judge would have to disregard their advice. The fear was expressed that if the assessors were given full judicial powers and outnumbered the professional judges, the administration of justice would suffer. It was concluded that the assessors should either be abolished or retained only in an advisory capacity.

The opposite view held that the system of assessors prevailing in the Southern Regions had been embodied in Article 95 of the Somali Constitution providing that "the people shall participate directly in assize proceedings in the manner prescribed by law". The intent of the draftsmen of the Constitution and of the Constituent Assembly was that the Somali Republic should continue the system of assessors which had been satisfactorily applied in the former Trust Territory since 1956. To reduce the role of the assessors would be inconsistent with the Constitution and a retrograde step.

In the end, a compromise solution was adopted. The assessors now participate in the decision on questions of fact, but it is for the judge to decide on questions of law and impose the punishment. Thus, except for sitting on the Bench, in the integrated system the assessors perform a role equivalent to that of jurors in a jury trial. In addition, the number of assessors was reduced from six to two in the Regional Court, and three in the Court of Appeal.

The Court of Appeal has a General Appellate Section, which hears appeals against judgments of the District Court and the General Section of the Regional Court, and an Assize Appellate

---

38. Ordinance No. 5 of 2 February, 1956, Arts. 6 and 7.

Section which hears appeals against judgments of the Assize Section of the Regional Court.

The Supreme Court has its seat in Mogadiscio and consists of a President, a Vice-President and four other judges. A Division Bench of three judges has appellate jurisdiction in civil matters, appellate and revisionary jurisdiction in criminal matters, and original jurisdiction in administrative and accounting matters. A full Bench of five judges decides on petitions challenging the qualifications of deputies elected to the National Assembly, controversies relating to conflict of jurisdiction among judicial organs, and other matters considered by the President of the Court to be of particular importance.

Law Administered by Courts

The extent of the application of the Shari'a law was another controversial issue. In the Northern Regions Shari'a law was applied by the Kadis' Court in all matters regarding marriage, divorce, family relationship, 'wakf', gift, succession and wills.[39] In the Southern Regions the application of Shari'a was governed by rather complicated provisions[40] whereby the Kadis had exclusive jurisdiction in matters of personal status, family law and succession, and any other controversy between Muslims, except where the plaintiff chose to submit to the jurisdiction of the Regional Judge. It was also provided that the Regional Judge, who applied Italian civil law, had exclusive jurisdiction over controversies based on a written document and those where "it appears that the juridical relationship has arisen or is governed by formalities different from those of the Islamic or customary law".

In view of the differences in the existing laws of the Northern and Southern Regions, it was necessary to find a solution applicable to the whole Republic. One view was that the application of Shari'a should not be in any way limited or restricted; the other view was that Shari'a should be applied only in matters of personal status and the parties should be given a choice of law.

After lengthy discussion, the following formulation was adopted:
"Subject to the provisions of the Constitution and this law,
the Courts shall apply:
(a) the Shariat law or customary law in civil controversies
where the cause of action has arisen under the said
law;

39. Surbodinate Courts Ordinance, 1944, S. 10(2)
40. Ordinance No. 5 of 2 February, 1956, Art. 2.

(b)   statutory law in all other matters."[41]

It has been said[42] that, while in other Muslim African countries, such as the Sudan and Northern Nigeria, the application of Islamic law is confined to personal matters, this provision entitles the courts of the Somali Republic to apply Islamic law in all civil matters so long as the dispute has arisen under that law. The solution adopted has also been criticized as being rather vague.[43]

Actually, the formulation of Article 9 is the outcome of a compromise. On the one hand it may have the effect of extending the application of Shari'a law beyond the categories specified in the law previously in force in the Northern Region; on the other hand, the parties appear to have been given freedom of choice as to the law governing their relationship. It will be mainly for the courts to draw the precise line of demarcation between Shariatic and non-Shariatic law.

The Rule of Law

The law on the organization of the judiciary implements in concrete terms three essential elements of the rule of law embodied in the Somali Constitution: independence of the judiciary,[44] judicial review of legislative acts,[45] and judicial review of administrative action.[46]

The law provides adequate safeguards to protect the independent exercise of judicial functions. Members of the Judiciary cannot be deprived of their judicial functions or transferred without their consent, except as a disciplinary measure in accordance with the binding advice of the Higher Judicial Council, which is entirely independent of the Executive.[47] The recommendations of the Higher Judicial Council are binding also with respect to the appointment, transfer, promotion, termination and disciplinary proceedings relating to members of the Judiciary.

The Supreme Court, with the addition of two members appointed by the President of the Republic and two members elected by the National Assembly, forms the Constitutional Court which has

---

41. Legislative Decree No. 3 of 12 June 1963, Art. 9.
42. Cotran, "Legal Problems Arising Out of the formation of the Somali Republic", International and Comparative Law Quarterly, July 1963, p. 1010 at p. 1021.
43. Santiapichi, op. cit., p. 26.
44. Constitution of the Somali Republic, Arts, 93 and 96
45. Ibid. Art. 98.
46. Ibid., Art. 39.
47. The Higher Judicial Council consists of the President of the Supreme Court, the Attorney General, the members of the Supreme Court and three members elected by the National Assembly

jurisdiction over the constitutionality of laws.[48] The decisions of the Constitutional Court have effect *erga omnes*. A law or a particular provision declared unconstitutional ceases to be in force on the day of the publication of the judgment.[49]

Any final decision of the Public Administration may be challenged before the Supreme Court.[50] Thus the Supreme Court acts also as the highest Administrative Tribunal. The powers of the Supreme Court are further strengthened by the provision that, where the Public Administration fails to comply with a Supreme Court judgment in an administrative matter, "the Supreme Court shall, at the instance of the party concerned, take the necessary action to carry out its judgment".[51] Thus the Supreme Court is authorized, if necessary, to use executive powers to ensure that its own judgments against the Public Administration are properly carried out.

The effectiveness of judicial review of administrative action in Somalia has been successfully tested in a recent case. On 26 November, 1963, Local Council elections were held in the whole Republic. The new Local Council of Mogadiscio met for the first time on 2 January 1964, and elected its Mayor. On the same day the Minister of Interior, having heard the Council of Ministers, issued a decree dissolving the Mogadiscio Council and appointing a Special Commissioner.[52] It was stated in the decree that the Council gave no assurance of being able to perform its functions, because the newly elected Mayor had also been the Mayor of the previous Municipal Council, which had been dissolved in 1962 on the ground of "serious administrative deficiencies and irregularities".

The Mayor and a number of Councillors petitioned the Supreme Court for the annulment of the Minister's decree. The Supreme Court noted that the Minister of interior was authorized to dissolve a Local Council "where a Council cannot perform its functions".[53] It held that this impossibility should be evaluated *a posteriori*, whereas the grounds stated in the decree were based on *a priori* judgment of how the Council would perform its functions in the future. Accordingly, the decree was annulled, and the Local Council reinstated.[54] Considering that the Government attached considerable political importance to the dissolution of the Mogadiscio

48. Legislative Decree No, 3 of 12 June 1962, Annex I, Chapter I.
49. Ibid., Art. 6, paragraph 4.
50. Legislative Decree No. 3 of 12 June 1962, Art. 5(3) (b).
51. Ibid., Art. 10(4).
52. Ministerial Decree No. 9 of 2 January, 1964.
53. Law No. 19 of 14 August, 1963, Art. 44(1).
54. *Ahmed Muddei Hussen and others* v. *the Minister of Interior* Supreme Court Judgment of 17 March, 1964.

Council, this Supreme Court decision, and its immediate implementation, is a fine example of the supremacy of the rule of law and the
independence of the Judiciary in the Somali Republic.

IV. IMPACT OF JUDICIAL INTEGRATION ON CUSTOMARY LAW

Where there is a dual system of courts, customary law and ordinary
law tend to develop as separate water-tight compartments. The
unification of the judiciary, instead, furthers the growth of unitary
case law, inspired by common principles and responsive to the
requirements of an evolving society. This means that customary law
is subject to objective scrutiny by the best qualified judges. As a
result, those rules of customary law that survive this critical analysis
emerge strengthened, while others may be discarded.

This is illustrated by two recent decisions of the Somali Supreme
Court, which in the first case upheld a rule of customary law, and in
the second case discarded another.

In *Hussein Hersi and another v. Yusuf Deria Ali* (Civil Appeal
No. 2 of 1964), the brother of a girl who was knocked down and killed
by a truck in the town of Hargeisa claimed 'dia' against the driver.

In a judgment delivered by Dr. Haji N. A. Noor Muhammad, J.,
the Supreme Court examined the following aspects of 'dia': (1)
whether the payment of 'dia' is consistent with the Somali Constitution and public policy; (2) whether 'dia' is applicable to motor
car accidents; (3) whether 'dia' for motor car accidents is applicable
in urban as well as rural areas.

The first question arose out of Article 43(1) of the Constitution
which provides that "penal liability is personal. No collective
punishment of any kind shall be imposed."

The Court considered two issues: the first was whether 'dia' is a
penal or civil liability; the second, whether the collective responsibility of a tribe is contrary to the above mentioned constitutional
provision.

The Court examined in some detail the nature of 'dia' under
Shari'a and Somali customary law and held:

"Under the Shariat law, 'dia' or blood money is a penal
punishment. In cases of premeditated homicide the
offender alone is liable for blood money; and in cases of
involuntary or voluntary homicide the 'aakila' of the
offender, i.e. the agnates of the offender on the collateral
line, are responsible for the blood money.
But Shariat law as applied in the Somali Republic has been
modified in certain respects by customary law. First, even

though the spread of Islam among the Hamitic tribes put an Islamic gloss upon the customary organization existing in the country, it did not produce any effective change in the tribal customs relating to compensation. The law of talion, which, as referred to earlier, is the principle of Shariat law, was never introduced, for there was no supreme authority to enforce it. Only the looser and less severe methods of compensation continued. When the Colonial Powers took over the administration of criminal law, the Indian Penal Code was made applicable in the former Somali-land Protectorate and the Italian Penal Code in Somalia. Under the above Codes, homicide became an offence against the State; the tribe of the victim, however, continued to exercise a right to claim civil damages, apparently as compensation for the loss of one of its members. Thus 'dia', which is a penal punishment under Shariat law, is considered civil damages in this country."

On the question of the collective responsibility of the tribe, the Court held that the constitutional prohibition applied only to collective punishment imposed on villages and communities in whose areas certain crimes were committed. As the collective responsibility for the payment of 'dia' is not a collective punishment, such a responsibility was not abolished by the Constitution.

The Court then considered the contention of counsel for the appellants that to hold compensation is payable by the tribal group would be contrary to the public policy of the State "of transforming the Somali society from the present largely tribal structure into a detribalized closely knit national State". The Court observed that the proceedings of the Constituent Assembly indicated there was no intention to abolish the collective responsibility of the tribe for the payment of 'dia'. Furthermore, the public order law recently enacted by the National Assembly implicitly confirmed collective responsibility for the payment of compensation. It was held:

"The Constituent Assembly which adopted the Constitution and the National Assembly both appear to approve the collective responsibility of the tribe regarding the payment of 'dia'. In the face of such approval, and in view of the long-standing nature of the custom, the Supreme Court cannot hold that the collective responsibility is against the public policy of the State."

Regarding the question whether 'dia' is applicable to motor car accidents, the Court held that "under Somali customary law, there is no distinction between deliberate and accidental homicide, and 'dia' is applicable in both types of homicide." The Court went on to say:

> "Traffic accidents are comparatively a new problem, and such problems could not have been contemplated under Somali customary law.
>
> Law, whether Shariatic or customary, is not static; and Shariat law definitely provides that, in the absence of specific provisions under Shariat to cover any particular matter or situation, analogy ('qiyas') should be resorted to. 'Qiyas' consists in the extension of the 'hukm' or rule contained in one text ('Nass'), or even consensus to somewhat different facts to be covered by the same 'illa' or efficient cause of the 'hukm'. The Court of Justice, which was the highest Court in the former Trust Territory of Somalia under Italian Administration, has laid down in *Dahabo Abdi* v. *Haleima Abdulla* (Judgment of 11 March, 1957) that:
>
>> " . . . in the absence of provisions in customary law for the payment of damages under Shariat law, the Judge can apply by way of analogy the criteria applied in similar cases."
>
> The above ruling approves the application of analogy in customary law, with which principle this Court respectfully agrees.
>
> When it is generally accepted that, under Somali customary law, a person must pay the 'dia' of the person he kills, it does not matter whether the homicide is caused by the person directly or through the vehicle that he drives negligently. The principle of 'dia' is that the offender has caused the death of another and thereby caused a loss to the latter's tribe, and it is his duty under Somali customary law to compensate the latter's tribe for the said loss. To deny compensation in motor car accidents cases would be contrary to the fundamental principle enunciated above.

As another ground for the extension of 'dia' to motor car accidents, the Court quoted with approval the following ruling of the Court of Appeal of Hargeisa:

> "Under the British (and I believe many other) legal system, the driver and owner of a vehicle causing an accident would be liable to compensate the victim, but this liability would normally be covered by compulsory car insurance. There is no compulsory insurance here and under the existing circumstances it would be impracticable to introduce it. Somali 'herr' provides a form of insurance. In natural

justice the victim of a traffic accident should be entitled to compensation where the accident is due to the other party's negligence. Obviously, if his only claim lies against the driver, the victim will have little hope of recovering compensation awarded, as in most cases the driver would be unable to pay. In the circumstances I feel I cannot agree with the defence submission that 'herr' should not apply to such cases."

The Court considered then the contention of counsel for the appellants that 'dia' should not be applicable to motor car accidents occurring in towns. It was stated by counsel that:

"Tribal groups accept collective responsibility for acts of individuals only in matters which directly affect the interests and security of the group as a whole. The extent of their responsibility is moreover clearly known to them. The tribe has no interest in the traffic misfortunes to which urbanized members of the group are parties and they have no control over townsmen who take to driving motor cars for business or pleasure."

This argument was not upheld by the Court, which ruled:

"If we accept the principle of collective responsibility of the tribe for the payment of 'dia' or other compensation, there is no reason why a distinction should be made whether the act was committed within a town or in the bush, or whether the act was committed by a person living in an urbanized area or a rural area."

In *Hassan Hussein and another* v. *Sulbub Aw Abdi* (Civil Appeal No. 5 of 1962), a girl was engaged by her brother against her will and she eloped with the respondent and married him. The man to whom the girl had been engaged claimed 'haal', i.e. compensation, against the respondent. The claim was based on a rule of Somali customary law providing that in those circumstances 'haal' is payable, regardless of whether the girl had given her consent to the engagement.

The Court rejected the claim on the following grounds:

"In view of the cardinal principles of Islamic law assuring that the legal status of grown-up females is as complete as that of a male, Courts are not prepared to concede the right of even the father to give his adult virgin daughter in marriage without the latter's consent . . . Even Minhaj Et Talabin states that an agnatic brother can give his adult virgin sister in marriage provided she does not oppose the choice. There cannot be, therefore, valid betrothal where she is opposed to the choice. The appellants' claim to 'haal'

could arise only if there was a valid betrothal, and if
Amina married the respondent during the subsistence
of a valid betrothal. The claim of the appellants for
'haal' cannot therefore be sustained."

This Conference is concerned with integration of customary law
and modern legal systems within African countries. I would like to
call the attention of the Conference to another aspect of the problem,
which might be called "trans-national" integration—to borrow
Professor Jessup's adjective, in other words, the integration or
harmonization of legal systems among different African States.

Up to now, African countries generally follow the Western legal
system inherited from the former colonial powers. This has brought
about conflicts and divergencies in legal concepts, resulting in
unnecessary complications that tend to impede economic progress.
These centrifugal legal forces also work against the aspiration to
closer African unity.

Recently, there has been an increasing awareness that some form
of integration is urgently needed, especially in laws affecting
economic development such as investments, land tenure, water
legislation. For example, the United Nations Economic Commission
for Africa includes in its work programme a number of projects for
the harmonization of laws in economic and social areas. In addition,
an organization of jurists was formed a few months ago for this very
purpose, and the International Juridical Organization for Developing
Countries is represented at this Conference.

The experience in Somalia of integrating two Western legal
systems and customary law has taught us that the work can most
effectively be done by teams of lawyers trained in different legal
systems. In the beginning, there was common ground between the
lawyers with British training and their Italian colleagues on only
one point: both sides were convinced of the superiority of their own
system. However, the constant exchange of ideas and experiences
gradually broadened everyone's vision. In the end, mutual suspicion
gave way to fruitful collaboration.

While it is natural for a lawyer to be reluctant to question the
validity of the legal concepts and traditions in which he has grown
up and been trained, it should be less difficult for African jurists to
be flexible about other peoples' legal traditions.

The approach to the work of integration can be described by a
story of ancient Greece: during the Peloponnesian War, a courier
was running to Athens with an urgent message. On his way, he met
an old shepherd and stopped to ask "How far is Athens from here?"
The shepherd did not answer. The messenger, thinking the old
man was deaf, started off again at a brisk trot. When he had gone

about 100 yards the shepherd shouted "Two hours away!" The messenger turned his head and shouted back "Why didn't you answer before?" And the shepherd replied "How did I know how fast you run?"

If we are to make real progress, we need the speed of the Greek messenger coupled with the wisdom of the old shepherd, who gave the right answer only after weighing all the elements of the problem.

THE JUDICIAL DEVELOPMENT OF CUSTOMARY LAW IN NIGERIA

by

DR. F. A. AJAYI

SOLICITOR GENERAL & PERMANENT SECRETARY,
MINISTRY OF JUSTICE, WESTERN STATE, IBADAN

THE JUDICIAL DEVELOPMENT OF CUSTOMARY LAW IN NIGERIA

Customary law being an integral part of indigenous social life in Africa, it is, as Lord Atkin once said, [1] the assent of the indigenous communities that gives it its validity, for without their recognition of it as an obligatory rule of conduct it could not properly be regarded as customary law. It is only too well known, however, that the European advent in Africa has had a tremendous impact on the growth and development of the customary laws in various parts of the continent. The pursuit of a policy of economic and social development has greatly changed the circumstances under which men live and thus the introduction of money, cash cropping, commercial and industrial development, rail and road communication, christianity and education, have all so changed African ways of life that the old customary laws with regard to such matters as land, marriage, property and inheritance have been changing too. [2] In some circumstances, all that has been necessary was to adapt customary law to suit the changed conditions, but in others where existing customary laws could not be applied, new laws have had to be formulated either by the decisions of the courts or with the authority of the legislatures or in some cases by the popular assent of the indigenous people concerned themselves.

Since law, in a real sense, is a reflection of the way in which people live, and since the African way of life is changing, it is only to be expected that the traditional laws of old Africa must change too. It is not the case that customary law in Africa derives all its dynamism making for change wholly from European presence on the continent, for indigenous communities, far from respecting all the time all immemorial customs, are, at any rate occasionally, disposed to make departures, even in fundamental rules, where these are considered to be in the social interest. [3] Customary law, like all forms of law, therefore, has to be adaptable in one form or

1. *Eshugbayi Eleko The* v. *Officer Administering the Government of Nigeria & Another,* [1931] A.C. 662 at p. 673.
2. T. R. Batten, *"Pattern of African Development"* (2nd ed.) Part II, p. 149.
3. See, for instance, Green, *"Ibo Village Affairs"* (1947), p. 132: "An Ibo community, far from resting on immemorial custom, seems always ready for new departures even to the extent of discussing, as Owerri was doing, the alteration of such apparently fundamental conditions as the rules governing exogamy."

another to meet changing socio-economic conditions if it is to continue surviving as an integral part of social life. As indicated above, it is possible for such development to take a variety of forms. Popular discussion with a view to securing general assent in favour of changes in old rules of customary law was not unknown under the indigenous legal system. The history of most known systems of law furnishes examples of legal development through this and other agencies as well, such as the use of procedural forms and the restrictive as well as the liberal method of interpretation in the judicial process; when the law becomes rather rigid and inconvenient in its application to day-to-day life, one finds evidence of the intervention of the discretionary and less rigid principles of equity for the purpose of modifying the asperity of the strict law; and finally where all other agencies prove incapable of generating further progress or of producing expeditiously enough legal changes considered necessary, one finds that legislation steps in as an agency of legal reform.[4]

A study of customary law in contemporary times would reveal more or less similar phases in its development, sometimes in succession and sometimes simultaneously. When one comes to consider in particular the development of customary law through the judicial process one finds that the courts have employed in this task a number of different judicial techniques. At one time, they may be relying on the methods of history, whereby one has to look back in order to find out what the customary rule of law had been in the past; and once the position in the past is revealed the old rule is applied to the new situation without question. Thus in the case of *Amodu Tijani* v. *The Secretary, Southern Provinces*,[5] where the question was whether Chief Oluwa, one of the White-Cap Chiefs of Lagos, was the owner of a piece of land at Apapa which had been acquired compulsorily by the Government, the court, before it could arrive at a decision, found it necessary to consider the whole matter in the light of the history of Lagos from about the beginning of the eighteenth century, including the invasion and conquest of the island by the King of Benin; the British intervention in the middle of the nineteenth century to suppress the slave trade; the resulting treaty of cession by King Docemo to the British Crown in 1861; and the effect, if any, which these historical events and upheavals had on the customary land tenure on the island of Lagos by the time the case came up for decision here in Nigeria. When the case

4. See *Julius Stone, "The Province and Function of Law"* (2nd printing) 1950, pp. 456-460 on Maine's famous generalisations in the present connection.
5. 3 N.L.R. 21

eventually went on appeal before the Judicial Committee of the Privy Council in England, the Committee stressed the importance of the historical method of inquiry, that is, the studying of the history of the particular community concerned and its usages before deciding issues of the type that had been raised before them and the avoidance of any resort to abstract principles fashioned *a priori* and likely to be of little substance as well as misleading.

Also, when, in the case of *Sakariyawo Oshodi* v. *Moriamo Dakolo & Others*,[6] the question first arose in 1928 as to who were the persons entitled to the ownership of a piece of land at Epetedo in Lagos, which had been acquired by the Government under the Public Lands Acquisition Ordinance, that is, whether the occupiers of the land who, in most though not in all cases, were descendants of slaves of Chief Oshodi Tappa, were entitled to the whole of the compensation to be paid by the Government or whether this should be paid to Chief Sakariyawo Oshodi, the head of the Oshodi Chieftaincy Family, it was eventually decided according to the customary law on land tenure in Lagos obtaining immediately after the return to Lagos in 1862 of Chief Oshodi Tappa with his family and entourage from exile at Epe. Various intervening events, like Crown grants in absolute terms to individuals (later held to be grants in trust for the individual grantees and the rest of the compound) and individual dispositions of land in some cases as between sons and daughters of the Oshodi Family and in others as between such members of the Family and strangers, were all in the end regarded as not having altered in any way the original position at customary law as between the Oshodi Family, the original owners, and the other claimants who were descendants or successors in title of those to whom Oshodi Family had allotted the land for purposes of occupation. There are a number of other cases in which similar methods of historical inquiry had been adopted in trying to find out what was the old rule of customary law, after which such rule was simply applied in the instant circumstances.[7]

On other occasions, the courts have shown themselves inclined to consider customary law as being in a continuous process of evolution and accordingly they have been disposed to take cognizance of changes in ancient rules where evidence has been produced that such changes have taken place and have been accepted by the society whose life the new rule of customary law is supposed to regulate. It is the use of this method of evolution, if one may call

6. 9 N.L.R. 13
7. See, for example, *Bassey James Bassey* v. *Archibong Cobham, Egbo Cobham and John Anthony Kouri*, 5 N.L.R. 92.

it that, that accounts for a number of cases where the courts have held that customary law has moved away from its ancient position, which did not recognise individual ownership or the alienability of land, and has reached a stage where individual ownership and alienability of land is accorded recognition. One may refer here as a matter of interest to the views expressed by Webber, J., in the case of *Brimah Balogun and Scottish Nigeria Mortgage and Trust Company Ltd.* v. *Saka Chief Oshodi*:[8]

"It seems to me that the native law existent during the last fifty years has recognised alienation of family land, even by a domestic, provided the permission of the family is obtained . . .

The chief characteristic of native law is its flexibility—one incident of land tenure after another disappears as the times change—but the most important incident of tenure which has crept in and become firmly established as a rule of native law is alienation of land."

Also, in the case of *Chief Joseph Wobo & Others* v. *Attorney-General for the Federation of Nigeria*, Viscount Simonds, in delivering the judgment of the Judicial Committee of the Privy Council, said as follows:[9]

"The learned counsel for the appellants laid stress on the importance of native law and custom in regard to the disposal of land, alleging alternatively that customary law made it impossible to sell such land or that a sale was so unprecedented a measure that it could not be supposed that the Chiefs understood what they were doing. Their Lordships see no reason to doubt the view of the learned trial Judge that native law and custom was not so inflexible as to render a sale of land to the Government illegal nor can they suppose that this aspect of the matter was not fully considered in determining the question of fact whether or not the Chiefs understood what they were doing."

And in 1943, in the case of *Kadiri Balogun* v. *Tijani Balogun & Others*,[10] Graham Paul, C.J. (of Sierra Leone), said at page 82:

"As a matter of historical fact and of judicial decision it is now too late in the day to say that under (Lagos) native law and custom family property is inalienable so as to give the grantee absolute ownership."

8. 10 N.L.R. 36 at 51, 53-54.
9. P.C. Appeal No. 18 of 1956, reported in the "*Journal of African Law*", Vol. 1, No. 1, p. 45 at p. 49
10. 9 W.A.C.A. 73.

Similarly, there has been a variety of new types of transactions which, strictly speaking, were not conducted under the old customary law but to which the courts have nonetheless been disposed to apply rules of customary law, albeit in an adapted form, in order to meet the changing requirements of society. Thus it has been held that estates of deceased persons disposed of by wills made in English statutory form could still devolve according to the customary law of succession governing family property;[11] or that the giving and taking of promissory notes by persons subject to customary law would not necessarily exclude the application to the transaction of customary law, which knows no concept of limitation of actions;[12] or that although a junior member of the family has no right under customary law to take action on his own in protection of family property, nevertheless where the senior members who have such right neglect or refuse to assert it, the court would allow the junior member to take such action in his capacity as beneficiary;[13] or that although a family head is not entitled under customary law to act on his own for the benefit of the family so as to render them bound without prior consultation or approval, nevertheless such a head may be taken to have this power in an emergency.[14]

In the case of *Ewa Ekeng Inyang* v. *Efana Ekeng Ita & Others*,[15] the issue which arose for decision before Berkeley, J., in the Divisional Court at Calabar in 1929 was as to the right of two rival claimants to the headship of the Ewa Ekeng house at Calabar. The defendant holder of the headship held it by virtue of the fact that he had been elected thereto by vote at a family meeting whilst the plaintiff claimed the headship by right of primogeniture, he being the eldest male member of the family. The plaintiff contended that any kind of popular election was contrary to customary law and therefore *ultra vires*. In the course of the judgment in the case, His Lordship had the following to say:-

> "Before the Government came to Calabar, and established law and order, it is certain that the headship of a house belonged as of right to the senior male member of that

11. *Abisatu Balogun & Another* v. *Amodu Ayinla Balogun & others*, 2 W.A.C.A. 290; *Mary Bolaji Jacobs* v. *Messrs Oladunni Bros.*, 12 N.L.R. 1; *In re Estate of Edward Forster, F. A. Coker* v. *G. B. Coker* 14 N.L.R. 83.
12. *Pearce* v. *Aderoku*, 13 N.L.R. 9
13. *Bassey Egbo Bassey* v. *Archibong Cobham & Others*, 5 N.L.R. 90 at p. 94
14. *Kasumu Aralawon* v. *Yesufu O. Aromire & Elo Aiyedun, Chief Aromire*, 15 N.L.R. 90
15. 9 N.L.R. 84.

house. But he took it at his peril. If he failed to find support within the family only two courses were open to him. Either he went into exile or else he stayed and was put to death. In either case the succession to the vacancy devolved on the next senior male, if he chose to take it up. Human nature is much the same all over the world, and it is absolutely certain that there must have been occasions on which the next senior male, knowing that he had no chance of winning the support of the family, had sufficient intelligence to stand aside rather than risk such perilous promotion . . .

It is obvious that even before the advent of the Government, the theory of election, though in a very rudimentary form, was already inherent in the family system of the Efik people of Calabar.

With the coming of the Government the rule of law was substituted for the rule of violence. It was no longer possible to put an unpopular head to death. Therefore an unpopular head, being no longer in fear of his life, was under no compulsion to seek security in exile. The family was saddled with the unpopular head and had no means of getting rid of him. The only remedy for such a state of affairs was to take steps to see that no man should become head of the house unless he had behind him the support of the family. No doubt in the majority of cases the senior man was sufficiently suitable, and became head without opposition. But when he was not suitable the family had no hesitation in selecting some other member in his stead. This was only common sense, and a natural adaptation of custom to make it conform to a change in condition.

The plaintiff is asking this court to put the clock back. He wishes to deprive the family of any choice in the matter of their head. He ignores the changed circumstances of the times and wishes to revert to a custom the safeguards and checks upon which can no longer be applied."

In conclusion, therefore, the court refused to uphold the plaintiff's claim and so applied the evolutionary method to the interpretation of customary law.

At still other times, the courts have used, in applying customary law, what one might call the methods of abstract justice or equity by trying to ensure that rules of customary law which are considered repugnant to natural justice, equity or good conscience are not enforced. The guiding principle here appears to be one like the maxim *malus usus abolendus est*. It is the application of this method that accounts for the great number of cases in which it has been held that although customary law knows no concept of prescription or limitation of actions, nevertheless, it would be unjust and inequitable to permit land owners under customary law to press stale claims with a view to ejecting from their lands those who had been in possession thereof for a long time.[16] Similarly where under the strict rule of customary law forfeiture of a customary tenant's interest would have been permissible on account of misbehaviour to his landlord, the courts have held on occasions that such a forfeiture would not be permitted where it would be inequitable.[17] Other examples of the application of the same method are to be found in the cases where the courts have refused to apply the customary rule of inheritance to the rights of survivors under Christian marriages[18] and their refusal to enforce alleged surviving incidents of slavery.[19]

There is nothing peculiar to customary law as such or to judicial experience in Nigeria in all the developments mentioned above, for every legal order, whatever its background, has to face the problem of the role of the courts in the evolution of law. As Friedmann has so clearly pointed out,[20] until the turn of the present century the opinion prevailed both in theory and practice that there was a clear-cut division between the respective spheres of the courts on the one hand and legislative bodies on the other, it being the function of the latter to make the laws and that of the former simply to apply them. But as another learned author has said:

"It is the case, whatever the form behind which it has been concealed, that the work of English courts from the medieval period onwards represents a great achievement in legislation by reference to the changing facts of social life as seen in the actual behaviours of associations of men for the time being."[21]

And as another learned writer has said with particular reference to the judicial role in the development of English Common Law:

"New combinations of circumstances—that is, new cases—

16. *Akpan Awo v. Cookey Gam*, 2 N.L.R, 100; *Chief Eferekuma Aro & Others v. Chief Mark Pepple Jaja*, 6 N.L.R. 24
17. *Chief Uwani v. Nwosu Akom & Others*, 8 *N.L.R.* 19; *Idowu Inasa & Others v. Chief Sakariyawo Oshodi*, 11. NL.R. 10; *Chief Mojolagbe Ashogbon v. S. Oduntan*, 12 N.L.R. 7.
18. *Cole v. Cole*, 1 N.L.R. 15; *In the matter of the Estate of Joseph Emodie Administrator-General v. Onwo Egbuna*, 18 N.L.R. 1.
19. *In re Effiong Okon, A. O. Ekpan v. Chief E. Henshaw & Another*, 10 N.L.R. 65
20. W. Friedmann, *"Law in a Changing Society"*, 1959, p. 24.
21. Stone, *op. cit.*, p. 167.

constantly call for the application, which means in truth the extension of old principles; or it may be, even for the thinking out of some new principle, in harmony with the general spirit of the law, fitted to meet the novel requirements of the time. Hence whole branches not of ancient but of very modern law have been built up, developed, or created by the action of the Courts. The whole body of rules, with regard to the conflict of laws (or in other words, for the decision of cases which contain some foreign element,) has come into existence during the last hundred and twenty, and, as regards by far the greater part of it, well within the last eighty, or even seventy years."[22]

It is also the view of Friedmann that when the French jurist, Geny, looked back in 1899 on nearly a century of legal development under the French Civil Code, he found that the courts had transformed it in many vital respects by a process of creative interpretation and Friedmann goes on to give other examples of the judicial development of the German Civil Code of 1900 and the Swiss Civil Code of 1907.[23]

A study of the work of the courts in the development of customary law in Nigeria would reveal a number of rather similar outstanding contributions which they have made. For instance, by the use of the historical method of interpretation, they have repeatedly enforced some of the old rules that make for the stability of the indigenous social structure and have thus assisted in preventing it from disintegrating completely under the impact of new and non-traditional aspects of life, whilst the very process of repeated judicial enforcement itself has led to better knowledge of the scope and content of the old rules. The distinctive contribution of the method of evolution when used by the courts for the purpose of interpreting customary law has been to render it as adaptable as possible to the ever changing needs of society. By the use of the method of abstract justice or equity the courts have tried to excise from the customary legal order such rules as they consider to be repugnant to natural justice, equity and good conscience, and in that way they have made the legal morality of the courts a precursor to the social morality of the people whose conduct is subject to the customary legal regime; in particular instances they have also, by the use of this method, ensured the maintenance and the security of various types of interests such as the economic interests of long

22. Dicey, *Law and Public opinion in England during the Nineteenth Century* (2nd. ed.) p. 363.
23. W. Friedmann, *op. cit.*, pp. 24-25.

possessors of land which would have been jeopardized by an application of the strict rules of the old customary law.

There is, however, a reverse side to the judicial contribution in relation to the development of customary law. There can be no doubt that the application of the doctrine of precedent in the present field might have led in some cases to a premature crystallization of the old rules when they were still only in a formative stage and, as a result, to a sacrifice of future development on the altar of history. Similarly, there are cases where it seems that legal certainty has been obtained only by perpetuating errors of interpretation which, once committed, are repeatedly followed in obedience to the doctrine of judicial precedent. Also, the rigid enforcement of local rules in various areas, where not accompanied by an attempt to recognise and distinguish between principles generally applicable and mere variations only of local application, could constitute itself into an impediment to rationalization and unification of diverse systems of local customary laws over such areas.

It should therefore not be surprising that the question of the development of customary law has not been left entirely to the judicial process with all its merits and demerits, and that in various ways the intervention of legislation has proved necessary for this purpose. Trial by ordeal of various types such as the eating of the poisonous *esere* bean or exposure to the attacks of crocodiles are now criminal offences[24] although nobody can deny that they were potent means of proof under ancient customary judicial procedure. Crucifixion, decapitation and drowning were legal forms of execution of condemned persons under customary law[25] but all these are now things of the past. It has for long been a criminal offence[26] for anyone to administer extra-judicial oaths of the customary types[27] either in proof or disproof of given facts, while now that

---

24.   Section 145(1) of the Criminal Code of Western Nigeria, Cap. 28. For a comparison with trial by the ordeal of cold water, the ordeal of hot iron and the ordeal of accursed morsel in medieval English law, see Potter, *"Historical Introduction to English Law"* (2nd ed.) p. 282.

25.   See Alan Burns, *"History of Nigeria"* (4th ed.) pp. 251 and 264

26.   Section 90 of the Criminal Code, Cap. 28. Cf. Compurgation or Wager of Law as a mode of proof in old English judicial procedure as discussed by Potter op. cit., where he referred to *King* v. *Williams* (1824) 2 B. & C. 538 as the last reported case of Wager of Law in England and also expressed the view that the fear of divine vengenanze for false swearing was a real one as shown by the case of *Gundulf v. Pichot*, Bigelow, Placita. p. 34 where a person who had sworn came and fell at the feet of the Bishop hearing the case and confessed that he had perjured himself.

27.   See *R.* v. *Udo Ebong*, 12 W.A.C.A. 139, where it is reported that a person accused of murder had, before the case came to court, offered to take an oath to prove his innocence.

even customary courts themselves are creations of statutes it is equally a criminal offence[28] for anyone to adjudicate upon cases without statutory authority, as was permissible under the old customary law.

The intervention of legislative authority has been carried to its highest pitch when in one fell swoop it was decreed that all customary crimes are abolished,[29] although here it is difficult to say whether this legislative abolition is as effective in the remoter parts of the country as it would appear to be in the urban areas where people have ready access to the services of legal practitioners for the purpose of enforcing their fundamental human rights under the Constitution. The case of *Taiwo Aoko* v. *Adeyemi Fagbemi and the Director of Public Prosecutions*,[30] shows clearly that some two years after the constitutional abolition of all unwritten, that is customary, criminal offences as being against fundamental human rights, a customary court in a locality some eighty miles away from the Regional capital of Western Nigeria convicted and sentenced a woman for committing the customary offence of adultery by living with another man without judicial separation. Proceedings had to be instituted in the High Court for the purpose of nullifying the conviction and sentence. There are other fields of course where one can find evidence of legislative interference with the strict rules of customary law. Under the Chiefs Law,[31] Chieftaincy Committees, which are composed of traditional members of local government councils, have power not only to declare the existing customary law relating to the filling of chieftaincy vacancies but also to make recommendations for the purpose of laying down for the first time, wherever necessary, an order of rotation in which ruling houses should exercise their right to provide candidates for the purpose of filling vacancies. Also, under the Local Government Law,[32] local government councils have power (in respect of matters not relating to chieftaincy) to make declarations as to the customary law in their particular areas and also to submit recommendations for the purpose of modifying such customary law, subject to the approval of the Governor in Council.

28. Section 56(1) of the Customary Courts Law, Cap. 31, formerly section 43(1) of the Native Courts Ordinance, Cap. 142 of the 1948 Laws of Nigeria under which the accused persons in *R. v. Bassey Mba & others*, 15 N.L.R. 53, were tried and convicted.
29. Section 22(1) of the Constitution of the Federation of Nigeria, Act No. 20 of 1963, reproducing similar provisions first introduced in the pre-Independence Constitution in 1959.
30. 1961 W.N.L.R. 147.
31. Cap. 19, section 4(2) (b).
32. Cap. 68, section 78.

In spite of both judicial and legislative attempts to ensure the development of customary law, there are still, as most people would agree a number of *lacunae* in the whole system. Today it is still the rule of customary law that an individual's interest in his family land cannot be alienated by him on his own. As a result, where there is no general agreement within the land-owning group, there is a lack of effective machinery for making titles to land in favour of purchasers even where disposition of the land away from the group is necessary for sound economic reasons. Here one's mind goes back to a more or less analogous position under the English law of strict settlement of land upon successive life tenants within the family, a system which, after centuries of its application, became a clog in the wheel of social and economic progress by rendering land not fully disposable. The legislature had to intervene[33] in order to ensure the free alienability of settled land and the attaching of the rights of those successively interested therein to the proceeds of sale. Another example of old customary law which is as potent today as it was in the past is the rule which excludes wives married under that law from any share in the property of their deceased husbands.[34] Under various systems of law and at different times in history rules of inheritance have provided opportunities for the legislative reformer. Thus we are told that the right to claim one-quarter of a deceased person's estate by means of the *quarela inofficiosi testamenti* of ancient Roman Law could be traced to the *lex Falcidia*[35] whereby it was permitted to bring what was known as the plaint of the unduteous will against a testamentary disposition disinheriting or in later times giving less than one-quarter to those who would have been entitled if the testator had died without making a will. English law did not permit anything in the nature of a similar plaint until the enactment of the Inheritance (Family Provisions) Act of 1938, and it is today still the rule that the widow of a customary marriage is not in her own right entitled to any share of the estate of her deceased husband. Lack of suitable provisions in customary law such as those mentioned above appear to call for legislative action in order to meet the needs of modern times.

In the development of customary law through the judicial process there is a need for greater awareness of the many-sided nature of that process and for a better understanding and evaluation of the respective effects of e ach of its facets on the course of legal develop-

---

33. See Cheshire. "*The Modern Law of Real Property*" (6th ed.) pp. 371-375
34. *Aileru & Others* v. *Anibi*, 20 N.L.R. 46.
35. Buckland, *A Text-Book of Roman Law*, (2nd ed.) pp. 327-328.

ment in particular and on national life itself in general. The number of features assumed by the judicial process in any country and the degree of reliance placed upon each depends to a large extent on local conceptions of the duties of the judicial office. In Nigeria the judicial process in relation to the application and development of customary law has come to acquire a threefold character and the degree of reliance that has hitherto been placed on each aspect of this compound nature has been to a large extent a matter of individual judicial choice either expressly or by tacit predilection. It was Cardozo who said of the application of legal principles in the general judicial process:

"The directive force of a principle may be exerted along the line of logical progression; this I will call the rule of analogy or the method of philosophy; along the line of historical development; this I will call the method of evolution; along the line of the customs of the community; this I will call the method of tradition; along the lines of justice, morals and social welfare, the *mores* of the day; and this I will call the method of sociology."[36]

One may not agree entirely with the terminology adopted in this statement, but its general validity as an accurate analysis of the judicial process does not appear open to question. It is this very fact of the many-sided nature of the judicial process and of the tendency of legal principles and rules in the hands of judges, now to veer in this direction, and now in that, that makes the judicial method one of the most important leavens of legal development. The current and counter-current, the tendency and counter-tendency, the antinomies in this process, as they are called, are inevitable features not only of the judicial method but of law itself.

It is suggested that there is now a pressing necessity for a legislative and judicial re-assignment of functions or roles with regard to the three different methods or techniques hitherto relied upon for the development of customary law in Nigeria by the superior courts. There is need for legislative provisions to facilitate conscious judicial preferences out of these three methods on teleological grounds and for rendering more comprehensive and more articulate the major premises of judicial decisions. As regards the difficult task of adjusting customary law through the judicial process to the changing conditions of contemporary Nigerian life, there should be some guide lines in order to prevent or at least greatly minimise, the development of the law according to different principles and

36. Cardozo, "Nature of the Judicial Process," in M. Hall (ed.), *Selected Writings of Benjamin Nathan Cardozo*, p. 117

with different tendencies in different parts of the country.

Writing on the "Effects of Culture Contact" in the Colony and Protectorate of Kenya, Arthur Phillips has said:

> "The magnitude of the effects of culture contact in this sphere can hardly be exaggerated. The foundations of native law are being undermined at all points. In the first place, the social system on which it is based is being profoundly disturbed and altered. Individualism is gaining ground. Centralized government has been established. Secondly, modern conditions generally and the setting up of permanent centralized judicial bodies in particular necessitate the crystallization of native law into a set code of rules, involving a clear distinction between law and non-enforceable custom. Thirdly, there is an urgent and ever-increasing need for native law to adapt itself to the conditions of modern African Society, and to take account not only of the changes which are affecting traditional institutions but also of the entirely new elements which are intruding. In other words, the slow, almost imperceptible processes by which indigenous law developed in the past are totally inadequate to keep pace with modern requirements. And fourthly, the institutions upon which the knowledge and preservation of native law depended are tending to pass more or less rapidly into desuetude."[37]

Although these statements were made with reference to conditions in Kenya well over some two decades ago, they are, it is suggested, even far more true of conditions in the Nigeria of today. They argue very strongly for a shift in emphasis from the purely historical to the evolutionary method in judicial interpretation.

In his Report on the Native Courts (Northern Provinces) Commission of Inquiry, 1952, Brooke has the following to say:[38]

> "Witnesses before the Commissions of Inquiry in the Western and Eastern Provinces, as well as in this Region, have complained of the uncertainty and unpredictability of any particular decision in such matters as matrimonial and testamentary causes as well as the absence of information as to the individual rights within the group in customary tenures. At the lowest stages it is always difficult to discover what custom actually is and social necessities are in advance of custom; the policy has been to let custom

---

37. Arthur Phillips, *"Report on Native Tribunals in the Colony and Protectorate of Kenya"* 1945, para. 820.
38. Para. 147.

evolve from within (words used in a despatch to the Secretary of State and clearly borrowed from *Law in the Making* by C. K. Allen) as a code puts an end to its spontaneous development. This accounts for the present fortuitous position."

There is therefore a need for new legislative provisions to allow the dynamic and evolutionary method of interpretation to emerge from its present relative obscurity in the general judicial process and to permit of its being consciously adopted by the courts with definite purposes in view. The observations of Brooke about "social necessities being in advance of custom" do not constitute the discovery of any facts peculiar to the developing processes of customary law in Nigeria. The view of Allen is that:

"It is a very characteristic quality of custom—perhaps, indeed, its strongest—that the mere fact of its practice and repetition invest it with a sanctity which is often more compelling than reason, logic, or utility."[39]

In this connection he also refers to the following observations of Maine:-

"The usages which a particular community is found to have adopted in its infancy and in its primitive seats are generally those which are on the whole best suited to promote its physical and moral well-being; and, if they are retained in their integrity until new social wants have taught new practices, the upward march of society is almost certain. But unhappily there is a law of development which ever threatens to operate upon unwritten usage. The customs are of course obeyed by multitudes who are incapable of understanding the true ground of their expediency, and who are therefore left inevitably to invent superstitious reasons for their permanence. A process then commences which may be shortly described by saying that usage which is reasonable generates usage which is unreasonable. Analogy, the most valuable of instruments in the maturity of jurisprudence, is the most dangerous of snares in its infancy. Prohibitions and ordinances, originally confined, for good reasons, to a single description of acts, are made to apply to all acts of the same class, because a man menaced with the anger of the gods for doing one thing, feels a natural terror in doing any other thing which is remotely like it."[40]

---

39.   C. K. Allen, *"Law in the Making"* (4th ed.) p. 96.
40.   Maine, *"Ancient Law"*, (World's Classics ed.) p. 16.

It is therefore essential to guard against the continued reign of particular customs after their reasons have departed, and to this end, new legislative provisions will be required not only to allow greater judical recognition of the evolutionary aspects of the nature of customary law, but also to endow the judicial office with distinctively creative functions in this field. If social necessities in specific cases can be shown to be in advance of custom then it will be necessary for the judicial task to transcend the limits of mere assimilation of previous or even present observances into the body of the law. It would be necessary, in other words, for the judiciary to be empowered by clear legislative mandate to play a creative role in this respect by the declaration and development of new rules designed to attune the contents of customary law to the social necessities of contemporary life.

The assignment of such a task by express statutory mandate will no doubt be novel even if, as a matter of fact, in Nigeria to an extent, and still more so in England, the need for its performance has occasionally been assumed by the courts, of their own volition. In England the creative role of the judiciary as a law-making agency has evolved over several centuries of national progress and legal development. In Nigeria there have been signs of the beginnings and even occasionally some fruition of the same process in relation to the judicial development of customary law. But in general, it can be said that what there are as yet are only the seeds of the idea and that for them to be able to germinate, develop really fully and fructify in abundance, as they ought to do, the legislature should give the judiciary an unambiguous and definite mandate to carry on and enlarge upon a task which has fallen inevitably within its province. Here it should be remembered that a number of important institutions (all of them with some bearing upon law) which have been "evolved" elsewhere over a very long period of time, and which have become veritable props and significant features of contemporary life in Nigeria, have had to be introduced into the country, as into many others, by processes savouring almost of a revolution. Examples are representative, responsible or parliamentary and cabinet government; the democratic principle in Local Government; public ownership or regulation and control of some of the means of production, distribution and exchange; modern conceptions of the "Welfare State"; and several other things which need not be detailed here. In many cases, for instance, the unwritten conventions of the British Constitution which in England are generally assumed and accepted as part of the established order of things have had to be expressly incorporated in statutory form in Nigeria as in many another country. It therefore need not appear strange that a suggestion has here been made for express statutory conferment on the Courts in Nigeria of powers the exercise of which has been generally and tacitly assumed in England and elsewhere. The suggestion is intended to remove all possible doubts as to the necessity, indeed, the inevitability of judicial resort to the dynamic method of interpretation which with express statutory authority would be enabled to emerge clearly into the open in the general judicial process. There is, as has been argued in various connections above, a very strong case for permitting "judicial legislation" which would go beyond the mere assimilation of old rules into the law or the application and enforcement only of customary law not repugnant to natural justice, equity and good conscience.

It should not prove an insurmountable problem to devise new juridical formulae by reference to which the power of "judicial legislation" by way of adaptation and modification of customary law should be exercised. The example of principles based upon the interests of the individual or the public at large is one that can usefully be followed by the courts for present purposes. Another that may be suggested here as eminently suitable for adoption is the maxim *cessante ratione legis cessat ipsa lex* which is based on sound legal reasoning and common sense. Others also can with some thought be devised with the mainsprings being the overriding necessities of social, political and economic development and progress in a society which is currently undergoing a very rapid process of transformation.

There is no suggestion here that the historical approach or method should be totally abandoned. A system of law which, in no respect whatsoever, has any features of stability would be the very apotheosis of juridical anarchy and chaos, rather than an instrument of orderly progress and development. However paradoxical this may appear in theory, it has to be admitted that the historical method of interpretation will always be a matter of practical necessity in any system of law judicially applied. All that has been suggested, therefore, is that the dynamic or evolutionary method should be given its own due measure or recognition, so that customary law may no longer have to be regarded as an archaic survival from a by-gone age but as an integral and vital part of modern life which in its various aspects is responsive in every possible way to the demands of modern society.

PART II

LAW OF CONTRACTS AND CIVIL WRONGS

INTEGRATION OF THE LAW OF CONTRACTS

by

B. O. NWABUEZE

FORMERLY LECTURER IN LAW, UNIVERSITY OF LAGOS

INTEGRATION OF THE LAW OF CONTRACTS

A paper on the integration of laws governing contracts in African countries should perhaps conveniently begin with a general picture of the pluralism of laws which characterises African legal systems. But the need for this has been admirably answered by the background paper prepared by Professor A. N. Allott and Mr. E. Cotran, entitled "Restatement of Laws in Africa. The need, value and methods of such restatement." I will therefore tackle straight away the main theme of this paper, and I will begin by considering the nature of contract.

Nature of Contract

Under the modern legal systems which have been introduced or "received" into Africa, contract is a fully mature institution, with many refinements and also complexities which are the result of the accumulated experience of many centuries of development. From a rather slender origin, it has blossomed into a general remedy for breaches of all serious agreements between persons of full legal capacity. In its present state of maturity, its constitutive elements are briefly:-

(a) mutual assent, signified by an offer made by one party and accepted by another;[1]

(b) an intention on the part of the offeror to be bound legally and not merely morally by his offer, for, as has been said, "to offer a friend a meal is not to invite litigation;"[2] and (in the common law systems only)

(c) consideration or *causa*.

Once these elements are present in any particular case, then the parties are legally bound to each other in contract; that is to say, the law will bestow its sanctions on the agreement, so that a party who tries to go back on his promise will be met by an action, at the suit of the other party, for breach of contract. It is not an answer to such an action that the party suing has not yet performed his part of the agreement, for an agreement is nonetheless enforceable by an

---

1. On the jurisprudential question whether the existence of this mutual assent should be ascertained subjectively, by regarding the actual mental state of the parties at the time of the agreement, or objectively, see Paton, *A Textbook of Jurisprudence* (1964) pp. 400-403.
2. Cheshire & Fifoot, *The Law of Contract* (6th ed.) page 93.

action at law although all the obligations arising under it remain in *futuro*.

Contract, under "civilised" law, is characterised, therefore, by the fact that it provides a comprehensive remedy for breaches of all serious agreements, executed as well as executory. When we turn to contract under customary law, it seems that we cannot attribute to it anything like the same comprehensiveness. Indeed, the view adumbrated by some of the older generation of writers on ancient or primitive law is that contract was only marginally known to that law. Perhaps the best known proponent of this view is Sir Henry Maine. Starting from the premise that the unit of the ancient society was the family, and not the individual as in the modern society, Maine asserts, not without plausibility, that the individual in primitive societies "creates for himself few or no rights and few or no duties. The rules which he obeys are derived from the station into which he is born, and next from the imperative commands addressed to him by the chief of the household of which he forms part. Such a system leaves the very smallest room for contract. The members of the same family ... are wholly incapable of contracting with each other, and the family is entitled to disregard the engagements by which any one of its subordinate members has attempted to bind it."[3] It must be said in fairness to Maine that he concedes that no primitive society was ever entirely destitute of the conception of contract. For, as he admits, "family ... may contract with family, chieftain with chieftain."

But present African customary law has so far developed beyond the stage described by Maine, that it will be naive to apply to it his observations. In the famous words of Maine himself "the movement of the progressive societies has hitherto been a movement from Status to Contract."[4] Changes in social and economic conditions have made contract a dynamic institution in present day African societies. The old system of family corporate life has virtually disintegrated, and the individual has emerged as the new unit of economic activity the spheres of which have widened beyond that of peasant agriculture. In the result, buying and selling have become a vital feature of economic life in all African communities.

Having said this, however, one is faced at once with the crucial

---

3. *Ancient Law*, 10th ed. pp. 276-277.
4. *Ibid*, page 151. It is perhaps a pity that Maine confined this statement to progressive societies only, which by his definition do not include African societies. Note that contract in modern industrial societies is becoming more and more "socialised" and less and less dependent on individual will: see Friedmann, *Law in a Changing Society* (1959) pp. 90-125; Sale, Standard Form Contracts (1953) 16 M.L.R. 318.

question as to whether, given its present enlarged scope and vitality, contract under customary law can be said to have acquired the same characteristics as under civilised law; more specifically, whether the customary contract now provides a general remedy for breaches of all agreements, particularly those in which the obligations arising thereunder remain still *in futuro* This point is a crucial one because most commercial contracts are of this kind (executory) and, without a law that enforces executory commercial engagements, no nation, it seems to me, can ever attain to an industrialised and commercialised society. It is therefore on this point that the whole question of integration seems to hang.

The familiar phenomenon presented by the customary contract is of an action for the recovery of money owed or for the recovery of specific articles of their value. If I sold and delivered my goat to you for £2, all African customary laws would certainly grant me an action for the recovery of the purchase price or of the goat itself. But if, after we have both agreed on the sale but before anything has been done in pursuance thereof, either you or I should refuse to go ahead with it, it seems on the better view[5] that few, if any, customary laws would grant an action against the defaulting party. It is scarcely surprising that this should be so, for the executory contract is the highest point in the development of the modern conception of contract. It is indeed a rather late development in English law. In spite of its ancient origins, the English common law did not provide any remedy for executory agreements until about 1528 when, through the ingenious device of an "Action on the Case", English judges began to hold a party liable on an executory undertaking.[6] Before this development the only remedies provided by the common law for breach of agreement were action for debt and detinue, much like the position just postulated for customary law today.[7]

Nor is the non-enforcement of executory contracts the only serious gap in the customary contract law. For example, bills of exchange, cheques and promissory notes, so indispensable to modern

---

5. Elias, *Nature of African Customary Law* (1956) p. 154, thinks however that executory contracts may be enforceable under certain circumstances.
6. The first case in which an executory contract was enforced by the common law appears to be *Jordan's case* (1528). Y.B. 19 Hen. VIII, F. 24.
7. For an account of the history of the enforcement of contract in English law, see Cheshire & Fifoot, *op. cit.*, pp. 3-15; Fifoot, *History and Sources of the Common Law*, particularly pp. 353-374 Smith & Thomas, *A Casebook on Contract* (2nd ed.) pp. 119-126.

commercial transactions, are unknown to it,[8] so are companies, hire-purchase agreements, etc.

From this brief picture of the nature of contract under the customary and modern legal systems emerges the significant contrast between them: the one is a developed system providing a general remedy for all contracts, both executed and executory; the other is a primitive, albeit a developing, system enforcing only certain kinds of contract of which the executory contract does not appear to be one.

Application of both Systems

I should be reluctant to inflict upon you any long discussion of the difficult and complicated subject of internal conflict of laws, that is to say, of the rules which determine the circumstances in which both systems—customary and modern—are to be applied. I apprehend, however, that the need for their integration may not be fully appreciated unless some account, however brief, is given of this, in order to enable you to perceive the extent of their respective application. I will adopt the position in Nigeria as a model. It is provided in the various courts enactments that customary law[9] "shall be deemed applicable in causes and matters where the parties thereto are natives and also in causes and matters between natives and non-natives where it may appear to the court that substantial injustice would be done to either party by a strict adherence to any other rules of law which would otherwise be applicable."[10] The application of an otherwise valid rule of customary law is limited by the provision that "no party shall be entitled to claim the benefit of any native law or custom if it shall appear either from express contract or from the nature of the transactions out of which any suit or question may have arisen, that such party agreed that his obligations[11] in connection with such transactions should be exclusively[12] regulated otherwise than by native law and custom or that such transactions are transactions unknown to native law and custom."

It will thus be seen that, in spite of the qualifications on the

---

8. See, e.g., *Bakare* v. *Coker* (1935) 12 N.L.R. 31; *Egebor* v. *Agbereghe* (Supreme Court) Suit 194/1933, unreported.
9. Customary law has validity, of course, only if it is not repugnant to natural justice, equity and good conscience nor incompatible with any local enactment.
10. See s. 27 (2), High Court of Lagos Act Cap. 80 Laws of the Federation 1958.
11. This limitation has no application where such party has no obligations but only rights under the transaction: *Rotibi* v. *Savage* (1944) 17 N.L.R. 77.
12. "Native Law and custom are not ousted when the parties had no clear conception in their minds and contemplated a mixture of English and Native law and custom;" *Ferguson* v. *Duncan* (1953) 14 W.A.C.A. 316.

application of customary law, contractual relations among the vast majority of the population in African countries are governed by customary law. A point that is perhaps worth emphasising is that the provisions just quoted do not appear to exhaust the circumstances in which customary law may be applied; as the words "shall be deemed" indicate, they appear merely to amplify the provision enjoining the courts to enforce customary law.[13]   It follows therefore that, apart from the circumstances expressly prescribed by the courts enactments, a non-native may agree either expressly or by necessary implication to be bound by customary law.[14]

THE NEED FOR INTEGRATION

It is pertinent to re-echo here (in a modified form) two questions once posed by Professor Anderson: Can a modern society long remain viable if its legal system enshrines an inter-personal conflict of laws? Can customary law so adapt itself—or be adapted—as to enable it to resolve the typical conflicts of an industrial society?[15] Professor Anderson answers both questions in the affirmative, so long, however, as they are limited to matters of marriage, divorce, and succession.[16] With this view I respectfully agree, though I would add also land. To this extent, my thinking remains unchanged that "the integration of customary and British law into one national system is not a desirable thing at our present state of civilisation.[17] It is gratifying that this is also substantially the view of the Conference on the Future of Law in Africa held in London from 28th December, 1959, to 8th January, 1960.[18] These are matters touching deeply on the life of the people and to abrogate the customs regulating them would be to knock the bottom out of our rural communities. Professor Rene David has put the point so vividly when he wrote: "The law becomes arbitrary and destructive of established order as soon as it attempts to regulate relationships between individuals who feel that they have worked out a fairly successful *modus vivendi* for themselves. The legislator begins to err as soon as he attempts to legislate between a husband and wife, between parents and children, between a village community or tribe

---

13.   Cf. *Shorunke* v. *R.* [1936] A.C. 316.
14.   Park, *The Sources of Nigeria Law* (1963) pp. 114-115, thinks otherwise, on the doubtful authority of *Savage* v. *Mac Foy* (1909) Ren. 504.
15.   The Future of Islamic Law in British Commonwealth Territories in Africa, *in African Law*, ed. Baade (1963) page 83.
16.   *Ibid*, page 96.
17.   Nwabueze, *Machinery of Justice in Nigeria* (1963) page 24.
18.   See *Record of Proceedings*, ed. by A. A. Allott. (1960)

which has as its major preoccupation not the affirmation of individual rights for the benefit of individual members but, on the contrary, has the idea of maintaining the cohesion of the group which it forms and the solidarity of its members, because they cannot conceive of life outside their particular community."[19]

But contract is on a different footing. As we have seen, it still operates within a narrow compass, so that its impact upon the life of the traditional communities is relatively small.[20] One of the greatest needs in Africa today is industrialisation. This is not only a desirable object but it is one that must be pursued with the maximum possible speed, and I conceive that an efficient, modern system of contract law is a *sine qua non* to its attainment. And by an efficient modern system of law I mean one which provides a comprehensive contractual remedy, and whose rules are sufficiently certain and can be changed with sufficient ease. I have tried to demonstrate the inadequacy of the customary law of contract. Customary law is undoubtedly flexible, yet it is not sufficiently so, at any rate in comparison with enacted law; moreover, it suffers from the cardinal disadvantage of uncertainty.

Integration would also have other advantages. By making contract law uniform it is expected to simplify not only its administration but also the study and teaching of it. The courts would be saved the trouble, of which the law reports show more than ample evidence, of having to decide in a contract case whether customary law or some other law applies. It would facilitate the work of our emergent universities in their study and teaching of the law.

WHAT I MEAN BY INTEGRATION

By integration I do not mean the total supersession of customary law by English law. I would define integration in the terms of the recommendation of the conference on the Future of Law in Africa: "There should be a general law of contract (that is to say, the law regulating agreements not covered by legislation nor concerned with land tenure nor with marriage, divorce or succession) uniformly applicable to persons of all communities, races or creeds, which should follow the general principles of the English law of contract but without some of the refinements and technicalities peculiar to it, and with such modifications or additions as would incorporate

19. Background paper on the Potentialities and Limitations of Legislation in the Independent African States.—— *Supra* p. 47.
20. Outside the Northern Region of Nigeria, contract has very limited application under Islamic law in Africa: See Anderson, *op. cit.* pp. 90-94.

those rules of native law and custom which it was desirable to recognise as part of the general law."[21] And I would modify English law (or other modern law) by customary law in the following main respects.

1. Capacity to Contract

Under English law (and perhaps other modern legal systems) the age of contractual capacity is twenty-one. Anyone under that age is by those systems designated an infant and is in general exempted from liability for contracts made by him, the only exceptions being in the case of contracts relating to the infant's person, such as contracts for necessaries—food, clothing and lodging—contracts of marriage; and contracts of apprenticeship and service.[22] Even as regards contracts so excepted they are not legally enforceable against the infant unless they are for his benefit; furthermore his obligation with respect to a contract for necessaries is to pay a reasonable price and not necessarily the contract price. Some other contracts are valid and binding on an infant unless he avoids them during infancy or within a reasonable time after attaining his majority. Also contracts under which an infant acquires an interest in a subject-matter of a permanent nature, such as land or company shares, are valid and binding upon him unless he repudiates them during infancy or within a reasonable time of reaching full age. Besides these, all other contracts made by an infant are void and no liability can attach to him thereunder and this is so even if such contracts are for his benefit or are ratified by him after full age.

Under customary law the age of contractual capacity has been held to begin at puberty (which is normally about 15 to 16).[23] Further, it is doubtful whether the position of an infant under customary law is as strongly protected as under English law. It is relevant to observe that the somewhat excessive solicitude shown to infants under English law is attributable, not to the common law but to the statute law, the Infants' Relief Act, 1874. For before it was modified by statute, the common law did not hold any infant's contract to be void; even those contracts which the statute now taints with absolute voidness were merely voidable at common law and as such were capable of ratification by the infant after full age.

One should not of course argue against protection for infants as such. Indeed, it is pre-eminently desirable that they should be

---

21. Record of Proceedings, ed. Allott page 40
22. See the English Infants' Relief Act, 1874.
23. *Labinjoh* v. *Abake* (1924) 5 N.L.R. 33; *Fagawa* v. *Kano N.A.* (1958) N.R.N. L.R. 64.

protected against the depredations of adults who might unfairly exploit their youthful inexperience and indiscretion to their own advantage. But to fix the age of contractual capacity at twenty-one seems to be going too far in a direction that is capable of producing, as indeed it has produced, absurd results. Let me illustrate. In *Cowern* v. *Nield*,[24] an infant (whose age does not appear in the report but who was in all probability about 20) carried on business as a hay and straw merchant. The plaintiff ordered some clover and hay from him, and sent him a cheque for £35: 19/- in payment. The infant duly delivered the clover, but the plaintiff rejected it, as he was entitled to do, because it was rotten. The infant took back the rejected clover. No hay was ever delivered by him. The plaintiff now claimed £35: 19/- as damages for breach of contract or alternatively as money had received on a consideration which had failed. To this claim, the defendant pleaded infancy in defence. The County Court judge who tried the action, quite reasonably in my view, rejected the plea of infancy. He held that an infant who earned his living by trading was liable on his trading contracts because such contracts would be for his benefit. The County Court judge was overruled on appeal by the Court of King's Bench, consisting of two judges, who held that, in the absence of fraud committed by the infant, an infant's trading contract, not being one of the contracts made binding on the infant if for his benefit, is void notwithstanding that it is for his benefit. The effect of this decision is therefore that the infant was entitled to keep both the money and the articles ordered. It seems to me so palpably unconscionable that a person who is old enough to engage in trade from which he derives his means of livelihood is to be allowed on facts such as those in this case to retain not only the articles he has contracted to sell but also the money paid to him in respect thereof.

Equally revolting is the case of *Mercantile Union Guarantee-Corporation Ltd.*, v. *Ball*.[25] The facts there were that an infant, aged 20, had been carrying on business as a haulage contractor for about two years, and his livelihood was derived entirely from this source. He bought a lorry worth £666 from the plaintiffs on hire-purchase. The lorry was bought and used for the purpose of his business as a result of which the business yielded increased profits. The infant paid his hire-purchase instalments regularly until he got into financial difficulties on account of increased tax imposed by the Government. He fell into arrears with his instalments and when sued pleaded infancy. It was held that the infant was not liable to

24. (1912) 2 K.B. 419.
25. (1937) 2 K.B. 498.

pay the instalments because the contract was not one of those upon which an infant could be made liable.

If we imagine that in these two cases the infant defendants had wives and children, the absurdity of the rule becomes perhaps even more glaring. To regard a person who has the responsibility of providing food, clothing and shelter for a family of four or five as an infant lacking capacity to enter into trading contracts has hardly anything in reason to commend it. If he orders food for himself and family, the law will hold him liable to pay a reasonable price therefore, but the same law will refuse to enforce a trading contract from which he derives the wherewithal to pay for the food. In an integrated law of contract I would, therefore, prescribe the age of contractual capacity to be 16 which is incidentally the age of capacity to marry. Furthermore, I would restore the old common law position that no contract is to be absolutely void against an infant who is old enough to exercise his will intelligently.

2. Formal Requirements

Customary and modern laws of contract differ also in their formal requirements. The remarkable point of departure is writing. Being itself unwritten, customary law does not prescribe writing for any kind of contract recognised by it, including even contracts for the sale of land. An unwritten customary contract for the sale of land is not only valid but (what is more remarkable) is also effective to pass the title in the land to the purchaser without a formal conveyance, for "a conveyance forms no part of a sale by native law and custom."[26] In their origins, the modern legal systems, like customary law, dealt with relations among communities that were wholly illiterate. For this reason, they could not have required any form of writing for contracts enforced by them. Indeed writing itself is a comparatively modern invention. The English common law, in its wisdom, still keeps to the circumstances of its origin in not generally requiring writing for the validity or enforceability of a contract. Indeed, not only did the common law not normally require writing for a contract, but it was prepared to relieve an illiterate person of the consequences of any contract to which he had affixed his seal or finger-mark without understanding its nature, either because this was fraudulently misrepresented to him or

---

26. Per Foster-Sutton P. in *Kwesi-Johnston* v. *Effie* (1953) 14 W.A.C.A. 254 at p. 256. See also *Alake* v. *Awawu* (1932) 11 N.L.R. 39 where it was held that an oral gift of land under customary law was effective to pass the title thereto to the donee. Also *Malomo* v. *Olusola* (1954) 21 N.L.R. 1; *Griffin* v. *Talabi* (1948) 12 W.A.C.A. 371; *Nelson* v. *Nelson* (1951) 13 W.A.C.A. 248.

through some other cause. It allowed him in such cases to deny that the seal or writing was his own—*non est factum*, as the Latin formula reads.

But the wisdom and simplicity of the common law in regard to the form of a contract have been assailed by the statute law (notably by the famous or rather infamous Statute of Frauds, 1677) which requires writing for the enforceability (though not validity) of a variety of contracts,[27] viz.:

   (i) a promise by an executor or administrator;

  (ii) a promise to answer for the debt, default or miscarriage of another person, called a contract of guarantee or suretyship;

 (iii) an agreement made upon consideration of marriage;

 (iv) a contract for the sale of lands or any interest in or concerning them;

  (v) an agreement that is not to be performed within one year from the making thereof;[28]

 (vi) a contract for the sale of goods of the value of ten pounds or upwards—unless the buyer has accepted and actually received part of the goods so sold or has given something in earnest to bind the contract or in part payment;[29]

(vii) a contract by a borrower for the repayment of principal or interest of money lent to him by a moneylender;[30]

(viii) a contract of marine insurance.[31]

These are some of the contracts required by statute to be in writing; the list is by no means exhaustive. The wisdom of the requirement of writing by the Statute of Frauds has been vigorously challenged by successive generations of English lawyers who have not hesitated to call their ingenuity into use in order to avoid its harsh operation. Lord Wright has described the Statute as "an extemporaneous excrescence on the common law."[32] And so persistent and vocal had been the demand for its abolition that, after the feeble step taken by the Sale of Goods Act (U.K.) in 1893, the

---

27. The writing must be signed by the party to be bound or by his duly duly authorised agent. It was the original intention of the framers of the Statute of Frauds to require writing for all contracts.
28. Nos. (i) to (v) are prescribed by s. 4 of the Statute of Frauds, 1677.
29. S. 4 (1), Sale of Goods Act, 1893, repealing s. 17 of the Statute of Frauds which declared such contracts to be not merely unenforceable but void.
30. Moneylenders Act, Cap. 124 Laws of the Federation 1958. For the Western and Mid-Western Regions, see. Cap. 78, Laws of Western Nigeria, 1959. The enactment requires that the writing must be signed by the borrower before the money was actually lent; the lender must also sign it, though this may be before or after the loan had been made.
31. Marine Insurance Act, 1961, s. 24 (1) (Nigeria).
32. *Legal Essays and Addresses, at p.* 226.

146   B. O. NWABUEZE

relevant provisions of the Statute were finally laid to rest in England
by the Law Reform (Enforcement of Contracts) Act, 1954, with
the exception of contracts of guarantee and contracts relating to
land; the reason given for excepting contracts of guarantee being to
"avoid the danger of inexperienced people being led into undertaking obligations which they did not fully understand" and to
"prevent unscrupulous persons from asserting that credit had been
given on the faith of a guarantee which in fact the alleged surety had
no intention of giving."[33]

If, in the middle of the 20th century, England, with its centuries
of civilisation and education, considers the requirement of writing
for a contract to be undesirable, it should be infinitely more so for
Africa where the bulk of the population is still illiterate. "We feel,"
says Dr. Elias, "that in our own law, especially considering the
prevalence of illiteracy in our country, the requirement of documents
in every one of these cases generally works hardship in many
cases."[34]   There is, for example, the difficulty of procuring a
competent writer in the remote villages. Furthermore, considering
the prevalence of sharp practices in many African countries, the
requirement of writing may indeed constitute a positive evil. It is
true that the Nigerian statute law, like that of some other African
countries, provides a measure of safeguard for illiterate persons in
this respect. The Illiterates Protection Act[35] provides that "any
person who shall write any letter or document at the request, on
behalf or in the name of any illiterate person shall also write on such
letter or other document his own name as the writer thereof and his
address; and his so doing shall be equivalent to a statement:-

(a)   that he was instructed to write such letter or document by
the person for whom it purports to have been written and
that the letter or document fully and correctly represents his
instructions; and

(b)   if the letter or document purports to be signed with the
signature or mark of the illiterate person, that prior to its
being so signed it was read over and explained to the illiterate person, and that the signature or mark was made by
such person."[36]

The courts in Nigeria have applied this provision so as to secure

33.   Report of the Law Reform Committee, April 1953 Cmd. 8809
(England.)
34.   House of Representatives Debates on the Law Reform (Contracts)
Bill, 23rd November, 1961, Col. 3341.
35.   Cap. 83 Laws of the Federation, 1958. For the Western and Mid-
Western Regions, see Cap. 47, Laws of Western Nigeria, 1959.
36.   Section 3. Contravention of this provision is punishable with £50 fine
or imprisonment for six months. Barristers and solicitors are exempted

maximum protection to an illiterate person. It has been held that if a document to which the Act applies "creates legal rights and the writer benefits thereunder those benefits are only enforceable by the writer of the document if he complies strictly with the provisions of the Act. If the document which does not comply with the provisions of the Act creates legal rights between the illiterate and a third party then evidence may be called to prove what happened at the time the document was prepared by the writer and the parties signed it. But the writer himself cannot adduce evidence in his own favour to remedy the omission."[37] Although the Act appears to have had public letter writers primarily in view, it has nevertheless been applied to a bond executed by an illiterate person to a company as a security for money owed to the company by a third person.[38] The word, "illiterate," has also been liberally interpreted, and it has been held that a person need not be totally illiterate in order to come within the protection of the Act, for a man may be sufficiently literate to sign his name and read figures, but not sufficiently literate to understand the meaning and effect of a document such as a bond."[39]

Admirable as this measure undoubtedly is, it cannot provide an impregnable protection; its efficacy depends on the availability of evidence showing that the writer has not correctly recorded the instructions of the illiterate. It is heartening, therefore, that some of the Legislatures in Africa have awakened to the danger inherent in the statutory requirement of writing for certain contracts. In Nigeria the Western Region (including the Mid-Western Region) has taken the lead in adopting the reforms introduced in England by the Law Reform (Enforcement of Contracts) Act, 1954.[40] The Federal Legislature has followed suit by the Law Reform (Contracts) Act, 1961, which applies only in the Federal Territory.[41] The

---

37. *U.A.C. of Nigeria Ltd.* v. *Edems & Ajayi* 1958 N.R.N.L.R. 33; approved by the Supreme Court in *S.C.O.A., Zaria* v. *Okon* 1960 N.R.N.L.R. 34. In *Ntiashagwo* v. *Amodu* 1959 W.R.N.L.R. 273 Charles J. went so far as to hold that a document to which the Ordinance applies, and which has not been signed in the prescribed manner, is a nullity and inadmissible in evidence even in a suit between the illiterate and a third person.
38. Cases in No. 3 above.
39. *S.C.O.A. Zaria* v. *Okon* 1960 N.R.N.L.R. 34 at p. 38 A person who is literate in, say, Arabic but illiterate in English is an illiterate in relation to a document written in English: *Paterson Zochonis & Co. Ltd.* v. *Gusau* (1961), N.L.N.L.R. 1.
40. See ss. 2 and 3, Contracts Law No. 22 of 1958, Cap. 25 Laws of Western Nigeria 1959; Sale of Goods Law, No. 43 of 1958 Cap. 115, repealing section 4 of the English Sale of Goods Act, 1893.
41. No. 64, 1961. Sections 5, 6 and 7. But contracts made before 1961 are not affected.

Ghana Parliament has done the same in its Contracts Act, 1960.[42]
For the Northern and Eastern Regions, the position remains
unchanged—i.e. the contracts enumerated above are still required
to be evidenced by writing. This is a situation that calls for
immediate action on the part of the appropriate Legislatures.
Indeed the wisdom of preserving the requirement in regard to
contracts of surety is questionable. Contracts of surety have gained
currency under customary law, and there is no doubt that the village
communities will be shocked to know that, in case of default by the
principal debtor, such loans are not recoverable from the surety by
an action at law because of the absence of writing. Alive to this, the
Ghana legislation also excepts contracts of guarantee under
customary law.

In an integrated law of contract, the requirement of writing should
be dispensed with except in respect of contracts relating to land; if,
however, it is thought necessary to maintain it in regard to contracts
of suretyship, an exception should be made for illiterates. Customary
contract law itself is not entirely destitute of form. For example, in
many places, the sale of land is attended with elaborate formalities
involving the killing of a goat and/or the doing of some other
ceremonial act, like the offering of libation. The contract of marriage
is also attended with elaborate formalities. One would not wish to
upset these, because the ceremonies in these cases are strictly
speaking, referable, not to the contract as such, but to the conveyance
of the land or to the transfer of the wife; they are intended to convey
the land and to transfer the wife and they have their counterpart in
English law; they sound therefore more in the field of land and
family law than in contract. In so far, however, as customary law
requires some ceremony for other contracts it should be abolished.

3. The Doctrine of Consideration

As already indicated, the doctrine of consideration as a constitutive element of contract appears to be a peculiarly English
concept, without any parallel in other legal systems, both modern
and primitive. As Lord Wright has said: "No other modern system
has any such notion; the *Civil Code* does indeed provide for 'cause'
as a condition of contract, but it seems to be agreed that the Scottish

---

42.   See J. S. Read, Changes in the Law of Contract (1961) 5 J.A.L. 48:
Daniels, *The Common Law in West Africa* (1964) p. 228. It should
perhaps be emphasised that all these enactments except contracts of
suretyships and contracts relating to land; indeed under the Ghana
Legislation a contract of guarantee which is not evidenced by a memorandum in writing is not merely unenforceable as in all the other common
law countries but is absolutely void: Part iv, section 14.

law know nothing of consideration; modern Codes, the German and Swiss, have disregarded the notion. Consideration is thus clearly no necessary part of a civilised law of contract."[43] It can also confidently be said that customary law knows nothing of it; should perhaps be so (not necessarily, though) if our thesis that customary law does not enforce executory contracts be tenable. For in English law the doctrine of consideration was introduced by English judges in the 16th century as a sequel to their decision to enforce executory contracts. Having thus evolved a general contractual remedy, they were immediately faced with the question whether to enforce all promises whether made for value or gratuitously. In the event, and impelled by a variety of circumstances,[44] they came down in favour of discriminating between the two types of promises; they decided not to lend their machinery and process to the enforcement of gratuitous promises, unless the same be under seal.

It is not easy to give a precise definition of the requirement of consideration. Perhaps the simplest way of portraying it is by the antithesis of benefit and detriment; that is to say, that consideration consists in some benefit conferred upon one party or some detriment suffered by the other.[45] In the context of modern commercial practices, this view of consideration appears rather over-simplified, and it has been suggested, with conviction, that the notion of consideration is better portrayed by regarding it as the price of the other party's promise. This price can be a counter-promise, as it usually is in modern commercial contracts, or the doing of an act.[46]

It will be recalled that, as stated above, one of the constitutive elements of a contract is an intention to create legal relations. The great difficulty about consideration is to justify why it should be an additional requirement to an intention to affect legal relations. The law of contract is predicated upon the will of the parties to an agreement and, if they have clearly manifested an intention to be bound to one another in contract, why ought they to be gainsaid? In strict logic, it seems that one can only require one or the other, but not both (i.e. consideration and intention). That indeed is the view taken by that great Chief Justice of England, Lord Mansfield, who denied the necessity for consideration,[47] and of Professor

43. *Legal Essays and Addresses*, page 375.
44. As to which see Cheshire & Fifoot, *op.cit.*, page 11.
45. See, e.g., Patteson J. In *Thomas* v. *Thomas* (1842) 2 Q.B. 851. *Also Currie* v. *Misa* (1875) L.R. 10 Ex. 153, at p. 162.
46. Cheshire & Fifoot, op. cit., pp. 57-660
47. See, e.g. *Pillans* v. *Van Mierop* (1765) 3 Burr. 1163; *Hawkes* v. *Saunders* (1782) 1 Cowper 289.

Williston of America who, admitting consideration, denies an intention to create legal relations as an additional condition of contract at common law.[48] Not only this, the rules governing the doctrine have made it into something of a mockery, especially those which stipulate that consideration need not be adequate to the promise by which it is bought.[49] Thus if I agreed with you to sell my Jaguar car to you for ½d. or in consideration of your going to the garage to collect it, your promise to pay ½d. or to go to the garage and collect the car is sufficient consideration to support the contract. I would be over-burdening this paper if I were to go into a detailed criticism of the doctrine of consideration,[50] and I would content myself with saying that it has a rather dubious function in the law of contract. It is not surprising, therefore, that the English Law Revision Committee of 1937, which was extremely critical of the doctrine, recommended a radical modification of it. Unfortunately, its recommendations have not found favour with the British Government. As far as African countries are concerned, the main recommendations of the Committee cannot also be acceptable, since it sought to prescribe writing as an alternative to consideration. But the Committee made other minor recommendations which have now been adopted and implemented in Ghana by the Contracts Act, 1960. Under it a promise to keep an offer open for a specified time, or to waive payment of a debt or part thereof, shall not be invalid only for want of consideration.[51] The performance of an act or the promise to perform, may be sufficient consideration although the performance is already enjoined by some legal duty,[52] and consideration need not move from the promise.[53]

Bold though the measures taken by the Ghana Parliament are, they do not seem to go far enough. An integrated law of contract should have no room for the doctrine of consideration at all. If, having regard to all the circumstances, it is clear that a person of full contractual capacity intended to create legal relations with another, he should be held to this promise, whether it was given for value or gratuitously.

48.   *Selected Papers on the Law of Contract* (1938) section 21.
49.   Consideration is also dispensed with if a contract is under seal.
50.   The arguments against it have been ably put by the English Law Revision Committee C.md. 5449 (1937). For an equally able, though unconvincing, defence, see Cheshire & Fifoot, *op.cit.*, pp. 89-91.
51.   Section 8.
52.   Section 9.
53.   Section 10.

4. Privity of Contract

Another curiosity of the English law of contract is the doctrine which ordains that only a person who is a party to a contract can sue on it. "Our law," says Lord Haldane, "knows nothing of a *jus quaestium tertio* arising by way of contract.[54] This is one of those questionable rules which percolated into the English law in the course of its development, and whose inconvenience in a modern commercial society has impelled the judges to qualify it almost out of existence.[55] Of the doctrine, Cheshire and Fifoot have written that it has "in its incidence worked injustice and proved inadequate to modern needs ... and business men, though they might be expected to welcome the notion of bargain upon which it rests, have been especially urgent in seeking to avoid it."[56] Accordingly, the English Law Revision Committee, 1937, has recommended that a person be enabled to sue on a contract to which he is not a party.[57] This accords with the position under customary law, for it can hardly be doubted that the customary law of contract enforces a *jus quaesitum tertio*, to the extent that it enforces contracts at all. The recommendation of the Committee has not been accepted in Britain but it has fortunately been implemented in Ghana.[58] An integrated law of contract should follow the example of Ghana and abolish the doctrine of privity of contract.

5. Limitation of Action

This is another subject on which there is a cleavage between customary and modern legal systems, Under the latter, a contract as well as any other cause of action ceases, generally speaking, to be enforceable by an action at law after a certain period of time—usually six years in the systems derived from English law—but without the cause of action itself being necessarily defeated. The purpose of limitation is therefore to bar a court action being brought to enforce a right, but it normally leaves the right itself still subsisting and demandable in any other lawful way.

It is well established, on the other hand, that customary law does not recognise any limitation of action. Thus in *Ferguson* v. *Duncan*,[59] the plaintiff in 1934 lent £200 to the defendant, who acknowledged it

---

54. *Dunlop Pneumatic Tyre Co. Ltd.* v. *Selfridge & Co., Ltd.* (1915).
55. There are also various statutory qualifications.
56. *Op.cit.*, page 384.
57. The recommendation of the Committee is limited to the enforcement of benefits arising under a contract by a person who is not a party thereto. Different considerations apply to the imposition of a duty on a stranger to a contract.
58. See s. 5 (1) Contracts Act, 1960.
59. (1953) 14 W.A.C.A. 316.

by a receipt in common form. Of this sum the defendant was able to repay only £20. When many years later the plaintiff sued for the balance, the defendant pleaded that the debt had become barred by the Statute of Limitations, which requires an action of contract to be brought within six years of the breach complained of. The West African Court of Appeal (W.A.C.A.) held, reversing the Supreme Court of the Gold Coast, that the plaintiff was entitled to maintain the action notwithstanding the lapse of nearly twenty years, because the contract was governed by customary law under which there is no limitation of action.[60]

Such, therefore, is the cleavage between customary and modern law in this vital matter of limitation of action, and the question that now falls to be answered is which of the two positions an integrated law of contract should adopt. Should the rule about limitation of action be applied to illiterate persons? The answer is not as easy as it may appear. The necessity for prescribing a period of limitation is to ensure that a plaintiff does not delay bringing action until such a time when relevant evidence may have ceased to be available (e.g. owing to the death of witnesses) or the parties' recollection of the matter has grown dim. As Kingdom C.J., has said: "in one sense there must always be an injustice when a plea under the statutes [of limitation] is set up and succeeds. The plaintiff may or may not have a good case, but good or bad it is refused a hearing on its merits. If I understand the reasoning of the Statute aright it is that a greater injustice is likely to be done by allowing stale claims than by refusing them a hearing on the merits."[61] In support of the view taken by his learned chief, Graham Paul J., observed: "I think there is commonly quite a wrong perspective in considering the question of applying the Statute of Limitations to an educated native of this country. This Statute of Limitations is not a recent invention of modern civilisation. It was applied to the state of education and civilisation which existed in England in 1623, and I find nothing at all startling in apply it to an educated African today."[62]

The underlying purpose of a limitation of action is therefore commendable and desirable, and an integrated law of contract should make provision therefor. The Western Region (including the Mid-Western Region) of Nigeria has again taken the lead. The

60. For an identical decision on similar facts see *Rotibi* v. *Savage* (1944) 17 N.L.R. 77. For other illustrative cases, see *Bakare* v. *Coker* (1935) 12 N.L.R. 31; *Pearse* v. *Aderoku* (1936) 13 N.L.R. 9; *Koney* v. *U.T.C. Ltd.* (1934) 2 W.A.C.A. 188.
61. *Koney* v. *U.T.C. Ltd.*, (1934) 2 W.A.C.A. 188.
62. *Ibid.*, page 196.

periods of limitation prescribed in its Limitation Law of 1959[63] apply to actions under the British-type law as well as under customary law except for a proviso which says that "Nothing in this Law affects actions in respect of the title to land or any interest in land held by customary tenure or in respect of any matter which is subject to the jurisdiction of a customary court relating to marriage, family status, guardianship of children, inheritance or disposition of property on death."[64] The necessity for this exception is not apparent. Although we have advocated that customary law on these matters be kept inviolable yet the need for a limitation of action is so great that one would welcome the modification of customary law in this connection in order to admit it.

It appears indeed that the customary laws of some of the East African countries now recognise limitation of action even in land matters.[65] Furthermore, the British-type courts in Africa have, in the exercise of their equitable jurisdiction, made vast inroads into the customary law rule as it relates to land. In a long line of cases they have held that, notwithstanding that customary law recognises neither limitation of action nor the acquisition of rights in land by prescription, acquiescence by an owner of land in the occupation or alienation of his land by another may not only preclude him from bringing an action to recover possession but may also in certain circumstances operate even to pass the title in the land to that other.[66] The Western Region Limitation Law, 1959, recognises this development by providing that nothing therein contained "shall affect any equitable jurisdiction to refuse relief on the ground of acquiescence or otherwise."[67]

6. Conclusion

It is impossible in a paper of this kind to deal with all the reforms that a scheme for an integrated law of contract should attempt. My aim has been to examine the broad departments of the law of contract, without going into a discussion of their detailed rules—an exercise which would take a voluminuous treatise; but a consideration of them will reveal numerous cleavages between customary and modern law. For example, it has been held in Nigeria that

63. Cap. 64 Laws of Western Nigeria, 1959.
64. Section 1 (2).
65. See Lloyd Fallers, Customary Law in the New African States, in *African Law* (1963) ed. Baade pp. 71-82, esp. pp. 73-78.
66. The cases on this are too numerous to be mentioned here, but the most important ones are *Awo* v. *Cookey Gam* (1913) 2 N.L.R. 100; *Oshodi* v. *Imoru* (1936) 3 W.A.C.A. 93; *Oshodi* v. *Balogun* (1936) 4 W.A.C.A. 1; and *Suleman* v. *Johnson* (1951) 13 W.A.C.A. 213.
67. Section 28.

under Moslem law a purchaser of a defective article may apply to the Qaidi, who will have the article examined by those who know about it and if the fault affects the value by a third or more, the sale may be revoked, or, if the fault affects the value by less than a third, then the purchase price will be reduced accordingly, provided that the purchaser stopped using the article immediately after discovering the fault.[68] This seems simpler and more sensible than the corresponding rules in English law. An integrated system might therefore wish to adopt this customary law position in preference to the English law. Modern law of contract also contains many out-moded rules which an integrated system should also try to remove.

METHODOLOGY

In general, I share the fears of Professor Réné David about precipitate legislative action in the field of customary law,[69] but on my thesis that the integration of contract laws is an object to be desired and pursued, there can be no question but that legislation is the best way to bring about the changes that I have adumbrated. But the great and naggling question is: What form should such legislation take? Should it take the form of an ordinary statute which will be concerned with effecting the desired changes while leaving the form of the existing law unchanged? Or should the integrated law be promulgated in a brand new code? I do not intend to traverse the old and familiar arguments about codification. But it seems to me that time is of the essence in this matter. I have advocated integration because I believe it to be urgently necessary in our march towards industrialisation. Whatever may be the merits of codification—and one does not wish to deny them—it is not going to be easy to codify the English common law of contract; it is a daunting job that will take some time to complete.[70] In contrast, ordinary legislation implementing our integration scheme will entail less onerous drafting effort and can be completed quite quickly. If a need is felt for codification of the integrated law, this may be undertaken later on.

By legislation I mean of course legislation by the supreme legislature. Judicial "legislation" can hardly provide a machinery for doing this. As presently conceived, its scope is seriously limited by

68.   *Alhaji Amodu & John Holt* v. *Idah* 1956 N.R.N.L.R. 81.
69.   See Potentialities and the Limitations of Legislation in the Independent African States.
70.   The Indian effort has been quite successful: see the Indian Contract Act which has been adopted in some Afro-Asian Countries.

various factors, particularly the rigid adherence of judges in the common law countries to strict legalism. A good illustration of this attitude is *Labinjoh* v. *Abake*[71] where, in a case thought to be governed by the English Infants' Relief Act, 1874, the Supreme Court, in order to avoid the hardship that might otherwise result from a strict application of English law, substituted the age of infancy under customary law for that under English law. On appeal the appeal court (the Full Court of the Supreme Court), emphatically disapproving of the trial judge's attempt at a synthesis of English and Customary law, held that "when any matter before the court is governed by the English law, whether the common law or a statute of general application the question in issue must be decided in accordance with the English law, and not as has been done by the divisional court in this case, in accordance with what the court considered would be a proper modification of the English law by customary law."[72]

Nor is it desirable or expedient that judges should be given *carte blanche* to reform the law. It is better that the law should be certain and rigid than that each judge should be enabled to remould it according to his conception of what the interest of society requires.[73] If that were to happen, the law would sooner degenerate into a confused jumble of conflicting decisions. Recent law reforms in Ghana seems to have invested the courts there with power to decide what rules of customary law are suitable to be integrated with the common law into a peculiarly Ghana common law.[74] Of this provision, a Ghanaian lawyer has written: "Short of legislative enactment by the national legislature, it is not easy to see how it can be left to the courts to decide which customary law rules to assimilate and generalise, and how communities subject to a different system of customary law of which they are equally proud are going to be induced to drop their own rule merely because the court has seen fit, in some particular case before it, to declare that a particular rule of customary law in one system is suitable for universal application and should be assimilated into the common law. This would seem to indicate that it would be preferable for the national

71. (1924) 5 N.L.R. 33.
72. At page 35. The Full Court thought that the case should be governed by customary law if it recognised the transaction in question.
73. Cf. the judicial process of the old courts of the administrative officers in British African territories, who were empowered to modify English law by customary law.
74. See s. 17(1), Interpretation Act, 1960; also Courts Act, 1960; and Chieftaincy Act, 1961.

legislature rather than the courts to tackle the general problem of customary law.[75]

One is not of course advocating that judges should be denied all creative discretion. Far from it. Within the restricted area allowed to them by the law they have an important contribution to make in the evolution of an up-to-date and intelligent legal system. In common law Africa they are usually empowered to adapt the rules of common law and equity to local circumstances;[76] the only exception being Nigeria where it appears that the courts lack this power.[77] It is submitted that the courts in Nigeria should be given this power.

On this issue of methodology it is important to emphasise the need for implementing legislation to be preceded by a thorough research and study, aimed at discovering the relevant rules of customary law and deciding which ones among them should be given a place in the integrated system.

PROBLEMS OF ADMINISTRATION

No discussion of the integration of customary and modern laws of contract in Africa would be complete unless it also took account of the problems connected with the administration of the integrated law. For the legal systems of most African countries accommodate a dualism not only of customary and modern laws but also of customary and modern courts. The difficulty here arises from the difference in their personnel. The modern courts are manned by professionally trained lawyers, the customary ones by lay people few of whom have good education while some are completely illiterate. It is true that since 1945 when the members of the courts began to be appointed on the "bestman" principle irrespective of traditional status, the majority of those who now form the benches of the courts possess some education, but their education is not such as will enable them to administer a law of contract based essentially on the English common law or some other modern system. In the common law African countries at the moment, they do not apply the British-type law in civil cases, except in the Northern Region of Nigeria where it is now provided that nothing is to be "deemed to

75. Bensi-Enchill, quoted by Burnett Harvey, The Evolution of Ghana Law since Independence, in *African Law* 1963 ed. Baade pp. 47-70 at p. 61.
76. See, e.g. *Nyali Ltd.*, v. *Attorney-General* [1955] 1 All E.R. 646; [1957] A.C. 253.
77. See Park, *The Sources of Nigerian Law* (1963) pp. 36-40. Cf. Allott, *Essays in African Law* (1960), page 25.

preclude the application by a native court of any principle of English law which the parties to any civil case agreed or intended or may be presumed to have agreed or intended should regulate their obligations in connection with the transactions which are in controversy before the court."[78]

As I have endeavoured to show elsewhere,[79] it is impossible under present circumstances to do away completely with these courts. Nor will it do to transfer their jurisdiction in contract cases to the modern courts. The problem is not, however, so difficult of solution as it may appear. A solution may indeed be found along the following lines :-[80]

(i) by requiring a higher standard of education for appointments to the benches of native or customary courts;

(ii) by providing short professional training for the personnel of the courts on the line of the course now being organised by the Institute of Administration, Zaria, in conjunction with the Law Faculty of the Ahmadu Bello University;

(iii) by producing simplified a re-statement of the law of contract for the guidance of the courts.[81]

---

78. Native Courts Law, 1956, s. 21 (5); see *Okolie v. Uke Ibo* 1958 N.R.N.L.R. 89 where the jurisdiction of an Alkali Court to apply the English law of contract under this section was confirmed.
79. Nwabueze, *Machinery of Justice in Nigeria* (1963) pp. 125-129.
80. Nwabueze *Ibid.*
81. See Allott & Cotran, The Need, Value and Methods of the Restatement of Laws in Africa, *Supra*. pp. 17-47.

THE LAW OF CONTRACT AND OF CIVIL WRONGS IN FRENCH-SPEAKING AFRICA

by

RENE DAVID

PROFESSEUR DE DROIT COMPARE A LA FACULTE DE
DROIT ET DES SCIENCES ECONOMIQUES DE PARIS

THE LAW OF CONTRACT AND OF CIVIL
WRONGS IN FRENCH-SPEAKING AFRICA

Writing a paper on the law of Contracts and of Civil Wrongs in French-speaking Africa is a dual task. It is, in the first place, a descriptive task; that is, in what manner is this part of the law itself regulated at the present moment in the various African countries? And in the second place, a critical examination; that is, to what extent is the present law (introduced into Africa for the most part during the colonial period) suitable for modern African states.

This study of the laws of French-speaking African countries excludes the Arab-African countries even though the law of these countries is based largely on French sources or utilizes the French language. The study, however includes the laws of most of Madagascar and Ethiopia, countries which are not French-speaking but have law of contracts, that can be considered as belonging generally to the family of French law.

The law of contract and of civil wrongs in the French colonies in Africa and Madagascar was the French law. In this field, which was not covered by particular local statutes, the civil code had been introduced as well as applicable portions of the commercial code; otherwise, the law follows the same general path in these territories as in the French judicial and administrative courts.

Such, at least, was the principle. Further studies, would be necessary to determine to what extent the principle was applied in practice. French law was undoubtedly applied as regards Western-type relationships established between individuals or between individuals and the administration. Speaking of regulation of traditional type relationships, the application of the law might have been very different in Africa and Madagascar from that in Metropolitan France, even though the underlying principles remained unchanged. The law of contract in French law rests upon *animus contrahendi;* the legal remedy rests in principle upon an *actionable wrong*. These two fundamental elements must normally, in an indigenous situation, have been conceived quite differently than in France, which implies the existence of a significant difference between African laws in relation to the French laws. The concept of *contract* could thus, even while existing in the code, remain unknown in the interior of certain communities—the inhabitants of these communities not having the *animus contrahendi* necessary for the conclusion of a contract and thereby limiting themselves to the conclusion of agreements between themselves "lacking in juridical character or qualities". The notion of actionable wrong-doing, resting on the idea of a wrong, could in the same way be rendered completely sterile in relation to the situation in France, if one takes into consideration that which, in certain African communities, would be regarded as an *"actionable wrong"*.

The situation thus created appears, on the whole, to have given satisfaction. In effect, it does not appear that the question whether or not to repudiate French law was posed in any country, until the dawn of independence. No constitution, it is true, judged it worthwhile to state precisely that the law of the colonial epoch in so far as it specifically concerned contracts or civil wrongs—re-mained in force. That, however, is precisely what happened.

This confirmation of the principles of the former law, however, does not signify stagnation. An intensive codification movement has developed in African countries and in Madagascar. This movement, in most cases, has had only a limited effect on the law of contract. Other tasks have appeared more urgent. Only in Senegal has a project to codify the law of contract (*Partie Generale*) been established.[1] A project to develop a civil code relative to the law of contracts is likewise in the course of preparation in Mada-gascar.[2] Only in Ethiopia has the law of contract recently been codified.[3] This can be explained by the fact that, before that date, Ethiopia did not possess any law of contract. Neither French law nor any other "modern" law had been introduced into this country, which has so consistently succeeded in preserving its independence.

Does this lack of activity signify that the law of contract, as it currently exists in French-speaking African countries is satisfactory? One can give a generally affirmative response to this question. It quite evidently does not follow however, that some improve-ments could not be made, and that a certain adaptation or adjustment to the African environment should not be desirable; in particular such improvements and adaptations as would favour the development of African societies under existing plans.

It is particularly interesting in this connection to study the Ethiopian experience. The recent codification project in that country did not in fact have to take account of a preceding and established tradition, French or otherwise. It was performed solely

---

1. Approved by Parliament, Spring 1962; The project is still to be carried into full effect. New Development have taken place since this article was written.
2. Three chapters have already been written
3. Civil Code 1960.

on the basis of the national interest of an African country as seen by the Ethiopian legislators.

There is no doubt that improvements can be made in the law of contract and of civil wrongs under a purely technical scheme. Even in France, the Civil Code appears in certain respects to be obsolete; a Commission of twelve members has, during the last 20 years, worked on the reform of the Code. It should be noticed, however, that this Commission has not addressed itself to the law of contract. The Commission does not wish to concern itself with this matter because it wishes, among other reasons, to see established, more than a French law, a *European* law of contract, which will be common to the different countries of the European continent. However, no initiative has so far been taken in this direction by any European government. It is necessary to note, the opinion of the French Commission, regarding the development of a European Law of Contract. In revising the law of contract in Africa, is valid for Europe as it is for Africa. This opinion one must take care that this work does not result in the destruction of the benefits of long usage and of the unity of the law existing among the French-speaking African countries.

The work which was thought to be undesirable in France has been accomplished in Senegal, with the 1962 codification project. The editors of this project had, however, only a modest ambition, and they did not compromise the unity of African law. They had in mind only a scheme of "consolidation", and re-formulation, that takes account particularly of judicial creativity. The project has likewise been involved in certain unsettled controversies, it has occasionally nullified, on the basis of criticisms levelled against it, certain of the recommended legislative or jurisprudential solutions. On the whole, the project is modest and is directed towards clarifying Senegalese law, until such time as a more vigorous reform of the law is deemed necessary.

The work completed in Ethiopia was, of necessity, more ambitious and more comprehensive than the Senegalese one, since there did not exist in that country the base of French law, nor did local customs offer a sufficient base for a code meant for a modern legal system The Ethiopian law of contracts has, by force of events, become an original law built on a base of comparative law and taking account of the peculiar conditions of Ethiopia as a developing country.

In explaining the principles and the solutions offered by the Ethiopian law of contract, and in stating why these original principles and solutions have been adopted, we shall also indicate the reasons why for a modern Code of Contract, in a modern system, is on a number of occasions led away from the French model, which continues to operate in the former French Colonies and Madagascar. Firstly we will treat the structure of the law of contract. The French regulation of contracts is complex, and it is necessary to search for it in three different places; that is in the Civil law which is the "common law", in the commercial law and also in the administrative law. In addition to the general works of the Civil Law relating to contracts like (COLIN-CAPITANT-LA MORANDIERE, PLANIO-RIPERT-BOULANGER, MARTY-RAY—NAUD, MAZEAUD, CARBONNIER), the French lawyer knows that he must occasionally consult the works on "commercial contracts" like HEMARD and of critics on "administrative contracts" like LAUBADERE.

The Ethiopian codification presents a different picture. No doubt one finds in Ethiopia separate civil and commercial codes, but the division thus preserved does not have the same character as it has in France. One never finds applicable to the same institution or the same contract two concurrent regulations, one from the civil code and the other from the commercial code. In spite of the separate codes, the unification of civil law and of commercial law has been achieved in Ethiopia.

As regards administrative contracts, it is noteworthy that in the special section of the Ethiopian Civil Code—(Title XIX) no less than 176 articles have been devoted to administrative contracts. In this way it has been made clear that the common (or commercial) law of contracts applies to these contracts (Article 3131), except when specific provisions have established a special regime for them. The inclusion of the rules relating to these administrative contracts in the Code itself, and the application of the ordinary principles of the civil law to them, was considered necessary, because of the importance that these contracts have for the development of an African country: A code which did not embrace these administrative contracts would not achieve its aim. It should, however, be noted that the Senegalese codification project, whilst embracing civil and commercial contracts, has (in conformity with the French tradition,) excluded administrative contracts from the Code.

Two other somewhat less fundamental observations regarding the structure of the Ethiopian Code are the following: In the first place, all special provisions concerning contracts relating to real estate have been isolated under a special title (Title XVIII). On the other hand, various other types of contracts (hiring of movables, loans, storage, deposit) which concern the safe keeping, usage or enjoyment of movable things—have been grouped under a single title (Title XVII). This later innovation will interest jurists of the English tradition; there they will find, established in a law of the Roman tradition, the notion of *bailment* which is known to the common law. The devotion of a special title to contracts relating to real estate is of interest from the point of view of an eventual unification of African law in the field of contracts. It would seem, in effect, that, that unification would have more chance of being realized, if it did not seek to extend to the unification of contracts relating to real estate. The structure of the Ethiopian Civil Code is such that one can see at a glance which are the provisions relating to such contracts.

Common law lawyers will also have noticed the presence in the Ethiopian Civil Code of a special title (Title XIV) devoted to agencies. This is purely the English notion of *agency* which it was desired to introduce distinct from contracts, to apply to particular situations such as those which develop between two people who establish a "relationship of representation" such as that existing between *principal* and *agent*. Because it does not derive necessarily from a contract, agency has been treated in Book IV of the Code (*of Contracts*) and not in Book V (*special contracts*).

When we examine the solutions devoted to basic changes, the originality of Ethiopian law appears, particularly in this regard, in the solutions concerning *civil wrongs*. This is easy to understand. "Contracts"—except those contracts relating to real estate—relate to a society in which there exists "commerce". Traditional or formal customs are not adequate to regulate commerce and one can, in this field, import without substantial change a European regulatory system, in the same fashion as, in the thirteenth century, one could in the same field on the European continent "receive" a Roman law which had been dormant for one thousand years. In the case of torts it is a different thing. One finds actionable wrongs in all societies, even those in which commerce is unknown; such wrongs are even recognized by custom. The task of codification must at least have, as its object, not only the "reception" of formal concept, but must also accomplish a unification, modernisation, and an improvement of existing customs.

Different sections of the law bear witness to the desire of the Ethiopian legislators to make place, here, for the customary concepts. Thus one can cite, as being typical in this field, three sections of the Code: Article 2067, Article 2113, and Article 2142. Article 2067 imposes an obligation upon a person who causes, by his act, any physical harm to another, to pay compensation *independently of any legal wrong whatsoever;* he who kills or injures another is responsible and must pay an indemnity, even if he has not committed what might properly be called any "legal wrong". Article 2113, on the other hand, resting on the same hypothesis, envisioned that in addition to material damage, "moral damage" can give rise to an indemnity to the benefit of the victim or, if the victim is deceased, to the benefit of his family. Articles 2116 and 2117 make more precise that which concerns the establishment of the indemnity thus payable and the determination of the people who may be called to represent "the family". Here again account has been taken of "local custom". Article 2142, finally, preserves in conformity with custom (*Afersasat*) a principle of collective responsibility: if it appears that the damage has been caused by the member of a group (e.g., village, tribe), in such a way that it may be impossible to identify among the members of this group the actual doer of the damage, the entire group can be declared by the judges responsible. Some may be astonished to see preserved by a modern code such a custom which qualifies as "primitive", but one can say in response to such an objection that the rule here preserved can be found in certain modern laws (notably hunting accidents) of the most developed countries. The individualism of the French Civil Code is not necessarily suitable for all societies and can be tempered for societies, whether traditional or modern, where a more collective spirit prevails.

It has appeared inappropriate on these points, as on certain others, in a matter of tort, to conserve the French rules. Above all it has appeared useful in these matters which are of interest to all the citizens, to put an end to the uncertainties which exist too often in French law, and to expose methodically in the statutes those poorly systematized solutions of French jurisprudence which have been elaborated by precedent after precedent through an empirical method, while at the same time rationalizing these solutions.

In contrast to the French Civil Code, which devotes only five articles to this field of law, the Ethiopian Civil Code devotes 135 articles to it (Articles 2027-2161) thereby taking a position on a great many points which remain uncertain or debatable in France. The Ethiopian Code regulates, in addition to the responsibility of private individuals to each other, that of officers or employees of the State, abandoning here, in conformity with the English model, the French distinction between civil law and administrative law. Systematizing the rules of law as it has not been possible to do in French jurisprudence, Ethiopians have not hesitated to recognize that there exists, two fundamental bases for legal responsibility which often result from a legal wrong and often can exist in the absence of any legal wrong. In the first case they sought to determine, much more vigorously than is done in French law, that which constitutes a legal wrong. While conceived according to the system of French law (which admits the general principle of civil responsibility in the case of a legal wrong (Article 1382-1283)), the Ethiopian Civil Code is modelled here again after the English law which recognizes a variety of "torts". In the second case (liability without legal wrong) the Ethiopian Civil Code proceeds, in a deliberate fashion, to depart further from French jurisprudence. It appeared to the Ethiopian legislators that in an underdeveloped country where liability insurance is less practical, the French solution would have to be modified, for it would not be possible to discourage individuals from acting in a menacing fashion without declaring them responsible.

In other ways the Ethiopian Civil Code seeks to perfect the system of French law. The responsibility for acts of another person have been regulated in such a manner that there always exists an individual legally liable for the acts of a minor, wherever the liability of a minor is involved. Some powers of equity have been conferred upon judges in a series of cases (Article 2099-2103) in order to permit judges to estimate the amount of the indemnity due in reparation for material damage. A shortened period has been fixed for stay of execution in reparation situations (Article 2143).

The law of contracts, as has been said, is concerned less with solutions that can be related to customs. The problem here has been to create a law designed for a new situation, and which must, for this reason, be entirely new.

Is it more suitable on this subject to take a European model or to establish a new model, uniquely African? One can detect a certain amount of hesitation from the beginning on this subject. The temptation has been present for the Ethiopians to adopt a "more simple" model than that offered by European laws. This temptation has been resisted and, we think, justifiably.

The country's stage of development is not very significant in the field of contracts. Granted that these regulations are made for the most developed section of the population, (that section which participates in commercial operations), this segment of the population is perfectly capable of assimilating a European law, and it is even easy to find judges to apply such a modern law. It is possible to reject, here and there, those complications which have their origin in the history of Europe, and for which it would be difficult to find a rational basis. On the whole, however, "over-simplification" has been avoided. It has been considered practicable, in doubtful cases, to preserve the structure offered by European models. There has been no effort, on principle, to make something uniquely "African". In this field of law, where there does not exist an African tradition, to act otherwise would have been, in reality, to act arbitrarily. The laws of Africa have the advantage of drawing upon a well-established family of law in a manner which permits one to utilize, for interpretation and development of these laws, the materials of doctrine and of jurisprudence elaborated in the foreign country. The legislators would have raised obstacles to development of the law and of the economy of the country if, inspired by a chauvinistic nationalism, they had repudiated the European models in this case which are the legacy of long centuries of experience.

In Ethiopia, however, in contrast to that which has happened in other French-speaking African countries and Madagascar, the model followed has not been that of any European law whatsoever. The Ethiopians have deliberately utilized, in combination, the materials offered by a variety of laws: Laws of the European continent principally, but also, as we have seen, English law.

The structure of the Ethiopian Civil Law is that of the laws of the European continent. It is difficult in review, in so far as fundamental solutions are concerned, to say which law has had the preponderant influence. The solution offered by the different systems of law to the various questions have been, in each question, considered. In each case, the Ethiopians have chosen that which appeared to be most in harmony with the general equilibrium of the system that which appeared must be the most in conformity with justice under the particular conditions of the times in Ethiopia. It has thus been possible, on this occasion, to preserve rules which come from English law as much as from continental law. Thus one would find in the Ethiopian Civil Code, articles devoted to the English theory of "anticipatory breach of contract" (Article 1759, 1789) or a regulation of damage to "interests" inspired by the English law (Article 1799-1802). In the field of sale of goods, they have adopted the solutions foreseen in the project which recently ended (la Haye, April 1964) at the conclusion of an international convention regarding uniform laws for the sale of goods. Here we must end our observations. We will of course be permitted to underscore again the Ethiopian legislators' primary concern for clarity. The Ethiopians strove to recapture the conciseness of the text of the Code Napoleon. Each Article of the Ethiopian Civil Code consists of no more than three paragraphs; each paragraph consists of no more than one sentence. The Ethiopian Civil Code is for this reason easy to read and to understand, even if, like all legislative works and like all human works, it often calls for interpretation and is not free of defects.

Because it is an original work, employing the French technique, but established on a basis of comparative law and for the use of an African country, the Ethiopian Civil Code, with its complementary commercial code, must be taken into serious consideration, if no taken as a model, when French-speaking African States decide to perform in concert the revision of their law of contracts. This is all the more true because the Ethiopian Civil Code, in many respects, has taken account of the solutions offered by English law, even more than any civil code deriving from the Romano Germanic systems, and it constitutes, for this reason, a step towards the rapprochement which one must also envisage between the legal systems of French-speaking and English-speaking African countries.

THE CODIFICATION OF THE LAW OF CIVIL WRONGS IN COMMON-LAW AFRICAN COUNTRIES

by

A. N. ALLOTT

PROFESSOR OF AFRICAN LAW, UNIVERSITY OF LONDON;
DIRECTOR, RESTATEMENT OF AFRICAN LAW PROJECT

THE CODIFICATION OF THE LAW OF CIVIL WRONGS IN COMMON-LAW AFRICAN COUNTRIES

The object of this paper is both (i) to discuss in general terms the problems that may arise in attempting to integrate the diverse laws which control liability for civil wrongs and which coexist in many common-law African countries, and (ii) to present an interim report on research which is already in progress at the School of Oriental and African Studies, University of London, by way of investigation of practical methods of dealing with these problems. An exercise of this kind inevitably involves the application of the comparative law method and of techniques of legal drafting; one can therefore learn a great deal by setting side by side the theoretical considerations and some of the practical possibilities. The relevant activities at the School of Oriental and African Studies comprise: (a) work which has been in progress for some years in the teaching of African law, both statutory and customary, especially in the field of torts; (b) the work of the Restatement of African Law Project, which is reported in another paper (the Project seeks, *inter alia*, to discover and describe the customary legal institutions of African peoples in such a way as to facilitate their application by judges primarily trained in the English common-law tradition); (c) the discussions of the Advanced Seminar in African Law, which has in its last two years examined codification and unification of laws in Africa in general, and the codification of the law of civil wrongs in particular; and (d) the papers and deliberations of the annual Colloquium on African Law, attended by representatives of a number of African countries, and which in June, 1964, discussed as one of its main themes the codification of the law of torts. Drafts as submitted by myself to the Advanced Seminar of parts of a tentative Code of civil wrongs are printed as Appendix I to this paper; and the background paper submitted by myself to the Colloquium, consisting mainly of questions rather than answers, is printed as Appendix II.

I. THE EXISTING LAWS IN AFRICAN COUNTRIES

The present or former British countries or territories in tropical Africa north of the Zambezi, which received the law of England (the common law, doctrines of equity and English statutes of general application as they stood at a particular date[1]) as the basis of their general legal systems, thus took over the English law of contract, tort, trusts, and marriage, with some variations, of which the most notable was the application of the Indian Contract Act (itself in large measure a codification of English law) in East Africa.

But this was not the only kind of law that was applied in these countries. The local African customary laws everywhere continued in force, and these laws, which were primarily applicable to the civil relations of the indigenous African populations *inter se*, dealt exhaustively with civil liability, whether arising from agreement, status, or some wrongful act or omission of a tortious kind. Islamic law too, which was in many places recognised either as the dominant law of a territory or its ruler, or as the personal law of Muslim adherents, contains copious rules dealing with civil responsibility.

If one is to criticise the legal situation thus created, the first point that one selects for criticism must be the wholesale application of a law evolved or fabricated in England for English conditions to peoples and their disputes in far-distant lands living a quite different way of life and with quite different conceptions both of social organisation and of appropriate behaviour towards their fellow-citizens. The ineptness of applying English law in Africa was mitigated by, for instance, the continued recognition of local customary laws, and by the requirement that the English law should only apply so far as local circumstances permitted; but generally speaking these qualifications have been of least significance in the fields of liability in tort and contract (i.e., the pre-eminently uncodified part of the law of England), and have been of the most significance in fields such as those of marriage and land law, where the substance of the English law is now to be found in statutory form.

Another criticism, growing in importance with the passing of time, is of the reception of English law as it stood at one moment in its history. Unless the judges or the legislatures in the African countries have been able, by a parallel process of development, to keep the law up to date as compared with that prevailing in England from time to time, the general "English" law as applied in Africa must inevitably have lagged more and more behind the times. This lagging behind social and economic progress and the refinements of juristic thought has been appallingly aggravated in recent years by

1. The "date of reception". This date varies from country to country: 24th July, 1874, for Ghana; 1st January, 1900, for Nigeria, and so on. In no case does the date correspond with any major legal event in England.

the revolutionary changes in social conditions which have been occurring on the African continent.

A third criticism of the legal systems of the African countries, as transmitted by the British at the moment of independence, would be that they were dualistic or pluralistic in character, i.e. recognising as coexisting within the same frontiers laws of completely different historical origins, equipped with different techniques and styles. The dichotomy or trichotomy between "English", customary, and in some places Islamic, laws was bad enough; the existence of dozens, and in some countries of hundreds, of different customary laws, each attaching to a particular ethnic group, was even worse, at least in the eyes of governments anxious to promote the social cohesion of their newly created states.

II. THE DEFECTS IN THE EXISTING LAWS OF CIVIL WRONGS AND POSSIBLE REMEDIES FOR THEM

The major defects in the existing legal systems, therefore, that face the government of an African common-law country are: (i) the reception of an unadapted English law of civil wrongs; (ii) the out-of-dateness of the received laws as far as present-day conditions are concerned; (iii) the pluralism of the national legal system and the internal conflict problems to which this gives rise.

The corresponding remedies for these defects might appear to be: (i) to reject, or at least substantially modify, the English law, so as to "africanise" or "acclimatise" it; (ii) to reform or modernise the general law in line with contemporary requirements; (iii) to unify the legal systems, eliminating the competing and coexisting systems already described. How far is such a programme feasible or desirable in the field which we are now examining, that of civil wrongs?

Africanisation

The clock cannot be put back. It is impossible to restore the "tribal" legal systems of the pre-colonial past. The communities which evolved these systems have radically altered or in some cases vanished. They are no longer closed and autonomous communities; their economic basis has altered; the social organisation of which the legal order was the expression is daily crumbling away. African countries are now part of the modern, industrialising, world; and their legal systems must recognize this fact.

But even if it is impossible to restore African legal institutions to their pristine state, it might be suggested that the answer is to try to recapture the essence of these institutions, and to build that essence into new laws which have been consciously and scientifically constructed for such countries. This conception is most attractive in theory, but it tends to prove frustrating or unattainable in practice, as we have discovered in our discussions at the School.

What, taking torts as our field of enquiry, are the essential features of the African customary laws? Strict liability and the absence of the notion of *mens rea*? This kind of idea might be suitable for societies where the only insurance company was the clan or lineage; is it suitable for today, with the expanding realisation in African countries of the notion of individual responsibility? Corporate or vicarious responsibility (a concept akin to that we have just discussed)? There is an increasing rejection in Africa of the mono-lithic solidarity of family or social groups, of the idea that a father or a husband should be automatically answerable for the wrongs of a dependent child or wife. Such dependency is vanishing with the emergence of women as possessors of equal social, economic, and legal rights, and with the gradual disappearance of the parental household and its autocratic *paterfamilias*.

One has to face the fact that in modern Africa, even where English law and African customary law originally started off with different institutions inspired by utterly different notions of legal liability there has been an inevitable convergence between the two types of systems. An excellent illustration might be found in the so-called "sexual torts," adultery and seduction. Adultery as a separate civil cause of action has been largely absent from English law for the last 100 years; it is now generally an appendage of a suit for divorce. In customary law, adultery, by the *wife*, has everywhere been a tort entitling the husband to sue the adulterer for damages, and in some places to obtain or impose criminal sanctions on him as well or in lieu. (Under the Indian Penal Code, as applied in East Africa until 1930, adultery was a statutory offence as well.) There are now signs that African countries may either eliminate adultery as a civil wrong altogether, or broaden its definition so as to make it more like the offence to English law, or else may convert into a criminal offence regulated by central or local legislation. In each instance the law inexorably moves nearer to the language and conceptions of the English law.

Much the same is true of the tort of seduction. The differences between the English and the customary torts of seduction, if one ignores the legal fiction upon which the English action is based, are not now as great as one might imagine; and a reconciliation between the twh systems is by no means out of the question.

What one might be tempted to reject in the English law of civil wrong is not that which is "English" in the sense that it is peculiarly and solely relevant to the problems of Englishmen living in England, but rather that which is found in English law for reasons of English legal history only. The classifications of the causes of action is a case in point. Many of the detailed ingredients of nominate torts, e.g. those specifying when one commits the tort of defamation or conspiracy or seduction, exist merely because English judges have evolved them over the centuries. It is these *accidental* features of the English law or torts, rather than any features of substance, that one might be tempted to reject for African purposes; but if one does so, the reason is not because they are English but because they are irrelevant, antiquated, unsatisfactory or illogical, in England just as much as in Africa.

MODERNISATION

In other words, the English law of civil wrongs is in urgent need of modernisation and simplification. There can be no justification (other than inertia) for the continued application of the unreformed English law of torts in modern African countries. What is needed is to rid the English law of all its clogging and inconvenient detail (mainly the accretions of generations of judicial decisions), to systematise the bases of liability and the remedies obtainable for different kinds of unjustifiable harm, and to express the results in a language which is consistent and, so far as possible, scientific. In fairness to the judiciary in contemporary England, one must admit that much is being done at the present by judicial decision to introduce reforms of this kind; but the results can at best be no more than piecemeal and imperfectly integrated into the remainder of the law. A much bolder revision or "new look" is required, such as can only be brought about by legislation.

Legislation in the common-law African countries would also enable the governments to acquire a law which conformed to the up-to-the-minute requirements of their peoples, and which harmonised or synthesized the laws other than those of English origin as recognised in their countries. That is, legislation could permit both the improvement of the law, and its "africanisation" (in the sense of adapting the law to contemporary African needs) and integration.

Unification

The achievements of greater consistency and uniformity in the legal system can vary enormously in scope and effect. Just as with the degree of political association between two independent countries, so the relationship between the imported English law and the indigenous laws can range all the way from a loose form of link through harmonisation to complete unification. In the past, the relationship between the introduced and the indigenous laws of civil wrongs was a loose one; generally these different kinds of laws were administered by different kinds of courts, acting under different statutes. The fact that the two types of law disagreed and were sometimes fundamentally incompatible did not matter at that relatively unsophisticated period.

Today the situation is changing rapidly and radically. Unification of the courts means that all kinds of courts may now be called upon to apply all kinds of law. Economic and educational progress means that persons are often faced with a choice between dealing with a legal problem according to the norms and procedures of the customary law on the one hand, and of the general "English" law on the other. A good illustration of this personal choice problem can be found in suits for breach of promise of marriage. If a girl is proposed to by a young man who later disappoints her, she may decide today, if the facts fit this course, to sue for damages in accordance with the "English" law; will such a remedy be available if the parties are Africans subject to customary law, and if it is uncertain whether the marriage proposed was intended to be under customary law or the law of the land?

Which sort of association between "English" and indigenous law is feasible in the realm of civil wrongs—harmonisation, integration, or complete unification? To answer this question, let us first clarify our terms:

> By *harmonisation* is meant the removal of discord, the reconciliation of contradictory elements, between the rules and effects of two legal systems which continue in force as self-sufficient bodies of law.

Harmonisation implies the maintenance of the existing legal systems in force, or some of them at any rate; neither the customary nor the English law would be abolished or merged in the other. The removal of discord between the systems would entail: (i) eliminating incompatible results between the two systems, as where customary law says that there shall be no remedy for breach of promise, and one is given by the English law, or where English law says that there shall be no remedy (outside divorce proceedings) for adultery, and one is given by the customary law; and (ii) eliminating doubt as to which is the applicable system in any given fact-situation—in other words, the making of adequate internal conflict rules, specifying which law is to apply in any case, with special reference to the application of remedies drawn from one law to claims made under the other.

> By *integration* is meant the making of a new legal system

by the combining of separate legal systems into a self-consistent whole. The legal systems thus combined may still retain a life of their own as sources of rules, but they cease to be self-sufficient autonomous systems.

This is the kind of combination that occurred in England with the "fusion" of law and equity in 1873. It is obviously a more advanced stage than that of mere harmonisation, since such integration probably needs legislation to bring it into existence; though there is little doubt that the courts, given sufficient time, might be able to devise a new integrated law out of the diverse elements—"English", statutory, customary—presented to them. Integration, in my view, does not imply the complete disappearance of the pre-existing legal systems, and the possibility of variation or choice between systems might still be found. Thus an integrated law of marriage might allow persons to choose their form of marriage and the type of matrimonial régime they should live under; an integrated law of succession might allow a testator to resort to local customary law; an integrated law of civil wrongs might recognise different kinds of relationships constituted under different local laws as being the subject of protection by the law.

Integration can be low-level integration, as where the customary laws are nationally integrated—the method of restatement is well adapted for procuring such integration; or it may take place at a higher level, between legal systems of different species. Legislation, probably of the "outline" or "framework" variety, is almost certainly needed to bring about integration of the latter kind. The customary laws in an integrated system may then become no more than "legal rules of customary origin".

The third possibility is of unification.

By *unification* is meant the creation of a new, uniform, legal system entirely replacing the pre-existing legal systems, which no longer exist, either as self-sufficient systems or as bodies of rules incorporated in the larger whole; although the unified law may well draw its rules from any of the component legal systems which it has replaced.

Unification implies the building of a novel law. This might seem the most attractive solution—a fresh start unencumbered with the dead legal lumber of the past. But it is exceptionally difficult, as legal history shows, to make a new and revolutionary legal start owing nothing to the laws which have been swept away or superseded. Even under the Kemalist reforms in Turkey, where the Ottoman law was entirely replaced in theory by new codes borrowed from Europe, the progress of the new law has not been plain sailing; the lingering on of the traditional social habits of the people (for example, in the field of marriage) has provoked a discrepancy between the written law and the norms followed by those subject to this law.

Discrepancies of this sort are to be avoided at all costs. They show that the law does not have the assent of the inarticulate majority of the people, and they bring both the law and those who make it into contempt. There is a particular danger that governments in Africa may be tempted to indulge in "phantom legislation" of this kind. Nothing could be simpler than making a new statute; nothing is harder than ensuring that in practice it will be accepted by those subject to it as a natural evolution from the old law.

Any new law must, in my submission, therefore try—so far as possible —to build on what is already there. That means, in the common-law African countries, the Western-type common and statutory law, as well as the indigenous customary and religious laws. To make a new law of civil wrongs, which replaces but at the same time incorporates and synthesizes, the existing multiple legal systems, is much more of a challenge than to bring in a quite different law from outside. To try to do as Ataturk did, and introduce a novel law having no previous connexion with the country, would be an exercise doomed to failure in the modern African context. To try to devise a new jurist's law, elaborated in the abstract and having no connexion with any particular legal system (inside or outside Africa), is an attractive task for the theoretical legal scientist, but is not practical politics, as the law reform commission in Israel have apparently come to realize.

III. THE NEW LAW OF CIVIL WRONGS

The pattern of development

What, then, is to be our choice—to have leave things as they are, letting the law evolve in response to the hidden groundswell of public opinion and the random piecemeal adaptations of the courts; or to step in with legislation to reform, renew, or replace those laws? In my opinion, there is only one possible line of action: the problems of modernisation, unification, and africanisation are too vast to be tackled other than by a major legislative effort.

As to the sort of legislation that should be introduced-harmonising, integrating, or unifying—there are arguments in favour of each. The decisive factors are: (i) the availability of jurists capable of providing the sort of draft law likely to prove acceptable to legislator, judge, lawyer, and common man alike; (ii) the availability of parliamentary time for discussing and improving such a draft; (iii) the urgency with which governments view a problem which might seem less pressing than those which confront them now, such as the expansion of education and the diversification of economic development; (iv) the vision that the governments and their legal advisers have of the eventual legal goal, the destination to which such reforms must move, and the urgency with which they wish to reach that goal.

My own opinion is that it is best to begin immediately with the preparation of the ultimate law, and that in the field of civil wrongs little will now be gained by spending too much time on the intermediate stage. In other words, the objective should be a unified law of civil wrongs, entirely replacing the existing systems. The rapid breaking down of the barrier between customary and English law would soon render any other solution out of date.

What is proposed is the unification of the law of civil wrongs, not of the legal systems generally. In other words, the diverse laws regulating marriage, the family, succession and the like would remain; what would be unified would be the remedies made available by the law against those who damage or interfere with those relations. It would be advisable, though, for a parallel activity to take place in these other fields, aimed at harmonising the laws (as a minimum), or preferably at integrating them by way of outline laws controlling their application.

The unification proposed can only be produced in the foreseeable future by way of legislation. Such legislation, if it is to be comprehensive, self-consistent and economical, must take the form of a "code". The code would have to regulate in an exhaustive manner the topics covered by it, to which the existing laws—English, customary, religious—would cease to apply.

The availability of models

The codification of the law of civil wrongs is a relatively novel exercise in the common-law world. England, and the Commonwealth countries with legal systems based on English law, generally have uncodified laws of torts. Only in Palestine and Cyprus was a code of civil wrongs introduced. This code is quite unsuitable as a model for the sort of law we should like to introduce. The California Civil Cede, enacted in 1872, has also been found by our seminar to be unsuitable for this purpose. The law of torts was never codified in British India, so that it is no use turning to this source of inspiration. There is, then, no legislative model available for us to follow in the common-law world.

The American Restatements, which restate at length the common law of tort, contract and trusts, might seem a better source to which to turn. A codification of the American Restatement of Torts would not be adequate, unfortunately. Our feeling has been that the Restatement is far too ponderous to form the basis of a code, although the legal learning and the reshaping of the common law which it provides represent an invaluable source of ideas for anyone preparing a code on this subject.

Outside the common-law world, the Ethiopian Civil Code of 1960 provides an unusually lengthy set of provisions dealing with liability in tort, contract, and restitution, Indeed, Professor David, the author of this Code, has incorporated many ideas from the common-law systems in this part of his work. In our seminar at the School we have made constant reference to the Ethiopian Civil Code, but we have felt that, although we have gained enormous inspiration from the clarifying and simplifying approach that the Code adopts, it would not be feasible to use the Code as in any sense a basis for a code of civil wrongs in a common-law country in Africa. There are several reasons for this conclusion: the first is the obvious one that the Ethiopian code is primarily inspired by the romanist tradition, which can be fitted only with some difficulty into the classifications, methods, and concepts of the common law. The second is that the author of the code has largely avoided any attempt to synthesize in this part of the code the existing customary and other local laws of different parts of Ethiopia; indeed, he rather doubts whether any such "laws" exist for this purpose. We, on the other hand, should like to build the ideas and principles of the customary laws into our code, if possible.

The style of the code

The third reason is that a judge or lawyer trained in the common law would require a rather ampler and differently presented kind of statute from that apparently needed by his colleague in the civil-law world. At the School we have spent a considerable time discussing how far a new code should try to be exhaustive, in the sense not merely that it entirely replaces the previous law, but that it provides in detail for every eventuality. Inevitably recognising the inability of the draftsman to legislate for every contingency, we nevertheless felt that something more substantial than the bare statement of a few principles was required. There are three main ways of meeting this requirement: (i) to provide a detailed set of general principles, but no discussion of special or nominate heads of liability (in other words, going away from the traditional English approach that the law of tort is the law of *torts*); (ii) to go to the opposite extreme, in effect codifying the existing English approach, and to provide detailed rules regulating each separate tort or wrong, but without any general statement of principle applying to them all; or (iii) to seek an intermediate solution, combining a statement of general principles with statements setting out the special rules applying to each several wrong. Our conclusion was in favour of this last approach, not least because it corresponds both to the advanced English handling of the subject and to the traditional African approach to civil liability, which generally incorporates both broad principles of liability for unlawfully causing harm and sets of specific rules regulating nominate torts such as adultery.

The rules regulating nominate wrongs then become special cases of the general principles, which they in some instances amplify and in other instances vary. Special rules regarding defences and remedies for nominate wrongs are particularly needed.

One recognizes that it is impossible to satisfy all sides, to be ample enough to provide usable rules for deciding every dispute, without being so prolix that the code becomes unmanageable, especially in the hands of lower court judges; but we hope that a *via media* can be found between this Scylla and Charybdis.

The content of the code

The code is intended to be exhaustive, in other words, it is to be the sole source of rules governing liability for civil wrongs. The pre-existing common, statutory, customary, and religious laws are *pro tanto* repealed. Any other solution appears to us to be unworkable, and to render valueless what should be the main advantage of a code, that it is self-sufficient and definitive in the fields with which it deals.

We felt, secondly, that there was little point in preparing a code of *torts* only. This would reflect an internal subdivision of the English law of wrongs which it is difficult to justify. Civil liability may arise as a result of the breach of various kinds of obligation; some of these obligations are imposed by law, others are assumed voluntarily, either by agreement or by the acceptance of some status or some other relationship or obligation. The breach of such an obligation constitutes a civil wrong. The English law of civil wrongs is found partly in the law of tort, and partly in other branches of the law (e.g. the law of family relations, trusts, contract, quasi-contract). We feel that the new code should so far as possible synthesize, without necessarily eliminating all distinction between, the laws relating to different kinds of wrongs; this distinction leads at present to anomalies or uncertainties. Examples of cases which lead to difficulty are differences in parties or remedies according to whether the claim is in tort or contract, and the classification of the wrong of adultery (which has found a place in Professor Street's latest work on torts, but which previously has not been generally classed as such).

In preparing the code, we therefore started off from the principle that it should cover proceedings in respect of every kind of civil wrong, and that the sections establishing general principles of liability, defences, damages, parties, etc., should be applicable not only to actions in "tort", but to those for breach of contract and breach of trust as well. The distinctions of English law between these kinds of wrong are entirely unknown in African customary law (which has, of course, its own classifications of wrongs). In the actual drafting of the code, however, we had to face the fact that we were not always able to follow this guiding principle to the letter; technical and drafting difficulties are inevitably encountered in such an attempt at subsumption of what had formerly evolved as separate compartments of the law. The basic distinction might seem to be between obligations imposed by the law, and those which are voluntarily assumed; but the latter category is not coextensive by any means with contractual obligations. Unilateral assumption of responsibility is possible both in English and in customary law; and looked at from a different point of view, the law may impose an obligation on those who voluntarily enter into an agreement. All actions for civil remedies appear to relate to the breach, or the anticipated breach, of some obligation which the law recognizes. This obligation has come into existence as the result of a legal relationship existing between the person obliged and the one who claims the benefit of it. Such a relationship may be particular to the two individuals concerned (as with a contract or a voluntary promise) or may apply to the obligee and a restricted range of persons implicated in the relationship (e.g. between neighbouring occupiers of land), or may be more general (as between an individual and any potential assaulter of him). A division of this kind might provide the theoretical basis for a code of obligations; but our seminar has not yet been able to work on this aspect of the problem, and we have proceeded on the basis that we should try to elaborate general principles covering relationships and obligations of all these types, and then to append specific rules governing certain of them.

The primary division of the code is therefore between a First Part, setting out General Principles of Liability, and a Second Part, setting out Specific Heads of Liability. Owing to shortage of time, we were not able to discuss the Second Part in detail; but at our Colloquium we were able to consider the broad arrangement of this Part, and some of our tentative ideas are reported below in the Commentary on the code. The general principles in the code are preceded by a Part dealing with definitions, interpretation, and application of the code, not all of which we had time to consider in detail.

Method of drafting of code

The actual contents of the code will not be completely strange to the lawyer trained in English law. Firstly, the code is in English. We consider this to be inevitable in view of the fact that the general legal systems in all the former British territories are operated in English and with English legal terms.

In countries where an African language is established as the national language, and where central legislation is habitually prepared in that language, the code might not be in English but in that language; thus in Tanzania and Northern Nigeria such a code might well be translated into, or even prepared in, Swahili and Hausa respectively; and the same might be true of Buganda (with Luganda) and Lesotho (Basutoland) with Sesotho. Furthermore, since the intention is that the lower courts (subordinate courts, local and "customary" courts) would also use the code, it might be decided to render the code into the appropriate local language for the use of such courts; though this might well be inadvisable on other grounds.

The use of English as the language of the code does not mean that all the technical terms of English law, encrusted with the barnacles of countless judicial explanations, should be used indiscriminately in the new code. But the first essential of the code, as I see it, is that it should be *compatible* with the pre-existing law; the introduction of a completely new terminology is likely to impede this policy until the courts have learnt the new legal language. Where, then, it seems possible to use English legal terms without thereby importing a mass of irrelevant rules and qualifications into the new law, they have been used; but the opportunity has been seized to get rid of a host of English legal terms which cannot prove their right to continued survival. Antique terms like "detinue" and "trespass to the person", and obscure terms like "malice", have no place in a new code.

Many of the arbitrary classifications and division of the English law of torts also have no place in a new model code. Where is the justification for a distinction between "assault" and "battery", for instance; or for the collection of separate actions dealing with interference with family relations?

But the code is not a mere codification of the current English law. A code can solve controversies: this we have done in various places. It can remove inconsistencies between different rules: this we have also tried to do. It can reject what is no longer in keeping with modern life. It can introduce a juster principle. All these possibilities have been constantly in our minds. Two others, of much greater significance, have also been constantly before us: first, that the law should be *systematised;* secondly, that it should be *adapted to modern African needs and wishes.* Systematisation is what the current English law of civil wrongs so conspicuously lacks; the few general principles tentatively put forward in the draft (for which see Appendix 1) try to introduce such a system. As for adaptation, the method has been to review, in respect of each aspect of the law, the current English law on the subject to see whether this can be re-expressed in a more logical, clear and modern form; to measure the rules so derived against the current customary and other laws existing in Africa; and to see how these different rules may be synthesized.

Sometimes synthesis is possible: for example, with the law of adultery or seduction. Sometimes it is not possible, as where English law generally denies the vicarious responsibility of a father for the torts of his child, whereas the customary law generally asserts it. In the latter case, one must choose, and if necessary create a new rule altogether. This we have done with the law of vicarious responsibility for the torts of "dependants" (of. s. 11(d) of the Code).

It is obvious that every African country must produce its own code in the light of the social and economic circumstances which exist there, and so as to accommodate the varying customary and other laws found within its borders. The code as drafted therefore offers merely a first step towards the synthesis of which I have just spoken. The legal draftsman in a particular country would have to take the local laws (e.g. as restated by a restatement of customary law project) and examine them in detail so as to incorporate their substance into the code.

Despite the local or national variations that would inevitably ensue, each African country would be able to use the same basic model for its Code of Civil Wrongs. The basic uniformity which exists today between the general laws of the different common-law African countries could therefore very happily continue. As so often, it is the first step (in this case, the drafting of a model) which counts; it is here that the legal science of the common-law world, and especially of those institutions which have made a special study of the laws and legal problems of Africa, can be of such enormous help.

IV. BRIEF COMMENTARY ON THE DRAFT CODE

Section 1. Principle of interpretation

The main difficulty with any code, indeed any statute, in the common-law world is that its text tends to form a battleground or bone of contention between the draftsman (representing the legislator) and the judge. Instead of looking at each other as partners in the process of law-making, there is a risk that each side will view the other as in a sense an opponent. The strict English rules regarding interpretation of statutes aggravate and explain this risk. The answer is to incorporate in the code a general provision, such as is finding favour in the U.S.A. and in New Zealand providing for the "liberal interpretation" of the code. Any code of general principles must be sympathetically interpreted by the courts if it is to work smoothly; a clause of this kind asks the judges to help in this task.

Whatever sort of interpretation the code gets, there are various difficulties which inevitably occur. The first is with regard to the status of the pre-existing, now repealed, laws. There is no point in having a new code if the judges continue to apply, in effect, the law as it was before codification. This code is not a mere consolidation of the old law; it supersedes that law. But, since its ideas and language derive in part from the old law, judges may well be tempted to refer to the old law for illumination in applying the code. How far should one permit or encourage them to yield to this temptation? I must confess to being baffled by this question. One's first, purist, reaction is to insist that no reference should be made to the pre-existing law at all. But this is asking too much of the judges, and may well be putting too much faith in the all-embracing wisdom of the draftsman. On the other hand, a code can easily be stultified by unhelpful judicial interpretation seeking to force the law back into old paths. One would like to discourage, without entirely eliminating, legal scholarship of this sort.

Tied up with the problem of the status of the pre-existing law (mainly to be found in judicial decisions) is that of the status of decisions and commentaries on the new code. One cannot prevent the courts interpreting and expanding upon the meaning of the new code. Short of abolishing the law reports, one does not see how to prevent the code becoming encrusted with the same sort of judicial interpretation as has attached to every other statute in the common-law world. The legislator and the draftsman must recognize that "their" code will in time become the judges' code. This conclusion must either be accepted, or machinery created to avoid it (as with the constitution of a permanent Law Revision Commission, able to recommend the swift introduction of legislation adding to, consolidating, or varying the interpretations put on the code by the courts).

Section 2. Specific definitions

Every law must have its own "dictionary". This is unusually important in a code which seeks to establish new meanings for old terms, and to effect a synthesis between institutions and ideas deriving from various legal sources. The term "civil wrong" must obviously be defined; but an example of another, and more complex, definition is that of "person". Here one must synthesize the English law relating to legal personality with that found in the relevant customary laws, which may recognize the legal personality of social and family groupings of a kind unknown to English law.

Section 3. Repeal of pre-existing laws

Pre-existing statutory, common, local customary, and religious rules regulating liability for civil wrongs must be repealed. Great care is required in such repeal. Not only will statutes concerning, for instance, joint tortfeasors, the liability of the state in tort, and limitation of actions, have to be incorporated in the code, but so much of the English and customary laws as relates to topics affected by the code will have to be repealed or modified, with consequent repercussions on other branches of the law.

The rules establishing, recognising, or prescribing the legal consequences of family, property and other relationships will continue in force unless repealed or otherwise dealt with.

Section 4. Rules governing conflict of laws

Many of the internal conflicts which formerly arose (e.g. with the breach of promise suit referred to above) should no longer apply. External conflict problems require to be settled according to the well-established rules of Private International Law, or suitable variants thereof.

Section 5. Actions by or against the State

Incorporates existing laws.

Section 6. Concurrent criminal and civil liability

A difficult problem, not least because the problem already arises in English law, and also because (i) English and customary law may not see eye to eye regarding the question whether a wrong should be treated as civil or criminal, and (ii) it is often asserted that the distinction between criminal and civil wrongs is not always clearly made in customary law.

Sections 7, 8 and 9.

A general definition of the circumstances in which one person may sue another for a civil injury. "Harm" and "injury" should be technical defined terms under the code. The actual obligations imposed by law would have to be set out in Part III of the code; the wording is wide enough to cover breach of any statutory obligation, however. It is felt that a more subjective definition of the "reasonable man" than is provided by English law is required in Africa: see s. 8(2).

Sections 10-12.

Joint and vicarious responsibility are of great importance in African law, given family solidarity and the dependency of wives and children in many areas. The rules under ss. 10 and 11 partly overlap; one has to distinguish today between group legal liability for wrongs committed by individual members, and the assistance which a group might voluntarily give to a member embroiled in a legal dispute. The general feeling in the seminar was that group liability, in the strict legal sense, is today greatly on the decline.

Modern English law has watered down the traditional conceptions of family responsibility, especially in relation to a father's lability for his child, and a husband's for his wife. Present African circumstances suggest that a much ampler law is required; the law has been accordingly framed in terms of responsibility for the wrongs "dependants" as defined.

Section 13.

Specific defences to particular wrongs (e.g. defamation) will have to be included, so far as they are not covered by this section. An attempt has been made here to cover most of the major defences recognised by the English law of torts. There are various customary rules and practices which do not correspond with current English rules on the matter: e.g in regard to the privileged infliction of harm by parents, husbands, and traditional authorities.

Chapter V

The details of this Chapter have not yet been worked out, but it should be noted that one will have to try to harmonise the remedies at present afforded for breaches of contract, torts, and quasi-contract.

Chapter VI

African ideas on the survival of actions after death may well differ from those of English law. The same applies to limitation of actions generally.

Part III

The details of this Part have not yet been worked out. The first step is to decide how to sub-divide the specific heads of liability. Several different bases for such a division exist:

(i) The traditional one: by named wrongs (e.g. trespass, nuisance), though even here one must distinguish between the nominate and innominate wrongs.

(ii) Division by type of injury:
physical injury to the person;
psychological injury to the person;
injury to property/economic injury;
injury to inter-personal relations/social injury.

(iii) Division by category of subject-matter: e.g.
injuries to animals.

(iv) Division by mental element:
intentional harm;   negligent harm;   strict liability.

None of these divisions is entirely satisfactory. The best answer is to look at the matter from the point of view of a legal practitioner advising on legal liability for harm suffered or inflicted. The first category is haphazardly and illogically constituted, and must be rejected. The third is purely arbitrary. Cases where one is liable without proof of intention or negligence need to be set out expressly in the Code; but these can be mentioned at appropriate places. One might adopt the scheme under (ii) as a broad classification, but if one does, one must recognize that some wrongs overlap several categories; e.g. seduction may well damage the girl complainant physically, it may inflict psychological injury on her and her guardian, it may cause economic loss to her or her guardian (as where she fails to get married as a result), and it may well damage her standing in the community. On the other hand, some wrongs are expressly injuries to one kind of interest only.

For each specific head of liability, it is necessary to set out the ingredients of the wrong; the defences if any to it (where they vary from the general defences); and the special remedies if any which attach to it.

APPENDIX I

(*Important Note:* The drafts that are given here are no more than *extracts* from a possible code, and do not represent a complete system. Equally, they do not represent the final version of any code devised for any particular African country, but are preliminary and tentative suggestions for consideration.)

CODE OF CIVIL WRONGS

PART I: DEFINITIONS AND INTERPRETATION OF CODE

Chapter I. Definitions
1. (Principles of interpretation of Code.)
2. (Specific definitions: e.g. "person", "civil wrong.")

Chapter II. Application of code
3. (Repeal of previously existing statutory common, local customary, and religious rules determining liability for civil wrongs)
4. (Rules governing conflict of laws)
5. (Actions by or against the State)
6. (Concurrent criminal and civil liability)

PART II. GENERAL PRINCIPLES OF LIABILITY

Chapter I. General circumstances in which causing harm to another gives rise to civil liability.
7. Any person who suffers harm as the result of an injury caused by another person shall be entitled to such remedy or remedies as the law provides against the person responsible in law for such harm.
8. (1) A person is said to cause an injury to another person if:
    (i) the law imposes upon him an obligation to act or refrain from acting; and
    (ii) he intentionally or negligently fails to act or acts, as the case may be, in breach of that obligation; and
    (iii) his act or omission, as the case may be, inflicts harm on that other person; and

    (iv) such harm is either
- (a) the direct and foreseeable consequence of the injurious act or omission and would not have occurred in the absence of such act or omission; or
- (b) of such a kind as is irrebuttably presumed by law to be the consequence of such injurious act or omission; and

    (v) the wrongdoer is not excused by incapacity, the consent of the injured party, or any other defence whatsoever.

(2) (a) In determining whether an obligation to act or refrain from acting exists, regard shall be had to the individual wrongs set out in PART IV of this Code.

    (b) In determining whether harm is the direct and foreseeable consequence of an injurious act or omission, regard shall be had to the physical connexion, if any, between the injury and the harm, and the conduct that might reasonably be expected of a person having the knowledge and physical and mental capacity of the wrongdoer.

    (c) For the removal of doubts, it is declared that;
- (i) a person may cause harm by a statement or gesture;
- (ii) [etc.]

(3) In this Code "Harm" means:-
- (i) Detriment to a person's mental or physical faculties.
- (ii) Detriment to his property or material interests.
- (iii) Detriment to his reputation.
- (iv) The infliction of mental anguish.

9. Where a person holds himself out as possessing any special knowledge or skill appropriate to any profession office or calling, he shall be responsible for any harm caused by his failure to exercise that knowledge or skill or when he exercises it negligently, in any event where the injured party has expressly or impliedly relied upon, and the wrongdoer has purported to exercise, such knowledge or skill.

Chapter II. Vicarious and joint responsibility

Group
Liability

10. A group, community, society or association having a corporate structure shall be answerable for a wrong committed by one of its members, representatives, agents, or servants if:-

(a) the group itself expressly or impliedly authorised the act or omission complained of, or has adopted such act or omission; or

(b) the wrong was committed by its representative, agent or servant, having general or special authority to act on behalf of the group, etc. and the wrongful act or omission was within the scope of the ostensible authority so conferred.

Explanations. (i) A group may be assumed to have impliedly authorised the act or omission complained of where the member, representative, agent or servant of the group has purported to act on behalf of the group or to deal with the property of the group as if it were his own, to the knowledge of the person or persons having the right to manage the affairs of the group. Such presumption shall be rebuttable.

(ii) A group shall not be answerable for a wrong committed by one of its members if the person claiming to be injured by such wrong was aware that the wrongful act or omission was not expressly or impliedly authorised by the group or was not within the actual authority of its representative.

(iii) "Group, community, society or association having a corporate structure" includes bodies deemed to be bodies corporate under English law; unincorporated associations; territorial family and other traditional or customary groupings having a defined membership and management structure; and other juristic persons and legal entities recognised by the law.

APPENDIX II

BACKGROUND PAPER SUBMITTED TO COLLOQUIUM ON AFRICAN LAW, JUNE 1964

CODIFICATION OF THE LAW OF CIVIL WRONGS IN AFRICAN COUNTRIES

The objective in this discussion is to examine the questions:-
I. Whether the existing laws of civil wrongs in African countries (including the statutory, common, and local customary laws) are:
(a) easily ascertainable;
(b) free from internal conflict;
(c) adapted to the needs of modern states.
II. If not, whether the answer is:
(a) to unify the laws, and if so, whether by elimination of all systems of law except one, or by synthesising the existing laws;
(b) to codify the law, in a unified form or not.
III. If the choice is codification, to examine the possible arrangement and contents of such a code.

I. The existing laws of civil wrongs

1. What is the source of the general or territorial law of civil wrongs? How far is this law based on that of another country, e.g. England; and if so, how far has it been adapted to local exigencies? How easy is it to ascertain the applicable rules of the general law of civil wrongs? Is this law integrated, or are rules governing civil wrongs to be found partly in the law of torts, and partly in the law of contract, of quasi-contract, trusts, marriage, etc?

2. To what extent are (a) customary, and (b) religious, laws of civil wrongs in force? How easy is it to ascertain the applicable rules of these laws?

3. In what circumstances may conflict arise as between one body of law and another in the sphere of civil wrongs (i.e. will a court be faced with the task of choosing between one system and another as the applicable law in the case before it)? Note especially conflicts between the general law and local customary law, between different systems of customary law (where the plaintiff and defendant belong to different ethnic groups), and difficulties where cases involve persons some of whom are subject to customary law and other of whom are not. Are the rules for dealing with such conflicts fully adequate?

4 To what extent are (i) the general law, and (ii) special (customary or religious) laws, governing civil wrongs felt to be out of date or out of tune with the needs, social, economic and political, of modern African states? In particular, are the categories and language in which the English law of torts is expressed accepted as being suitable for continued application?

II.   The policy to be adopted

5. Is the establishment of a unified law of civil wrongs, replacing existing laws, advocated [cf. the general adoption of the principle that criminal law should so far as possible be unified and applicable equally to all sections of the community]?

6. If unification of the law of civil wrongs is favoured, by what means may this be brought about:

    (i) elimination of the imported law (general or common law);
    (ii) elimination of the local, customary and religious laws;
    (iii) synthesis of the different kinds of law;

7. Whether unification is advocated or not, does the reform of the existing law(s) of civil wrongs necessarily imply the codification of that law? Is the idea of an exhaustive code of civil wrongs generally supported [cf. experience in Ethiopia with the Civil Code]?

III.   The main characteristics of a New Code of Civil Wrongs

8. It is suggested that:-

    (i) the law of civil wrongs should be unified;
    (ii) this unified law should be universally applicable;
    (iii) it should be couched in the form of a legislated code;
    (iv) this code should in general scope embrace not only the equivalent of the English law of torts, but also other kinds of civil wrongs, including those arising from breach of contract (so as to achieve, for instance, a single system of measure of damages, defences, vicarious liability, etc.);
    (v) the language of the code must necessarily be English, but the terms employed need not necessarily be those established in English law;
    (vi) the arrangement should be logical and comprehensive;
    (vii) the code should, if possible, pay due regard to African conceptions, rules and institutions.

9. *The general arrangements of the topics.* A possible arrangement might be to divide the CODE OF CIVIL WRONGS into *Parts* as follows:-

Part I.   General Principles of Liability
    —Definition of a civil wrong.

—General circumstances in which causing harm to another gives rise to civil liability.
—Vicarious and joint responsibility.
—Defences.
—Remedies.

Part II. Specific Heads of liability

[i.e. listing specific wrongs, with their ingredients and special rules *re* defences, remedies, etc: e.g. defamation, adultery, physical harm to person].

10. *Interpretation and application of the code.* It is assumed that the code would be applied by all grades of courts (including local or customary courts). The form and language of the code would have to be adapted to this requirement. Translation into indigenous languages may be required, and this should be borne in mind in drafting the code.

If the code is exhaustive, no reference to the prior law would be permitted.

Special rules governing the judicial interpretation of the code would probably be required, e.g. providing for "liberal interpretation." (It is probably impossible in the common law system to prevent the accretion of judicial interpretations of the code through case-law: is there any special provision that can be made to avoid diminishing the special virtue of a code, e.g. that it is clear and certain?)

> *Explanation.* An act or omission is not committed within the course of the wrongdoer's employment if:-
>
> (i) the wrongdoer was not authorised to do the kind of work which resulted in the harm complained of; or
>
> (ii) the wrong was not committed at or near a time or place within which such work was to be performed; or
>
> (iii) the wrong was an intentional contravention of a direction issued by the defendant to the wrongdoer.
>
> (c) The wrongdoer was the agent of the defendant, either generally or for the specific transaction concerned, and the wrong complained of was committed by the agent within the scope of his ostensible authority.
>
> Provided that a defendant shall not be answerable for a wrongful act or omission of his agent in circumstances where the defendant did not in law have effective control

over the manner in which the wrongdoer was to perform his duties.

(d) The wrongdoer was at the material time a dependent of the defendant.

Explanations. (1) One person is said to be a dependant of he her person where:-

(i) he is ordinarily resident at the home of that other erson, and

(ii) he is under the authority and control of that other person, and

(iii) he is entitled in law to rely, in whole or in part, upon that other person for his maintenance.

(2) "Dependant" includes the spouse, parent, child or other relative of a person, or an inmate of his household, if the personal law applying to the person upon whom it is claimed that he is dependent provides to that effect.

(e) The defendant has assumed or accepted responsibility forthe wrongful act or omission of the wrongdoer·

parents   12. Without prejudice to any claims under other sections of this Part, the partners in a commercial or professional partnership formed under the statute, common, religious or customary law shall be jointly and severally responsible to any person not being a partner for a wrong committed by any one of them (i) in the ordinary course of the business of the partnership or (ii) authorised by them.

Chapter III. Defences

13. A person is excused from responsibility for harm caused by his wrongful act or omission if:-

(1) He did not intend, nor foresaw, nor could be normally expected to foresee, that harm of the kind suffered by the injured party would be a consequence of his act or omission:

Provided that a person may be liable for harm which he neither intended nor foresaw nor could reasonably expected to foresee if—

(i) the harm was the direct consequence of his act or omission; and

(ii) his act or omission was in contravention of a statute imposing strict liability or formed part of or was connected with an ultra-hazardous activity in which he had voluntarily engaged himself.

(*Note:* The circumstances in which a person will be strictly liable for breach of a statutory obligation or as a result of engaging in an ultra-hazardous activity are set out in PART III of this Code.)

(2) The harm suffered by the injured party was not the direct consequence of the wrongdoer's unlawful act or omission.

(*Note:* Harm is said to be not the direct consequence of the wrongdoer's act or omission where it has been occasioned by a subsequent (i) voluntary and unconstrained act of another person, or (ii) accidental occurrence which could not have been within the contemplation of the wrongdoer at the time of his act or omission.)

(3) The injured party consented to the infliction of the actual harm, or harm of the kind which he suffered.

(*Note:* Where it appears to the court that the injured party has, by his presence at a particular place, his participation in any public or private event, or otherwise, voluntarily assumed the risk that he will be injured by a wrongful act or omission of the kind which has actually resulted in harm to him, he shall be deemed to have consented to the infliction of the harm complained of.)

(4) The injured party contributed to the harm by his own intentional or negligent act or omission.

In this event, the court shall assess the respective extent to which the defendant and the injured party should be fairly held responsible, and compensation for such harm shall be awared in a like proportion.

(5) He was privileged to inflict harm of the kind suffered by the injured party, by reason of his act or omission authorized by law.

Examples. (i) The State and its duly authorized servants are not responsible to any alien for harm inflicted on him in time of war outside the territorial jurisdiction of the State.

(ii) A judge, magistrate, or officer of any court is not responsible for any judicial, quasi-judicial or administrative act performed without intention to injure by him which he reasonably believes to be within the limits of his jurisdiction and powers.

(iii) The act took place in the course of the business

of [either] House of Parliament.

(iv) The harmful act or omission was expressly authorized by statute.

(v) He is a parent or person *in loco parentis* to the injured party, and the harm was directly and soley intended for purposes of reasonable correction and is not disproportionate or excessive.

(vi) The harm was inflicted by a peace officer or by a private citizen in the course of effecting a lawful arrest or in lawfully restraining a person already under arrest.

Exceptions. The defence of privilege by reason of the harmful act or omission being authorized by law shall not be available to any person except where:-

(a) there was reasonable cause for his doing or failing to do the act which resulted in the harm; and

(b) the act or omission was not intended solely or substantially to inflict harm on the injured party or to serve any personal advantage; and

(c) the harm inflicted was not excessive or disproportionate in the circumstances of the case.

Chapter IV.   Remedies
Chapter V. Extinction of liability: limitation: death
Part III.   Specific heads of liability

Other Vicarious Liability

11. Without prejudice to any claim under the foregoing section, a person (hereinafter called the defendant) may be answerable for a wrong committed by another person (hereinafter called the wrongdoer) if:-

(a) The defendant instigated, counselled or procured the commission of the wrong by the wrongdoer;

(b) The defendant was the employer of the wrongdoer at the material time, and the wrong was committed by the wrongdoer within the course of his employment.

PART III

LAND LAW

INTEGRATION IN THE FIELD
OF LAND LAW

by

CHIEF F. R. A. WILLIAMS
M.A. CANTAB, BARRISTER-AT-LAW

INTEGRATION IN THE FIELD
OF LAND LAW

Part A—Southern Nigeria

It is widely assumed that the scope of alienations or dispositions of land permissible by native law and custom among the peoples of West Africa in olden times is extremely limited. The most recent restatement of this is to be found in the judgment of the Federal Supreme Court in *Okiji and Anor.* v. *Adejobi (Bale and Ors)*[1] where Brett, F.J., said as follows:

"It is clear from the questions which the Chief Justice put to the witnesses that he was sceptical about the story of a sale of the land to a stranger two hundred years ago, and in his judgment what he says is 'Much as I realise how difficult it is to prove a transaction of this nature so many years ago, I do not believe the plaintiffs' assertion that there was a sale. The plaintiffs' ancestor Molusewu was a total stranger from Ikorodu. It is most unlikely 200 years ago that land would be sold to a total stranger or that land at Ijebu-Igbo would be sold at all. It was unlike Yorubas to sell land at that period of their history, especially to a total stranger. He could be given land on payment of the usual tribute but an out and out sale was rare, if made at all.' It is not necessary for the purposes of the present appeal to consider whether every word of that passage can be justified either as a matter of judicial cognisance or on the evidence in this case. It is enough to say that the Chief Justice was fully entitled to make use of his own knowledge in regarding the story of the sale as improbable, and to hold that on the evidence it had not been proved. *I am not prepared to dissent from this finding, which is in accordance with the general trend of judicial decisions or dicta about the sale of land among the Yoruba and other West African peoples.* In *Lewis* v. *Bankole* (1909) 1 N.L.R. 82, 104, Osborne, C.J. stated that 'The idea of alienation of land was undoubtedly foreign to native ideas in olden days', and in 1955 the West African Court of Appeal held that in Accra alienation of land, though well established by then,

1. (1960) 5 F.S.C. 44 at pp. 47-48

was 'originally unthought of': *Golightly* v. *Ashrifi* 14 W.A.C.A. 676, 681. See also the judgment of the Privy Council in *Oshodi* v. *Balogun* (1936) 4 W.A.C.A. 1, 2. It is true that these cases involved family or stool land, whereas we are asked in this case to assume that the land in question belonged to Olaribido personally, but, as I have already said, that assumption seems open to doubt and agree with the Chief Justice in not being satisfied that a sale to Molusewu ever took place.''

The position is very different today and the changes which have taken place in southern Nigeria have been brought about almost exclusively by the integration of ideas derived from the English law of property and conveyancing with those of native law and custom.

The limited forms of disposition of land or interest in land permitted by native law and custom are hopelessly inadequate to meet the economic and social requirements and needs of a modern African society. It is consequently not surprising that everywhere in southern Nigeria, recognition has come to be given to various forms of estates and interests in land which are derived almost entirely from English law. In every such case, the original title from which such estate or interest has been "created" or "carved out" is title under native law and custom, and the method adopted for giving effect to the various transactions is based upon English conveyancing technique. But the amount of land covered by such transactions or subject to the rules of English law is still comparatively small and its greatest incidence is in the big towns where the pressure of modern commerce and industry is greatest. The need of business enterprises for large scale plantations has also resulted in creation of leasehold interests in remote areas of the country.

It is therefore true to say that in this field, integration has been brought about principally by the need to make land or interests in land more easily disposable than they would have been had there been a strict adherence to native law and custom. The main problem which has frequently come before the courts is whether the grantors of family or communal land have the consent of the family or community to make the grant. It was never doubted that a family or community which is the absolute owner of land can grant any estate or interest known to English law by a deed in English conveyancing form. In the case of *Sakariyawo Oshodi* v. *Brimah Balogun & Ors.*,[2] the Judicial Committee of the Privy Council expressly stated that they did not entertain any doubt "as to the

2. (1936) 4 W.A.C.A. 1 at p. 6

possibility of a title equivalent to a fee simple being obtained as the result of a sale with the general consent of the family."

Since the estates and interests created by deeds in English conveyancing forms are unknown to native law and custom, it follows that all the cases arising therefrom are dealt with exclusively in the High Court (formerly the Supreme Court of Nigeria). It is well to bear in mind that up to the late forties, all the judges of this Court were British. Apart from statutory restrictions on the jurisdiction of the native courts, it would have been impracticable to expect most of the members of such courts to understand English conveyancing jargon.

In approaching and resolving the problems posed by the various transactions which came before them, the High Court judges proceeded on the analogy of the law of Trusts. The head of the family or the community was said to be analogous to a trustee and the members of the family or community were said to be analogous to the beneficiaries. The whole concept of family or communal property was regarded as analogous to a trust or settlement. Since it is well established in the law of Trusts that beneficiaries of full age and *sui juris* may modify or extinguish the trust, the courts had no difficulty in deciding that provided the general consent of the community or family is secured, the head or representatives of such community or family may convert the interest of the other beneficiaries into cash or otherwise dispose of it for any estate or interest recognized by law.

I leave aside for the moment, the problems created by the need to secure the general consent of the family or community. This will be considered later (see below). It is to be observed that, so far, I have been dealing with land vested *absolutely* in the family or community. It is necessary to consider next how land so vested, but which at the same time is subject to other rights or interests by native law and custom, has been affected by the English law of property and conveyancing. The cases of which I am aware belong to two categories:

(i) dispositions by the overlords of family or communal land in which other persons have occupational and farming rights as customary tenants; and

(ii) dispositions by customary tenants of their interest in such land.

I do not know whether there is anything in native law and custom anywhere in Southern Nigeria which is analogous to an English mortgage. If there is, I doubt if any case has ever come up to the High Court respecting any such transaction.

One of the basic rules of English law of conveyancing is that contained in section 63 of the Conveyancing Act, 1881, which is still in force throughout Nigeria except in Western Nigeria (as to which, see section 88 of the Property and Conveyancing Law which is to the same effect). The provision is as follows:-

"63. (1) Every conveyance shall, by virtue of this Act, be effectual to pass all the estate, right, title, interest, claim, and demand which the conveying parties respectively have, in, to, or on the property conveyed, or expressed or intended so to be, or which they respectively have power to convey in, to, or on the same.

(2) This section applies only if and as far as a contrary intention is not expressed in the conveyance, and shall have effect subject to the terms of the conveyance and to the provisions therein contained."

If the above rule is applied to conveyances by the overlords of family or communal land in which there are customary tenants, it would follow that the purchaser would take the whole of the reversionary interest of the overlords. Any tribute formerly payable to the overlords would henceforth be payable to the purchasers who will also acquire all other customary rights exercisable by the former overlords in respect of the land. But the tribute payable by customary tenants to their overlords is in most cases no more than a mere token in acknowledgment of the rights of the overlord. There is, in consequence, hardly any market for the overlord's reversionary rights. Where voluntary dispositions have been made at all it is likely that the purchasers or grantees were ignorant of the existence of occupational or possessory rights of customary tenants. The only reported case of voluntary disposition of the overlords' rights I know of is *Kugbuyi* v. *Odunjo*[2a] where Tew, Acting C.J., referred to a number of other unreported cases.[2b] In practice, any grant in fee simple or for a term of years or any other disposition intended to pass rights of user or possession to the purchaser or grantee should be made by the combined representatives of the overlords and the tenants and with the consent of their respective communities or families.

Attempts to assign the possessory or occupational rights of customary tenants have, however, received an unfavourable reception in the courts. In all cases that I have come across, it would appear that native law and custom throughout southern Nigeria regards all customary tenancies as being subject to a condition that the rights of the tenants cannot be assigned or sublet. The courts have always treated any purported assignment or underletting without the

2a. VII NLR p. 51
2b. VII NLR at p. 52

consent of the overlord not only as void but also as making the customary tenants liable for forfeiture of their interest under native law and custom. In the case of *Buraimo* v. *Gbamigboye*,[3] Butler Lloyd, Ag. C.J., treated the native law and custom on this point as being "so notorious that the Courts have taken judicial notice of them." In lieu of forfeiture, the court often awards a fine payable to the overlord.

I now turn to the problem of securing the general consent of the family or community. In this respect, there are, I think, two lines of authorities which are in conflict one with another. According to one line of authorities, it is not necessary to get the consent of every member of the community or family concerned and it is enough if a majority of the members of the family gave their consent (e.g. *Adewoyin & Ors.* v. *Ishola & Ors.*,[4] per Ademola, C.J.). In a later case, the same judge sitting in the Federal Supreme Court observed that "where a member of the family is not available, this should not stand in the way of the Head of the family and others, *if they are in agreement*, from disposing of family property. The case of *Adedubu & Anor.* v. *Makanjuola*[5] and other cases cited by Counsel are not authority for saying that every member of the family must agree to a sale."[6] It would seem on these authorities that although only members of the group who are "available" need be consulted, it is the consent of a majority that is required to effect a valid disposition of family land.

According to the second line of authorities, a sale of family property at the instance of a majority of its members and against the wishes of "a not unimportant minority" of the family is voidable and will be set aside.[7] It is however very difficult to follow the reasoning of the West African Court of Appeal in this case. To begin with, it is not quite clear what criterion determines a "not unimportant minority of the family." Furthermore, the Court itself recognized that "no sale could ever take place in this country if every individual member of the family had to signify his or her consent." I doubt whether this case can be regarded as a satisfactory authority.

I think the rule as laid down by Ademola, C.J.F., is to be preferred. That rule is however not quite consistent with the principles laid down in actions for partition or sale of family land. Such actions usually arise because of difference of opinion within the family as

3.   (1940) 15 N.L.R. at p. 139
4.   (1958) W.N.L.R. 110
5.   (1944) 10 W.A.C.A. 33
6.   *Mogaji & others* v. *Nuga* (1960) 5 F.S.C. 107 at p. 109
7.   *Esan & Ors.* v. *Bakare Faro & Anor.* (1947) 12 W.A.C.A. 135

to whether or not family property should be sold. The court, in deciding whether or not it should order partition or sale, proceeds on the principle that no such order would be made unless it is impossible to continue to use the property as family property, *Bajulaiye* & *anor.* v. *Akapo*[8]. The significant thing about *Bajulaiye's* case is that two were in favour of sale and one was against and the court refused to make the order for sale. If the rule in *Adewoyin's* case is valid, it was unnecessary for the majority to have bothered to take action since a valid sale could have been effected by the majority of the members of the family.

In the case of family property, there is usually little difficulty in ascertaining and identifying the members of the family whose consent is necessary. In the case of communal property, however, the position is different. The "community" is a very large unit and it is impracticable to consult all of the members thereof. Usually one can identify a "traditional authority" or "principal members" who are the acknowledged spokesmen for the community. But in modern conditions, the so-called "consent of the community" to dispositions of communal property is becoming more and more artificial. A possible solution to the problem is by legislation on the lines of the Communal Rights (Vesting in Trustees) Law now in force in Western Nigeria and Mid-Western Nigeria. The idea behind this type of legislation is to make provision for appointing a body of persons who will be trustees of the rights of the community and accordingly empowered to make necessary deeds disposing of communal rights in land.

Care must be taken by the conveyancer to make it perfectly clear that the grantors are the family or the community. In other words, those who execute the conveyance must be shown to be doing so in a representative capacity, for, otherwise, the deed may be held to be void on the ground that the grantors purport to grant what they have not got. A good example of this is the case of *Adedubu* & *Anor.* v. *Makanjuola*,[9] where Kingdon, C.J., said:

> "We must further point out that the conveyance in this case does not in its terms even profess to convey Bashorun Oluyole Family land but only certain hereditaments of which the Vendors, a number of individuals, not in any representative capacity, were 'seised in fee simple'. In this respect the conveyance differs from the sale agreement on which it was supposed to follow. The conveyance was ineffectual to convey to the Defendant the legal estate in

8. (1938) 14 N.L.R. 10
9. (1944) 10 W.A.C.A. 33 at 36

the Family land and the question which still has to be decided in this suit is whether the agreement of sale of the Family land had the consent of the Family and so gave to the Defendant an equitable right of occupation which would prevent the Court granting the injunction sought or awarding damages for trespass."

The general policy of the courts is to exercise their jurisdiction in equity and to set aside any sale or conveyance of family or communal property in cases where there is no consent of the family or community to the sale or conveyance as required by native law and custom. In this connection, the Federal Supreme Court in *Ekpendu & Ors.* v. *Erika*,[10] after referring to the apparent inconsistency between two former decisions of the West African Court of Appeal, concluded as follows:

"Briefly then, the joint effect of the two decisions is that a sale of family land which the head of the family carries out, but in which other members of the family do not concur, is voidable, while a sale made by principal members without the concurrence of the head of the family is void *ab initio.*"

If this decision can be supported, then it must stand as a further qualification to the rule in *Adewoyin's* case. In other words, if there is a head of the family, an intending purchaser must see not only that he obtains the consent of the majority of the members of the family, but also of the family head. But with all due respect, I fail to see the justification of this distinction which may have been made as a result of the reluctance of the court to overrule a previous decision of the West African Court of Appeal. If the decision is pressed to its logical conclusion, it would mean that there can never be a sale against the wishes of the head of the family, even if he is the sole opponent. It is true that he is usually charged with the management and control of family property. But it must be remembered that he cannot be called to render any account of his administration of family property—*Konobi, etc.* v. *Onano V-La Mantse & Ors.*[11] This is a Ghana case but there is no doubt that the same rule applies in Nigeria.[12] Whether a purchaser was, at the time of the sale, able to identify the head of the family or not, it seems to me, on principle, that if he gets a grant expressed to be made on behalf of the family, he should be regarded as having acquired the title of the family. If it is the case that the head or

10. (1959) 4 F.S.C. 79 at 81
11. (1946) 12 W.A.C.A. 102
12. Coker, *Family Property Among the Yorubas*, p. 143

majority of the family did not in fact, authorise the sale, then the conveyance will be liable to be set aside at their instance on the ground of fraud on the part of those who falsely claimed that they had the authority of the family. I fail to see how any distinction can properly be drawn between a false claim of authority to act on behalf of the family (including the head thereof) and a similarly false claim made by other persons including the head of the family. In each case, it is surely neater to treat the transaction as voidable rather than void, particularly since, in each case, the sale should be capable of ratification by the members of the family who have been defrauded. It is, indeed, not uncommon nowadays to find conveyancers preparing Deeds of Ratification for their clients in cases which would otherwise have led to court actions to set aside sales of family land.

I think that at this stage I ought to make a brief reference to one of the very important innovations which English conveyancing practice has introduced to Nigeria and which is not unconnected with the subject matter of this paper. It is the precise survey of land and marking of boundaries by survey pillars. Among every ethnic group the traditional method of demarcation was by well known boundary trees (e.g. the "porogun" tree in Yorubaland or the "akpu" tree in Iboland). "Natural" boundaries, such as streams, rivers, hills or valleys as well as "artificial" ones such as roads or footpaths often demarcate the boundaries between families or communal owners. But firms or individuals who require grants of land for commercial or other purposes would normally insist on a survey which is essential not only for an accuratede limitation of what they have purchased, but also in order to comply with the requirements of legislation which regulate such transactions and require the registration of deeds or title to land. Furthermore, boundary disputes often reach the courts and the courts invariably order that one or both parties should make a survey of the area in dispute. Action for a declaration of title will not be entertained unless the plaintiff files or submits a plan of the area over which he seeks such a declaration. This process has helped to define more accurately the areas of land vested in families or communities in the comparatively few cases that have reached the courts.

The compulsory acquisition of land by the Government for housing or industrial estates or for other Government purposes has resulted in the creation of estates in fee simple or for a term of years absolute in a number of companies, statutory corporations, or individuals. But this is a very recent development. The original Public Lands Acquisition Ordinance in force throughout Nigeria did not authorise the compulsory acquisition of land for the propuse of leasing or selling such land to commercial companies or other individuals since this is not a "public purpose" within the meaning of the Ordinance.[13] Recent amendments to the relevant legislation in every part of the Republic have however altered the legal position.

The courts in Nigeria have always assumed jurisdiction to order the partition or sale of family property. The effect of a court order for partition or sale is to divest the property of all incidents of native law and custom because, in case of a sale, purchasers usually insist on a conveyance in fee simple and, in case of partition members of the family similarly insist on having a conveyance in fee simple. I am however at a loss to trace the legal basis for the exercise of this jurisdiction. Dr. Coker, in *family property among the Yorubas*[14] thought that the jurisdiction was derived from the "inherent jurisdiction to do whatever justice demands." On the other hand, Dr. Elias in his book on *Nigerian Land Law and Custom*[15], seemed to think that it was an assumption by the Courts of a jurisdiction exercised by the Elders in former times. It is pertinent to observe that the jurisdiction is certainly not derived from the U.K. Partition Acts of 1868 and 1870 which are statutes of general application which have been held to apply in Nigeria. These Acts merely enable the court to order a sale in cases where before the passing of the Acts the court could only have declared a partition. Consequently, it would apply only to land held under English law. One of the very few cases in which an order for sale has been made in Nigeria under these Acts is *Giwa & Ors. v. Ottun & Ors.*[16] None of the reported cases in which partition or sale of family property has been ordered gives any clue to the question of the legal basis of the court's assumption of jurisdiction. In *Lewis v. Bankole*,[17] Osborne, C.J. entertained no doubt that the jurisdiction existed nor did Butler Lloyd, J., in *Bajulaiye & Anor. v. Akapo.*[18] The latter case was followed in *Ajibabi v. Jura & Ors.*[19] But none of these cases gives any clue to the question.

I find it difficult to understand the suggestion of Dr. Coker that this jurisdiction can be supported on the basis of the court's "inherent jurisdiction to do whatever justice demands." For that is to give jurisdiction to the court to do practically anything, which I respectfully submit, cannot be right. Dr. Elias's solution has some

---

13. See Waddington, J. in *Chief Commissioner E. Provinces* v. *Ononye & Ors.*, (1944), 17 N.L.R. 142 at pp. 143-144.
14. pp. 89-90
15. at p. 151
16. (1932) 11 N.L.R. 160
17. (1908) 1 N.L.R. at 105
18. (1938) 14 N.L.R. at p. 10
19. (198) 419 N.L.R. 27

support in the sense that it is undoubtedly correct that Elders or chiefs do make partitions of family land between members of the family. But the jurisdiction conferred upon the High Court by law is to enforce the observance of native law and custom. In other words, whilst the High Court must give effect to a partition made in accordance with native law and custom by those entitled to do so, I do not see how this confers jurisdiction upon the court itself to assume functions vested by customary law in chiefs or Elders of the family. One might as well say that because the chief or head of the family is entitled to the control and management of family property, this authorises the High Court to do the same.

It is arguable that the exercise of this jurisdiction by the courts derives from the following provision of the old Supreme Court Ordinance:

" . . . in cases where no express rule is applicable to any matter in controversy, the Court shall be governed by the principles of justice equity and good conscience."

But this particular provision has been omitted from the High Court of Lagos Act and the High Court Law of Western Nigeria, Mid-Western Nigeria, and Eastern Nigeria. It is only in Northern Nigeria that the provision has been retained. Notwithstanding my observation, it is unlikely that the High Court would refuse to exercise jurisdiction to order partition or sale of family property.

But if the jurisdiction is to continue to be exercised, I think there is a need to bring the rules which govern the exercise of the court's discretion into conformity with the rule which Ademola, C.J.F., laid down in *Adewoyin's* case, i.e., the courts should be more ready to order a partition whenever the majority of the family desires it. As already remarked, the rule in *Adewoyin's* case is that the majority can sell against the wishes of the minority. The logical consequence of this is that it is no longer necessary for the majority to bring legal proceedings if all that they desire is a sale. But if they desire partition, and the minority objects, it might be proper to bring legal proceedings. The court should refuse to give judgment for the plaintiffs only where the proposed sale would, in the circumstances, prejudice in some way the rights of the minority.

Although legislation providing for the registration of titles to land has been on the Statute Books of Nigeria for almost twenty years, it is only in Lagos that it has ever been put into practice. Its expansion has been hindered partly by shortage of staff, but probably more (at least in the earlier period of its introduction to Nigeria) as a result of indecision on a question of policy—whether to register only titles based on English law or customary titles as well (Report of the Lloyd Committee on Registration of Title to Land in Western

Nigeria, 1962, para. 7-8. This report is hereinafter referred to as "Lloyd Report.") From its inception, the scheme of the legislation which was put into effect in Lagos was designed to promote only the registration of titles based on English law and no application to register titles based on native law and custom can be considered. This policy, which was reflected in the Registration of Titles Act of 1935, was very effectively criticised by Mr. S. R. Simpson in his Report on the Registration of Title to Land in Lagos, 1957, para. 52 (this Report is hereinafter referred to as the "Simpson Report"). Mr. Simpson accordingly recommended that provision be made for registration of titles based upon native law and custom and the Lloyd Report was of the same opinion in so far as Western Nigeria is concerned. The Simpson Report has been implemented in respect of the Federal Territory of Lagos by the Registered Land Act of 1964 and the Lloyd Report may also be implemented in due course in Western Nigeria. Although these developments will make for greater stability of titles to land and easier identification of those entitled to execute a conveyance, there will be hardly any repercussions insofar as the subject matter of this paper is concerned. Indeed the change of legislative policy is to ensure "coexistence" rather than to encourage "integration".

As a general rule, succession on intestacy to land, whether held under English law or by native law and custom is governed by the latter, that is, those entitled to inherit the deceased's property will be determined by native law and custom and, further, they will hold the land in accordance with that law irrespective of the fact that the deceased had held the property in fee simple during his life time (*Miller Bros. (of Liverpool) Ltd.* v. *Ayeni*.[20] But there is an exception to this rule which probably affects only a small but important minority of individuals. This exception owes its origin to section 36 of the Marriage Act, Cap. 115 of the Laws of the Federation, which provides that—

"36. (1) Where any person who is subject to native law or custom contracts a marriage in accordance with the provisions of this Ordinance, and such person dies intestate, subsequently to the commencement of this Ordinance, leaving a widow or husband, or any issue of such marriage; and also where any person who is the issue of any such marriage as aforesaid dies intestate subsequently to the commencement of this Ordinance—

"The Personal property of such intestate and also any real property of which the said intestate might have dis-

20.   (1924) 5 N.L.R. 42

posed by will, shall be distributed in accordance with the provisions of the law of England relating to the distribution of the personal estates of intestates, any native law or custom to the contrary notwithstanding. . . ."

The above provisions came into force in 1914 and originally applied only to "the Colony" i.e. the present Federal Territory of Lagos and the Administrative Divisions of Ikeja and Badagry. They still apply to Lagos but since 23rd April 1959, their broad effect has been applied by section 49(5) of the Administration of Estates Law to the whole of Western and Mid-Western Nigeria. The provisions do not apply to Eastern Nigeria.

It was at first thought that the effect of the above quoted section of the Marriage Act was to exclude the widow and children of the deceased from any share in the estate notwithstanding the validity of the marriage and the legitimacy of the children by native law and custom—*Re Williams*.[21] This decision was followed in Nigeria until November, 1951 when it was overruled by the West African Court of Appeal in *Re Adadevoh*.[22] The latter decision, which has been followed in later cases and approved by the Privy Council, decided that although the persons entitled to distribution in cases coming under the above provisions must be ascertained by reference to the laws of England, nevertheless by such laws, the legitimacy of the children will ultimately be determined by native law and custom which is the law of the domicile of the intestate. The status of the widow must also be determined in this way, i.e. by reference to native law and custom—(*Coleman* v. *Shang*[23] dealing with the similarly worded Marriage Ordinance of Ghana). It seems to me beyond question that the widow and children of an intestate whose estate is governed by section 36 of the Marriage Ordinance will hold the beneficial rights to any real property of the deceased in accordance with English law rather than native law and custom irrespective of the system of law under which the intestate held the property.

I agree with the observations in para. 29 of the Lloyd Report that "although there are two systems of tenure—customary tenure and the non-customary system drawn from English Law—land may be 'converted' from one system to another, either wholly or partly, and back again." Among the consequences of this process has been the tendency to keep "the family" as a unit within the society in urban areas of southern Nigeria by providing something valuable

21. (1941) 7 W.A.C.A. 156
22. (1951) 13 W.A.C.A. 304
23. [1961] A.C. 481

of common interest or (perhaps more often) something for the members of the family to quarrel about!

Part B—Northern Nigeria

Tenure of land in Northern Nigeria was, until 1st October, 1962 regulated by the Land and Native Rights Ordinance which came into force on 25th February, 1916 and the various regulations made thereunder. The Ordinance has since been repealed and replaced by the Land Tenure Law, 1962, which did not appear to make many fundamental changes in land tenure, the changes introduced being related rather to the administration of the law.

Apart from those specified in section 4 of the Law, all lands in Northern Nigeria are declared to be under the control and subject to the disposition of the Minister charged with the responsibilities for land matters. He is, however, under a public duty to hold and administer such lands for the use and common benefits of the natives. Any individual or firm who wants land for commercial or other purposes can only acquire one of two types of occupational rights. He could either acquire a statutory right of occupancy or a customary right of occupancy. There is in addition power vested in the Minister to grant a licence under section 16 of the Law to any person to extract any stone, gravel, clay, sand or other similar substance.

The statutory right of occupancy is for a term of years subject to the right of the Minister to revoke the grant on grounds prescribed by law. Bairamian, S.P.J. (as he then was), has described this right as being "in substance a lease" and the right of revocation as corresponding to a proviso for re-entry,[24] and the High Court has invariably imported ideas based upon the English law of landlord and tenant into the interpretation of these rights.

The customary right of occupancy, on the other hand, is an occupational right granted by a native or native community lawfully using or occupying land in accordance with native law and custom. All grants are subject to the approval and consent of the Minister. I am not familiar with any transactions in respect of such land. Nor can one derive any assistance from reported cases, since the High Court has no jurisdiction over cases involving title to such grants.[25] It is well known that the Northern Government, proud of its heritage of Moslem law, is not particularly anxious to encourage "integration" between indigenous and English law and I can only guess that approval will probably be given to grants made on terms

24. See *Majiyagbe* v. *A. G. & Ors.* [1957] N.N.L.R. 158 at 159
25. *Kosoko* v. *Nakoji* [1959] N.N.L.R. 15

similar to those under a statutory right of occupancy. In addition, it is almost certain that grants in fee simple will not be tolerated.

CONCLUSION

Integration between native law and custom and English law occurs only in Southern Nigeria and its incidence is greatest in the urban areas. In the North, ideas based on the English law of landlord and tenant have been used to interpret statutory rights of occupancy but I doubt whether there has, as yet, been any integration of the two systems of law on the lines which have taken place in the South. In the South, the two systems based on English law and customary law are likely to coexist for a long time to come and titles based upon English law will continue to be created from or "carved out" of titles based upon customary law. On the other hand, the direction of policy in the North is to discourage any similar development.

PROBLEMS OF HARMONIZATION OF TRADITIONAL AND MODERN CONCEPTS IN THE LAND LAW OF FRENCH - SPEAKING AFRICA AND MADAGASCAR

by

XAVIER BLANC-JOUVAN

PROFESSEUR A LA FACULTE DE DROIT ET DES
SCIENCES ECONOMIQUES D' AIX-EN-PROVENCE

PROBLEMS OF HARMONIZATION OF TRADITIONAL AND MODERN CONCEPTS IN THE LAND LAW OF FRENCH-SPEAKING AFRICA AND MADAGASCAR

All the newly independent African countries are today confronted with the problem of developing a new legal system. Constitutions and political laws have already been drafted, administrative apparatus established, and extensive reforms in judiciary organization undertaken. African nations now are extending their efforts to private law and are trying to find rules and institutions better suited to their new situation.

In French-speaking African countries, the movement for the development of new laws began with accession to internal autonomy following the *loi-cadre*, or fundamental law, of 1956, and thus actually preceded the proclamation of independence. It was then that the need for a new legal system taking into account upheavals in the political sphere began to be felt. In several countries, the decision to begin drafting new laws and even new codes (after the French example) was made at that time. Since then a great deal has been done. It could even be feared that the evolution might take place too quickly, for certainly a good system of laws cannot be elaborated overnight and the reform of private law is not of such urgency as to justify a hurried job. In any case, numerous laws have already been enacted in the majority of French-speaking African states and are now being widely applied.

The movement, however, is not equally marked in all areas of law. The task of codification is further advanced in criminal law, commercial law, and civil procedure than in matters which are in the area of our Civil Code. And even within this area, a distinction must be made. It is easy enough to legislate in contracts or torts, areas where rules are necessarily somewhat abstract and may easily be transposed from one country to another without regard for individual differences. The greatest difficulties occur in family law and land law, and, as a result, codification is considerably less advanced in these areas. In most countries, of course, statutes have already been drafted and promulgated to resolve those difficulties which demand immediate solution. As to land law in particular, it was necessary to establish without delay procedures permitting the allocation of vacant lands to those who would develop them, and the recovery of lands left uncleared by their owner; it was also necessary to provide means by which real property rights in land law could be officially recognized. Nevertheless, no country has yet succeeded in developing regulations for the whole of this area; no country has yet proposed a true reform of land law. Even in countries such as Madagascar, Mali, Guinea and Ivory Coast where chapters of the future Civil Code have already been developed covering family law, the preparation of a real property law has had to be postponed.

Why this delay? It is certainly not that the need for a reform is less urgent in this area than in others. On the contrary, nowhere is the development of a new set of laws more important as a preliminary step to social and economic progress. The imprecision of present land regulation as well as its often archaic and obsolete character are great obstacles to the development of a country dependent on agriculture. It is imperative that new solutions be found, and it is a fact that no French-speaking African state has come this far without including in its plans an agrarian and land law reform. There is no doubt, however, that land law is the area where the indigenous populations show the greatest attachment to their customary laws and traditions. It is in the methods of allocation of lands, and in the rights in land that are conferred on individuals and the powers of control conferred on the group that the local populations cling most to their ancestral practices, which are generally local in nature. Land law is the chosen area of traditional law.

One sees from this the problem which arises and which is at the root of the difficulties African legislators have run up against so far. Land law must take into account the traditions, customs, and habits of each country as well as the needs of modernization and economic development. It must at the same time be rooted in the past and provide a foundation for the future, and this forces the reconciliation of apparently contradictory requirements. A way must be found to integrate the concepts of traditional law with those of modern law.

This integration becomes all the more necessary as one realizes that until now the two systems of law, traditional and modern, have existed side by side and have been applied simultaneously in all French-speaking African countries. During the colonial period, France followed the same policy everywhere, based on the idea that the indigenous populations should remain subject as much as possible to their traditional customs and practices in all areas of private law. Special courts were set up to insure the application of this customary law. That explains why, in all countries, the system of tenure inherited from customary law and corresponding to certain forms of family and social organization of each population has been able to survive. Even so, there has been a certain number of cases in which customary law has been declared inapplicable or has been abandoned in favour of modern law. This has been done particularly when it was a question of defining the right of the State in land or of defining the methods by which lands may be put at the disposal of individuals (for example, by concessions) or of organizing procedures for granting official recognition to the existence of property rights. In these cases, the public interest has been found to justify the replacement of the rules of traditional law by those of modern law, the latter not being rules of French law but rather those created by the colonial government for individual countries. Similarly, it was recognized that the traditional law should apply only to the indigenous populations, not to foreigners, particularly French settlers, occupying these territories. The latter were subject to modern law, in this case French law. Thus, the lands acquired by French citizens were governed by the rules of the French Civil Code; they were also transferred *inter vivos* or upon death according to French law. Finally, the indigenous populations themselves could opt in favour of French law and request, for example, that their lands be subject to the rules of the Civil Code. To do this, they had only to go through a registration procedure that was available to them. In certain countries, like Madagascar, two procedures were provided for the recognition of real property rights: the cadastral procedure was reserved to natives and left their lands under the jurisdiction of customary law; the registration procedure was open to everybody, and if natives went through the latter, their lands fell automatically under the regulation of the Civil Code.

One could discuss extensively the question of whether this juxtaposition of two such different legal systems has allowed them to influence each other's development or whether, on the contrary, it has "frozen" them both, paralyzing particularly the customary law. The essential thing to note is that this duality of the law can no longer be maintained for obvious political and psychological reasons—it appears as a vestige of the old colonial domination, whose survival cannot be tolerated by the indigenous populations. The reforms which have already been realized demonstrate clearly the concern of the governments in elaborating a single law which will be applied equally to all citizens.[1] And this law cannot be

---

1. Thus, in Madagascar, the law of February 15, 1960, abolished the procedure of cadaster.

simply a transposition of customary law without recognition of the solutions reached in modern law, for that would constitute a disastrous step backwards in the economic and social development of the country. Clearly the ancestral customary laws are not always the best suited to an effective and rational use of the land. The need to free the native populations from certain traditional duties that hinder their action and keep them in a state of stagnation is widely recognized today. It is necessary, therefore, to modernize customary law and to unify it on a national basis, since it often varies greatly within national borders. But some traditional values are certainly worth safeguarding. It is especially important to insure the cohesion of the group and to prevent the land from becoming an object of speculation, as is too often the case in our Western societies. It is therefore essential that the new land law not be simply an adaptation of modern law, without reference to local customs and practices—it must be deeply rooted in tradition. If not, it would run the risk of not being accepted by the populations and thus of not being applied. A reconciliation between the fundamentals of traditional law and those of modern law is clearly important for the development of a new law.

But the basic premises of the two systems are so different that their reconciliation frequently raises serious difficulties. More specifically even, one could say that such a reconciliation sometimes appears impossible, thus forcing a clear choice between opposing tendencies. African legislators find themselves faced today with certain fundamental choices which will determine the future of their land law.

Throughout the colonial period, development has been about the same in all African territories from those of French West Africa to French Equatorial Africa and Madagascar. Everywhere modern land law tended to predominate over traditional land law, and everywhere this resulted in a more and more marked abandonment of the old forms of collective tenure and a clearer tendency toward the individualization of real property rights. Moreover, the development of the system of concessions of land accorded to the settlers, the changes in the methods of cultivation and techniques of production, and the habit of the judges of applying French law as "written reason" to fill in gaps left by the silence or ambiguity of the customary law accelerated the process. Thus, when the African states achieved independence, modern land law was on the verge of replacing customary law. Even though the customary law continued to be widely enough applied outside the towns and cities, it appeared as the remains of a system condemned to disappear. More and more the rules of the Civil Code were applied to land law problems;

more and more judges recognized property rights of the French type, that is, individual and absolute rights, to the detriment of ancestral rights that were often collective and were considered too vague and imprecise.

But the important transformations in the political sphere that accompanied the independence of the African countries affected the legal sphere, and the new states find themselves today at a crossroads. They must choose between the different directions which are available to them. Of course, none of them is seriously tempted to adopt extreme solutions, and one could say that all are, fundamentally, seeking a certain balance, but this balance can still be achieved in different ways, and there is no doubt that different tendencies are already appearing in the more or less partial reforms which are taking place in a certain number of countries. Each state reacts in its own way, according to its own traditions, and to the ideology and orientation of its politics. The solutions are not necessarily the same in the countries in which traditional law has remained at a very primitive level and those in which an important evolution had already occurred in the 19th century, before the beginning of colonization, such as Madagascar (at least in certain areas of the *Grande Ile*). Neither can the same rules be adopted in the countries where respect for the Negro-African tradition has been emphasized, and those which place more emphasis on the needs of modernization; finally, the evolution cannot be the same in countries tending to be liberal (Madagascar, Ivory Coast . . .), socialist (Senegal) or collectivist (Guinea, Mali). Sometimes the new legislation marks a return to the concepts of traditional law, and sometimes, on the contrary, it tends to align itself with the concepts of modern law which have little by little penetrated Africa through the colonial administration.

Let us examine how this conflict of concepts presents itself with reference to the ultimate rights that the State is thought to hold in land. We will see that this question poses two others: first, the kinds of rights in land that the State recognizes in groups or in individuals, and then the extent to which these rights can be restricted in the general interest.

I. What is the nature of the right in land held by the State?

All legal systems admit that the group which holds political power over a territory also has certain rights over the land which makes up the territory. The same idea is found in the traditional law of African societies and in modern law, in the law of liberal countries as well as that of socialist countries. But the nature of this right of the group is far from being the same in all cases. There are, in fact, fundamental differences on this point which dominate the organization of land administration.

A. There is an astonishing similarity in the traditional concepts of all the African countries and of Madagascar. The idea is well-established that the group has important rights over the land which it occupies. These rights, however, are not exactly rights of ownership, for it is fundamental to the Negro-African tradition that land cannot be owned. The land is thought of as a person or a spirit, with which the leader of the people (the king or chief) has signed a pact permitting its use. When the chief declares himself "master of the land," and asserts his right over the land, it is not really in his own name that he speaks, but rather in the name of the group which he represents—a group, moreover, very broadly conceived since it includes not only living members but also deceased ancestors and descendants not yet born. The rights of this group in the land, through the intermediary of its chief, are of a very particular nature. They do not constitute absolute ownership, but rather confer only the privilege of distributing the land to those who will cultivate it and of controlling the manner in which the land is to be used. The distribution is made first to smaller groups, the extended family, village, etc., and then finally to household heads, each one receiving an allotment commensurate with his needs. The allotments are originally temporary, but as time passes, they tend to stabilize and become inheritable, at least when a lasting investment has been made in the land. Correspondingly, the ultimate right of the group tends to diminish in its extent and its prerogatives, until it becomes little more than a right of eminent domain, although, of course, it still extends to the whole of the territory held by the group.

This was the concept in effect in the majority of African countries before the colonial period. In Madagascar, in the land of the Merina, the king Andrianampoinimerina asserted, "The land is mine," even at the beginning of the 19th century, and provided for the division of the lands of the kingdom among the six tribes which composed it so that each tribe could redistribute the lands among the "fokono-lona." All the Merina kings up until the colonial period followed the same formula in continuing to assert their superior right over all the lands of the kingdom. The same concept prevailed in many other African countries as well. In 1912, a chief of Nigeria affirmed before the West African Lands Committee, "As I see it, the land belongs to a great family of which many members are dead, some are living, and the largest number is still to be born." President Senghor has just confirmed that the same idea exists in Senegal and it has been shown that it also exists in Uganda. In the tradition of all Africa, the land is thus regarded as belonging to the entire group.

B. The idea of ultimate state rights in land was retained by the colonial legislation in French-speaking African countries, but for completely different reasons. In appearance, the legislatures only continued the old tradition by stating everywhere as was done in Madagascar in article 1 of the local law of March 9, 1896, "The land belongs to the State," but in fact a completely different concept inspired this statement. It was the statement of a principle of French law, and the right to which it referred in claiming the land for the State was actually a right of ownership. This right could not be exercised, of course, over lands already belonging to individuals, and was only applicable to lands that were considered vacant or unowned. Although such lands are relatively rare in a country like France, they were, on the contrary, extremely plentiful in the countries of Africa and in Madagascar, since individual property was less widely known and it was relatively difficult to prove ownership. There was also a presumption of vacancy which applied to most uncultivated lands, and which led to a presumption of "domainality." These lands made up what was called the private domain of the State, or in other words, they were considered the property of the State.

The importance of this presumption of "domainality," from a political as well as a judicial point of view, is obvious. It played an extremely important role in allowing the State to take over almost all the territory of the colonies. This was one of the points where the inadequacy of customary law and of modern law was most noticeable. Among the indigenous populations, these lands were generally considered occupied, and were therefore the object of real customary rights which deserved protection and respect. But from the point of view of the colonial legislature and administration, attached as they were to judicial concepts inherited from Roman law and thus considering the right to ownership the only real property right worthy of protection, these lands were not appropriated. They were thus considered vacant and able to be transferred to the State, which could, of course, decide to respect the rights of use and possession that were exercised over them, but which could also decide otherwise. Experience shows that, in practice, these rights of use and possession were respected in the great majority of cases, although not in all. The State, as owner of the lands, was free to dispose of them as it chose, and sought to redistribute them by sale or concession to colonial settlers who came to the country. This redistribution of full ownership was a vital political instrument of the colonization. Much land which was, in fact, occupied and cultivated by natives was given as concessions to new owners, often foreigners, giving rise to many abuses and many difficulties.

This situation lasted throughout the colonial period. The rule according to which the State was owner of all vacant and unowned lands was retained until the end, in Madagascar as well as in the countries of Africa, although there was an attempt, in certain cases, to improve the condition of the indigenous people, either by offering them some means for contesting the presumption of vacancy by proof of an ancestral property right (e.g., in Madagascar, the decree of February 28, 1956); or by suppressing the presumption of vacancy (e.g., in French West Africa and French Equatorial Africa, the decree of May 20, 1955); or by putting at their disposition a certain number of procedures permitting them to become owners of the lands themselves, by concession or otherwise. But the idea remained that all lands must be, in the end, the object of ownership by someone—and those lands which were not appropriated by individuals either through their ancestral rights or through modern law, had to be the property of the State.

Thus one sees the extent to which concepts of traditional and modern law differ concerning the nature of the State's rights in land. During the entire colonial period, one could say that these two sorts of concepts survived. Certainly, officially, the concepts of modern law prevailed, because they were imposed in the name of public order and also because the local leaders, who were invested with some authority in land matters according to customary law, had their prerogatives reduced by the establishment of the colonial administrative organization, the disturbance of ancestral structures, the splitting up of old groups, etc. But in spite of all this, these local leaders did not disappear and they continued to exercise some of their traditional powers. This explains the misunderstanding that existed in this area between the colonial authority and the indigenous population.

C. When the African states achieved independence, the problem arose of which direction they were to follow. Ought one to continue on the way indicated by modern law, or ought one, on the contrary, to attempt a kind of return to basic traditional ideas?

The majority of French speaking African countries today tend toward the first solution, and many statutes which have been promulgated since their independence repeat statutes from the colonial period, modifying them only in details. One finds especially the idea that the State must own all lands which are not appropriated by individuals. The only difference is a political one, it being thought today that the State must distribute the lands not to favour the policy of colonization, but rather to favour the economic develop-

ment of the country. Since it is the State which is in the best position
to organize and direct this development, it is necessary that it be
able to concentrate in its hands as much land as possible. That is
why it has been proclaimed that the State has a right of ownership
over all vacant lands, and consequently that it has the power to
dispose of these lands in the general interest (either by redistributing
their full ownership or by ceding their use to individuals). Thus
the conflict between the concepts of traditional law and those of
modern law has been resolved by the triumph of the latter, which
tends to replace definitively the former.

Such is certainly the situation, for instance, in the Malagasy
Republic. The new statutes promulgated since 1960 are directly
inspired by old laws. Article 11 of the law of February 15, 1960,
takes up the presumption of "domainality" and reasserts, "The
State is presumed owner of all lands which are unregistered and
unappropriated." The property right of the State is exercised even
over lands which are already being cultivated but for which the
appropriation by individuals cannot be proved. Article 54 of the
same law of February 15, 1960, affirms that individuals will continue
to "enjoy traditional rights of use and the possibility of cultivating
annual crops necessary for the subsistence of their families," but
it only recognizes their right as a temporary one, that is, with no
guarantee against eventual repossession since these lands are
unquestionably part of the private domain of the State. An ordinance
of October 1, 1962, even provides as we shall see, that the State
can repossess appropriated lands that are not cultivated or are
insufficiently cultivated. The full ownership of these lands may be
transferred to the State and they thus become part of its private
domain. As important as the private domain may be, it does not
however include all lands, for it conflicts with the property rights
of individuals, and it is only on lands considered legally vacant
that the State may assume full ownership.

More radical are the rules which have been adopted by some
African countries with collectivist tendencies, such as Guinea.
Speeches and circulars by Guinean leaders have, in fact, proclaimed
that the entire Guinean land is nationalized, and a circular of
November 1961 affirmed that the land was the property of the
Guinean people. Although the statutes actually promulgated have
not always gone as far as the official declarations and although all the
proposals have not yet been carried out, notably because of a desire
to avoid upsetting already vested private rights in property, there
is no doubt, that a tendency exists toward the suppression of
traditional land tenures and an allocation of full ownership to the
State of all lands not held under title by individuals. The official

declarations become thus, if not a present reality, at least a goal toward which the State will aim, a goal much more extreme than the old colonial practice of claiming vacant lands. Even though the right of the state is considered as a right of ownership, it should be noted here that it refers to a socialist idea of ownership that is quite different from that which we have inherited from Roman law. It is certain that the concept thus proclaimed by the Guinean leaders draws its inspiration directly from the concepts in practice in countries of socialist law, which tend to attribute the ownership of land to the State, and in this way it still marks the penetration of concepts of modern law into new African legislation. But it must be mentioned also that it rejoins, in certain ways, the Negro-African tradition, and represents a kind of convergence of modern and traditional African law.

Other countries, such as the Republic of Senegal, hope to build a socialist society based solely on traditional African ideas, without making use of Roman law concepts at all. Recent statutes—and notably the law of June 17, 1964—show the concern of the Senegalese authorities for a return from Roman law to African law, from modern law to traditional law, or, in the words of President Senghor, "from the bourgeois concept of land rights to the socialist concept of traditional Black Africa." It is proclaimed once again that land cannot be owned, even by the State. Of course, the State is to exercise a right over the land, and in fact over all the land (with the single exception, in order not to disturb vested rights, of land already registered or about to be registered), but this right is not ownership in the Roman sense. The State is considered rather as a master of the land who can exercise prerogatives in the general interest and in favour of economic development. It could even be said that the land belongs to the nation, that is, to the whole group conceived as a permanent entity in perpetual development; and this is why Senegalese leaders prefer to speak of the national domain" rather than the domain of the State. But the nation must be organized, and is organized in the framework of the State. Thus it is the State, legitimate heir to the old traditional rulers, which exercises the rights over the land, in the name of the nation; it is the State which insures that the land is put to a use that will profit the whole group.

This is the essential idea that allows today's Senegalese leaders to claim that they are returning to the old "communalist principle" which is "the ethical foundation of the nation" and which constitutes "one of the component elements of negritude."[2] Clearly the old

2. Declaration of President Senghor on May 1st, 1964.

Western concept of ownership has been abandoned; all that is said is that the State possesses the land on the basis of a superior right, in the exercise of which it allots parcels of land to those who use them effectively.

In fact, whatever may be the nature of the right which the State is thought to have over land, the problem arises of knowing what use it is to make of this right, since it will not cultivate the land itself, but will entrust its cultivation to others, either individuals or groups. Therefore we must examine specifically the kind of rights that are conferred on these individuals or groups.

II What kinds of rights in land does the State recognize as belonging to groups or individuals ?

The property rights held by groups of individuals in traditional law differ greatly from those held under modern law.

A. In the Negro-African tradition, we have found that land is generally regarded as being owned neither by the State nor by individuals nor by groups. One speaks sometimes of collective ownership of the tribe, clan, village, or family, but this notion of collective ownership is primarily a result of an effort by European jurists to account for a phenomenon that is not in their usual frame of reference. No doubt one should avoid using the term ownership and speak simply of collective tenure and of various kinds of usufructary rights. The lands are distributed among the members of the group by the king or political chief. Normally, the distribution is made to heads of households and in consideration of the development of the land. The allottee does not become owner of his lot; he can use it, but not alienate it, and the group retains some rights to control its use. At least at the beginning, the allotment is not definitive and can be revised, according to the needs of the society and variations in the size of the house-hold group. It generally tends, however, toward a certain stability in the case of a fixed investment, and comes to resemble a kind of ownership without, however, any right to dispose of the land.

It is, of course, dangerous to overgeneralize in these matters. In Madagascar, for example, a movement had already begun in the last century, before the beginning of the colonial period, toward a system of private property to the detriment of the old forms of collective tenure. When the French administration was established in 1896, this movement was already well advanced in certain parts of the country (on the Highlands Plateaus and in the Merina and Betsileo areas) and for certain kinds of lands (particularly those used for rice cultivation). No doubt Christian missionaries from

Europe had already had an influence during the 19th century, and the country had some methods of cultivation that were peculiar to it, but it is equally important that the favour granted to the idea of private property corresponded perfectly to the Malagasy character. The peasants were deeply attached to the land they cultivated and anxious to have a stable and definite right in it. Let us add, however, that this private property was not always absolute and exclusive; it was not always free from control by the group, and the owner was often deprived of the right to alienate his land outside the group of which he was a part. In any case, it should be emphasized that, even in Madagascar, this sytem of private property did not replace old forms of collective tenure, and the latter continued to be wide-spread, especially in the south, the southeast, and the north.

B. The introduction of colonial rule and modern law greatly modified the basis of the problem. The question arose of what to do with traditional rights in land. Ought they to be respected or abo-lished? In fact, the legislator acknowledged the existence of these rights, but he did not always give them the same force.

The legislator was quite hostile to collective rights and to rights that confer only vague and imprecise prerogatives, as was the case with the great majority of customary rights; particularly did he not want to sanction a kind of collective property that did not fit into any of his usual categories (there had been a vain effort to analyse it in terms of joint possession, or as property belonging to a corporate body). That is why he decided to classify these rights as temporary and revocable rights of use that need not be respected absolutely by the State. The latter could thus claim the land for redistribution by concession, which permitted many abuses and created the feeling that customary tenure enjoyed little protection under colonial rule.

Traditional rights that were individual, conferred important prerogatives, and seemed to present sufficient guarantees of durability and stability were considered by the legislator as amounting to ownership. Certainly these rights were hard to prove, since documentary evidence was often required, and the ownership thus recognized was only ownership "in traditional law," remaining subject to customary laws and carrying with it restrictions on the power of alienation outside the group. It was, nevertheless, recog-nized as ownership, and offered an alternative to the presumption of "domainality" instituted in favour of the State. By assimilation, and especially by the influence of the traditional courts, which were composed in part of colonial government officers who did not hesitate to apply French law as "written reason," private, exclusive, and absolute property rights of the Roman law type tended to become established. A new concept was introduced into the African countries and Madagascar which had not existed there before.

The colonial legislator went even further in this direction, and expressly introduced the private property system of modern law by organizing the possibility for the State to redistribute land from its private domain to members of society. This redistribution operated in full ownership, by sale or concession, the latter being used extensively. Property rights thus created were regulated entirely by the rules of the French Civil Code; they conferred on individuals the right not only to use the land but also to dispose of it. Also the legislator, in order to favour individual ownership and to give it more guarantees, instituted procedures designed to grant official recognition of rights in a deed, so that the rights would be more secure and stable. In all French speaking African countries, a system of registration inspired by the Torrens Act,[3] which was then much more advanced than the system existing in France, was established. The procedure of registration was open to all property owners, French or indigenous, and brought them automatically under the rules of modern law. In some countries, such as Madagascar, another procedure was also instituted for the benefit of the indigenous populations: this was the cadastral procedure, and left the land under the jurisdiction of traditional law. Both procedures tended to develop private ownership.

The new concepts borrowed from modern law did not, however, replace traditional concepts; the two sets of concepts were simply juxtaposed. Certainly one must recognize that the customary system was affected by contact with new ideas. It was also influenced by events outside the law, such as the development of a money economy, the introduction of industrial cultures, the institution of tenant farming and of hired farm labour, etc. It also suffered from upheavals in the social and family structures: the dying out and splitting up of traditional groups, the transition from the extended family to the immediate family, etc. This resulted in a certain evolution toward individual acquisition, a tendency to stabilize tenures, a weakening of the rule which forbade the concession of land to foreigners, etc. All this amounted, in fact, to a real agrarian reform. Nevertheless, this did not mean at all that the indigenous populations had abandoned their traditional concepts nor that they rallied easily to the solutions of modern law. It is necessary to note, in particular, that the institution of private property has not always been received

---

3. The Torrens Act had been promulgated in South-Australia on July 2, 1858; it had been later amended under the name of "Real Property Act" on August 7, 1861, then extended to other Australian colonies

by the indigenous peoples with great success. It could even be said, generally, that it encountered considerable resistance from traditional ideas. There was a particular hostility to the modern law idea of absolute ownership that removes the land from all control by the group. This explains the popular hostility in many regions to the registration procedure, a hostility which was so serious that members of the community who registered their land risked social ostracism. The indigenous populations were afraid of seeing their lands, which until then had been regulated by customary law, placed under modern law rules. In Madagascar, only 4% of the lands were registered, and much of that was in the name of the State; in Senegal, registration affected only 1% of the lands. Much more generally, Roman concepts were blamed for altering the traditional nature of land tenure; private ownership of land was thought to be too exclusive and absolute, to take insufficient account of the needs of the group, and to foster a spirit of speculation among holders of the land, as if the land were in itself an element of wealth. And, in fact, it often happened that the registration of land was a way for alleged holders of customary rights (usually professional speculators) to try to be recognized as the real owners in the place of the present occupants. Lastly, the recognition of individual rights complicated the operations of regrouping of land, interfered with cultivation, and thus hindered the economic development of the country.

C. The criticisms were not, however, universal. When the problem arose, following independence, as to which of the various solutions to select, some countries sought to continue the evolution begun under the influence of modern law while others sought to return to a system closer to the traditional African concepts. It is precisely because the choice between the different possibilities is a difficult one that the majority of countries have not yet undertaken a reform of the whole system and have restricted their legislation to particular points.

Some countries, in particular Madagascar, seem to have opted for the generalization of the system of individual ownership. This can be explained no doubt by the already important evolution which took place in the country before the beginning of colonization, and by the peculiar attachment that the Malagasy people have for the ownership of a small parcel of land. The legislature has not been able to avoid consideration of this sentiment in seeking to define the orientation of the land law of the future; anxious to favour the economic development of the country, it has also been aware of the indisputable advantages which private ownership offers from the point of view of security and permanence of rights, the possibility of selling land, the institution of a system of credit, etc. It has therefore promulgated numerous statutes since independence which tend to encourage the acquisition of private ownership of land. Those traditional land rights which confer broad enough prerogatives continue to be considered rights of ownership. The Preamble of the Constitution expressly guarantees them, and article 11 of the law of February 15, 1960, declares that if the holders of such rights can prove their claims, they can upset the assumption of "domainality" instituted in favour of the State. Article 54 of the same law reserves only the case of traditional rights which cannot be considered as ownership because they are not well enough established or do not confer broad enough prerogatives. These rights are well-recognized by law, but only as provisional rights: they are simply rights of usage and enjoyment and can be withdrawn at any time by the State. On the other hand, the Malagasy legislature has undertaken an extension of the procedures allowing members of the public to acquire land from the private domain of the State. The procedures existed previously, but they have recently been clarified and simplified. The common condition of these procedures is that the acquisition of property is always subject to its development. He who effectively cultivated the land or built upon it may demand that the administration issue a deed of ownership (articles 18, 26, 42 of the law of February 15, 1960), and he who wants to develop land can request that the State grant it to him in concession, but he will only obtain a permanent deed of ownership at the end of a certain period, after a commission has ascertained whether the land is being effectively cultivated (article 45 ff. of the law of February 15, 1960). In any case, the ownership is that of modern law and is now even regulated by the rules of the French Civil Code.[4] Also, the ordinance of October 3, 1960, expressly continues the procedure of registration permitting the official recognition of ownership and the issuance of a definitive and irrevocable deed that implies the application of modern law. But this is simply a possibility open to all holders of rights and is by no means obligatory.

The Malagasy legislature has thus favoured and encouraged the

4. These property rights, moreover, can only be granted to individuals, not to groups. Groups can request the recognition of rights in land that are part of the State's private domain, but they only received usufructary rights and never full ownership. These are called "group donations" and have replaced the former "indigenous reserves" that had been created in 1926. This is one case where the legislature has not encouraged full ownership of land, but this is explained by its hostility to the idea of communal property.

private acquisition of property for purposes of development. It is true that this ownership is still of a double nature, traditional and modern, but the Malagasy legislature has decided to enact a single system of property law to be included in the future Civil Code. The elaboration of this system will require the resolution of many conflicts that the legislature has thus far avoided. Perhaps observation of the effects of recent regulations will facilitate the task which must soon be undertaken. The present orientation of Malagasy law is nevertheless very clear; it corresponds to a tendency toward liberalism that is also found in other African countries, such as the Ivory Coast and Upper Volta. It contrasts, on the other hand, with the orientation of countries of socialist tendencies, such as Guinea and Mali, which are trying to establish socialist systems, and those, like Senegal, who want to arrive at socialism through a return to traditional African concepts. In all these countries, the legislature today is hostile to private ownership of land; it prefers to favour economic development only by granting rights of use and enjoyment.

Certainly, in no French speaking African country has private ownership of the land yet been completely abolished. Everywhere, the legislature has respected individual ownership where it already existed and especially where it was registered (except in rare cases of confiscation which we will discuss later); private property rights have even been recognized by Constitutions. The goal is rather to prevent the future development of a private ownership system.

This is particularly true in the Republic of Guinea. The statutes promulgated so far, while awaiting the formulation of a single code, have respected rights of ownership that are recognized by deeds. They are, however, oriented toward the suppression of traditional land tenures and the attribution to the State of all unclaimed lands. These lands will certainly not be redistributed to individuals with full ownership rights. They will remain the property of the State and individuals will have only a simply usufructary right guaranteed by the government (decrees of October 20, 1959 and February 20, 1961). This procedure has given rise to the fear that distribution of usufructary titles will be done by a simple administrative measure (ministerial authorization), with no participation by the traditional groups of which the individual is normally a part. It is realized that this could have serious effects on the cohesion of the social group as well as on the stability of rights.

In Senegal, on the contrary, the newly established system (law of June 17, 1964) seems much more firmly rooted in native African customs and tradition. It is true that the lands which are now registered will remain under the jurisdiction of the Civil Code, and that occupants of lands not yet registered who have made a permanent investment in their land (construction of buildings, lasting plantations, development of rice beds) are given a period of time in which they can still begin this registration and obtain a right of complete ownership. Nevertheless, at the end of this period, new registrations will only be possible in the name of the State for the realization of projects of public utility. All other lands, about 98% or 99% of the country, will be incorporated into the National Domain, and individuals will no longer be able to acquire full ownership of them. They will be distributed in different ways depending on the zones in which they are located.

In already developed zones, called "*zones de terroirs*," the State will delegate its powers to rural Councils, composed of some government officials and some locally elected or designated representatives. These Councils will make decisions pertaining to the rural group concerning development projects, methods of exercising the usufructary rights, general plans of utilization of the lands, organization of fallow lands, regulations of roads, fencing, the use of water, etc. The presidents of these Councils will make and modify allotments of usufructary rights to individuals according to legislatively formulated standards. These operations must be equitable and the law provides for the protection of the usufructary rights in the land. Those who are already using it must be able to keep it. On the other hand, no right is given to those who do not use the land personally. The allocations will be made for indefinite periods. At the death of the occupant, his heirs may claim his allotment as successors if they use the land personally themselves. The principal concern is to give the land to someone who will develop it effectively and personally.

As for the zones which are not yet cultivated, they are called "pioneer zones" and special laws provide for their development by various types of organizations: new rural cooperatives, state organizations, mixed private-state enterprises, agricultural schools, etc.; other experiments may be tried. Once the area is developed, the lands will pass into the ordinary system as "*zones de terroirs.*"

Such is the regulation by which the Senegalese legislature intends to return to the authentic Black African law. It intends also to assure, by this means, an equilibrium between the stability necessary to the cultivator of the land and the higher rights of the community; also it intends to arrive at a modern legal system which is suited to development, makes speculation impossible, and reinforces the cohesion of the group. In the words of President Senghor, the new system of land law is "equidistant from egoistic individual ownership and levelling collectivism; founded essentially on personal use and development, it represents the original direction of African socialism."[5]

We must emphasize that, for the average Senegalese peasant, this reform makes few changes from the situation during the colonial period, since in the great majority of cases the rights which were granted to natives were only usufructary rights and not rights of ownership. Only those who had rights over lands which they did not use personally and from which they drew revenue will have their position impaired. Those who have cultivated the lands in the past will be able to continue to use them. The old customary tenures will thus be preserved and their stability will be increased since they will be guaranteed by law. Moreover, the occupants of the land will find their situation improved since from now on they will participate, through their representatives, in the daily administration of the lands. They will also be released from various payments that many of them had to make, for example, as tenants to landlords who collected more or less abusively.

This is certainly not to say, that the rights thus conferred on individuals are free from all control, nor that the new occupants may do as they wish with the land which is allotted to them. Their right is not absolute nor definitive since it is the result of an allotment by the State: the administrative authorities can control the manner in which this right is exercised and the development carried out. Such a power of control is nothing very special nor very new, for it is rooted in African tradition. It is this control that we will examine now.

III. In what ways can the rights of groups or individuals be restricted in the general interest ?

The ways in which real property rights can be restricted in the interest of the society varies according to the nature of these rights.

A. To the extent that the essential rights belong to the group which in turn simply apportions the usage of the land among its members; the problem of control by the group is not even posed. The apportionment made by the holder of the rights, whether he be a king, a tribal chief, or a village head, is never made definitively; it is always precarious and revocable. Each individual, or at least each household head, receives a lot corresponding to his needs, but the allotment can always be revised in the face of changed circumstances. Certainly, there is a tendency toward stability of allotments in the case of a lasting investment, but this is never

5. Declaration of President Seghor on May 1st, 1964.

absolute and if the land is badly cultivated, it can always be taken back and realloted to another member of the group. Even in cases where private property already existed, such as Madagascar, property rights were far from absolute; they remained subject to group control. On the one hand, the holder could not alienate his land outside the community to which he belonged, and on the other hand, he was subject to sanctions for the non-use or misuse of the land. It was thus admitted that the land must serve the interest of all and that the group had a supervisory right over its use.

B.   The system introduced by colonial legislation was, of course, very different, since it drew its inspiration directly from French law. Where property rights were those of the modern law, they were subject to the rules of the Civil Code and thus were exclusive and absolute. Where they were ancestral property rights, they were theoretically governed by customary law; but in fact there was a tendency to apply the same rules to them (except that it was usually impossible for the land to be alienated outside the group). It is true that the issuance of a title was sometimes subject to the use and development of the land, especially in the "concessions" system. An individual who requested a concession of land was at first given only a provisional title that carried with it an obligation to develop the land. It was only if this development was effectively realized within the prescribed time limits that the provisional title could be exchanged for a title of full ownership. Nevertheless, once this title was granted, the property right became absolute and irrevocable. The individual could do whatever he wanted with his land or do nothing with it at all: there was no possible control over what he did. Of course, an individual could still be deprived of his property when this was required in the general interest, by means of a procedure of expropriation, but this was rather exceptional and unusual.

These rules reflected the liberal, individualist concept of property rights. Even during the colonial period, however, this concept had been criticized and disparaged both in metropolitan France and in the territories of Africa. The idea developed that property has a social function and that the State cannot remain indifferent to the manner in which property rights—especially rights in land—are used. The ideas of social control eventually prevailed and it was admitted that the omnipotence of the property owner could be restricted in order to oblige him to develop the land he held. The first measure of this kind was a designation of zones in which a special development effort was to be made and in which special obligations could be imposed on property owners. Then, in the last years of the colonial period, special mechanisms were sought that could induce all land owners to use their land. In particular, a system of tax measures was instituted with the object of forcing land owners guilty of not using their land to relinquish it to the State. But these were only indirect sanctions and no one dared go further for fear of violating quasi-sacred property rights.

C. With independence, African countries were immediately faced with the necessity of adapting land law to the needs of the economic development. It is today generally accepted that individual rights in land have to be restricted considerably in the public interest.

Where these rights are only rights of usage and enjoyment granted by the group to the individual, the problem is easily solved, for the group can exercise a control over the development of the land. The capacities of the individual can be considered at the time of allotment, obligations can be imposed as to the manner in which the land should be cultivated, and the land can be reclaimed totally or in part if the obligations are not fulfilled. Senegalese law, for example, has devised a system of this kind. The law provides for a limited number of situations in which the occupants of the land can be deprived of their usufructary rights: misuse of the land, non-personal exploitation of the land, decrease in the size of the family. There is also a provision that the land may be reclaimed if the general interest requires the redistribution of land for its more effective development or for the cultivation of new crops. In all these cases, the State, as "master of the land", has broad powers to oblige the holders of usufructary rights to use the land in a way that conforms to the general interest.

The problem is more difficult where it is admitted that individuals can acquire ownership of the land. Even in this case, however, means have been provided by which the State can continue to exercise a certain control and impose a rational development of the land. Even in France, rights in land no longer are considered absolute and exclusive. *A fortiori* this is true, then, in countries which have to fight under-development and where the demands of a planned and directed economy are perfectly consistent with the old communal concepts of customary law. There are only some small differences from one country to another in the forms of the restrictions which may be brought to the rights in land.

These restrictions sometimes relate to the fact that, in a given territorial area, the State has decided to undertake projects on a communual scale in order to speed or orient the economic development of the area. Such projects imply an obligation on the part of all property owners within the zone thus defined to comply with a common discipline. It is this idea that is the basis for the Malagasy institution of *aire de mise en valeur rurale* (A.M.V.R.), or areas of rural development. It was recognized that the possibility of cultivating certain areas depended on the execution of drainage, irrigation, or clearing projects. These projects required the cooperation of all the area's property owners, and thus implied the active intervention of the government for the elaboration of a common policy and the rational coordination of efforts. The fundamental law in this area today is the ordinance of September 19, 1962. It provides that the administrative body in charge of the A.M.V.R. can reorganize, "restructure," the plots of an area, either by division or regrouping, in such a way as to form rational units of cultivation. In addition, the government can impose a regulatory scheme determining how the development program shall be carried out. Owners who refuse to submit to the obligations imposed on them can be deprived of their lands in favour of the State, with compensation for land thus taken. There are thus important limitations on the rights of individual owners of land—on all owners, whether their rights derive from customary law or modern law.

Although these limitations are only admitted in specific geographic areas where the State has decided to make a special development effort, the legislature has desired that economic development not be limited to these regions and has thus generalized the obligation to cultivate the land. Penalties for the non-cultivation of land are no longer limited to tax penalties. Several African states have taken radical measures in this direction, providing that the non-use of rights in land be sanctioned by the loss of the right itself. Some have provided for a system of forced leases; others have had recourse to a system of expropriation with compensation. Still others have admitted the principle of a confiscation without compensation, and that is, it seems, the logical conclusion of the evolution. Several laws of this sort have already been enacted in a desire to operate a kind of agrarian reform and to fight the development of large estates.[6] Madagascar has recently enacted such a law, the ordinance of October 1, 1962, which penalizes the abuse of property rights and transfers rights in non-cultivated land to the state. The adoption of this law, however, was not accomplished without

6.   Already during the colonial period, decrees of 1935, 1936, and 1938 in French West Africa organized an extinctive prescription of 30 years in favour of the State, thus limiting the perpetual character of registered property, and allotted to the private domain of the State unregistered concessions that were left vacant or uncultivated for a period of ten years. (This latter provision, however, was never applied.) Other laws were enacted at a latter date, toward the end of the colonial period, particularly in application of the fundamental law of 1956, but these laws which dealt particularly with concessions, were, in fact, never applied.

difficulty, since it was necessary to modify a constitutional provision which had declared that property rights were inviolable and that no one could be deprived of these rights without a just and immediate compensation. It was necessary to specify that land could be taken without compensation if it was unused or misused. Here again, it should be noted that the sanction applies both to owners under customary law and to owners under modern law.

Similarly, the Republic of Mali enacted a law on January 20, 1961, by virtue of which any registered land left vacant during ten consecutive years would be considered ownerless and thus part of the domain of the State. This law, of course, can be seen as an extinctive prescription rather than a confiscation. In Guinea a temporary decree of February 20, 1961, allowed the taking of land without compensation during a certain period if the land was not being cultivated, and this decree was clearly confiscatory.

The idea is the same in each case. Unexploited lands are to be transfered without cost from individual ownership to the domain of the State. This is the most efficacious means of fighting the concept of intangible and absolute property rights.

CONCLUSION

The examination of the land law reforms realized in the last several years by the states of French-speaking Africa reveals a remarkable diversity. The single common element of these reforms is their goal: in every case the goal is development of the land, and this is true both in the way in which rights are allotted and in the restrictions to which the rights are subject. The diversity of the legislative approaches that have been used in spite of the common goal was not always foreseen when the problem of the orientation of African land law was first faced on the morrow of independence. It was thought by many that the evolution would lead inevitably to the triumph of modern law concepts over customary law concepts. It was thought that the multiplicity and ambiguity of customary tenures constituted an obstacle to rural development. It was thought that the foundation of the new system of land law ought to be the notion of private property, which alone could permit a real economic development. The only thing to do, in this opinion, was to continue the evolution begun in the colonial period, without undertaking any revolutionary reforms, since, during the last fifty years, modern law had already tended to prevail over traditional law, with which it was juxtaposed.

Time has shown that this conception was not shared by everyone and that, in fact, the conditions favourable to economic development could also be sought in another direction. By abandoning the private property system and returning to the traditional ideas of African law, under which land is an object whose usage should be allotted to those who will cultivate it, one can arrive at a system of land law which is more in conformity with the customary laws of the African populations as well as with their social and familiar organization.

What this shows is that no evolution is inevitable. The choice between the various systems depends on such circumstances as the political orientation and the psychological basis of the society, and these are peculiar to each state considered. It is in taking account of all these factors that the newly independent states have been led to assure the predominance of concepts of traditional law or concepts of modern law in their new real property legislation. On the one hand, it is hard to imagine a real fusion between these two sets of concepts, but on the other hand, it is hard to imagine, in the present context, a deliberate purging of one set in favour of the other. The new land law that is being elaborated by the states of Africa needs to make allowances for the fact that the two sets of concepts have long been juxtaposed and have mutually influenced and penetrated each other. Thus the evolution of modern law itself, which has tended to limit the scope of the private property right on the basis of the need for development, converges somewhat with the peculiarly African tradition that only recognizes to individuals precarious and revocable rights in land. There is not as great a distance as one might have imagined between the traditional and modern concepts, and there even appears to be a convergence of the two. Often the same solutions are arrived at by different paths. Thus, the return to traditional ideas and methods can be reconciled perfectly with the aspirations for progress and the pursuit of economic development.

PART IV

LAW OF SUCCESSION

INTEGRATION OF THE CUSTOMARY AND THE GENERAL (ENGLISH) LAWS OF SUCCESSION IN EASTERN NIGERIA

by

DR. NWAKAMMA OKORO

SOLICITOR AND ADVOCATE OF THE SUPREME COURT OF
NIGERIA, FORMERLY WILLIAM SENIOR SCHOLAR IN
COMPARATIVE LAW, CLARE COLLEGE, CAMBRIDGE

INTEGRATION OF THE CUSTOMARY AND THE GENERAL (ENGLISH) LAWS OF SUCCESSION IN EASTERN NIGERIA

INTRODUCTION

A characteristic of the legal system in Eastern Nigeria, as in many African territories, is the existence, side by side, of customary and general laws, the latter modelled on English law. Because Nigeria was not a settled Colony, the former colonial administration had no urge to impede the development of customary law, more so as most of the rules satisfied the principles of natural justice, equity and good conscience[1]. Indeed, the colonial administration left a remarkable record by preserving and even tolerating some objectionable rules of customary law to an extent which surprises Nigerians. This was a wise political judgment. There is now evidence of a great desire for customary law reform in Nigeria, disagreements arise only as regards the scope and the method of reform.

An efficient administration of customary law in Nigeria has been confronted with serious, though not intractable problems. The principles of the law are not certain in many respects. Because the evolution of customary law did not contemplate modern economic and social standards, customary law has failed to provide answers to many contemporary problems. To these may be added the problem created by the existence of variations not only between the laws of the different ethnic groups but also within the laws of different sections of the same ethnic group. Of the Ibo, Miss Green has commented:[2]

"There are, however, countless variations of customs from district to district and even within a small area. And peripheral or intrusive communities such as Onitsha or Arochuku or places bordering on other tribes will tend to show cultural features differing from those of the interior or central Ibo, particularly those of Owerri Division ... "

There are 18 ethnic groups in Eastern Nigeria, a Region of over twelve million people. These are Ibo, Ibibio, Annang, Ijaw, Ogoni, Oron, Yakurr, Efik, Andoni, Mbembe, Boki, Yala, Ukelle, Biase, Abuah, Obanliko, Ejegham and Ngenni. The variations in

1. Supreme Court Ordinance, S. 19. No. 4 of 1876.
2. Igbo Village Affairs (2nd edn. 1964) p. 5.

the customary laws of these 18 ethnic groups are numerous. A classification of the customary laws of succession in Eastern Nigeria is relevant here. This classification is based on the patterns of distribution of property. The three main patterns of distribution of property corresponding to different methods of reckoning relationship in the succeeding group are the patrilineal, matrilineal, and bilineal. The patrilineal is the pattern in which a man's estate is inherited by his patrilineage. In the matrilineal system, the matrilineage is entitled to the estate to the exclusion of a man's children and his patrilineage. In the bilineal pattern, each of the two lineages, matrilineal and patrilineal, succeed to different parts of the estate.

The matrilineal pattern is found only among the Andoni. The bilineal pattern is the law of the Ejegham, Mbembe, Yalla, Yakurr and a few Ibo societies. The bilineal rules of succession in all these societies are based on similar principles, any variations there may be between the societies are few and are variations within the broad general principles on which the system is built. These variations relate to the concessions which the matrilineage in different societies have made to the patrilineage, and the variations arise from the willingness of matrilineages in recent times to concede to the children of a deceased person more of their father's property than they were entitled to in the past under the strict customary law. The extent of these concessions is not uniform in all the bilineal societies.

The succession laws of the patrilineal societies are not, however, as homogeneous as those of the bilineal societies, especially as regards the choice of successors within the patrilineage. It is therefore convenient to sub-classify the patrilineal societies, following their patterns of choice of the succeeding group. Four types are found.

Type A

In these case of a man's property, the successors are his sons, brothers, father, uncle, excluding daughters, wives, sisters, and mother. This type is male-biased and is found among the Ibo, Ibibio, Annang, Oron, Obanliko, Ngene, Abua, and Ogoni.

Type B

The difference between this and type A is that in Type B, the form of marriage entered into by a woman determines the family to which her children belong. The children of an *igwa* marriage belong to and have succession rights in their mother's family, whereas the children of an *iya* marriage belong to and have succession rights in their father's family. The line of succession in type B is the same as that in type A but for this important difference we have just indicated. Type B is found among the Ijaw.

Type C

The difference between this type and type A is that whereas type A is male-biased, type C is not. Daughters, together with their brothers, have succession rights to their father's property. This is the law of the Efik and Umon (Biase).

Type D

Here, the line of successors to a man's property comprises father, eldest brother, uncle, etc., excluding children, wife, and sisters. One person succeeds to the estate at a time. This is Boki law. The difference between this type and the others is that children are excluded from succeeding to their father's property. It resembles type A in being male-biased. It resembles the matrilineal pattern in the denial of children's rights of succession to their father's property but differs from it in that the successors are chosen from the patrilineage rather than from the matrilineage.

Despite the differences in the patrilineal societies in the choice of successors, it has been seen that the one principle which runs through the four type is that succession is based entirely on the patrilineal principle. A learned author has observed that "legal historians have not found any universally common origin to the law of succession; nor does that branch of the law seem to have developed in different systems along uniform lines."[3]

THE INTEGRATION OF THE CUSTOMARY LAWS OF SUCCESSION

Any attempt to integrate the general and customary laws of succession in Eastern Nigeria must be preceded by an assimilation of the different patterns of customary law into a unity of law. The impact which the elimination of the local variations in customary law within each pattern of succession would make on the society would not be as great as the impact which a unification of the different patterns of customary laws of succession into one law would produce. It may be asked whether it is desirable to unify the matrilineal, bilineal and patrilineal patterns of succession. Many lawyers will be tempted to oppose any such scheme. They would emphasize that customary law by its nature presupposes variations

3.   Parry, *The Law of Succession*, (1953), pp. 1-2.

and differences which inevitably arise from the different localities, economic lives and ethos of different societies. They would argue that customary law has never been justified by the standards of sophisticated and enlightened men but derives its force from the immemorial usages of the society. In other words, customary law is not what people think it ought to be but what people came to find it to be.

The theoretical merits of this argument cannot be denied, but those who have been engaged not only in the academic study of customary law but also in its administration would prefer to lay emphasis on the role which customary law is playing in modern society and the role which it will play in future. In Eastern Nigeria, there is a remarkable evidence of willingness by the society to modernize their rules of succession[4]. The bilineal societies frown at the custom which denies children and the patrilineage rights of succession to a man's estate. Already the matrilineage have conceded substantial succession rights to the patrilineage. In the patrilineal societies, the exclusion of women from inheriting a man's property and from succeeding to immovable property is regarded as outmoded in many circles.

A practical reaction to the present situation is the increasing number of people who make Wills under the general law in order to avoid the rules of customary law. With the introduction of partially free primary education in Eastern Nigeria, a new generation is growing up who will have little or no patience for outmoded customary succession laws. If customary law is to play a useful role in modern society, it must be a mirror of modern attitudes, beliefs, and usages; it must command the respect of those whose lives it regulates. Customary law should no longer justify itself by its immemorial antiquity only but also by the respect which it commands in contemporary society. This qualification is necessary to discourage the growing habit of regarding customary law as inferior to the general law and the growing trend of resorting to fictions designed to circumvent unpopular rules of succession.[5]

The view taken here is that the integration of the different patterns of customary law in Eastern Nigeria is both desirable and practicable. This can be done in the matrilineal societies by removing the

---

4. This conclusion is based on my observations during the 6 months' field work I conducted in 1962 on the customary laws of succession in Eastern Nigeria.
5. e.g. The fiction in the matrilineal societies that a woman who is married from patrilineal into a matrilineal society is, along with her issue by that marriage, her husbnda's matrikin. In some patrilineal societies, an unmarried daughter may be initiated into a 'son' so as to qualify her to inherit as a man.

disqualification placed on the patrilineage; and as far as the patrilineal societies are concerned, by abolishing the bias against female successors. It is important to emphasize the role which a unified system of customary law can play in welding national unity.

Whether complete unification is desirable or not must be determined from the reaction of the people. The observations contained in this paper are based on the writer's personal assessment of the reactions of Eastern Nigerians. The government should be urged to appoint a Commission to test public opinion. No such step has been taken in Eastern Nigeria; the people will welcome this opportunity in the field of succession.[6]

THE DUALISM OF SUCCESSION LAWS

The Marriage Act[7] regulates the celebration of monogamous marriages throughout Nigeria. The only legislation which regulates succession to the property of those who contract monogamous or Christian marriages is contained in section 36 of the Marriage Act, but this section applies only to the Colony of Lagos.

It provides:-

(1) Where any person who is subject to native law or custom contracts a marriage in accordance with the provisions of this Act and such person dies intestate subsequently to the commencement of this Act, leaving a widow or husband or any issue of such marriage, and also where any person who is the issue of any such marriage as aforesaid dies intestate subsequently to the commencement of this Act, the personal property of such intestate and also any real property of which the said intestate might have disposed by will, shall be distributed in accordance with the provisions of the law of England relating to the distribution of the estates of intestates, any native law or custom to the contrary notwithstanding: Provided that—

(a) Where by the law of England any portion of the estate of such intestate would become a portion of the casual hereditary revenues of the Crown, such portion shall be distributed in accordance with the provisions of native law and custom and shall not become a portion of the said casual hereditary revenues; and

(b) real property, the succession to which cannot by native

6. The experience in this field in Kenya will be valuable. See the account given in *The Future of law in Africa* p. 44.
7. *Laws of Nigeria* (1958 Revision), Cap. 115.

law and custom be affected by testamentary disposition shall descend in accordance with the
provisions of such native law and custom, anything
herein to the contrary notwithstanding.

(2) Before the registrar of marriages issues his certificate
in the case of an intended marriage either party to which is
a person subject to native law or custom, he shall explain to
both parties the effect of these provisions as to the succession to property as affected by marriage.

(3) This section applies to the Colony only.[8]

The limitation of the application of English law of succession to
Lagos and the absence of any other legislation for Eastern Nigeria
have created considerable speculation as to which law of succession
applies to Eastern Nigeria.

On this question, there are two conflicting views: one supports
the application of English law, the other that of customary law. It
is important to note that there is no statutory authority for the
former view, the authority is the case of Cole v. Cole[9]. In that case,
Brandford Griffith, J., was of the opinion that because Christian
marriage was unknown to customary law, the estate of persons who
contracted Christian marriages should not be governed by the
customary law of intestate succession. His Lordship argued:

"Were such a contention to hold good then an educated
Lagos gentleman—may—be a doctor, or a barrister, or a
clergyman, or a bishop (for there are all such) marrying an
educated native lady out of the Colony and coming to
reside permanently in Lagos would have his estate subject
to native law in case he died intestate, his widow being
required by a strict undiluted, native law to act as wife to
her brother-in-law in order to obtain support."[10]

His Lordship was of the opinion that parties to a Christian marriage
would be presumed to have intended that English law should
regulate suscession to their property, the presumption being
rebuttable by the circumstances of each case.

A detailed examination of this judgment is outside the scope of
this paper. Its weakness lies in the assumptions (a) that the law of
marriage also regulates succession to the estate of the spouses, and

---

8. A section of the former Colony of Lagos now constitutes the Federal
Territory of Lagos and the other section is now a part of Western
Nigeria. It is submitted that s. 36 of the Marriage Act does not apply
to that part of the former Colony of Lagos which is now a part of
Western Nigeria.

9. (1898), 1 N.L.R. 15.

10. Ibid. at p. 22.

(b) that the law of intestate succession is based on the unexpressed rebuttable intention of a deceased person.[11] *Cole's* case was followed in Eastern Nigeria in *The Administrator-General* v. *Onwo Egbuna.*[12] Ames, J., argued:[13]

> "Because section 36 of the Marriage Ordinance applies only to the Colony, it does not follow that the opposite, so to speak, is the law of the Protectorate. It only means that one must look elsewhere than to this section for guidance on this point. I do not think it necessary to look very far. It seems to me that the principle enunciated in the well-known case of *Cole* v. *Cole* covers this point. It is true that the matter of *Cole* v. *Cole* occurred in the Colony, although the parties were married outside both the Colony and Protectorate. I do not know if the Marriage Ordinance then in force had a section corresponding to section 36 of the Ordinance now in force; and it does not matter whether it did or not, because the decision in *Cole* v. *Cole* was not based on the provisions of any Ordinance but on general principles concerning the application of native law and custom to such a case."

Onwo Egbunna's case did not go on appeal to the then West African Court of Appeal. The High Court of Eastern Nigeria has never had another opportunity to decide the same issue. The question remains to be tested in future in the Supreme Court of Nigeria. The present writer has argued at length elsewhere that *Onwo Egbunna's* case was wrongly decided.[14]

THE DIFFERENCES BETWEEN THE CUSTOMARY AND THE ENGLISH LAWS OF SUCCESSION

An account has been given of the different patterns of customary laws of succession in Eastern Nigeria. It is necessary to summarize the differences between the customary rules and those of the English law as imported by *Onwo Egbunna's* case in Eastern Nigeria. This knowledge is essential in a discussion of the integration of the

---

11.   For eloquent criticisms of *Cole's* case, see Allott: *Essays in African Law* (1960), pp. 182 & 219; see also *Onwudinjo* v. *Onwudinjo* (1957), 2 E.R.L.R. 1 at pp. 4-5 for Ainley, C.J.'s criticisms.
12.   (1945) 18 N.L.R. 1.
13.   *Ibid.* at p. 2.
14.   See Chapter 9 of the writer's book: *The Customary Laws of Succession in Eastern Nigeria.* (1966).
      The same view was held by Dr. G. B. A. Coker (now a judge of the Supreme Court) in his book *Family Property among the Yorubas* (second edn. 1966).

two systems of law. We saw that section 36 of the Marriage Act did not introduce the English law of succession before 1900 in its entirety but altered it in two respects. Firstly, reality is to be distributed as if it were personalty, and secondly, the rights of the Crown to *bona vacantia* were abolished and such property is to devolve in accordance with customary law. The subjection in Eastern Nigeria of the estates of spouses of Christian marriage to English law of succession was initiated by judicial decision and not by legislation. The result is that the entire body of English law of succession as it stood on 1st January, 1900 was introduced into Eastern Nigeria without any adaptations to local conditions as were made for Lagos by section 36 of the Marriage Ordinance.

The following eleven differences may be noted:

(i) Whereas wives have no succession rights in customary law, other than the ill-defined and vague right to live in their late husband's compound and to be maintained by his successors, English law gives them much ampler rights.[15]

(ii) The succession rights of daughters in customary law have been discussed in the preceding pages.[16] In English law before 1900 the principles of primogeniture and co-parcenary applied to the inheritance of real estate. When there were two or more males in equal degree, the eldest only inherited, and if there was no male issue, the daughters inherited together as co-parceners.[17]

As regards personal estate, sons and daughters had equal shares. If English law of succession before 1900 were to apply in Eastern Nigeria, then the rights of daughters on an intestacy would be identical to those just described.

(iii) In the matrilineal societies, the application of English law produces more significant and radical consequences. Children would be entitled to inherit their father's estate to the exclusion of the matrilineal kindred; thus succession becomes patrilineal. Again, spouses would have succession rights in each other's estate, rights which they are denied by the matrilineal rules of succession (with the sole exception that if a man from a matrilineal society marries a wife from a patrilineal society, both would be entitled to succession rights on the death intestate of either).

(iv) With the application of English law of succession among the Boki, children would be entitled to succession rights in their father's estate, a right denied them by the Boki customary law.

(v) With the application of English law among the Kalabari and

15. Parry: *op. cit.* (5th edn. 1966) pp. 153-4.
16. See pp. 2-3 *post*.
17. Parry, *op. cit.* p. 150.

Nembe of the Ijaw, the children of *Igwa* marriages would be entitled to succession rights in their father's estate and not in their mother's family which is in accordance with Ijaw law.

(vi) In customary law, the succession rights of a husband in his wife's estate, where they exist, are inferior to and are subjected to the rights of the wife's sons. In some places, these rights are ill-defined and in other places non-existent if the wife bears a male child to the husband. English law gives a husband defined rights in his wife's estate.[18]

(vii) A distinctive feature of customary law of succession is group succession. Usually the children of a deceased person succeed to his property as a group in undivided shares. The property is thus constituted into family property. This system of plural succession is popular in customary law. The total application of the English law of intestate succession would utterly destroy the institution of family property, since the principle of primogeniture would apply in the inheritance of real estate.[19] The first son would inherit such property. Family property could then be created only by making a will.

(viii) Furthermore, successors in English law succeed to assets. The result is that succession is beneficial rather than onerous. In the customary laws of Eastern Nigeria, succession is not limited to inheritance of assets only. It includes an assumption of the debts and other obligations of the deceased which attached to the estate at all times until discharged. Thus, a successor in customary law may find that he has to use his personal money to discharge all the deceased's debts and obligations. In English law, the deceased's debts and obligations which were not in law terminated by his death can be met only from the estate and if it is insufficient, the creditors have no other recourse.

(ix) The application of the English law of succession before 1900 gives the Crown a right of succession to the personal estate of a deceased intestate who was not survived by a next-of-kin. This anomaly struck Ames, J., in *The Administrator-General* v. *Onwo Egbuna.*[20] He commented.[21]

> "The fact that section 36 of the Marriage Ordinance applies only to the Colony appears to me to have the following consequence. It provides that any part which under English law would go to the Crown shall not do so but shall be distributed in accordance with native law and custom.

18. Parry, *op. cit.* pp. 152, 154-5.
19. *Ibid.* p. 150.
20. (1945), 18 N.L.R. 1.
21. *Ibid.* at p. 3.

There is no such provision applying to the Protectorate. It is not for me to make one. Consequently the rights of the Crown to any portion of this estate remain unaffected and are those which it has by the law of England."

To the Crown's right of *bona vacantia* in personalty must be added his right of *escheat* in the realty of a person who died without an heir capable of succeeding to it.[22]

(x) Finally, it is to be noted that some of the rules of testamentary succession in customary law differ from those of English law. Whereas in customary law a person may make oral death-bed declarations affecting the distribution of his estate after his death, this method of testate distribution of property may be ineffectual in English law except as a *donatio mortis causa*.

TESTAMENTARY SUCCESSION

The two branches of the law of succession namely, testamentary and intestate, are common features of both customary and the general laws of succession. But whereas testamentary succession in the general law is effected by written Wills, testamentary succession in customary law is effected by oral declarations, hence it is described as a nuncupative Will. It is to be pointed out that testamentary succession is the exception rather than the rule in customary law; it is normal to die intestate. The opposite seems to be the case under the general law.

The essential elements of a valid testamentary disposition of property in customary law are that the disposition must be voluntary, the testator must have the mental capacity to alienate property, the subject-matter must be disposable, the identity of the subject-matter must be certain or determinable and the beneficiary must be known. These are not different from the requirements under the general law.

There are certain problems in the general law which are absent in customary law of testamentary succession. Because Wills under the general law are written, problems arise from their construction, especially in relation to the use of technical terms and the rules of vesting of property; but oral testamentary dispositions under customary law do not occasion these problems. Another difference in the two systems is that whereas under the general law, a testator can dispose of his property as he pleases,[23] customary law imposes

22. Parry, *op. cit.* p. 152.
23. The Inheritance (Family Provisions) Act 1938 which imposes certain restrictions on testators in English law is not applicable in Eastern Nigeria.

restrictions in the patrilineal, matrilineal, and bilineal societies as to property which may be disposed of and dependants or successors who may be deprived of certain rights or specific property.[24]

The simplicity of and the restrictions imposed by the rules of customary law of testamentary succession are to be preferred to the general law system. From this brief account, it could be said that an integration of both systems is practicable. In the exercise, customary law would undoubtedly surrender its nuncupative character but will lend a lot of its principles to the new product.

RECONCILIATION OF CONCEPTS AND INSTITUTIONS

An integration of the customary and the general laws of succession must take into account the differences in the concepts and institutions of both systems.

Monogamous and polygamous marriages

The future of polygamous marriages in Nigeria is still very bright even amongst a class of educated men. There would be no difficulty in determining the rights of a husband in a polygamous family. He will be entitled to his share on intestacy in the estate of each of his wives. In monogamous families, there is no difficulty in ascertaining the rights of a wife in her husband's estate. The rights of wives in polygamous families in their husband's estate, it is submitted, can easily be determined if provision is made for the wives to share equally among themselves, the share which a wife is entitled to in a monogamous family. The polygamous institution of marriage, it is submitted, is not an impediment to the integration of succession laws.

Legitimation

Under the general law, legitimation is governed by the Legitimacy Act[25] which provides for legitimation by subsequent Christian marriage of the parents of the child. The Act sets out the succession rights of such persons and regulates as well succession to their estates. Under the customary law, there are at least four modes of legitimation. The first is by the subsequent marriage of the parents. This custom exists among the Efik, Umon, Ibibio, Annang, Ngene, Ijaw, Oron, Ogoni, Obanliko, and among the Ibo at Abakaliki, Onitsha, Owerri, Ngwa, Ekpeye and Ogba (Ahoada).

24.   For a fuller account of the two systems, see Chapter 4 of the present writer's book: *The Customary Laws of Succession in Eastern Nigeria.* 1966.
25.   *Laws of Nigeria,* (1958 Revision) Cap. 103.

This custom is of recent development. Before this change, only children born after marriage belonged to their natural fathers. For this reason, fathers do not accept marriage payment during the pregnancy of their daughters so as to be entitled to the paternity of the child to be born, and husbands do not accept a refund of the marriage payment made in respect of their wives without making sure that their wives are not pregnant even by another man. The spread of legitimation *per subsequens matrinonium* is one of the direct results of modern attitudes and current public opinion.

Another method by which illegitimate children may be legitimated and thus acquire succession rights is by acknowledgment by their natural fathers. Acknowledgment takes different forms, the popular ones being the footing of maternity expenses and the naming of the child by its natural father, (in which case the child takes his natural father's surname), provisions by the natural father for the accommodation, maintenance, and education of the child, according to the child rights and privileges due to the natural father's legitimate children. These examples are not exhaustive and all of them need not be fulfilled. What constitutes sufficient acknowledgment depends on the circumstances and facts of each case. The custom of legitimation by acknowledgment is popular among the Yoruba[26] and the Kwale of Western Nigeria.[27] In Eastern Nigeria, the custom is found chiefly among the Boki, Ngene, and among the Ibo, in Awgu.

Among the Efik society, a child born of men and women from the well known Efut Royal Families is legitimated from birth solely on account of the royal blood of the child's parents, without any form of marriage by them.

There is yet another form of legitimation in Eastern Nigeria. In some societies, the natural father of a child may without marrying the child's mother, pay some money and give drinks to the mother's family for the only purpose of legitimating the child. This custom is found among the Ibo in Enugu—Ezike-Nsukka, Onitsha, Agwu, among the Efik, also in Oron, Ogoni, Eket (Ibibio), and Umon (Biase). Among the Efik, the child himself may be instrumental to the performance of the ceremony by providing the money and drink. He cannot, however, deliver the money and drinks personally to his mother's family but must cause people in his father's family to make the payment on his behalf. The ceremony could be

26. See *Phillip* v. *Phillip* (1946), 18 N.L.R. 102. *Young* v. *Young* (1953) W.A.C.A. Civil Appeal No. 3631 May 1953 W.A.C.A. cyclostyled Reports. *Alake* v. *Pratt* (1955), 15 W.A.C.A. 20; *Lawal* v. *Younan* (1961). All. N.L.R. 245.
27. See *Jirigho* v. *Anamali* (1958), W.R.N.L.R. 195.

performed at any stage of the child's life, even when he has become an adult and after the death of his mother. A suggested reconciliation is the recognition of legitimation by both subsequent Christian and customary law marriages and by no other process.

Illegitimacy[28]

Customary law is not uniform on the succession right of illegitimate children. In the following societies, an illegitimate child has succession rights in the family to which he belongs: Annang, Ibibio, Oron, the Efut (Efik), and among the Ibo—Agwu, Mbaise-Owerri, Udi, Aba-Ngwa, and Nsukka. In the following societies he has not: Boki, Ijaw, Efik (excepting the Efut), Umon, and among the Ibo—Arochuku, Ogidi, Opobo and Onitsha. Only by legitimation can an illegitimate child acquire succession rights in the latter societies.

In all the societies, however, an illegitimate child can succeed to her mother's pre-nuptial property. He cannot succeed to the estate of his half-brothers and half-sisters of the same mother since these belong to other families. He can, however, succeed to the estate of his illegitimate brothers and sisters who belong to the same family as himself and who die without other eligible successors with a prior claim to the estate.

On the principle of public policy which eschews promiscuity, the general law on the rights of illegitimate persons may be preferred to the liberal provisions of customary law. The list of concepts discussed above are not exhaustive.

THE CASE FOR THE INTEGRATION OF THE GENERAL AND CUSTOMARY LAWS

It is hoped that preceding pages have revealed the unsatisfactory state of the laws of succession in Eastern Nigeria. There are some Nigerians who talk of "strength in diversity." This must be regarded as politicians' logic. The existence of different patterns of and variations in customary laws in one territory, the inadequacy of customary rules, the problems of their ascertainment, and the undeveloped state of rules of administration of estate in customary law constitute a serious defect in the legal system. The introduction of English law of succession into Eastern Nigeria without adapting it to its new environment has in turn contributed many problems. Thus, the existence in one legal system of customary succession rules

28.   Illegitimacy does not disqualify a successor under the matrilineal rules.

with many deficiencies and variations and the general law with numerous imperfections left Eastern Nigeria with an unsatisfactory corpus of succession laws!

The question now is not whether the present health of the law needs treatment but what the drug should be. Integration is the panacea. It must be realised that the retention of some principles of English law in Nigeria is now the deliberate choice of a sovereign Nigeria and not an imposition by a colonial power. There is, therefore, no justification for Nigerian nationalists to frown at those rules of English law which have been imported and adapted. The Nigerians of today live in societies different from those of the Nigerians who fashioned the present customary laws. Since customary law should reflect the consciousness of the people whose lives and property it regulates, every generation has an unquestionable right to modernize its customary laws. A modern legal system should aim at a unified system of law within a territory. This should be the aim even if it is achieved in stages and over a long period of time, and even if it results (as it is bound to) to the disappearance of customary law as a separate body of law.

GENERAL PRINCIPLES OF INTEGRATION

An integration exercise must not be limited to a fusion of what is good in the existing customary and general laws of succession. It has been shown that neither of the two systems is satisfactory. It would be misleading to suppose that an integration of the existing systems would produce an unimpeachable substitute. The opportunity must be taken to look beyond the existing laws with a view to building up a new body of law suitable to contemporary Nigerian society.

Customary law of succession has to a great extent successfully resisted the influence of English law . . . It is the predominant law of succession in Eastern Nigeria and the estates of most Eastern Nigerians are subjected to it. It is desirable that unified law of succession in Eastern Nigeria, to be acceptable and popular, should preserve most of the cherished principles of customary law. An example is the principle of plural succession which ensures economic inter-dependence within a family and which has had the effect of binding families together rather than separating them.

A new law of succession should, as far as possible, create little room for technicalities and should not place emphasis on form. Not many Nigerian lawyers, let alone laymen, appreciate these characteristics of English property law.

Any attempt to integrate and reform the existing laws of succession

must be preceded by an ascertainment of both the existing customary rules and the English rules before 1900. The practice of
incorporating English laws by reference to the body of law[29] and not
by reference to the distinct rules of that law should be discontinued.
Apart from being a lazy man's method of legislation, it renders the
imported law uncertain and denies the law makers the opportunity
of reconciling the provisions of the law with the new environment in
which they are to thrive.

MODE OF INTEGRATION

An effective and radical method of integration is by legislation.
The acceptance of the principle of integration implies the willingness
to build a new body of law which is neither customary nor alien. It
implies an acceptance of the principle of codification.[30]

29.   There are many such provisions in the High Court Law (Eastern
      Nigeria): E.R. No. 27 of 1955.
      s. 10(1)   The Court shall be a Superior Court of Record and in
                 addition to any other jurisdiction conferred by this Law or
                 any other written law shall, within the limits and subject
                 as is mentioned in this law or any other written Law, possess
                 and exercise all the jurisdiction, powers and authorities
                 vested in the High Court of Justice in England.
      s. 14   Subject to the provisions of this section and except in so far
                 as other provision is made by any law in force in the Region,
                 the common law of England, the doctrines of equity and the
                 statutes of general application that were in force in England
                 on the first day of January, 1900, shall in so far as they relate
                 to any matter for which the Legislature of the Region is for
                 the time being competent to make laws, be in force within
                 the jurisdiction of the Court.
      s. 16.   The jurisdiction of the Court in probate, divorce and matri-
                 monial causes and matters shall, subject to this law and
                 to any rules of court, be exercised by the Court in conformity
                 with the law and practice for the time being in force in
                 England.
30.   The principle of codification of customary laws seems to have been
      accepted by the Eastern Nigeria Government. The Ministry of
      Customary Courts Policy Paper (Official Document No. 12 of 1963)
      states:
                 "With the task of establishing Customary Courts throughout
                 the Region virtually accomplished, the aim of the Ministry is
                 to embark on collecting important decided cases on Customary
                 Law with a view to providing material for an eventual codification
                 of our native law and custom".
                 "A lot of emphasis is still being placed on the English common
                 law as if no indigenous law exists in the Region. Most of the
                 decisions in some of the courts of the Region are based on the
                 English common law. A halt must be put to this and, to achieve
                 this, it is hoped to arrange for a regular and systematic reporting
                 of important and interesting decisions of Customary Courts
                 dealing with native law and custom to be done. This will provide
                 material for research students in our Universities."

CONCLUSION

An attempt has been made to spotlight the case for and the problems of integration of customary and English laws of succession in Eastern Nigeria. Some of what has been said of Eastern Nigeria may be relevant to Western Nigeria and to other African territories. It has not been thought necessary to make recommendations on the rules of a new law of succession. Such an attempt would be premature and presumptuous. No useful suggestions can be made without ascertaining the wishes of the people. All that has been urged in this paper is that an integration is both desirable and practicable. The customary law of Eastern Nigeria is not, like Moslem law, based on religion; changes thereto are not a matter of conscience or faith but of practicability, reasoning, and convenience.

"With the task of establishing Customary Courts throughout the Region virtually accomplished, the aim of the Ministry is to embark on collecting important decided cases on Customary Law with a view to providing material for an eventual codification of our native law and custom."

"A lot of emphasis is still being placed on the English common law as if no indigenous law exists in the Region. Most of the decisions in some of the courts of the Region are based on the English common law. A halt must be put to this and, to achieve this, it is hoped to arrange for a regular and systematic reporting of important and interesting decisions of Customary Courts dealing with native law and custom to be done. This will provide material for research students in our Universities."

INTEGRATION IN THE FIELD OF THE LAW OF SUCCESSION IN THE MID-WESTERN REGION OF NIGERIA

by

MUDIAGA ODJE

LL.M., Ph.D. (Lond.) DIP. AIR LAW, LEGAL PRACTITIONER,
WARRI, NIGERIA

INTEGRATION IN THE FIELD OF THE LAW OF SUCCESSION IN THE MID-WESTERN REGION OF NIGERIA

A. INTRODUCTION:
THE NEW REGION AND ITS LEGAL SYSTEM

It may be of help if we begin this paper with a brief introduction of the Mid-Western Region, including an outline of its legal system so far as this affects the subject of this paper.

1. The establishment of the Mid-Western Nigeria

"The British created Nigeria; Nigerians created the Mid-West".[1] Up till the 8th August 1963, the area known as the Mid-Western Region of Nigeria formed an integral part of a much larger territory—the old Western Region of Nigeria. Following the due observance of the procedures laid down by the Nigerian Constitution with respect to the creation of a new Region,[2] Mid-Western Nigeria was on the 9th August 1963 established as an autonomous Region within the Federation of Nigeria.[3]

Within three days of its creation, the administrative machinery of the Region was set up: an Administrator and a team of Commissioners—known collectively as the Administrative Council —were appointed to administer the young Region for an interim period of six months in accordance with the provisions of a special Act of the Federal Parliament designated as the Mid-Western Region (Transitional Provisions) Act.[4]

During the life of the interim administration, steps were taken with regard to the eventual setting-up of a normal government and to the provision of a written constitution for the Region. Arrangements were also made in connection with the establishment and composition of the Regional House of Assembly, the fixing of

1. This was the popular cry at Warri in the Mid-Western Region on the 14th July 1963 when the results of the referendum held the previous day with respect to the creation of the Region had conclusively shown that the requisite percentage of affirmative votes (at least 60% of those entitled to vote) had been secured.
2. See now the Constitution of Nigeria (1963), s. 4 (3).
3. The Mid-Western Region Act 1962 (No. 6 of 1962) Appointed day Order 1963; L.N. 96 of 1963.
4. No. 19 of 1963.

electoral constituencies and the holding of elections to the House of Assembly.

Elections were held to the newly constituted Regional House of Assembly on the 3rd February 1964.[5] The present government took office four days later when also the provisions of the Constitution of Mid-Western Nigeria came into force.[6]

2. Position and size of the Mid-Western Region

The Mid-Western Region actually occupies the middle part of south-western Nigeria and is situated right on the western portion of the delta formed by the country's historic and largest river, the Niger. On the north, it has administrative boundaries with both the Northern and the Western Regions, taking the position from east to west. The administrative boundary with the Northern Region follows closely latitude 7° 30' N.; while in the case of the Western Region the boundary stops roughly at latitude 7° N. To the south is the Atlantic Ocean, curving into the Bight of Benin. Eastward, the lower reaches of the River Niger constitute the natural boundary between it and the North—Region on the one hand, and the Eastern Region on the other. The western boundary is partly an administrative one running near longitude 5° E., which it again has with the Western Region; and partly that offered by the Atlantic Ocean or more precisely, the Bight of Benin.

The area so defined covers some 14,923 square miles of territory and has a population of 2,535,839 according to the figures obtained from the last country-wide Population Census taken in November 1963.[7] Barring the Federal Territory having an area of 27 square miles, and a population of 665,246 this Region is easily the smallest autonomous unit, both in area and population in Nigeria. It consists of two provinces: the Benin and the Delta Provinces, split up into ten administrative divisions.[8] The regional capital is at Benin, an ancient and well-known city.

3. Peoples

Inhabiting this comparatively small area of territory is what may be described as a wealth of peoples of various languages, dialects

5. Federal Government Notice No. 57 of 10th January 1964.
6. Mid-Western Nigeria Notices No. 1-24 of 13th February 1964; L.N. 7 of 1964, the Constitution of Mid-Western Nigeria Act (Commencement) Order 1964, S. 1.
7. See the Nigeria Sunday Times of the 30th August 1964 and The Nigeria Year Book 1966 pp. 12 and 13.
8. These are Aboh, Afenmai, Akoko-Edo, Asaba, Benin, Ishan, Isoko, Urhobo, Warri and Western Ijaw.

and ethnic affiliations. Broadly speaking, the indigenous ethnic groups found in the Region are the Akoko-Edo, Bini, Etsako, Ibo, Ijaw, Ishan, Isoko, Itsekiri, Ivbiosakon and Urhobo: In the heart of the area occupied by the Ibo of the Asaba administrative division, there occur three communities of Yoruba origin who have settled here some seven centuries ago.[9] They still speak a dialect of the Yoruba language as well as Ibo which they use as a second language; they have adopted Ibo culture and customs in almost all other respects.[10] The establishment of the administrative divisions has, to a considerable extent, followed the ethnic distribution occurring in the Region·

Too much, however, must not be made of the multiplicity of the ethnic groups inhabiting the Region. For, despite the semblance of what may appear to the foreigner's eye as the bewildering number of ethnic variations exhibited by the peoples, one significant and, it is generally believed, uniting characteristic is shared by almost all the groups—their common Benin origin. Thus, the premier, Chief Osadebay, has justified the choice of Benin as the regional head-quarters on the ground that the city is "the ancestral and cultural home of almost all of us in the Mid-West."[11] In addition to this common Benin (Edo) origin and, no doubt, because of it, seven of the ten major ethnic groups have linguistic affinities and other common cultural features; they are collectively known as the Edo-speaking peoples.[12]

THE LEGAL SYSTEM

The legal system of the Mid-Western Region, including the judicial system and the types of law administered by the Regional courts, offers no material difference from the systems in other jurisdictions within the Federation of Nigeria; the Federal Territory of Lagos having no customary or native courts being excepted with respect to the judicial system.[13] The common patterns of these

---

9. Thomas, N.W., *Anthropological report on Ibo-speaking peoples* (1914) pt. IV, p. 2; Beier, H.U. "Yoruba enclave" (1958) 58 Nigeria p. 238.
10. Thomas, Loc. cit.; Beier, op.cit. pp. 238, 247 and 251.
11. See the Nigeria Sunday Times of 8th August, 1963.
12. On this see: Thomas, *Anthropological report on the Edo-speaking peoples* (1910). pt. I, pp. 5 and 64 ff.; Thomas, "Marriage and legal customs of the Edo-speaking peoples" (1910). 11 J.Comp. (N.S.) 94 at pp. 94-5; Thomas, "The Edo-speaking peoples (1910) 10 J. Afr. Soc. p. 1; Bradbury, R.E., *The Benin Kingdom*, pp. 13-17, 16, 81, 84, 100, 110, 123 and 127.
13. Allott, A. N., *Judicial and legal systems in Africa* (1962), p. 47; Nwabueze, B. O., *The machinery of justice in Nigeria* (1963), p. 32; Park, A.E.W., *The sources of Nigeria law* (1963) pp. 68 and 118.

Nigerian systems—duality of courts (English and customary or native courts, except in the case of Lagos) and of law English or general law and customary law or native law and custom)—as well as other aspects of the systems have been fully covered by the standard works now available.[14]

In one respect, however, the legal system of the Mid-Western Region with respect to the general law now in force therein is in marked contrast with the position obtaining in any of the other jurisdictions in the country. This is because, as will appear shortly, Mid-Western Nigeria is at present the lone jurisdiction applying practically the whole body of the general law of another Region. It is this rather interesting aspect of the legal system of the new Region, together with one or two related topics that will occupy our attention in the remaining part of this section. The related topics are: a brief indication of the two types of law governing succession in the Region; and mention of the appropriate courts in which disputes and claims arising out of succession are determined.

The general law in force in the Region

The bulk of the general law at present in force in the Mid-Western Region is the *corpus* of the Laws of the Western Region of Nigeria[15] as it stood on the 9th August, 1963, when the new Region was established.

The provisions by virtue of which this general law continues to be in force in the Mid-Western Region are now contained in paragraph 6 of the second schedule to the Constitution of the new Region.[16] This paragraph substantially embodies the earlier relevant provisions of sections 2, 3, and 4 of the Mid-Western (Transitional Provisions) Act[17] which regulated the position during the period of the interim administration of the Region.

The paragraph provides:

(1) Any law which, immediately before the appointed day [i.e. the 9th August 1963, when the Mid-Western Region was created], is in force in or in any part of the Region by virtue of section two, three or four of the Transitional Provisions Act shall, until it is changed by an authority having power to do so and subject to paragraph 5 of this Schedule [i.e. the paragraph dealing with the assets, liabilities and the Consolidated Revenue

14. See: Allott, *op. cit.* pp. 44-75; Nwabueze, *op. cit.* chaps. 1-12; Park, *op. cit.*, chap. 1; Elias, T. O., *Groundwork of Nigeria Law* (1953), chaps. 1-11, Elias, *The Nigerian Legal System* (1962), chaps. 1-11.
15. Published in 1959, these Laws run into seven volumes.
16. The Constitution of Mid-Western Nigeria Act, No. 3 of 1964.
17. (1963), No. 19 of 1963.

Fund of the Region], continue in force in the Region or part with such modification (whether by way of addition, alteration or omission) as may be necessary to bring it into conformity with this Constitution.

(2) Without prejudice to the provisions of the foregoing sub-paragraph, where any matter—

  (a) falls to be prescribed under this Constitution by the Legislature of the Region or any other authority; and

  (b) is prepared by any law having effect by virtue of that sub-paragraph or paragraph 5 of this Schedule, that law shall, as respects that matter, be deemed to have been made by the Legislature or other authority in question.

(3) For the avoidance of doubt it is hereby declared that the provisions repealed by section 154 of the Constitution of the Federation [i.e. the Act of the British Parliament entitled the Nigeria Independence Act[18] and the Nigeria (Constitution) Order in Council[19] (other than the third, fourth and fifth schedules[20] to that Order)] ceased to have effect as respects the Region on the coming into force of this Constitution, and accordingly nothing in sub-paragraph (1) of this paragraph shall be construed as continuing those provisions in force as respects the Region.

(4) For the purpose of sub-section (1) of section three of the Constitution of Mid-Western Nigeria Act, 1964 [i.e. as to composition of the Mid-Western House of Assembly,] electoral constituencies, etc., which were deemed to have come into purposes, the reference in this paragraph to the appointed day shall be construed as a reference to the relevant date mentioned in that subsection [i.e. the 9th August, 1963].

BRIEF INDICATION OF THE TWO TYPES OF LAW GOVERNING SUCCESSION IN THE MID-WESTERN REGION

The two types of law governing succession in the Region are the general or English law and the customary law.

The general law

The general law of succession (including the administration of estate) in the Region is contained in local statutes which include:

18.   (1960), 8 and 9 Eliz. 2, c. 55.
19.   (1960), S. I. No. 1652.
20.   These schedules contain the Constitutions of the Northern, Western and the Eastern Regions respectively.

(i) the Administration of Estates Law;[21]
(ii) the Administrator-General's Law;[22]
(iii) the Legitimacy Law;[23] and
(iv) the Wills Law.[24]

Where the general law of succession applies

It may be simply stated that the general law relating to intestate succession applies where a person married under a monogamous or Christian system of marriage dies intestate domiciled in the Region; or where such a person—whether or not he was also domiciled in the Region—dies intestate, leaving real property situated in the Region.

As regards testate succession, the general law governs the position where a testator makes a will in English form or the general law form; irrespective of the system under which a marriage is contracted. The law of wills is treated fully in section 4.

Customary law

In respect of the Western Region, it is possible to speak of a broad uniform system of customary law of succession—Yoruba customary law. As regards the Mid-Western Region, however, this is dangerous; and one must refer specifically to the society one has in mind, since the various ethnic groups already enumerated have their own systems with local variations sometimes occurring within one and the same system. We are, therefore, concerned with at least ten main systems (corresponding with the number of the main ethnic groups) together with any local variations which may exist under one or more of the ten main systems of the customary law.

Despite this multiplicity of systems, however, it is possible, as will be shown later, to classify the various bodies of indigenous law governing succession into three main patterns in the essentially patrilineal societies; with a fourth pattern for the groups in which both the patrilineal and matrilineal principles exist side by side. The basis of this classification, which will be mentioned later, is whether only eldest sons, or all sons, or all children are entitled to inherit from one or both of their parents.

The four main patterns of successoin found in the Region we may refer to as:

(a) Type "A" which covers the Ishan and holders of hereditary

---

21. Laws of the Western Region of Nigeria, 1959, Cap. 1.
22. *Ibid.*, Cap. 2.
23. Laws of the Western Region of Nigeria, 1959, Cap. 62.
24. *Ibid.*, Cap. 133.

titles among the Bini, under which the eldest son takes exclusively;[25]

(b) Type "B" which is found among the Ibo and Ivbiosakon, where only sons inherit;[26]

(c) Type "C" which is followed by the Bini (other than the holders of hereditary titles), Aoko-Edo, Isoko, Itsekiri and Urhobo, under which all children participate in the benefits of inheritance;[27] and

(d) Type "D" which represents the system found among the Etsako and Ijaw, where the inheritance rights of children are determined largely by the type of customary marriage ("big dowry" or "small dowry") contracted by their parents.[28]

Warning must however be given in connection with our arrangement of the patterns of succession already outlined. These patterns must not be considered in water-tight compartments since quite striking similarities on specific points are detectable between groups having otherwise divergent rules of succession. Thus, the Ishan people included in Type "A" practise the now dying custom of *arebhoa*[29] or *arewa*[29] which is also found among the Ibo who are included in Type "B". Briefly, under this custom, a man having only daughters may make his eldest daughter an *arebhoa*[29] or *arewa*[29] (Ishan) or *idegbe*[30] or *idebwe*[30] (Ibo) who is then regarded

25. Roth, H. L., *Great Benin* . . . (1903) p. 97; Talbot, P. A., The peoples of southern Nigeria (1926) Vol. 1, pp. 684-6; Egharevba, J. U. *Benin law and custom* (1949) pp. 37-8; Okojie, C. G., Ishan native law and customs (1960) p. 92; *Ehigie* v. *Ehigie* (1961) W.N.L.R. 307; (1961) All N.L.R. 842.

26. Thomas, *Anthropological report on Ibo-speaking peoples* (1914) pt. IV, pp. 127 ff.; Talbot, *op cit*. pp. 686-7; Jones, G. I., "Ibo land tenure" (1949) 19 Africa 309 at p. 315; Esenwa, F. E., "Marriage customs in Asaba Division" (1948) XIII Nigeria Field 71 at p. 80; Chubb, L. T., *Ibo land tenure* (1961) para. 101; Obi, S.N.C.; *The Ibo law of property* (1963) pp. 154-5; Thomas, *Anthropological* report on the Edo-speaking peoples (1910) pt. I, p. 74; Bradbury, R. E., The Benin Kingdom (1957) p. 96.

27. Thomas, (1910) *pt. I.* pp. 66 ff. and 86 ff., Egharevba, *op. cit*; p. 38; Omoneukanrain, C. O., *Itsekiri law and custom* (1942) p. 74; Bradbury, *op. cit.* p. 152.

28. Thomas, (1910) *pt. I*, pp. 75 ff., Thomas, (1910) 11 J. Comp. Leg. (N.S.) 94 at pp. 96 and 99; Rowling, C. W., *Land tenure in Benin Province* (1948) Para. 49; Bradbury, op. cit., pp. 106-7.

29. Thomas, *Anthropological report on the Edo-speaking peoples* (1910) pt. I, p. 79; Thomas, "The Edo-speaking peoples" (1910) 10 J. Roy. Afr. Soc., 1 at pp. 7-8; Thomas, "Marriage and legal customs of the Edo-speaking peoples" (1910) 11 J. Comp. Leg. (N.S.) 94 at p. 99; Rowling, C. W., *Land tenure in Benin Province* (1948), para. 65; Bradbury, R. E., *The Benin* Kingdom (1957) p. 80; Okojie, C. G., *Ishan native laws and customs* (1960) pp. 88, 93 and 118.

30. *Thomas, Anthropological Report on Ibo-speaking peoples* (1914) pt. IV, pp. 5, 60-61, 79, 128 and 1301; Rowling, *op. cit.*, para. 99.

as an "eldest son" for the purposes of succession. Further warning need be issued to the effect that even in some of the essentially patrilineal societies, the matrilineal principle of inheritance still asserts itself and the maternal relatives of a deceased person may be included in the list of the beneficiaries of his estate.[31]

The forum or the appropriate court in which proceedings relating to succession are brought

Where succession is governed by the general law

Where the succession is governed by the general law, the appropriate court in which proceedings may be instituted is the High Court of Justice.[32] Neither the magistrates' courts[33] nor the customary courts[34] have jurisdiction in causes and matters relating to succession governed by the general law.

Where succession is governed by customary law.

Where customary law applies to the succession, customary courts have exclusive original jurisdiction.[35] Appeals from these courts go to the magistrates' courts[36] and the High Court,[37] the last court also exercising appellate jurisdiction over magistrates' courts.[37] In appropriate cases an appeal lies from the High Court to the Supreme Court of Nigeria.[38]

In addition to the channels of appeal from the customary courts to the non-customary or English courts, there is the avenue of review by means of which chief magistrates, acting as supervising authorities, exercise powers of review in respect of all cases tried by the customary courts.[39]

31. Thomas, *Anthropological Report on the Edo-speaking peoples* (1910) pt. I, pp. 86-8.
32. The High Court Law (Mid-Western Region), No. 9 of 1964, S. 10(1); The Administration of Estates Law (Western Region); Cap. 1. S.2(1); The Administrator-General's Law (Western Region), Cap. 2, S. 2.
33. The Magistrates' Courts Law (Western Region), Cap. 74, S. 20(b).
34. W.R. No. 34 of 1959, the Customary Courts (Amendment) Law, 1959, Second Schedule; amending the Second Schedule to the Customary Courts Law, 1957, cap. 31, *op. cit.*
35. W.R. No. 34 of 1959, the Customary Courts (Amendment) Law, 1959, Second Schedule; amending the Second Schedule to the Customary Courts Law, 1957, Cap. 31, *op. cit.*
36. Cap. 31, S. 47.
37. *Ibid.*, S. 48.
38. That is, where the amount in dispute is £50 or more; Cap. 31, s. 49.
39. Cap. 31, ss. 44A-44E.

Original jurisdiction of the High Court and of the magistrates' courts where succession is governed by customary law

The High Court

It has always been assumed that the High Court is precluded from exercising original jurisdiction where the cause or matter is governed by customary law. This seems to be the interpretation put on the provisions of the High Court Law which exclude the original jurisdiction of that Court in any matter "which is subject to the jurisdiction of a customary court relating to. . . inheritance or disposition of property on death."[40]

It has, however, never been argued that where such a cause or matter involves an amount in excess of the jurisdiction of the appropriate customary court or courts; or where, in fact, no customary court exists in the area concerned (for example, where the establishing warrant is temporarily withdrawn as was the case with the majority of the courts in the Delta Province in 1963), it would amount to misuse of language to insist that such a cause or matter is "subject to the jurisdiction of a customary court." This is because in one case, the customary court would be incompetent in law to exercise jurisdiction; in the other, there simply would be no such court to whose jurisdiction the cause or matter would be subject. It is submitted that in the cases instanced, it would be open to the High Court to assume original jurisdiction.

It is a matter for regret that no thought has been given to a clear wording of the excluding provisions contained in the High Court Law[41] which has instead copied the relevant provisions of the High Court Law of the Western Region. Had some consideration been given to the matter model provisions would have been found in the Magistrates' Courts Law[42] which will be discussed in the next paragraph.

Magistrates' courts

In contrast to those contained in the High Court Law just discussed, the relevant provisions of the Magistrates' Courts Law[42] are distinguished by their clarity. These latter provisions exclude the original jurisdiction of magistrates' courts in causes or matters "relating to inheritance upon intestacy under customary law and the administration of intestate estates under customary law."[43]

---

40.   Cap. 44, *op. cit.*, S. 10(1) No. 9 of 1964.
41.   *Op. cit.*, S. 10.
42.   Cap. 74, Laws of the Western Region of Nigeria, 1959.
43.   *Ibid.*, S. 20(d).

Summary

We may summarise what has gone before. Mid-Western Nigeria is a newly established Region with an area of some 14,923 square miles, and a population of 2,533,337, shared among no fewer than ten indigenous groups.

There are two types of courts. There are the English courts (the High Court of Justice and the magistrates' courts) which administer, principally, the general law; with provisions enjoining them to observe and enforce any applicable customary law where this does not offend the repugnancy doctrine. Then there are the customary courts which normally exercise exclusive original jurisdiction in causes and matters relating to succession and administration of estates under customary law.

Only the High Court of Justice has jurisdiction in causes and matters relating to succession and the administration of estates governed by the general law. Both the High Court and the magistrates' courts exercise appellate jurisdiction over customary courts in all causes and matters. Appeals to the High Court from customary courts may be direct or may go through the magistrates' courts hearing appeals from customary courts. Chief Magistrates generally act as supervising authorities with respect to customary courts whose proceedings they (Chief Magistrates) supervise and review.

The general law in force in the Region is that "received" from the old Western Region, and the date of the "reception" is the 9th August, 1963, when the Region was officially established. The general law relating to succession and administration of estates is contained in a number of laws (Laws of the Western Region) which include the Administration of Estates Law, the Administrator-General's Law, the Legitimacy Law and the Wills Law.

B. DEGREE OF INTEGRATION DETECTABLE IN THE PRESENT LEGAL SYSTEM

Under the present legal system, there are no specific instances of integration in the field of the law of succession. This is not surprising. The question of succession is so essentially personal that it is extremely difficult to unify the divergent rules of the general law and the customary law into a single system that will not disrupt the people's way of life. In one or two general aspects of the present legal system, however, steps have been taken which might facilitate the eventual process of integration of both types of law. The steps so far taken are in connection with the organization of the judicial system, and the principles governing the administration of justice. These may be briefly considered.

The organization of the judicial system

Strictly speaking, the organization of the judicial system does not fall within the topic under discussion, which the background papers pertaining to the Conference have so abundantly made clear, i.e. how significant elements of the general law and the customary law may be unified into a single modern system, at once comprehensive and harmonious. Nevertheless, it is hoped that the Conference might like to consider the somewhat less important topic concerned with the linking of the customary courts organization with the main judicial system through the avenues of appeal and or review, since it may well be the first step towards complete integration of the general law and the customary law.[44]

The old judicial system

Under the old judicial system, the native courts organization was, to a very great extent, insulated from both the "English" courts (the old Supreme Court and the magistrates' courts). This insulation was particularly more far-reaching in the spheres of customary succession and administration and in family matters governed by customary law. The reason for this was that "it was thought that the law with regard to those matters was peculiarly within the knowledge of Native Courts and a right of appeal might swamp the English Courts with more business than they could cope with."[45]

The native courts had exclusive jurisdiction in customary succession and administration suits, and native courts of appeal exercised appellate jurisdiction in these suits heard by the native courts below. Further rights of appeal lay on administrative officers (District Officers, Residents and Governors,); or to the "English" courts only if the Governor so directed by means of a special endorsement on the warrant establishing a particular native court.[46]

The powers of review by means of which native courts were controlled and their proceedings scrutinized were exercised by administrative officers.[47]   The use of the prerogative unit and

44. See, The Record of Proceedings, Judicial Advisers' Conference, 1953, Special Supplement to the Journal of African Administration, Oct. 1953, p. 7; and Record of Proceeding of the Conference held in 1956, special Supplement to the Journal of African Administration, April, 1957, p. 5.
45. Report of the Native Courts (Western Provinces), Commission of Inquiry 1952, paras. 45 and 155.
46. The Native Courts Ordinance, s. 30(i) (iii), Laws of Nig. 1948, edn., cap. 142.
47. Op. cit. s. 28(i) (a) and (b).

orders for the removal of native court proceedings into the High Court, though not excluded by law, was not favourably viewed by the authorities.[48]

The present integrated judicial system

Since 1957, when the present system of customary courts was established in the Region, the old "parallel" system of the courts organization has been abolished; and in its place we now have a judicial system under which the customary courts organization is integrated with the main judicial system by the channels of appeal and review.

There now exist rights of appeal from the customary courts to the "English" courts, including the highest and most authoritative tribunal in the land—the Supreme Court of the Federal Republic of Nigeria. The powers of review formerly exercised by administrative officers with regard to the judicial functions of the old native courts have now been replaced by judicial supervision performed by judicial officers—generally, Chief Magistrates and legally qualified presidents of customary courts known as supervising authorities. The use of the prerogative writ and orders in respect of the proceedings of customary courts is no longer frowned upon.

The principles governing the administration of justice

The basic principles governing the administration of justice under the general law and the customary law have been unified. The process of unification has not meant that there now exists the unified set of rules observed by all courts in the administration of justice. It does mean, however, that there is hardly any difference between the rules of practice and procedure observed in the "English" courts and those followed by the customary courts. In both sets of rules the basic principles, such as those relating to the observance of natural justice, etc., can be found.

The process of integration (if we may so term it) here has resulted in the virtual exclusion of the customary rules of procedure. Indeed, it has been said that "very little of the customary rules of procedure remains."[49] The existing Customary Courts Rules, 1958, made under the Customary Courts Law, 1957, prescribe common practice

---

48. Report of the Native courts (Western Provinces), Commission of Inquiry, 1952, paras. 133-5; especially para. 134 and view expressed by the Acting Attorney-General to the effect that it would be disastrous if it became a general practice to use the prerogative writ and orders in relation to N. courts.
49. Report of the Native Courts (Western Provinces), Commission of Inquiry, 1952, para. 113.

and procedure for all customary courts in the Region; and they may be described as a modified form of the practice and procedure observed in the "English" courts. When the Customary Courts Rules were first made, the policy then was to assimilate the practice and procedure in customary courts to those observed in the magistrates' courts. Thus, Ord. XIX of the earlier rules—now repealed[50]—provided as follows:- "Where no other provision is expressly made by the Law or by these Rules, the provisions with respect to procedure, practice and process for the time being observed in magistrates' courts (except in so far as those provisions may be inconsistent with the law or these Rules) shall be adopted and followed in customary courts so far as those provisions may be appropriate and with such variations as the circumstances may require . . . "

The basic objective of the present legal system, so far as procedure is concerned, has been stated as "the assimilation of the legal standards of both systems (i.e. the general law and the customary law) as far as is practicable and the widest possible uniformity in the principles governing the administration of justice in all courts."[51] In this regard, the channels of appeal and review existing under the present system must be regarded as going a long way in ensuring that the basically uniform rules of procedure are complied with by the customary courts; and that these courts do not return to arbitrary and orthodox customary methods of procedure, as happened in the case of *Queen* v. *The President and members of Akugbene grade C customary court, Ex. p. Chief Carter.*[52] There, the High Court, Warri, quashed (by means of the order of certiorari) the proceedings of the customary court which had convicted and sentenced the applicant to a term of three months imprisonment for (as the customary court stated it): "the fact that the accused really disrespected the court and quoted section in his evidence while he is not authorised by law."[53] It is interesting to note that the disrespect complained of amounted to no more than that the applicant, who was a defendant in a civil case, had sought to transfer his case to another court, and had cited a section of the Customary Courts Law in support of his contention. Morgan, J., who corrected this arbitrary procedure on the part of the customary court, observed: "It is unthinkable that any persons considered fit for appointment as members of a Customary Court should be so

50.   W.R.L.R. 260 of 16th July, 1959, with effect from 1st August 1959.
51.   Ajayi, F. A., "The interaction of English law with customary law in Western Nigeria" (1960) Journal of African Law, 40 at p. 50.
52.   (1960) W.N.L.R. 146
53.   (1960) W.N.L.R. at p. 147.

ignorant as to think that it is disrespectful to their court for reference to be made to the law in the court."[53a]

C. OTHER ASPECTS IN WHICH INTEGRATION BE ATTEMPTED PROBLEMS AND SUGGESTED SOLUTIONS

The topics selected for consideration in connection with future attempts at integration of the general law and the customary law include the following:
   (1) the jurisdiction of the courts in causes and matters relating to succession and the administration of estates;
   (2) the administration of estates;
   (3) intestate succession; and
   (4) wills.

1. Jurisdiction of the courts in causes and matters relating to succession and the administration of estates

The jurisdiction of the courts in succession and administration suits has been considered.[54] It will be recalled that but for the avenues of appeal and review, the "English" courts would have normally had nothing to do with causes and matters relating to succession and the administration of estates under customary law. Customary courts, of course, have no jurisdiction whatsoever in these causes and matters where the applicable law is the general law.

As a step towards the integration of both systems of law, it is suggested that jurisdiction should be conferred upon both types of courts—with the exception, for the time being, of the lowest grade of customary court, the grade C court[55]—in succession and administration suits, irrespective of the system of law that applies. In other words, whether a court has jurisdiction or not should depend upon the value of the claim before it and not the type of law governing the claim.

Law to be administered

The foregoing suggestion implies that all courts would have to administer the general law of succession as well as the customary law

---

53a. See pp. 8-10.
54. See pp. 8-10.
55. The exclusion of the grade C customary court is based on the grounds that (a) its jurisdiction is limited to £50; and (b) it will, for some time to come, be manned by lay members.

of succession just as the courts in Ghana are empowered to do under the provision of Part III of the Courts Act, 1960.[56]

(a) Problems and suggested solutions
(i) The administration of the general law of succession in customary courts

One of the problems that will arise concerns the ability of customary court members to apply the provisions of the general law relating to succession and administration. As regards the grade A customary court, this problem does not exist, since only a legally qualified person is appointed as president of such court. We are left only with the grade B customary court, grade C being deliberately excluded from our consideration.

The first suggestion is that the less informed lay members of grade B customary courts should be replaced by persons having a higher standard of education and enlightenment. These more educated and enlightened members should be assisted to acquire good working knowledge of the general law. Such assistance should take two forms. The government should prepare a manual similar to the Customary Courts Manual, embodying the relevant provisions of the general law governing succession and administration. These provisions should be embodied in a manual together with explanatory notes in simple straight forward language or, alternatively the provisions could be translated into the principal languages spoken in the Region—Edo, Ibo, Isoko, Urhobo, Itsekiri, Ijaw, etc. Regular courses of instruction or in-service training organised on the basis of those now run for teachers might serve a useful purpose in facilitating the court members' grasp of the relevant provisions of the general law that they will be called upon to administer.

A second suggestion is to attract legally qualified persons to the "customary" bench. At the moment, a number of grade B customary courts have legal practitioners as their presidents on full-time or part-time basis.

(ii) The administration of the customary law of succession in the "English" courts

Granting that there is integration in the jurisdiction of the courts and both types of courts are empowered to administer both types of law as suggested, how can we be sure that the magistrates and judges, some of whom may not be well acquainted with the customary law, would be furnished with evidence of the correct rules of the applicable customary law? This is a real problem which

---

56.   Sections 66 and 67

has been pointed out in several cases in which the rules of customary law have either been deliberately twisted by parties and their witnesses, or stated in genuine ignorance.[57] Thus, in one case,[58] evidence of Yoruba customary law was given by a witness to the effect that where a man had provided living accommodation for his wife in his house during his life time, such accommodation, on the death of the man, became the property of the wife; and that it went to her family on her death if she was not survived by children. Graham Paul, J., was forced to observe: "I have heard a good deal of nonsense talked in the witness box about Yoruba custom but seldom anything more ridiculous than this. Even the defendant's Counsel himself had to throw over his witness, and I really do not blame him for that."[59] In yet another case,[60] Brooke, J., remarked: "There was conflict in their testimony which was so considerable that doubts might have been felt whether there was any certainty to be found in the local custom. The versions of the claimants were clearly influenced by their interests . . . most of the witnesses did not know what the . . . native law and custom as to succession was and some had invented or adopted it to support their claims to share in the estate."[61]

In connection with the ascertainment of customary law, steps should be taken to investigate and record the inheritance rules of the various systems of customary law obtaining among the different ethnic groups inhabiting the Region. Sources to be consulted in such investigation and recording include the following: textbooks; manuscripts written on the customary law whether these were written by persons having legal qualifications or by others not so qualified, for example, anthropologists and sociologists; records of customary courts; statements of informants and opinions of the appropriate authorities authorised to declare and/or modify the customary law.[62]

The recording should be in the form of textbooks, digests or restatement; the idea being to produce a record of customary law which, although authoritative in the sense that it accurately represents the law, would not be binding on the courts. It would be

---

57. See for instance: *Savage* v. *Macfoy* (1909) 1 Ren. Rep. 504 at 508; *Oloko* v *Giwa* (1939) 15 N.L.R., 41 at 323. *In re Alayo* II E.R.N.L.R. 1 at 5.
58. *Oloko* v. *Giwa* (1939) 15 N.L.R. 31.
59. Ibid., at pp. 32-3.
60. *In the Estate of Alayo* (1946) 18 N.L.R. 89.
61. (1946) 18 N.L.R. at p. 93.
62. Local government councils may declare and/or modify local customary law if so empowered in the Instruments establishing them. See Local Government Law, Cap. 68, s. 78.

a guide to them in their administration of the law. The next step would be to reconcile the divergences existing among the customary systems of law which have already been indicated. It is important that we know the customary law which we propose to integrate into our modern legal system; it is equally important that attempt should be made to reconcile the different customary systems before we can think of integrating them into the modern legal system.

Once customary law is made available in the form suggested, the attitude of the general law and the "English" courts in regarding it (customary law) as a question of fact would have to be reconsidered. One of the obstacles to the process of integration has been the ungracious attitude of the "English" courts in looking down on the customary law, and in treating it as inferior law. In Ghana, both systems have now been placed on an equal footing and "any question as to the existence or content of a rule of customary law is a question of law for the Court and not a question of fact."[63]

2. The administration of estates

The integration of the law governing the administration of estates is not likely to raise as many serious problems as the case of the integration of the law of succession. There are two reasons for this rather optimistic view. There is the fact that quite substantial agreement exists between the general law and the customary law as to the considerations governing the right to administer the estate. Generally speaking, the grant of administration follows the interest, that is to say, the right to administer the estate is granted to the person or persons entitled to inherit it or a substantial part of it. Furthermore, it may not matter much who administers the estate as opposed to who inherits it—so long as it is properly administered and the remuneration for administering it is not unreasonable. Thus, the fact that all unrepresented estates are administered under the Administrator-General's Law does not thereby exclude the rights of those entitled to inherit it either under the general law or in accordance with the provisions of the customary law. Thus, where the unrepresented estate is governed by customary law, s. 28(2) of the Administrator-General's Law provides that "the Administrator-General may apply to a customary court administering such law for information as to how . . . the estate shall be distributed."

Problems and suggested solutions

Certain problems are bound to arise in connection with the integration of the law governing the administration of estates.

63. The Courts Act (Ghana), s. 67(1).

These problems are due to the differences existing between both systems of law on a number of points. These will be discussed briefly before any suggestions for their solution are offered. There are divergencies between the general law and the customary law on the following points:-

(a) the machinery for administration;
(b) the recognition accorded to the authority under which the administrator is appointed;
(c) the preservation of the assets comprised in the estate, especially where minors are entitled; and
(d) the position of the surviving spouse with respect to the administration.

(a) **The machinery for administration**

The administration of the estate under customary law is the exclusive business of the family. It does not normally require the intervention of the court unless there is a dispute as to who is entitled to administer it. Under the general law, however, the estate is administered by the order of Court and in accordance with the rules and directions of Court. Anyone dealing with the estate otherwise than in accordance with the order, rules and directions of Court runs the risk of rendering himself liable.

It is suggested that there should be one common machinery for the administration of estates, namely: the court which includes both the customary and non-customary courts. This would ensure that estates are preserved pending their distribution. More will be said on this point later.

(b) **The recognition accorded to the authority under which the administrator is appointed**

Even where the customary administrator has been appointed by a customary court, the order of court so appointing him does not command the same amount of respect as the letters of administration granted to the administrator under the general law. To the Superior Courts, the order by which the customary court grants administration to the customary administrator is merely "an authority",[64] "power", "grant" (but without the additional words—"of administration") or "judgment."[65] It cannot be invoked in respect of claims arising under the general law, or at any rate, where the claim is regulated by an English statute applying to Nigeria as a statute of general application. This point arose in the case of *Lawal and ors. Ekun and ors.* v. *Younan and ors.*[64] There, the High Court of Western

64. *Lawal and ors.: Ekun and ors.* v. *Younan and ors.* (1959 W.N.L.R. 155 at p. 158

Nigeria held that customary administrators could sue for damages on behalf of the wives and children of two deceased persons under the English Fatal Accidents Act, 1846. This decision was reversed, on appeal, by the Supreme Court.[65] Ademola, C.J.F., delivering the main judgment of the Court, observed: "On the view I have taken of this matter, it is clear that a person to whom power is given under Customary Law to administer the Estate of a deceased person is a person empowered where Customary Law can be invoked, and such a power cannot be extended to matters which are statutory rights under English law and to which statutory remedies apply."[66]

The obvious solution to be recommended for the distinction so sharply drawn between letters of administration and "grants" made by customary courts is to assimilate the latter to the former. All grants of administration, whether made by the High Court or the customary courts should be designated letters of administration; and those granted by the latter courts should be recognised for all purposes in respect of which the existing letters of administration are recognised. Legislation would be the best method of achieving unification on this ponit.

(c) Preservation of the assets comprised in the estate especially where minors are entitled

Under whichever system of law—the general law or the customary law—the estate is administered, the preservation of the estate pending the distribution is regarded as a most important aspect of the administration, since otherwise, there might be precious little left for distribution.

Under the general law, there are fairly stringent rules to ensure that the assets are not wasted or converted by the administrator. Apart from acting under the directions of the Court, he is required to enter into a bond, with a number of suitable sureties, conditioned for his proper administration.[67] He is also required to file the accounts of his administration as often as the Court may direct.[68] He is accountable for wasting the assets or converting same to his own use.[69] and, above all, he is liable to be criminally prosecuted

---

65. Lawal's case (Supreme Court) (1961) All N.L.R. 245 at pp. 252-3; (1961) W.N.L.R. 199 at pp. 202-3. In Idowu and another. v. Adisa and another. (1957) W.N.L.R. 167, Ademola C.J. (Western Nigeria), as he then was, referred to the order of the customary court as "letters of Administration", i.e. letters of administration in inverted commas!.
66. (1961) All N.L.R. at p. 253; (1961) W.N.L.R. at p. 203.
67. The Administration of Estates Law, Cap. 1, s. 31; Order 33, r. 32, High Court (Civil Procedure), cap. 44.
68. Order 33, r. 43, High Court (Civil Procedure) Rules, cap. 44.
69. Cap. 1, s. 19, The Trustee Law, cap. 125, s. 21(1).

under a special provision of the Criminal Code for his conversion of the assets.[70] The customary administrator, on the other hand, is apparently immune from all the obligations and liabilities attaching to the administrator under the general law, with the possible exception that the misappropriation of assets may amount to stealing and attract general criminal liability under the Criminal Code. Under customary law (strict orthodox customary law, at any rate), the real sanction for improper administration is the doubtful intervention of the supernatural powers ascribed to the departed ancestors.[71] That the superior courts are aware of the laxity of the rules governing customary administration is evident in the case of *In re Hotonu*[72], where the old Supreme Court of Lagos refused to insist upon a strict account being rendered by a customary administrator. The Court said: "When the defendant (i.e. the customary administrator) took out letters of administration he states he had in view the discharge of the duties of an administrator from a native point of view and did not contemplate a distribution according to English law."

There is another important point of difference between the general law and the customary law relating to the administration of the estate. This is in connection with the protection of the interests that a minor may have in the estate. Under the general law, if a minor is entitled to any property comprised in the estate, at least two individuals or a trust corporation, with or without an individual, must be appointed to administer the estate.[73] No such rule exists under customary law with the result that wicked uncle, acting as sole administrator, may very well convert to his own use the property to which his minor nephew is entitled without a timely means of checking him.

Suggested solution

In order to protect the rights of those entitled to inherit under customary law, especially where interests of minors are concerned, the rules of the general law designed for the proper administration and preservation of estates, should be extended to include estates administered under customary law. The majority of the people no longer believe that the departed ancestors constitute an effective sanction for the misdeeds of the customary administrator. That once-powerful restraining influence has been on the wane with the

70. Cap. 28, s. 373.
71. Thomas, *Ibo-speaking peoples* (1914), pt. IV (Asaba district) p. 135; Okojie, *Ishan native laws and customs*, pp. 90-92, and 146.
72. Discussed by Stopford, J. G. B., in "Glimpses of native law in West Africa" (1901) 1 J. Roy Afr. Soc. 80 at p. 88.
73. The Administration of Estates Law, cap. 1. s. 24.

advent and spread of the Christian and other religions whose tenets are opposed to the worship of, and belief in, ancestors.

(d) The position of the surviving spouse with respect to the administration

A surviving spouse married under the general law (Christian marriage) has a right to administer the estate of the deceased spouse.[74]   The position of the surviving spouse, especially the wife, under customary law is different. Under no circumstances is a wife married under customary law permitted to administer her deceased husband's estate in her own right.[75] As regards the right of the husband, a distinction is drawn between the deceased wife's post-nuptial property, which he is entitled to administer; and her ante-nuptial property in respect of which he generally has no interest.[76]

The position of a wife married under customary law to a man after the determination of his Christian marriage with another woman

The point considered here may be stated thus: if X marries Y in accordance with Christian rites, and, on the determination of his Christian marriage with Y, marries Z under customary law, what is Z's legal position with respect to the administration of X's estate if she survives X, who dies intestate? The answer to this question is that Z's legal position is enhanced and she is entitled to administer X's estate under the general law.[77] In *Re Adadevoh and others*, [78] the West African Court of Appeal indicated, in the directions remitting the case back to the trial court, that the widow or widows of customary marriages contracted by the deceased after his Christian marriage had been determined would be entitled to share in his estate on proof of the customary marriages. The Ghana case of *Shang* v. *Coleman*[77] has now put the matter beyond doubt. There the Privy Council affirmed the decision of the Ghana Court of Appeal recognizing the right of a widow of a customary marriage to the grant of administration of the estate of her husband who had married her after the determination of his prior marriage under the Ghana Marriage Ordinance.

---

74. Cap. 1, s. 26(1) (b).
75. *Aileru and ors.* v. *Anibi* (1952) 20 N.L.R. 46.
76. *Uwugege* v. *Adigwe and other* (1934) 11 N.L.R. 134.
77. *Shang* v. *Coleman* (1959) Ghana Law Reports, 309, [1961] 2 All E.R. 406, [1961] A.C. 481—P.C.
78. (1951) 13 W.A.C.A. 304 at p. 311, overruling its earlier decision in *Re Somefun* (1941) 7 W.A.C.A. 156, on this as well as on another point.

It may be open to some doubt whether it was ever the intention of the legislature to benefit the widow of a customary marriage in this way. It cannot, however, be doubted that these decisions must be greeted as valiant attempts at judicial manipulation which constitutes one of the methods of integrating the law. It is suggested that a surviving husband in similar circumstances should be treated in the same way on the ground that what is sauce for the goose is sauce for the gander.

Suggestion

The customary rules precluding a surviving spouse from administering the estate of the deceased spouse should be modified so as to bring them in line with the position under the general law. This may appear to be a revolutionary step in view of some of the incidents of customary marriage which assign a rather lowly position to the wife.

In practice, however, the suggestion does not appear to be a startling one. Under customary law, widows sometimes administer estates on behalf of their young children. The only likely problem is where the deceased is survived by a good number of wives. Here, one of the wives, preferably the senior wife, could be appointed administratrix (to represent the interests of the other wives) jointly with the children or relatives of the deceased.

In view of the judicial decisions standing in the way of the recommended solution, the suggested change should be brought about by legislation. Before this is done, however, the people must be educated on the requirements of contemporary society with its stress on the emancipation of women.

3. Intestate succession

The rules governing devolution upon intestacy which are selected for consideration with respect to their integration are those relating to the inheritance rights of the following perhaps:-

(a) Children;
(b) Surviving spouse or spouses (wives); and
(c) Members of the extended family.

(a) Children

Under both systems of law, the children of a deceased person inherit his or her property. But while they inherit in equal shares under the general law,[79] their shares under customary law are

---

79. The Administration of Estates Law, cap. 1, s. 49 (5)

neither equal nor, indeed, fixed. Again, under the Ishan system which also governs succession to the holders of hereditary titles among the Bini, the eldest surviving son takes all the property, with a moral, not legal obligation to give some part of the inherited property to the younger children.[80] Finally, while the children (and the surviving spouse) inherit to the exclusion of other classes of relatives under the general law, the rules of the customary law also permit other classes of relatives—brothers, sisters, nephews, nieces, and cousins several times removed—to share the inheritance with the children, who however, take the lion's share. Daughters in some systems receive smaller shares than those given to sons.

In order to achieve uniformity in the divergent rules of both systems in respect of the inheritance rights of children, the rules of the customary law relating the quantum of shares should be modified so that all children take equally irrespective of age and sex. Under traditional customary law, the eldest son took a disproportionately large share of the estate on the grounds that he was charged with the performance of certain ritual functions; and he helped to maintain the other children. Under modern conditions, there exists little or no justification for his receiving such share, and equality should be the guiding principle.

(b) The surviving spouse or spouses (wives)

Under the general law, if the intestate leaves a surviving spouse and issue, the surviving spouse takes the *personal chattels*[81] absolutely, together with a sum equal to one-third of the residuary estate free of costs, charged on the residuary estate with interest at £2½ per cent per annum from the date of death until the date of payment. In addition, the surviving spouse takes a life interest in one-third of the residuary estate.[82]

If the intestate leaves no issue but leaves a surviving spouse, a parent, a brother or sister of the whole blood or issue of a brother or sister of the whole blood, the surviving spouse takes on the lines indicated above, save that he or she is in this case entitled to a sum

---

80.   *Ehigie* v. *Ehigie* (1961) All N.L.R. 842 at 845; (1961) W.N.L.R. 307 at 309; Okojie, *Ishan native laws and customs* (1960) p. 90; Egharevba, J. U., *Benin law and custom* (1949) pp. 37-8.

81.   *Loc. cit.* The definition of *personal chattels* contained in s. 2 of the Law comprises a long list of things, instruments and apparatuses. Briefly, however, it includes indoor and outdoor furniture and effects also motor cars, jewelry, plate, books and consumable stores, but does not include chattles used for business purposes or money, or securities for money. See *Parry, The law of succession*, 4th edn. (1961), p. 151.

82.   The Administration of Estates Law, *op. cit.* s. 49(1)(i)(2).

equal to two-thirds of the residuary estate; and, in addition, one-half of the residuary estate is held in trust for him or her.[83]

Where, however, the intestate leaves surviving spouses and there are no issue, no parent or brother or sister of the whole blood or issue of such brother or sister, the residuary estate is held in trust for the surviving spouse absolutely.[84]

Under customary law, a surviving wife is not entitled to inherit anything from her deceased husband.[85] A surviving husband may inherit his deceased wife's post-nuptial property in default of children.[86]

Here, again, the rules of the customary law regarding the rights of the surviving spouse should be brought in line with those under the general law. Under most of the existing systems of customary law, the surviving husband's inheritance rights in respect of his deceased wife's post-nuptial property are generally recognised. It is only a short step towards the mutual recognition of each spouse's rights of inheritance in respect of the other's property. The recognition of the wife's inheritance rights in respect of her deceased husband's estate is bound to be more difficult than that of the rights of the husband since customary law assigns a position of inferiority to the wife. The death of her husband does not terminate the marriage, and the authority which her husband formerly exercised over her may be taken over by his kinsman. Nevertheless, the fact that this practice popularly termed widow inheritance, is now increasingly disregarded[87] would suggest that the suggested change might be now more easily effected. Another factor which would help in bringing about the suggested change is the fact that husbands usually make *inter vivos* gifts of some of their property to their wives.

However revolutionary the notion of a wife inheriting her husband's property under customary law may appear, it has one merit. It recognises the contemporary conception of the family as primarily consisting of a man, his wife and children rather than the extended family based on the agnatic system of old.

(c) Members of the extended family

Under both systems of law, some members of the extended family, such as brothers and sisters, etc., may inherit the estate of a deceased

---

83. Ibid., s. 49 (1) (i) (3).
84. Ibid., s. 49(1)(i)(1).
85. *Caulcrick* v. *Doherty* (1926) 7 N.L.R. 48; *Sogunro-Davies* v. *Sogunro and ors.* (1929) 7 N.L.R. 79; *Suberu* v. *Somonu* (1957) II F.S.C. 33.
86. *Nwugege* v. *Adigwe and anor.* (1934) 11 N.L.R. 134.
87. Esenwa, F. E. "Marriage customs in Asaba Division", (1948) XIII Nigerian Field 71 at p. 74; Okojie, *op. cit.* p. 102.

member. But while under the general law these members inherit only in default of children or classes of persons specified in the order of preference laid down, under most of the customary systems of law found in the Region, these members inherit jointly with the children who, however, take the bulk of the estate. Again, while parents and grand-parents may inherit under the general law where there are no closer relatives, they are normally excluded from the inheritance under customary law, the rule being that relatives older than the deceased should not benefit from his estate unless there are no surviving younger relatives.

(i) The integrated law relating to intestate succession Underlying principle—Striking a balance between the rights of the immediate family and the claims of the extended family

Under the general law governing succession on intestacy, the principal beneficiaries of a deceased person are his or her children and his wife or her husband. The rules of the customary law with regard to the inheritance rights of children have changed or are changing in the direction of the general law, the rights of the surviving spouse under customary law remaining comparatively unchanged.

On the other hand, the strict traditional rules of the customary law made the brothers and sisters of the deceased the principal beneficiaries; the children enjoying, at the most the right to be maintained by the brothers and sisters who took. This was not surprising. The old agnatic system was based on age and on the fact that the extended family was both a social and economic unit. In the past men married late and had a shorter expectation of life. Consequently, when they died before their children grew up, a younger brother was nearly always preferred in the scheme of inheritance to the young and inexperienced children of the deceased.

Today, all this has changed. Men now marry younger and live longer; children usually attain the age of discretion and acquire the necessary experience with respect to the management of their own affairs (assisted, if need be by their now assertive mothers) long before their fathers die.[88] The customary rules have therefore changed or are still changing; and the benefits of inheritance are no longer being dispersed among the members of the extended family, but are gradually being concentrated on the children of the deceased.

But though the stress is now on the rights of the immediate

---

88. Lloyd, "Yoruba rules of succession" (1959) J.A.L. 7 at p. 14; Lloyd, *Yoruba land law* (1962) pp. 284-5.

family, yet it would not be entirely correct to say that the claims of the extended family have been or should be wiped out completely. This latter unit still plays an important role in the life of a man in the modern society. This can be easily seen in the parental responsibility sometimes assumed by a brother of the deceased in respect of the orphaned children left by the dead man. In the words of Ames, J., in *In re Agboruja:*[89] "When there are minor children it means that the father's heir becomes their new father. This is a relationship and the new fathers regard the children as their own children."[90] A good many of the educated men in Nigeria today were sent to universities through the concerted effort and sacrifice of their brothers and sisters, uncles and aunts and other kinsmen; and thousands are still today studying at universities, at home and abroad, as "extended family" scholars.

The foregoing account at once reveals the conflict between the rights of the immediate family and the claims of the extended family. The interests of one group have received higher recognition under the general law as well as under the changed and changing rules of the customary law; those of the other group have been placed in the background under the general law, and are being assailed under the changed and changing rules of the customary law. In these circumstances, the primary functions of the integrated law governing intestate succession—indeed, this should be the funcion of every law —is to ensure that these conflicting interests are reconciled and adjusted in such a manner that the goods of existence are made to go round with the least possible friction—social engineering.[91]

MODEL SCHEME OF DISTRIBUTION

A model scheme of distribution applicable to all persons (irrespective of tribal affiliation or the system of law under which a marriage was contracted), comprising elements drawn from both the existing general law and the customary law and designed to harmonize the conflicting claims of the immediate family and the extended family, appears hereunder.

There are two parts—A and B—reflecting the composition of the family in the two senses in which the word is used. Parents and grandparents are however grouped with the biological family in order to give them inheritance rights before the other members of the

89. (1949) 19. N.L.R. 39.
90. *Ibid.*
91. Pound, "The theory of social interests" in Papers and Proceedings of the American Sociology Society, May, 1961, quoted in *Hall's Readings in Jurisprudence*, p. 245.

extended family. This has been done in order to eliminate the problem of unwanted old people, in view of the almost complete lack of social or welfare services catering for old people in the society today. Also, as jobs and trade take people out of their local areas to other and more distant parts of the country or to other countries, those formerly responsible for providing for aged parents might not be in a position to do so today.

Under this model scheme of distribution, the estate is divided into two parts, the members of the immediate family (and parents and grandparents) share the larger part, while the extended family share the smaller part. This will ensure the continued solidarity of the family as understood by the African.

PART A

Husband or Wife, Children, Parents and Grandparents

(i) One-fifth of this part of the estate goes to the husband or wife for life, the reversion going to the children who share equally. Where a husband is survived by more than one wife (customary widows), they take equally the one-fifth share.

(ii) One-tenth of this part of the estate goes to any surviving parents and grandparents in equal shares for life, the children taking the reversion as in (i) above.

(iii) The children take seven-tenths of this part of the estate in equal shares, together with the reversion as to one-fifth and one-tenth specified in (i) and (ii) respectively, which they also share equally.

(iv) If the intestate leaves only children and no husband or wife, no parents or grandparents, the children share this part of the estate equally.

(v) If the intestate leaves a husband or wife, parents or grandparents but no children, the issue of any children pre-deceasing the intestate shall take on the principle of representation i.e. *per stirpes;* and the same principle of representation shall be observed where the intestate leaves children, but some of his children had pre-deceased him.

(vi) Where the intestate leaves a husband or wife, a parent or grandparents, but no children or the issue of children, the seventh-tenth of this part of the estate which should have gone to the children or their issue had they survive dthe intestate, shall be distributed among the classes of persons specified in Part B of this scheme or table, and in accordance with the provisions contained therein.

(vii) If the intestate leaves a husband or a wife, but no children, and no parents or grandparents, then the one-tenth share the parents should have taken had they survived the intestate shall fall to be distributed among the classes of person specified in Part B of this schedule or table, and in accordance with the provisions contained therein.

(viii) If the intestate leaves no husband or wife, no children, no parent and no grandparents, this part of the estate shall be distributed among the classes of persons specified in Part B of this scheme or table, and in accordance with the provisions contained therein.

PART B

Brothers and Sisters, Uncles and Aunts, and Nephews and Nieces

(i) Two-thirds of this part of the estate shall go to the brothers and sisters in equal shares.

(ii) One-third of this part of the estate shall go to the uncles and aunts, and nephews and nieces in equal shares.

(iii) The principle of representation, i.e. division *per stirpes*, shall apply so that the children (not issue of these children) shall take equally among themselves in the event of their parents predeceasing the intestate.

(iv) In default of any class or classes of the persons specified in (i) and (ii) under this part of the scheme or table, the interests which such defaulting class or classes of persons should have taken had they survived the intestate shall be distributed among the surviving class or classes in the manner specified under (i) and (ii) and (iii) of this part of the scheme or table.

(v) In default of all the classes of persons and their children taking under this Part of the scheme or table this part of the estate shall go to the children of the intestate or the issue of such children in the manner provided in Part A of this scheme or table.

(vi) In default of children of the intestate or the issue of such children, this part of the estate as well as any part of the estate falling to be distributed in accordance with the provisions of this Part of the scheme or table shall belong to the head of the intestate's family.

(iii) Ratio in which the estate should be divided between the immediate family and the extended family

The ratio in which the estate is divided between members of the immediate family, on the one hand, and those of the extended family, on the other, will be determined largely by the ultimate objective of the policy pursued by the government. Be that as it may, it is essential that the assessment of the ratio should only be determined after some investigation of the conditions existing in the society. For example, it is desirable to find out what proportion of the people are married under the general law, and whose intestate succession would be governed by the general law; and what proportion are married under the customary law, and whose intestate succession would be governed by the rules of the customary law. It is, however, not possible to fix a ratio valid for all times. Society is in a state of flux, and a ratio which is considered sensible today may be rendered meaningless within a few years by a change in the marriage pattern on which the earlier ratio was based.

At the moment, the review may be hazarded that the majority of the people still contract customary unions,[92] hence more intestate estates would devolve in accordance with the provisions of the customary law. On the other hand, the conditions of modern society require that the emphasis in succession matters should shift from the extended family to the immediate family. A ratio of something in the region of 4:1 may be considered as an equitable adjustment of the interest of the biological family, on the one hand, and the claims of the extended family on the other. This means that while some four-fifths of the estate would be distributed among the members of the immediate family (parents and grandparents are included in this group in our suggested scheme), one-fifth would go to the members of the extended family.

4. Wills
(a) The general law

The general law governing wills is, of course, contained in the Wills Law[93] which is based on three relevant English statutes. These are the Wills Act, 1837; the Wills Act Amendment Act, 1852, and the Wills (Soldiers and Sailors) Act, 1918. There are, however, two original provisions in the Wills Law which are designed to give recognition to some of the rules of the customary law. The first excludes from the category of "disposable property" an estate (real and personal) which cannot be affected by testamentary disposition under customary law;[94] the second excludes a customary union from the definition of a marriage that may revoke a will.[95]

92. See Callow, J.'s, dictum in *Phillip* v. *Phillip* (1946) 18 N.L.R. 102 at 103.
93. Cap. 133.
94. *Ibid;* s. 3(1).
95. *Ibid.,* s. 15

(i) **When is the general law applicable?**

It should be emphasized that the general law relating to Wills (the Wills Law) applies in all cases where a testator makes a will in writing notwithstanding that he had not contracted a Christian or monogamous marriage;[96] and notwithstanding that his intestate estate would therefore, have devolved in accordance with the provisions of some system of law—Moslem law or customary law in its narrow meaning[97]—differing from the general law.[98] Thus in *Apatira and another* v. *Akanke and others*,[99] Ames, J., said, *inter alia:* "The fact that the deceased was a Nigerian and a Mohammedan cannot make any difference to the necessity of complying with the requirements of the Wills Acts."[100]

(ii) **Requirements of a valid will**

The Wills Law contains provisions similar to the relevant English Wills Acts with regard to:-

(a) disposable property;[101]
(b) the capacity of the testator;[102] and
(c) writing, signature and attestation.[103]

(b) **The customary will: Usual features**

The usual features of a customary will are that:

(i) it is oral;
(ii) It is a wish made with due publicity, in the presence of witnesses, often as a "death-bed" declaration; and
(iii) it takes effect only with the general consent of the deceased's family.

The last requirement of the customary will—its taking effect with the consent of the family—may well constitute a stumbling block to its enforceability; and, indeed, raises the question as to whether it is ever possible for a man to make a valid and enforceable will under customary law. One result of the far-reaching requirements of the customary law in this regard has been to discourage the practice of making customary wills, and to render meaningless the

---

96. *Apatira & anor.* v. *Akanke & ors.* (1944) 17 N.L.R. 149; *Onwudinjoh* v. *Onwudinjoh* (1957) II E.R.N.L.R. 1; *Nelson and ors.* v. *Akorifanmi* (1959) N.L.R. 143.
97. In its narrow meaning because customary law includes Moslem law. See the Native Courts Law (Northern Region), No. 6 of 1956, s. 2
98. (1944) 17 N.L.R. 149.
99. (1944) 17 N.L.R. 149.
100. *Ibid.*, at p. 151.
101. Cap. 133, s. 3,
102. *Ibid.*, s. 5.
103. *Ibid.*, s. 6.

distinction between testacy and intestacy under customary law.[104]
A man's last will and testament under customary law tends invariably
to be that his property shall be distributed by his administrator in
accordance with the provisions of the customary law relating to
intestacy well known to him and all men.[104] As an eminent writer
put it: "There is accordingly no need to divide the customary rules
of inheritance into testate and intestate . . . "[105]

(iv)   The effect of reducing a customary will into writing

With the spread of literacy, the practice has grown up whereby
the terms of the traditional oral or nuncupative will are sometimes
reduced into writing. The idea behind such a practice may be the
clarification of the wishes of the deceased which, despite the form in
which they have been expressed, are not likely to differ in substance
from the customary rules observed in the distribution of intestate
estates. The effect of such writing, however, is an entirely different
matter; and the view has been that the use of writing in the making
of a customary will takes the document out of the realm of customary
law, and the question as to its validity and enforceability are to be
decided in accordance with the provisions of the general law relating
to wills.

(c)   The Wills Law: Necessity for its observance of some of the stringent but, perhaps, desirable requirements of the customary law

It may be questioned whether some of the requirements of the
customary will are not hopelessly out of touch with the conditions of
modern life, having regard to the modern trend towards the
individualization of property; and the freedom of the individual in
the alienation of his private or self-acquired property. Against this
view, however, must be set the equally weighty reason why some
restrictions (such as those imposed by the customary law) should not
be placed on the testamentary powers of a man to leave away all his
property or the bulk of it from his family (especially the biological
family) whom the law required him to provide for while he was alive.

Suggestions

The Wills Law should be amended so as to ensure that it adheres
to the following rules of the customary law:

104.   Lloyd, P. C., "Some notes on the Yoruba rules of succession" (1959)
       Journal of African Law, 7 at pp. 17-18; Lloyd, *Yoruba land law*, 1962,
       p. 290. See page 37n.
105.   Elias, T. O., *Groundwork of Nigerian law*, 1953, p. 337; Elias, *Nigerian
       Land Law and custom*, 1962, (3rd edition). p. 228.

(i) S.3 of the Law empowering a testator to dispose of all his real and personal estate should be amended so that the major part of the estate—say, four-fifths—shall not be left away from the members of the immediate family (we include parents and grandparents in this group) without their consent.

(ii) The Wills Law nowhere prescribes the language (English, Yoruba, Bini) that a testator should use in expressing his intention. This would mean that any language may be used. This should be expressly provided in the law so that people literate in a language other than English might employ that other language.

(iii) The requirement as to writing contained in section 6 of the Law should be qualified so as to admit as a will, a "death-bed" declaration on satisfactory proof of the circumstances necessitating such a "death-bed" declaration.

(d) Some of the obstacles to the making of wills

The practice of making written wills has not been a popular one. This must have been due to some extent, to the fact that customary wills were almost invariably oral. With the rising general standards of education, it is hoped that people would be able and willing to make written wills.

One of the greatest obstacles to the making of wills, however, has been the belief that some causal connection exists between the making of a will and the occurrence or, indeed, the hastening of death. As late as the year 1946, this belief was still popular, and a writer observed: "At present people are unwilling to do so (i.e. to make wills) partly because of a superstitious fear that such an action would somehow hasten death."[106] In this regard, the story is worth telling of a rich, old and illiterate man in the Region who caused his customary will to be reduced into writing by a school-boy specially engaged for the purpose. The latter had, so he thought, completed his task when the old man requested that a rather important provision which had escaped him (the old man) should be inserted in the document. And what was this rather important provision? It was no other than (in the words of the school-boy) "Not that I am going to die but for a remembrance."

106. Childs, S. H., "Christian marriage in Nigeria," (1946) 16 Africa 238 at p. 246.

THE LAW OF SUCCESSION IN GHANA

by

HON. N. A. OLLENNU

JUSTICE OF THE SUPREME COURT OF GHANA

THE LAW OF SUCCESSION IN GHANA

In Ghana as in every other country, the law of succession is part of the personal law. Its application is now regulated by Section 66 sub-section (1) Rules 4, 5 and 6, and sub-section 3(a) of the Courts Act, 1960 (C.A. 9). A brief history of the development of the judicial and legal systems is necessary for a full understanding of that law and the proper application of its rules.

As in many other countries in Africa, there was originally no central government or judicial organ prior to the time when Britain assumed administrative control. In Ghana we may say the period of assumption of administrative and judicial control of the country by the British began roughly between 1830 and 1844. Before that period the natural rulers, that is, the Chiefs and elders of each tribe constituted a council which in addition to general administration carried out the judicial functions of the state. Usually when sitting purely as a judicial body, they were known as Native Tribunals. This name was changed by amendments to Native Court Acts. At present the court that has assumed most of the powers and juris- diction of that body is called a Local Court; it first acquired that name under the Local Courts Act, 1958 (No. 23); and it is so known under the Courts Act, 1960 (C.A.9) which consolidated and re-enacted in substance, the essential features of all the laws which, prior to July 1, 1960, provided for the administration of justice in the land. The enactment so consolidated are the Courts Ordinance (Cap.4) as subsequently amended, the Court of Appeal Ordinance 1957, the Commissioner of Assize and Civil Pleas Act, 1958, and the Local Courts Act, 1958 as subsequently amended, all of which were repealed by the Courts Act 1960 (C.A.9). We shall for convenience refer to the tribunal of the aboriginal rulers and its successor, the Native Court, simply as Local Court.

Each Local Court enjoyed sovereign rights, but its jurisdiction was limited in certain respects, firstly as regards the territorial limit of its authority; secondly as to the law it administered which is the customary law existing within the area of its jurisdiction; and thirdly as regards persons, namely persons of African descent "whose mode of life is that of the general community". When the Local Court first came to be recognised by enactment, its jurisdiction was limited, as far as personal suits were concerned, to claims for debt or damage not exceeding £100 and in criminal cases, to petty offences. Regarding persons, its jurisdiction was extended to include "persons whether of African or non-African descent who have at any time instituted proceedings in any Native Court". As regards the law, there was included in its jurisdiction any law binding between parties who were subject to the jurisdiction of the Local Court, and also "English law", where it shall appear that the parties either by express contract or from the nature of the trans-action out of which the cause or matter may have arisen have agreed that their obligation arising out of such transaction should be regulated by "English law".[1]

The jurisdiction of the Local Court under both the Local Courts Act, 1958 and the Courts Act, 1960 as regards persons is unrestricted. But while the Local Court prior to 1960 had unlimited jurisdiction in land suit and in succession suit, the Local Court under the Courts Act, 1960 as amended, has no jurisdiction in land and succession suits relating to land, the value of which in either case exceeds £200.[2]

Between 1830 and 1844, one Captain Maclean, appointed by the Committee of Merchants in London which administered the Government of the Gold Coast, began to exercise jurisdiction over the people, irregular though it was, partly through persuasion of the Chiefs and their people, and eventually upon the authority of treaties and bonds entered into with the Chiefs and elders of some of the tribes.[3] Maclean exercised jurisdiction in two capacities; one as a Magistrate or Commissioner of the Peace within the British ports, and the other as an Assessor, an Assistant or Adviser to the Chiefs and elders in exercising their aboriginal judicial functions. This exercise of the function of Judicial Assessor later received statutory sanction from the British Government under Imperial Statutes 6 & 7 Vic. C 13, and 6 & 7 Vic. C 94 respectively, entitled "An Act to enable Her Majesty to provide for the Government of Her Settlements on the Coast of Africa and in the Falkland Islands" and "An Act to remove doubts as to the exercise of power and jurisdiction by Her Majesty within divers countries and places out of Her Majesty's dominion, and render the same effectual". By

---

1. See *The Native Jurisdiction Ordinance*, 1888 sections 10 and 11. *The Native Administration Ordinance*, 1927. sections 43 and 44. *The Native Administration (Togoland, Southern Section) Ordinance*, 1932 sections 43 and 46. *The Native Courts (Ashanti) Ordinance*, 1935 sections 7 and 8. *The Native Courts (Colony) Ordinance*, cap. 98 (1951 Rev.) sections 10, 11, 13 and 15. *The Native Courts (Southern Section of Togoland) Ordinance*, Cap. 106 (1951 Rev.) sections 10, 11, and 15.
2. Section 98 of the Courts Act, 1960 (C.A. 9) as amended by section 27 of Act 130.
3. See for example, the Bond of 1844, March 6, 1844, reproduced in Sar F. C.L. (1897) 263.

section 9 of "The Supreme Court of Her Majesty's Forts and Settlements on the Gold Coast, Act 1853", the "Judicial Assessor" described as "Assistant to the Native Sovereigns and Chiefs, Magistrate of the countries adjacent to Her Majesty's Forts and Settlements on the Gold Coast", was appointed Chief Justice. The office of Judicial Assessor continued until 1876 when it was abolished by the Supreme Courts Ordinance, 1876, and its jurisdiction vested in the Supreme Court created by that Ordinance.

At first the duty of advising the Chiefs in the Local Courts was the most important of the duties of the Judicial Assessor; he advised them on matters of procedure and evidence, and especially about customs which were contrary to natural justice and equity in the broad sense, and good conscience which should be discarded. Ultimately his judicial duties as Magistrate or Commissioner of the Peace holding commission from the British Crown took precedence over the advisory duties, and instead of advising the Chiefs and elders in their judicial functions, he had the Chiefs and elders as advisers to him in his court on customary law.   One of the Judicial Assessors, Sir James Marshall (Judicial Assessor 1873-1874) described his duties as follows:-

> "As Judicial Assessor I was a sort of head Chief and sat with the local Chief in Court, hearing cases brought by natives among themselves."

By this means the Judicial Assessor did a great deal to help mould the customary law and to systematise the practice and procedure of customary law, and thereby lay the foundation for bringing out the best in the customary law of the tribes among whom he worked; and above all he produced the first written records of cases on customary law. Sarbah, a celebrated Ghanaian jurist, the centenary of whose birth was celebrated on June 3, 1964, who was called to the English Bar in 1887 and practised up to the date of his death— November 27, 1910, paid tribute to the work of the Judicial Assessor as follows:-

> "By reason of his office, and being in close touch with the Chiefs and leading men, the Judicial Assessor made his influence for good felt. For, as Cruickshank explains, the Court played a most important part in effecting useful reforms. It became a species of lecture-room, from which the principles of justice were disseminated far and wide throughout the country whilst Maclean was in office. It was daily crowded by listeners from even the most distant districts. The presence of the Chiefs, who were constantly surrounded by a large body of retainers, gave greater publicity to the doctrines inculcated by the free access of

all classes to a knowledge of sentiments which influenced the Government. The Chief then learnt that an injustice done in his judicial capacity would recoil on himself; the master, that he owed duties to his slave, the neglect of which, or an undue severity, would lead to the slave's unconditional emancipation. In a word, the Court served admirably the purpose of a pole to indicate the extent of the reformation which the country was at any time capable of bearing, consistent with the degree of confidence in the Government, without which no progress in Government could be general."[4]

As far back as 1843, the British Government accepted in principle that Judges, Magistrates, Assessors and other officers who exercised jurisdiction in this country on behalf of the Queen, should observe these local customs where they may be compatible with the principles of the law of England, but in default of such custom they should proceed in all things as nearly as may be according to the law of England.[5]

The Supreme Court Ordinance, 1876 which abolished the office of Judicial Assessor, gave the Supreme Court unlimited jurisdiction as regards persons, subject-matter and law to be administered, and made it obligatory upon the Supreme Court to administer customary law in "matters relating to marriage and to tenure and transfer of real property and personal property and to inheritance and testamentary disposition."[6] This provision was re-enacted in 1935.[7] To assist the Judge of the Supreme Court to administer customary law in those special subjects, Section 74 of the Court Ordinance gave him power to invite one or more Chiefs or other persons conversant with the customary law, to act as referees and to assist him in trying any such case. This provision was re-enacted in 1935.[8] It was however repealed in 1944, and a new provision was enacted empowering the Land Court created by the Courts (Amendment) Ordinance No. 23 of 1944, to try a land cause such cause to be tried by the Land Judge with the aid of Assessors. Moreover, powers were given to the Divisional Court of the Supreme Court, and the Magistrate's Court to refer any question of "native law and custom" which may arise in a civil cause or matter, to a Local Court for

4. Journal of the African Society 1909-1910, 349 at p. 356.
5. See Order-In-Council of September 3, 1844.
6. S. 19 of the Supreme Court Ordinance 1876.
7. S. 87 of the Courts Ordinacen, Cap. 4, 1951 Rev.
8. S. 87 of the Courts Ordinance, Cap. 4, 1936 ed.

determination, and the Local Court to report its decision to the Court which referred the matter to it.[9]

The power to refer a point of customary law to the Local Court to decide and report thereon was used by the Divisional Court more in succession suits than in any other case. The court had a discretion to accept the decision of the Local Court, as it did in *Emmanuel W. K. Tamakloe* v. *Attipoe & Anor.*[10] to reject in whole,[11] or in part.[12]

Another important aspect of the Courts Ordinance as far as cases involving customary law are concerned is prohibition of a court to exercise its jurisdiction in a case which is properly cognizable by a Local Court[13] and the provisions in the various Local Courts Ordinances or Acts, making it mandatory upon a court to stop the hearing of any such case before it and refer the parties to the competent Local Court.[14] This provision has now been modified by Section 132 of the Courts Act, 1960, as amended by Section 37 of Act 130, and the High Court, the Circuit Court or the District Court may now remit a case to the Local Court instead of stopping its progress and referring the parties to the Local Court.

Prior to July 1, 1960, a sharp distinction was drawn between courts in the English system and the Local Court, the courts in the English system administering the customary law as at first instance or on appeal from decision of a Local Court.

The customary law was regarded as foreign law by the courts in the English system, and therefore had to be proved by evidence of expert witnesses.[15] In the Local Court, it is not foreign law, but the indigenous law, and the Chief and elders are deemed the repositories thereof. Therefore decisions of the highest Local Court are authoritative and binding even upon the highest court in the English system unless it is shown to be repugnant to natural justice, equity and good conscience. We must observe that the existence of a previous decision to the contrary given by a superior court is not enough justification for rejecting the opinion of a Local Court on a point of customary law. If it can be shown that the previous decision made by the superior court is based upon evidence which is not authoritative, or upon wrong inference drawn from evid nce of the custom, the opinion of the Local Court should not

---

9. S. 89 of the Courts Ordinance, Cap. 4, 1951 Rev.
10. Suit No. 78/44.
11. *Jones Nelson* v. *Ocansey & Tackie* W.AC.A., March 11 1950 unreported.
12. *Sackeyfio* v. *Tagoe* 11 W.A.C.A. 73.
13. S. 18, Courts Ordinance, Cap. 4, 1951 Rev.
14. S. 58, Native Courts (Colony) Ordinance, Cap. 98, 1951 Rev.
15. *Binba* v. *Mensah* (1897) Sar. F.C.L., 137, *Hughes* v. *Davies* (1909) Ren. 550.

be rejected. Proof of custom before a court in the English system is regulated by all the rules of procedure and evidence, e.g. pleading the specific custom if it is relied upon, to make it an issue for trial. Evidence of tradition of the family is received as exception to the hearsay rule. In the proof of the customary law treatise and text-books on the subject are always of great assistance in testing their suitability for retention as part of the law of the land.

Any particular customary law which has been proved so often by a Local Court or proved many times before a court, and has been accepted as having passed the test of repugnancy requires no further proof, for it becomes part of the law of the land which may be cited to a court as case law and a legal authority.

The Privy Council in *Angu* v. *Attah*[16] summed up this principle as follows:-

> "As in the case of all customary law, it has to be proved in the first instance by calling witnesses acquainted with the native custom until the particular customs have, by constant proof in the Courts, become so notorious that the Courts will take judicial notice of them."

Another test which the courts in the English system have applied to establish that native custom qualifies for acceptance, is that it must be shown to have existed and to have generally been accepted among the community of a locality as binding. It is not enough to show that it is a practice which has sprung up within recent years for the convenience of some sections or families in the community,[17] at the same time it need not be shown to have existed from time immemorial in the English sense.[18] That is a modification to suit local conditions since writing was unknown in customary law. But the memory of man as to tradition may not extend beyond two or three generations, i.e. to the custom as narrated by the grand-father or the great grand-father. There are other respects in which English law has influenced customary law.

A Local Court established under the Courts Act, 1960 is presided over by a lay magistrate; no special qualification is prescribed for this office, and there is no guarantee that as in the case of members of the former Local Courts, the lay magistrate has any special knowledge of the customary law. Besides the customary law is no longer a question of fact, it is a question of law for the court.[19] We shall revert to this point at a later stage.

From the time of the Judicial Assessors up to now, a large body

16. [1916] P.C. '76-'28, 43 at 44.
17. *Welbeck v. Brown* (1897) Sar. F.C.L. 188.
18. *Golightly v. Ashrifi* 14 W.A.C.A. 676.
19. Courts Act, 1960, s.67 (1).

of case law has been built upon the law of succession, all of which have passed tests applied by the rules of procedure and evidence either strictly according to English rules and regulations, or special rules and regulations of procedure as near as possible to the English rules.

Now basically, the customary law is a usage or custom which exists in a particular locality or community and is accepted as binding upon the people of that community. From the decisions on these customary laws, certain important basic principles emerge. The first of these is that some of the customs exist in the same form as in many localities and have a lot in common. The next point is that the real unit of Ghanaian society is the family, and that Ghanaian society is communal, not individualistic or communistic. In such a society the individual is not only expected but is also inspired to employ his physical and mental faculties to make achievements which will eventually enure to the benefit of his family and the general progress of the community. By this concept the individual and all he acquires are property of his family with this significant qualification: that is when he is of age and is possessed of his full mental capacities the family allow him complete dominion and control of himself and his self-acquired property; he has full liberty to alienate any self-acquired property in any manner during his lifetime, subject to certain conditions. These conditions are intended mainly for the protection of the purchaser or grantee from him. He can also make any testamentary disposition which should take effect after his death, and to do so according to the law of the land. But the moment he dies or becomes incapacitated by insanity or otherwise and so unable to exercise such functions, the family will then assert control over his person (including his corpse in case of death) and over any property acquired by him which has not been disposed of previously. In short then the general principle is that upon a person's death intestate, any self-acquired property of which he was possessed, vests in his family, and he is succeeded by his family as a whole.[20]

Another principle which emerges from the case law of succession is that for purposes of succession, Ghana is divided into two main classes with regard to members of a family which succeeds upon intestacy. These are (i) the matrilineal, that is, the family of blood connection, a group of persons each of whom traces descent in the direct female line from a common remote ancestress;[21] and (ii) the

20. *Pappoe v. Wingrove* (1922) 1921-25 Div. Ct. 2. *Captain v. Ankrah*, 13 W.A.C.A. 151; *Akwei v. Deedei & anor.* 3 WALR. 132. *Okoe v. Ankrah* (1961) P.C.L.L. G., 245.
21. *Amarfio v. Ayorkor* 14 W.A.C.A. 554.

patrilineal, that is, the spiritual personality, (and this) consists of a group of persons all of whom trace descent in the direct male line from a common remote ancestor.[22]

Another principle of general application is that when the family succeed they appoint one of their number who is considered worthy, to take charge of the property and administer it for the benefit, principally, of those nearest in relation to the deceased. The person so appointed is called the successor. Closely connected with this matter is the principle that no person has an inherent right to be appointed a successor, though a person may belong to a group or class of persons out of whom a successor may be appointed.[23]

But while there are a lot of customary laws peculiar to various tribes which are shown to be common, others are known to conflict, while even among those which apply universally or to more than one community, local variations exist which may amount to internal conflict. However, except to a very limited extent, as we shall see presently, there are no principles regulating internal conflicts in the laws of Ghana.

Of course, succession in Ghana is not regulated solely by customary law. In two instances, it is regulated either entirely by laws other than customary law, or by the customary law in conjunction with other law or laws. Again although succession is not regulated by a person's religion, yet under one particular enactment a person's religious persuasion is taken into consideration in determining the succession of his estate. We shall consider each of these enactments very briefly.

The first enactment in point is the Marriage Ordinance.[24] Section 48 of this ordinance provides that upon the death intestate of a person who was married under the ordinance or who is issue of such a marriage, self-acquired property shall be distributed or descend as to: "two-thirds in accordance with the law of England relating to the distribution of personal estate, and as to one-third in accordance with customary law."

When this ordinance was originally passed in 1884, it provided that English law should apply to the whole of the estate of an intestate who married under the ordinance or who was the issue of such a marriage.[25] That provision must have been influenced by the false interpretation which foreigners placed upon succession by the family. For example Bosman describing the customary law of

22. *Carboo v. Carboo* H. Ct. Feb. 3, 1961 unreported.
23. *Mankata v. Ahorli & Ors.*, 1 W.A.L.R., 169.
24. Cap. 127, 1951 Rev.
25. S. 39 of Ordinance No. 14 of 1884, and see *In the matter of James Hagan deceased:* Mary Hagan-Caveatrix, Sar. F.L.R. (1886), 92.

succession said: "On the death of either the man or the wife the respective relations come and immediately sweep away all, not leaving the widow or widower the least part thereof though they are equally obliged to help to pay the funeral charges."[26] The learned author was talking of succession in the matrilineal system. Bosman made these sweeping remarks because he understood the custom only superficially, and did not realise that the family who succeed have the responsibility to maintain the wife and the children.[27] Sarbah who knew the implications of succession by the family stated the correct view of the law when he pointed out that succession as provided under Section 39 of the Marriage Ordinance, 1884, is alien to the Ghanaian conception because by the application of English law, it enabled the wife and children or the husband alone to take away all the property of a deceased spouse or parent while, unlike the customary law, it did not impose upon such beneficiaries any obligation to provide for an aged parent or other dependants of the deceased. It was in consequence of these clarifications that the ordinance was amended in 1909 to its present form.

The present position therefore is that English law applies to two-thirds of the estate in the following cases:

(1)   As regards a person married under the ordinance if he died intestate and was survived by either
(a)   a spouse whether or not the deceased spouse married under the ordinance, or
(b)   issue of the marriage, and

(2)   As regards issue of the marriage unconditionally if he dies intestate.

This subject is fully discussed in *Coleman* v. *Shang*.[28] The Nigerian case of *Bamgbose* v. *Daniel*[29] discusses the same principle except that under the Nigerian Ordinance the English law applies to the whole of the estate of such a deceased person and not only to a portion of it as under the 1909 amendment to the Ghana Ordinance.

Islamic law of inheritance may also apply to the estate of a deceased Ghanaian by virtue of section 10 of the Marriage of Mohammedans Ordinance;[30] but it applies only if the Ghanaian married under the provisions of the Marriage of Mohammedans Ordinance, and had his marriage registered as provided in Section

26.   Bosman; *Gold Coast of Guinea,* 172
27.   Many v. Kumah, Supreme Court, May 27, 1963, unreported.
28.   (1959) G.L.R. 390; [1961] A.C. 481
29.   14 W.A.C.A. 116.
30.   Cap. 129 1959 Revised Laws.

5 of the ordinance.[31] As the word "intestate" is not used in section 10 of that ordinance, it would appear that although a Will or Samansiw (noncupative Will) made by such a Muslim will be valid if it conformed with the law of the land relating to testamentary disposition, yet it would seem to limit his freedom as to the portion of his estate he may so dispose of to meet the requirements of Islamic law. Here too another problem arises. Will the Islamic law applicable in such a case be that of the pure *Maliki* School of the *Sunni* class, the School of Islamic law which exists in Ghana[32] or the Islamic custom as would be proved to exist in the particular community to which the deceased belonged.[33] And this is so because in almost every community in Ghana where Islamic law is said to exist, it will be found that what prevails is Islamic influenced customary law, and not the pure Islamic law. The influence of Islamic law on customary law may be great or small; but basically what is practised is the customary law.

It has earlier been pointed out that customary law (this includes Islamic influenced customary law) is now a question of law for the court and not a question of fact by virtue of section 67(1) of the Courts Act, 1960. But it cannot be truly said that the court knows the customary law. In the first place, it must be admitted that the influence of the Judicial Assessors in assisting in the moulding of customary law and recording judicial decisions on it, was confined to the southern section of the country; and further that though Local Courts and Commissioner's Court including Chief Commissioners', Provincial Commissioners' or District Commissioners' Courts have operated in suits all over the country at least since the beginning of the present century, record of cases tried in some parts of the country is negligible; this applies particularly to the Northern and Upper Regions. Therefore at the moment there is no case law of any appreciable magnitude built either from decisions of Local Courts or of the superior courts, from which the court may acquire knowledge of the customary law of some tribes or localities.

At this stage it should be pointed out that the position of the courts is not much better in respect of the Ghana Common Law either. The Ghana Common Law as defined in Section 17(1) of the Interpretation Act, 1960 (C.A.4) comprises the Common Law of England, the doctrines of equity, English Statutes of general application in force in Ghana prior to July 1, 1960 which by Section 154 sub-section 4 of the Court Act, 1960 continue to apply in

---

31. *Kwakye v. Tubah & Ors.*, H. Ct. Nov. 27, 1961; unreported *Brimah & anor. v. Asana*, H. Ct. Feb. 20, 1962, unreported.
32. Anderson, *Islamic Law in Africa*, 7
33. *Ayoola & Ors. v. Folawiyo & Ors.* 8 W.A.C.A. 392.

Ghana, and also rules of customary law suitable for general application and assimilated into the common law by a semi-statutory method provided in Part VII of the *Chieftaincy Act*, 1961 (Act 81).

The English statutes of general application retained in Ghana Common Law are those in force in England on July 24, 1874,[34] and with special reference to succession, the English law retained are the provisions of the law of England relating to the distribution of the personal estate of intestates in force on November 19, 1884.[35] The relevant English laws include The *Statute of Distribution*, 1670[36] the Statute of Frauds, 1677[37] the *Administration of Estate Act*, 1685[38], the *Matrimonial Causes Act*, 1857[39] and the *Statute of Distribution*, 1865.[40] It is needless to say that except to research students, these statutes, almost all of which have long been repealed in England, are not taught to students in the faculties and schools of law in England save as part of English legal history. And since they are of no practical importance, the English text-books and reported cases on them are nearly all out of print and difficult to obtain in Ghana.

The Courts, therefore, cannot be said to be seized of accurate knowledge of them either. The statute, i.e. the Courts Act, 1960 (C.A.9) recognises the courts' handicap as far as the customary law is concerned; it therefore provides in Section 67 sub-section 2 that in addition to submissions made on the law by counsel for the parties to a suit and reference to reported cases—This must refer to decisions of courts of competent jurisdiction whether such decisions are reported or not, the court should consult text-books and other sources (these may include official and unofficial reports, learned articles and so on) as may be appropriate. The subsection further provides that if after it had considered all those materials, the court should still be in doubt as to the existence and content of a rule of customary law relevant to any proceedings, it should hold an enquiry which should form part of the proceedings before it, and summon persons whom it should consider knowledgeable about customary law relevant to the particular issue before it and who are prepared to testify on oath, their opinion as to the existence and content of the particular customary law. In this regard the court may request a House of Chiefs, or a Traditional Authority or other

34.   S.154 of the Courts Act 1960. C.A. 9)
35.   S. 48 of the Marriage Ordinance, Cap. 127, 1951 Rev.
36.   22 & 23 Car. 2 C 20
37.   29 Car. 2 C 3 s. 24.
38.   1 Jac. 2 C 3 sections 12 & 24
39.   20 & 21 Vic. C. 85, sections 7 & 25
40.   1 Jac. 2 C. 17, s. 7

body possessing knowledge of the customary law in question, to submit to it in writing its opinion of the customary law in question to be laid before the enquiry. In the provisions of sub-sections (2) and (3) of Section 67 of the Courts Act, 1960, we find the following:-

(i) the ideal to aim at in a Court for ascertaining the customary law is a body of case law; which of course, will take considerable time to build;

(ii) until that ideal situation is attained, textbooks, treatise, learned articles in journals and other forms of restatement of the customary law of particular areas or communities, are a desideratum, as these will not only fill a gap, but will also assist the progress towards the ideal, and

(iii) in the meantime purely as an emergency measure, and to help build case law, the Court, *suo motu*, should hold an enquiry to inform itself of the customary law, which it is presumed to know, for to leave it to parties to a suit, each to tender expert evidence on existence and content of the customary law, as was the case prior to July 1, 1960, would be to reduce the customary law to a status of foreign law in its own native land, and that would be ridiculous.

Needless to say that the enquiry method is an *ad hoc* measure designed to meet emergency situations, therefore in order of priority, text-books, articles and other forms of re-statement of the customary law is the country's greatest need of the moment.

At this stage it is well to observe that the customary law is not static, for it is developing and unfolding itself, and its existence and administration side by side with the common law and the enacted law, is conducive to progress and adptability. We have already pointed out how its existence and recognition influenced amendment to the rules of succession under the Marriage Ordinance. We may refer to one or two instances in which the customary law of succession has itself been influenced directly or indirectly by the common law or enacted law. According to strict customary law, the family of a deceased person are liable to pay all debts the deceased owed; consequently the successor appointed by the family was responsible to pay all such debts even if the deceased died a pauper; this means that the successor may have to pay his predecessor's debts out of his self-earned money. The only way in which the family could avoid this obligation was to disown the deceased, which of course, is one of the lowest depths of degradation to which a Ghanaian family could permit itself to sink. On the other hand, if the appointed successor took letters of administration in respect of the estate of the deceased according to English law, his responsibility as a personal representative is limited to the extent of the estate of the deceased which actually comes into his hands. Blending the two together, the present position of the law as to the responsibility of the successor for the debts and liabilities of the deceased appears to be that it is limited to the estate he succeeds to and at the highest to any ancestral property in his possession, but not to his self-acquired property except where such self-acquired property has become merged into family property by operation of law.[41]

Another instance is succession to a former slave or descendant of an emancipated slave. By customary law a slave was the property of his master, and upon his death his master or his master's family succeeded to his estate. Again by customary law an emancipated slave belongs to the family of his former master or of any other family to which he elects to attach himself. Although in a matrilineal system the family in such a case is the maternal family of his former master, or of the persons with whom he attached himself, therefore by customary law, the children of an emancipated male person would strictly not belong to that family, yet succession in those circumstances by the family to the exclusion of his blood descendants would be illegal, as it savours of slavery. In such a case the blood descendants of the emancipated person are treated as constituting his immediate family. In other words the emancipated male person is by legal fiction treated as female, therefore his children would belong to his immediate family, and the head and principal members of the entire family would in choosing a successor to such emancipated person, give prior consideration to the persons in that group and would appoint his successor from that immediate family. But in case there is no such descendant, the family to which he attached himself may appoint any one of themselves, i.e a uterine brother or sister of the former master or the person to whom he was attached, or descendants and ascendants in the direct female line of the sisters of such a person, and so on.[42]

We have earlier observed that except to a very limited extent there are no problems of internal conflict of laws in Ghana as far as succession is concerned; that is so because the customary law of succession is determined by personal law, while succession under the Marriage Ordinance is by the common law and customary law jointly, and in the case of inheritance under the Marriage of Mohammedans Ordinance, the Islamic law as locally observed. Thus where a

41. *Asiedu v. Ofori* H. Ct. Dec. 6, 1932 unreported.
42. Nimo v. Donkor, Div. Ct. (Kumasi) Feb. 21, 1949, unreported.

woman whose home was Gomoa, where the law of succession is pure Fanti (Akan) customary law, died and left real property at Winneba, where the law of succession is said to be a variation of the Fanti customary law of succession, it was held that internal conflict of law did not arise, because the personal law of the deceased upon which succession to her estate should be determined is fixed, and is the one which attached to her at her birth, therefore the pure Fanti customary law of succession which prevailed at her place of birth applied, and not the varied customary law of the place where the property she left was situated.[43] So that no question of *lex domicil* or *lex situs* arises internally.

Now section 66 of the Courts Act, 1960 which we said at the beginning regulates the law of succession to be applied in any given case, lays down rules for the determination of the rule of law— the common law or the customary law—to be applied in any particular proceedings. In succession suits the relevant rules of that section are rules 4 and 5 of sub-section (1), and sub-section (3). These provide that in the case of succession to land, the customary law to which the deceased through whom the claim is made was subject, would apply, or if the claim is made through different predecessors or families then the customary law to which both persons or families, through whom the claim is made were subject, would apply; where the persons or families through whom the claims are made belong to different systems of customary law, then the law of the place where the land is situated would apply. In the case of devolution of property other than land, the personal law of the deceased would apply, i.e. the common law or the customary law as the case may be; and where the law prevailing in any other place is involved, the principles of the common law relating to private international law would apply.[44] These statutory provisions are the only clear rules, if we may say so, providing for conflict of laws.

During the debates in the Legislative Council in 1906, on Sarbah's proposals for the amendment of the law of succession as laid down in section 39 of the Marriage Ordinance 1884,[45] A. Willoughby Osborne, the then Attorney-General, proposed that a Commission of Enquiry should be appointed to consider whether it could be desirable and feasible to have a law of succession applicable to all tribes of this country. The Attorney-General recommended that if it should be so found, steps should be taken to promulgate such a

43. *Wobill v. Kra & Anor.* 12 W.A.C.A. 181
44. *Davies v. Randall & Anor.*, Supreme Court April 29, 1963 unreported.
45. now s. 48, Marriage Ordinance Cap. 127, 1951 Rev.

law. However, no definite steps were taken on these proposals, although consultations took place between Government and state councils and provincial councils—the councils of the Chiefs and traditional elders. Some of these consultations culminated in resolutions passed or proposals made by some councils of the areas where succession is matrilineal, for modification of their customary law to provide a one-third of the estate of a deceased male for his wife and children. But nearly everyone of these resolutions became abortive because the procedure laid down in the enactments governing the respective councils for giving legal effects to amendment of the customary law was not followed,[46] and the position has remained the same ever since.

In May 1959, the Ghana Government appointed an Inheritance Commission* with the following terms of reference:-

   (1) to examine the existing statutory law of inheritance;
   (2) to record existing forms of customary law of inheritance in respect of self-acquired property, both real and personal;
   (3) to ascertain the views of the public on existing rules of Statutory and Customary Law governing intestacies and whether there is any public demand for a limitation on the powers of a testator to dispose of his property outside his family; and
   (4) to recommend ways in which the statutory and customary law relating to inheritance could be rationalised with a view to the adoption of a unified system.

The Commission submitted its report in or about October, 1959, but the report has not been published.

What seems evident from public opinion is a desire for modification of the matrilineal family system in such a way as to give the wife and children of a deceased person interest in a definite portion of his estate, since it is felt that the right to maintenance and training of the children and support for the wife out of the estate though legally enforcible, is not generally regarded as sufficiently substantial. But, in our opinion, a modification of that nature can better be achieved by resolution of the traditional councils of the matrilineal areas, than by enactment of the central legislature.

In May 1961, the Ghana Government published a White Paper making certain proposals on Marriage, Divorce and Inheritance, and requested free and dispassionate discussion of the problems and invited public opinion on the proposals made. Since then two Bills

---

46.   See e.g. resolution of the Ashanti Confederacy Council of Feb. 21, 1948 and judgment in *Kosi & Ors. v. Nimo* L. Ct. (Kumasi) June 12, 1958, unreported.
* The Ollennu Commission.

on Marriage, Divorce and Inheritance have been initiated but each has had to be withdrawn in view of public opinion expressed both in and outside the Legislative Assembly.[47] Perhaps the lumping together of all these three important branches of the personal law, was one of the chief obstacles to the passage of the Bills. It is believed that Bills are now in the course of preparation dealing separately with the subjects. Therefore, there is every probability, that within the next few years, there will come into existence, enacted law of succession universally applicable to all Ghanaians, which will be a blending and rationalisation of the existing statutory and customary law of succession.

CONCLUSIONS

1. The law of succession in Ghana is the personal law of the deceased.

2. The relevant personal law may be the customary law, the common law as defined in section 17 of the Interpretation Act, 1960 or Islamic-influenced local custom, and in the case of land owned by a non-Ghanaian, the customary law of the place where the land is situated.

3. The customary law like the common law, is now a question of law for the court, and not a question of fact as in pre-Republic Ghana; the customary law is not uniform, it varies according to tribes, although there are common features in the different systems.

4. There are proposals for enacting statutory law of succession in the near future which will apply to all persons irrespective of tribe or community.

5. The common law in this regard consists of the English common law providing for distribution of personalty, and the English statutes in force in England on November 19, 1884, relating to distribution of personal estate of an intestate, and the Wills Act, 1837.

6. The ideal source from which the court should gain its knowledge of the law, both the customary law and the common law is case law, which at the moment is most inadequate in certain fields, and particularly in respect of the customary law of some tribes and communities, especially those in the Upper and Northern Regions. There is great need to build this up, but the time within which that can be done, is from the nature of case law, very indefinite.

47. Mention should be made of Ollennu's comments which formed the basis of symposia on the 2nd Bill in the University of Ghana, Memoranda of the Christian Council, the Roman Catholic Church and the Presbyterian Church, and a memorandum of the Sarbah Law Society.

7.   The sources of information on the law which are and should be more readily available are text-books, learned articles, reports and other forms of restatement of the law, both the common law and the customary law. These too are inadequate at the moment but can be built up with efficiency more quickly than can case law.

The first need therefore is such material; consequently its production is an urgent necessity which should engage the immediate attention of teachers of law, research fellows, and members of the profession both on the Bench and at the Bar.

8.   In the meantime, and purely as an interim measure to meet the emergency and help build the stock of case law, enquiries held by the courts as part of proceedings before it, are to be employed and facilitated. Opinions of persons or bodies of persons, e.g. Linguists to Chiefs, or House of Chiefs and others who are repositories of the customary law by reason of their up-bringing and the facilities they have had to know the customary law should be made available to the courts either orally or in writing, at such enquiries, their opinion of the customary law.

THE LAW OF SUCCESSION IN UGANDA

by

DR. H. F. MORRIS

SCHOOL OF ORIENTAL AND AFRICAN STUDIES
UNIVERSITY OF LONDON

THE LAW OF SUCCESSION IN UGANDA[1]

The law of succession in Uganda provides a particularly interesting study in relation to the problems of integration. Many of the problems which arise from a dual system of law are, of course, by no means peculiar to Uganda, but there are certain purely local circumstances which accentuate these and make the position particularly relevant to the question of conflict and integration. First a brief outline of the current position must be given.[2]

The territorial law of succession

The Succession Act,[3] enacted as an Ordinance in 1906, introduced the Indian version of the English law of succession. This Act follows closely the Indian Succession Act of 1865, which represented a considerable advance on the pre-1926 succession law in England: indeed the 1925 reform in the English law brought the latter fairly closely into line with that operative in Uganda. The Act provides *inter alia* for the making of wills along the lines of the Wills Act, 1837, and lays down rules of distribution on intestacy. These briefly are that a widow inherits one third of the estate if the deceased has lineal descendants and one half if the kindred he leaves are not his lineal descendants. Where an intestate has died leaving such descendants, those who are nearest in degree to him share his estate (or two thirds of it if there is a surviving widow), the *per stirpes* rule applying where one or more of this group of beneficiaries has predeceased the intestate and left descendants. Where the intestate has no lineal descendants, then his father, if alive, succeeds to the whole (or half if there is a surviving widow). If he is dead, then the mother, brothers and sisters of the intestate share equally, the children of a deceased brother or sister sharing in what would have been their parent's portion. If the intestate leaves neither lineal descendants nor parent nor brother nor sister, the property is divided equally among those who are in the nearest degree of kinship to him.

1. Since this paper was presented in 1964, a number of important developments have taken place affecting the law of succession in Uganda. I have thought it best to leave the paper substantially as it was presented and to add a final section outlining development since 1964.
2. See MORRIS and READ, *Uganda: the Development of its Laws and Constitution*, London 1966, Chapter 16 passim and pp. 399-402.
3. Laws of Uganda 1964, Cap. 139. All ordinances enacted during the colonial period and still in force have been redesignated "Acts".

The Administrator-General's Act,[4] passed in 1933, enables the administrator-general, where a deceased has appointed him executor or has appointed no executor or an executor who is unable or unwilling to act as such, or has died intestate, to apply to the court for letters of administration of the estate which the court, except for good cause shown, shall grant.

Such is the general territorial law of succession, a seemingly comprehensive body of law. In actual fact, however, it affects only a minute proportion of the population. By an Order[5] issued in 1960 under the Succession Ordinance it was declared that the Ordinance did not apply to the estate of natives of Uganda and that the sections dealing with intestate succession did not apply to the estates of Muslims. Similarly, the Administrator-General's Act contains a clause stating that it does not apply to the estates of natives of Uganda.[6] There are no provisions in the Uganda Marriage Acts, as there are in the similar legislation of Ghana, Nigeria and Malawi, making the English law of succession applicable, in whole or in part, where there is a statute marriage and the deceased has left no will; in Uganda, Africans are subject to the customary law of succession and to that alone, regardless of whether or not the deceased has had a family by a statute marriage.

Customary laws of succession

It will be evident that in a country with some twenty or more different bodies of customary law, there will be considerable variety between rules of succession prevailing in different parts of the country, although, since all the people of Uganda are patrilineal, the divergences are not likely to be too wide. Without going into details, some general characteristics common to most of these systems of customary law (and indeed to much customary law throughout Africa) may be mentioned.

When a man dies an "heir" is chosen from among his family if the deceased has not before his death made it known who his heir is to be. The heir is normally one of the deceased's sons if he has any. The use of the term "heir" as a translation of the vernacular word in Uganda, as elsewhere, is time-honoured but misleading, since its significance in a customary law context is very different from that

4. Cap. 140. Unless otherwise stated references to chapter numbers are those in the 1964 Revision.
5. Laws (1951 Revision) Vol. VII p. 907.
6. Sec. 40 (2) In the 1964 Revision of the Laws, the phrase "natives of Uganda" in the Administrator—General's Act and the Order under the Succession Act has been replaced by the phrase "any person to whom any customary law relating to succession in force in any part of Uganda' applies'.

which it bears in an English law context. The heir will normally receive the largest single share of the estate, often one half or more, but he will also have duties to perform, comparable in some ways to those of the English executor and guardian. He takes the dead man's place as head of his family and is responsible for certain ritual ceremonies and also for the care of the younger members of the family and other dependants. The balance of the estate is then divided, the bulk going usually to the other sons of the deceased, that is to say those sons whom the deceased had recognized as his own; a portion may also go to other close relatives of the deceased such as his brothers. Daughters do not share equally with sons but among some Uganda peoples they get a share, if a small one, and among some of the pastoral people if a man has no son it is possible for a daughter to inherit the bulk of his estate. The deceased's widow has customarily no rights of inheritance; traditionally she was herself "inherited" by his heir. Today she has the right to return to her own family if she wishes to.

The right to make an oral will whereby a man states his wishes as to who his heir is to be and as to how his property is to be divided is generally recognized. The discretionary powers of the testator in this respect are, however, limited; the broad rules of inheritance are laid down in the customary law, and he cannot radically alter their application to his estate so as to upset what customary law considers to be a fair distribution. If his wishes as expressed in his will are considered by the family to be unjust, they will not be given effect on his death. So too he may, for good cause, disinherit a son, but unless the disinheritance is justified by customary law on account of the son's fault, the testator's wishes will be set aside. The making of written wills is becoming increasingly common. Such wills, however they may be framed, remain customary wills; that is to say they do not purport to be wills made under the statute law, and, though they may carry more weight in the family council, or more particularly in the court if the matter comes before it, than an oral will, their effectiveness depends upon their conformity with what is considered right and just according to customary law.

The above remarks refer generally to Uganda as a whole, but something must now be said about Buganda in particular, where the position is in certain respects exceptional. In the first place, the Buganda (Clan Cases) Agreement of 1924[7] stated that "any case relating to the headship, membership or other matter affecting clans" was to be dealt with by the clan councils who would lay their recommendations before the Kabaka, the courts being excluded from

7. Laws (1951 Revision) Vol. VI p. 54

all jurisdiction in such matters; this exclusion of the court has been incorporated in the Buganda Courts Ordinance 1940. What constitutes a "matter affecting clans" is, however, by no means clear, though it has been decided[8] that intestate succession is such a matter and cannot, therefore, be adjudicated upon in a court of law. Reference will be made again to this Agreement. In the second place, the Buganda Government during the early years of the century passed a number of laws considerably modifying the customary law and reflecting to a certain extent the influence which the Christian missions had, on the kingdom. The Land Law of 1908[9] and the Land Succession Law of 1912[10] deal with succession to *mailo* land, a form of tenure which the Agreement of 1900 had created. The owner of such land is permitted to dispose of it by written will to people of Uganda who are alive or have been conceived at the time of his death. If he leaves no will, "a successor will be ascertained according to the rules of succession of the Baganda". The Wills Law of 1916[11] provides for the making of written wills which must be signed in the presence of two witnesses. This law has not, however, in effect invalidated the traditional oral will and neither type of will can depart too radically from the customary rules of succession. In 1926 a draft Succession Law[12] was passed by the Lukiiko but was never promulgated as a law, because, apparently, it was thought that its enactment would encroach upon the jurisdiction of the clan authorities which the Clan Cases Agreement had protected. Although it thus never became a law, this Succession Order, as it is called, has been followed as though it had the force of law by the courts and the clan authorities. This Order represents in certain respects a compromise between mission and feminist demands on the one hand and traditional views on the other. The Order amplifies the Wills Law and states *inter alia* that a man may not by his will make a person who is not of his clan his heir, although he may leave a portion of his property to anyone he likes. In fact, however, the Kabaka, whose confirmation of a will is necessary, will not normally give this confirmation if the testator has a son whom he has disinherited without good cause. On intestacy, the eldest son is to be chosen as heir and is to have the largest share of the estate. Provision is made for female members of the family to have a share in the succession:

8. *Kajubi* v. *Kabali*, (1944) II E.A.C.A. 34
9. Laws (1951 Revision) Vol. VII p. 1219
10. *Ibid* p. 1225
11. Laws (1951 Revsion) Vol. VII p. 1233
12. Reproduced with commentary as an appendix to *Law and Justice in Buganda*. E.S. Haydon, London 1960.

daughters receive a share as do also the widow and the testator's mother if she survices him.

Problem arising from the present legal position
1. Statute marriage and succession

The first problem to be considered is whether, since the legislature has enacted legislation[13] providing for monogamous marriages and establishing that the contraction of any customary union with other women during the continuance of such marriage is a criminal offence, the "legitimate" children born of the statute marriage should have a privileged position as against those born of customary marriages which in the eyes of the territorial law (but not of customary law) are unlawful. This, of course, raises the whole vexed question of the unsatisfactory state of present marriage law in Uganda, as in many other African countries. A "church marriage" under the Act (normally coupled with a customary marriage contract) has long been looked on as a superior type of marriage and one which is socially obligatory upon persons of high status. This has never inhibited a large proportion of Uganda husbands from later contracting further marriages by customary law. In so doing they commit, of course, a criminal offence and are liable to a term of imprisonment of up to five years:[14] in practice prosecutions are extremely rare and the penal sections of the Marriage Act are in fact a dead letter. Such subsequent customary marriages are declared by the Act to be void and children by such unions would accordingly by territorial law be illegitimate. Nevertheless, since succession for Africans is determined according to customary law, such children have the same rights as those born of the statute marriage. An extreme view, and one which has never been entertained by the Uganda courts, would be that, since customary law can only be enforced in so far as it is not in conflict with territorial law, it would be *ultra vires* for the courts to enforce customary law which gave "illegitimate" children the same rights as "legitimate" children. An answer to this argument might be that there is no direct conflict here since the rights which the "illegitimate" children enjoy under customary law do not arise in any way from their parents' marriage, but rather from the fact that they are the recognized issue of their father. Nevertheless, although the succession rights of all of a man's children, regardless of the nature of their father's marriage, are generally accepted by the bulk of the population, criticism of the present position from time to time arises

13. Marriage Act cap. 211, Marriage of Africans Act cap. 212.
14. Marriage Act s. 52.

particularly from church and feminist organizations. In Buganda, where the advanced opinions of educated women are most vocal, there was pressure as early as the nineteen-twenties for the children of a statute marriage to be put in a privileged position; the Buganda Succession Order did meet their views so far as to say that the heir should be the eldest son (although in fact the eldest might, of course, be a child of a customary marriage prior to a church marriage). Their argument is that if a couple choose to marry under the Act it should be presumed that they intend to be bound by all the consequences of monogamous marriage as in English law. This argument has been heard for nearly a century in many parts of Africa and need not be dwelt on here.

2. The position of the widow

Under customary law a widow could not expect to inherit from her husband. Provided, however, that the traditional society remained intact, she could expect support from her husband's heir or her own family. But in present-day conditions, when, on the one hand, traditional obligations are often found irksome and evaded, and, on the other, dependence on her husband's family or her own may be unacceptable to the sophisticated woman, the customary rules of succession may well afford her inadequate protection. It is not merely that on intestacy the widow will in most customary societies be ineligible to receive a share of her husband's property, but that, since a customary will must conform to the general rules of distribution on intestacy, and since, as will be seen below, it does not appear to be possible for an African to make a will under the territorial law, it is impossible for a man to leave his property to his wife if his family object that the will is contrary to custom. Progressive feminist opinion would insist that adequate provision from a man's estate should be made in all cases for his widow, whether he dies intestate or makes a will. In this, feminist opinion goes beyond the current territorial law as contained in the Succession Act: for, although the Act provides (so far as non-Africans and non-Muslims are concerned) adequate provision for the widow on intestacy (one half or one third of the estate) and, of course, enables a man to will all his property to his wife if he wishes to, nothing prevents him from leaving everything away from his wife and family if he chooses. No legislation has been passed to safeguard his dependents regardless of the terms of his will as was done in England in 1938 by the Inheritance (Family Provision) Act.

3. Intestate succession to estates of non-African Muslims

Before turning to the question of the ability of an African to make

English-type will, it will be convenient to consider the complex question of what law applies in the case of intestacy where the deceased is a non-African Muslim. This is necessary because a series of cases bring out clearly the problems in this area which also have some bearing on the position of African testators.

First the source of the High Court's jurisdiction must be considered. The Africa Order in Council of 1889, which applied to Uganda on the establishment of the Protectorate in 1894, states that jurisdiction should "so far as circumstances permitted be exercised upon the principles of, and in conformity with, the substance of the law for the time being in force in England". The Uganda Order in Council of 1902 set up a High Court with full jurisdiction over all persons and matters and stated that jurisdiction should be exercised as far as circumstances permitted in conformity with certain Indian codes. No mention was made of the general English law; on the other hand the 1902 Order in Council, in repealing that of 1889 so far as Uganda was concerned, added a saving proviso which might or might not have retained the operation of English law in so far as the Indian codes did not apply.

This doubt was resolved in 1911 by an amending Order in Council to the effect that in so far as the Indian codes did not apply, jurisdiction would be exercised in conformity with common law doctrines of equity and statutes of general application in force in England on 11th August, 1902. The usual proviso was added: such law was to be in force only so far as the circumstances of the country and its people permitted and "subject to such qualifications as local circumstances render necessary". The 1902 order in Council also contained the usual provision that the High Court was to be guided by native law and custom in cases to which Africans were parties. The Order in Council was of course repealed in 1962 but the Judicature Act of that year has in substance retained the provisions concerning the applicability of English law. The provision for guidance by native law and custom has, however, disappeared.[15]

The Succession Act was passed in 1906, that is in the period between the Order in Council of 1902 and the amending Order of 1911. The sections dealing with intestacy were declared not to apply to the estates of Muslims. What law then did apply in such cases? If the Muslim were an African of Uganda, it has never been questioned that customary law applied. But what if he were an

---

15.   The High Court now has, under the Judicature Act of 1967, express authority to exercise jurisdiction in conformity with "any established and current custom or usage".

immigrant Muslim? This was considered in 1920 in the case of *Re Mohamed Habash: Vasila* v. *Worsta*[16] and the rather surprising conclusion was reached that, since the Act, or part of it, did not apply to Africans and Muslims, the law of succession in respect of those people reverted to the position in which it had stood prior to the passing of the Act; this meant that:

> the law of inheritance for immovables was English law (that for movables depending on domicile) as far as regards foreigners and native customs as far as regards natives of the Protectorate. There is no room anywhere for the application of Mohammedan law to land and it would lead to hopeless confusion if the course of descent to land depended both on tribe and religion.

Yet this judgment does not appear to have inhibited later judges from applying, on occasion, Islamic law to the estates of intestate Muslims. In 1949, Ainley, J., without in fact referring to *Re Mohamed Habash* underlined the illogicality of a situation in which the legislature had specifically exempted Muslims from the operation of the alien rules of intestate succession in the Act based on English law, only to make them subject to the equally alien law of England itself; he decided that the exemption Order must be interpreted as having the effect of requiring the court to administer Islamic law in cases of Muslim intestacy.[17]

The decision of Mr. Justice Ainley is of particular interest as one approach towards the gnawing doubt as to whether the High Court has any authority to administer a body of law when jurisdiction in respect of such law has not been specifically given by the Order in Council in the first place and then by the Judicature Act. Since it is clearly desirable for Islamic law to be enforced in certain cases, the courts in the East African countries (the jurisdiction of whose High Courts stems originally from similarly worded Orders in Council) have relied on different arguments to justify its application. In *Malek Sultan* v. *Sherali Jeraj*,[18] a Tanganyika case, the East African Court of Appeal disagreed with an earlier decision of the Appeal Court in *Bachoo* v. *Bolia*[19] to the effect that the High Court had no such jurisdiction and decided that it had. Two different arguments were advanced. The first was that the proviso that English law was applicable only so far as local cir-

16. (1920) 3 U.L.R. 26.
17. This unreported case, *In the Estate of Cookman Mugnal Imam Din (deceased)*, Administration Cause No. 36 of 1949, is fully discussed by Professor J. N. D. Anderson in [1963] J.A.L. 201-206.
18. (1954) 22 E.A.C.A. 142
19. (1946) 13 E.A.C.A. 50

cumstances permitted could have the practical effect of requiring
the application of some other body of law, an argument considered
but rejected in *Bachoo* v. *Bolia*. The second argument was that the
High Court derived its power to apply Islamic law from the fact
that it had full jurisdiction over all persons and matters under the
Order in Council.

4. Can an African make an English type will?

It has always been assume that an African of Uganda cannot
make a will conforming to the requirements of the Wills Act of
1837, which will be upheld by the courts even though it might
conflict with the customary rules of distribution, though in fact
the question does not appear ever to have come before the courts.
It has never been argued, as it was in the case of non-African
Muslims, that on the non-application of the Succession Act the
applicable law on intestacy was the English law; even in *Vasila* v.
Worsta it was asserted that in the case of Africans the applicable
law was customary law. Obviously the argument applied in relation
to Muslims in the case of *Imam Din*, that it would be illogical to
exempt a class of the community from one body of alien law only
to make it subject to another, applies equally to Africans as far as
intestate succession is concerned, but has far less force regarding
the right to make a will. Certainly since 1911, if not continuously
since 1894, statutes of general application in force in England at
the date of reception have been operative in Uganda in so far as the
local law does not apply, and it may be argued that the Wills Act
has been operative as far as Africans are concerned to fill the gap
left by the non-operation of the Succession Act. The law is there,
the argument would be; any African who wishes to do so may avail
himself of it and make a will according to its requirements and the
High Court must then, of necessity, enforce its provisions if required to do so. A counter argument would be that once again the
proviso making the operation of English law dependent on local
conditions would be operative and would render the Wills Act
inapplicable, since the idea of unfettered power of testamentary
disposition is completely foreign to Uganda African society and
would be an inequitable interference with the legitimate expectations
of the heir under customary law. At all events the question whether
an African can make such a will has not been argued in the courts
since it has been accepted that he cannot do so. What has been
contended is that the law should be changed to enable him to do so,
though there does not appear to have been widespread desire for
change, such pressure as there is coming largely from Buganda
and from feminist opinion which wants a husband to have the

power to provide by will for his wife or wives without the danger of such provision being overruled by the husband's family, after his death.

5. The Clan Cases Agreement 1924

Reference has already been made to this Agreement by the terms of which certain types of cases, the exact nature of which is not clear but among which those concerning intestate succession are definitely included, were excluded from the jurisdiction of the courts and reserved solely for the decision of the clan councils which might forward matters to the Kabaka's Ddiro Council. By the terms of the Agreement not only were the Buganda courts excluded from entertaining such cases, but it was also stated that the High Court should not take cognisance of any appeal from, or exercise any revisional jurisdiction over, any decision given in clan cases. The Agreement, of course, lapsed on independence; but a Buganda Law has been passed, the Clan Cases Declaratory Law, 1962,[20] stating that "It is declared, confirmed and enacted that the Kabaka and his Lukiiko Council have, and always have had, under the customary law of Buganda the right power and jurisdiction to hear and finally and conclusively to decide all cases relating to headship membership and all other matters affecting clans to the exclusion of all other courts whatsoever, appellate or otherwise, and that the revocation of the Buganda Agreement (Clan Cases) 1924 does not and shall not in any manner whatsoever affect such rights power and jurisdiction".

That this is a satisfactory state of affairs is certainly open to question.

The prospect of reform

Where there are two different bodies of law operating in one country, there is bound to be a potential for conflict. In fact, however, in Uganda cases of conflict regarding succession rarely come before the courts. Nevertheless, it cannot be said that the present position is satisfactory. Any reform must, however, be closely connected with the whole question of the appropriateness of the marriage, and other family law which has been inherited from the colonial period, and which not only provides scope for conflict but also does not necessarily meet the needs of a society which is becoming increasingly individualistic and in which the force of traditional obligations is steadily weakening.

In January 1964 a Commission was appointed[21] with the following

20. L.N. 21 of 1963.
21. L.N. 2 of 1964.

terms of reference:

> To consider the laws and customs regulating marriage, divorce and the status of women in Uganda bearing in mind to ensure that the laws and customs while preserving existing traditions and practices as far as possible should be consistent with justice and morality and appropriate to the position of Uganda as an independent nation and to make recommendations.

It is to be hoped that the Commission's investigations will prepare the way for a comprehensive revision of the existing succession laws in Uganda.

Recent developments

Since 1964, a number of important developments have taken place in Uganda in the field of succession law. The Report of the Commission on Marriage, Divorce and the Status of Women was published in October 1965[22] and this contained a number of proposals for the radical reform of the law of succession. Briefly these were as follows.

If a man dies intestate, then his self-acquired property should vest in a public trustee, who would be a civil servant and able to appoint any person as his agent with full powers. If the widow had been married to the deceased by a registered marriage[23], then she would take a life interest, terminating on re-marriage, in one third of the self-acquired property of the deceased, the reversionary interest therein devolving on the issue of this registered marriage as tenants in common. The remaining two-thirds of the self-acquired property would pass to the children, whether or not they had been born of the registered marriage, as tenants in common. If there were a surviving parent of the deceased, then he also would get a share with the children, but with a life interest in it only. Any person, man or woman, who is of age and of sound mind should be able to make a will, the provisions of which would be enforceable regardless of any conflict with the customary law. Such wills would have to be in writing and witnessed and the law regarding them should, in general, follow the provisions of the English Wills Act. If such a will did not make reasonable provision for the maintenance of the testator's children, then the High Court should be able, on application, to

22. Government Printer Entebbe, 1965. See H. F. Morris, "Uganda: Report of the Commission on Marriage, Divorce and the Status of Women" [1966] J.A.L. pp. 3-7.
23. The Commission recommended that there should be facilities for the registration of all types of marriage, but that no one should be permitted to register more than one marriage, although a subsequent marriage could be registered if the earlier marriage has been dissolved.

direct that such provision should be made out of the estate. In commenting on this recommendation, the Commission indicates that consideration was given to the inclusion of a recommendation that a widow should also be able to claim for reasonable provision out of the estate as under the English Inheritance (Family Provision) Act, 1938, but that they had come to the conclusion that "taking the structure of our society into account . . . at least for the time being our recommendations should be restricted to the impeachment of a will" in respect of a child's maintenance only.

When it published the Report of the Commission, the Uganda Government did not commit itself either to acceptance or rejection and invited comments from the public. Legislative action has, however, now been taken to ensure that any person who wishes to may make a will under the terms of the Succession Act, the provisions of which will be put into effect on the testator's death regardless of whether or not they are in conflict with the customary laws of succession. This was done in November, 1966 by a statutory instrument[24] revoking the Order made in 1906 exempting certain classes of people from the operation of the Succession Act and, at the same time, re-exempting persons to whom customary law applied from the provisions of the Act dealing with intestate succession: the provisions of the Act dealing with testate succession accordingly now apply to all members of the community. Moreover, the Administrator-General's Act was amended in 1967[25]: the section disapplying the Act to the estates of persons subject to customary law has been repealed and provision has been inserted to enable chiefs to be appointed as agents of the Administrator-General.

As far as intestate succession is concerned, the estate of a person subject to customary law is still divided in accordance with the relevant body of customary law. It is, however, unlikely that this state of affairs will long continue. In April, 1967 a Succession (Amendment) Bill was published under the terms of which the whole of the Succession Act would apply to all members of the community and a completely new set of rules for the distribution of property on intestacy would replace those at present in the Act. These proposed rules, although they make some concessions to customary law, particularly in providing for the customary "heir" to receive a portion of the estate, broadly follow the English law pattern of distribution according to degree of consanguinity rather than customary law principles. Reference can only be made here to a few of the new proposals. A wife would be entitled to a share in

24. Succession (Exemption) Order 1966., S.I. No. 181
25. Administrator-General's (Amendment) Act, Act 14 of 1967.

her husband's estate, which would vary from 25% to 90% depending on the proximity of the deceased to the other beneficiaries. If there should be more than one surviving wife, this share is divided between them, but a distinction is drawn between a "legal wife" and a "customary wife": the customary wives receive equal shares each being one half of that which the legal wife receives. In general, children share equally, but an illegitimate child, that is to say a child not born of a valid marriage, whether statutory or customary, but who was recognised by the intestate before his death as his child, takes half the share of a legitimate child. The customary heir, in addition to any share to which he may otherwsie be entitled, gets 10% of the estate.[26] As yet,[27] this proposed legislation has not been enacted.

Finally, it is necessary to consider briefly how far the recent constitutional changes, which have eliminated all federal elements from the constitution of Uganda,[28] have affected the position relating to succession law. Under the 1962 Constitution, the legislatures of the federal states had exclusive legislative power in respect of "traditional and customary matters relating to the state alone". This would appear, although the matter is by no means free from doubt, to have given to these states the exclusive right to legislate regarding customary law operative within the state and to have denied to the Parliament of Uganda the competence to enact legislation operative within these states on the lines of, say, the 1967 Succession Bill. Under the Constitution of 1966, the legislatures of the kingdoms retained their power to legislate on traditional and customary matters, but such power was no longer exclusive and any laws made would be void if they were in conflict with legislation enacted by Parliament. Under the terms of the 1967 Constitution, the kingdoms as such were swept away completely.[29] Parliament now has, subject, of course, to the fundamental rights provisions of the Constitution, unfettered power to enact legislation operative throughout Uganda.

As far as Buganda is concerned, these constitutional changes have had another, and far-reaching, effect in the field of succession.

26. But, if there are surviving lineal descendants, the customary heir takes either 10% or one half of the share to which a legitimate child would have been entitled, whichever is the lesser amount.
27. By March 1968.
28. The Constitution of 1966 considerably modified the federal nature of its predecessor, the Constitution of 1962, and the Constitution of 1967 removed all remaining federal elements.
29. District councils with bye-law making powers replaced the federal legislatures, whilst in Buganda there is now not even a central council, the former kingdom being divided into four districts.

As has already been explained earlier, matters involving intestate succession have been classed as clan matters and as such have been excluded from the jurisdiction of the courts. Since independence, the authority for this exclusion has lain, in the first place, in the Buganda Clan Cases Declaratory Law of 1962 and, in the second place, in the Buganda Courts Ordinance. Neither of these pieces of legislation could, while the 1962 Constitution was in force, be overriden, amended or repealed by Central Government statutes: the first was a Law passed by the Buganda legislature acting presumably within the scope of its exclusive powers, whilst the second, though a Central Government enactment, stood in an especially entrenched position under the Constitution, by the terms of which this Ordinance could be neither amended nor repealed without the consent of the Buganda legislature. Once the 1962 Constitution had been superseded, the Ordinance ceased to be in an entrenched position and opportunity was taken shortly afterwards to apply to Buganda the Magistrates' Courts Act, which by its terms repealed the Buganda Courts Ordinance. The Buganda Clan Cases Declaratory Law, however, remained in existence, since the Constitutions of 1966 and 1967 preserved existing laws. Nevertheless, it appears that this Law is void, in so far as it purports to deny to the courts jurisdiction over matters which would otherwise properly be within their jurisdiction, as being in conflict with the Constitution and statute law. Under the Constitution, the High Court has unlimited jurisdiction throughout Uganda, subject only to the provisions of the Constitution and of any law enacted by Parliament. Under the Magistrates' Courts Act, the varying grades of magistrates' courts are empowered to administer the customary law and there is nothing in the Act, or in any other statute, excluding from their jurisdiction aspects of the customary law within the ambit of "matters affecting clans" in Buganda. The present position in Buganda, therefore, appears to be that the clan councils, though now deprived of their apex, the Kabaka, continue to exist and may deliberate upon clan matters, including matters of succession, but that if any person wishes to institute proceedings, regarding succession in a court, he is entitled to do so and the courts judgment and orders will be enforced even if contrary to the clan council's decision on the matter.

In conclusion, it is clear that Uganda is in the process of rationalising the complex, and in many ways unsatisfactory, position regarding succession law which was inherited from the colonial period. Moreover, it seems likely that before long a comprehensive statutory body of law on succession, combining elements of the customary law with much of the English law, suitably modified, will be in force throughout the country.

PART V

MARRIAGE AND DIVORCE

INTEGRATION OF THE LAW OF HUSBAND AND WIFE IN WESTERN NIGERIA

by

A. B. KASUNMU

FACULTY OF LAW OF THE UNIVERSITY OF IFE

INTEGRATION OF THE LAW OF HUSBAND AND WIFE IN WESTERN NIGERIA

The problems of integrating the customary and statutory laws of husband and wife in Western Nigeria will be discussed under four main headings: (a) Marriage Preliminaries (b) Essentials of a valid marriage (c) Dissolution of Marriage and (d) Incidents of such marriages with particular reference to legitimacy and legitimation, but excluding succession. Our approach will be to state briefly the legal requirements of each of the various systems of marriages and to see how far integration is possible.

There are three forms of marriages possible under the law: Customary, Moslem and Statutory marriages. The first two forms are polygamous while the last is monogamous. Another form of marriage which is 'recognised' is a Christian monogamous marriage contracted outside Nigeria. The law governing the validity of a Statutory Marriage is the 1958 Marriage Act.[1]

The legal position of Moslem marriages needs further clarification in Western Nigeria. Even though Moslem marriages are polygamous, they differ from a customary marriage in that, whereas under the latter the husband can take as many wives as he wants, under the former he can take only four. Moreover, under a customary marriage the wife has exclusive rights to her property, while under Mohammedan law the husband has some right over the wife's property, there is also some restriction on the amount of property she can dispose of.[2] Mohammedan marriages occupy a unique position in Western Nigeria in that even though such a marriage is recognised, it has the same incidents as a customary marriage. Various factors account for this. Mohammedan law is applied (if at all) under the section of the High Court Law dealing with the application of 'native law and custom'.[2a] There is also the difficulty of deciding which of the various schools of Mohammedan law applies.[3] This difficulty was one of the reasons

---

1. Laws of the Federation of Nigeria, 1958 ed. Cap. 115. Statutory marriage is a matter within the exclusive Federal list.
2. Vesey Fitz-Gerald, *Mohammedan Law*
2a. Laws of Western Nigeria, 1959 ed. Cap. 44, s. 12.
3. Unlike Northern Nigeria where it is the Maliki school, (Northern Nigeria Native Court Law 1956), various schools have been suggested for the West: *Apatira* v. *Akanke* (1944) 17 N.L.R. 149—Maliki; *Ayoola* v. *Folawiyo* (1942) 8 W.A.C.A. 39—Sunni School, on appeal, held to be "Local Mohammedan custom".

why Brooke, J., applied customary law incidents to a Mohammedan marriage, holding that "there is no personal law in this country as there is, e.g. in India; and under section 17 of the Supreme Court Ordinance, native law and custom shall be deemed applicable in causes and matters where the parties are natives and in this case they are natives of Ijebu. This may include Mohammedan law, and in the Northern Emirates it is Maliki Code . . . but Ijebu is not a Mohammedan area".[4]

There is therefore complete integration between customary marriage and Mohammedan marriage in so far as incidents are concerned. The formation of a Mohammedan marriage is also very similar to that of a customary marriage. The same marriage negotiations are necessary, and parental consent is also important. It is the actual ceremony that distinguishes a Mohammedan marriage from a customary marriage. The presence of a Muslim priest is always necessary at the marriage or "Yigi" ceremony in a Mohammedan marriage. The 'Yigi' is usually performed in the house of the bride's father or anyone in *loco parentis*. Much of what is said and suggested in this paper in respect of customary marriages, will apply to Mohammedan marriages

A. Marriage Preliminaries

For a customary marriage, this is the period of negotiation. It begins from the time when the girl or her parents are approached on behalf of the intended husband. The intended husband as a rule does not approach the girl or her parents himself, but goes through a middleman known as "Alarina". This happens when the intended husband is old enough to find a wife himself. However, in most cases, the marriage negotiations take place when the parties are too young to participate, and such negotiations are usually transacted between the parents. Should the preliminary negotiations be successful, a meeting is then arranged between the couples and their respective families. This is the formal betrothal. The negotiation, hitherto informal, is now given family recognition by the payment of a consent fee called the "Ijohun". This is a token fee, symbolical rather than substantial in nature. These are the usual preliminaries to a customary marriage. In respect of a statutory marriage, there is what is called the 'engagement' which fulfils the same purpose as a betrothal. It is a combination of both the betrothal and the normal engagement as known in English law. The intended husband in asking for the girl's hand in marriage makes some presents to her and her parents. Included in the presents are

---

4. *Alayo* v. *Tunwase* (1946) 18 N.L.R. 88 at p. 92

an engagement ring and a Bible. It is also here that he pays the dowry, which, though not necessary for a statutory marriage, is normally paid.

The legal effect of an engagement is that it is regarded as a contract between the boy and the girl. If broken, either of them can bring an action for breach of promise. The only right against a third party is for inducing a breach of that contract. However, the legal consequences of a betrothal are not clear. It is generally agreed by writers that an action for a breach of promise is not known under customary law. If the termination was not due to any fault of his, he could recover the consent fee. As against third parties, he is said to have an 'action in adultery' against them. 'Adultery' here is used in a loose sense for it covers sexual intercourse by the wife before marriage. It is also said that any child born to a betrothed woman 'belongs' to the intended husband.[4a]

One of the methods adopted in effecting integration between the legal consequences of an engagement and a betrothal is through the application of the repugnancy doctrine. Under this doctrine, the courts are given the right to reject any proved custom which is against natural justice, equity and good conscience.[4b] As a result of this doctrine, the courts have always rejected the claim of an intended husband to any child born to the woman. Such a child will be given to the natural father.[5] Another way in which the courts have unconsciously integrated the legal consequences of a betrothal and an engagement is by their failure to classify the nature of the promise before deciding on whether there is any liability on an action for breach of a promise to marry. If A makes a promise to marry B and then breaks it, B can bring an action for breach if A's promise is to marry her under the Statute. No action can be maintained if the promise is to marry under customary law. The courts however do not classify the promise as analysed above but simply assume that the promise was to marry under the Statute.[6] This approach has made it possible for one to maintain an action for a breach of a promise to marry under customary law. There is therefore a certain degree of integration in the legal consequences of a betrothal and an engagement.

4a. Ajisafe, *Law and Customs of the Yorubas*, p. 73
4b. High Court of Lagos Act, s. 27(1). There are similar provisions in the High Court Laws of the other Regions.
5. *Edet* v. *Essien* (1932) 11 N.L.R. 47. *Amacheree* v. *Goodhead* (1923) 4 N.L.R. 99. See also s. 13 of the Divorce and Custody of children adoptive Bye-Laws 1958. The bye-laws have no force of Law. They are only models for guidance.
6. *Aiyede* v. *Norman Williams*, (1960) L.L.R. 253, *Uso* v. *Iketubosun* (1957) W.R.N.L.R. 187, *Ugboma* v. *Morah* (1940) 15 N.L.R. 78

B. Essentials of a valid Marriage:

The essential requirements for a valid customary marriage in Western Nigeria may be stated as follows: (i) Consent, (ii) Capacity, (iii) Dowry, (iv) Taking the bride to the bridegroom. These points will now be discussed in turn. They will be followed by a discussion of the requisites for a Statutory marriage, and how far, if at all, it is possible to integrate the two systems of marriages.

Customary law

1. (a) **Consent of Parties**

Despite the views of some early writers on Yoruba law to the effect that the consent of the parties to the marriage is unnecessary,[7] it would appear from judicial decisions that consent is necessary. Thus in *Re Soluade and Beckley*,[8] Ames, J. held that an Idano ceremony is not the actual marriage, and that even if it was, it was not valid since it was celebrated without the consent of the prospective bridegroom. Similarly, in *Savage v. Macfoy*[9] Osborne C.J. expressed the view that the consent of the bride is equally essential to a valid marriage.

(b) **Consent of Parents**

Parental consent has always been considered necessary before a valid marriage could be said to exist. Various reasons have been given for this. One reason for requiring parental consent when a man is getting married is that it is his parents who eventually will be responsible for paying the dowry and it is only fair that they should have a say as to whom he marries. The need for parental consent when a woman is getting married arises from the fact that under customary law, dowry is payable directly to the girl's parents and their refusal to accept it signifies their disapproval of the association. A man could defy the wishes of his parents if he is able to pay the dowry without their assistance, though it is doubtful if the wife's parent will give their assent to such a wedding.

Apart from the attempt made in section 5 of the Western Nigeria's Marriage, Divorce and Custody of Children Adoptive Bye-Laws Order 1958, it is difficult to say how much of the above is still law. Osborne C.J. for instance in *Re Sapara*[10] holds the view that while parental consent is necessary in the case of a girl, a man does not need the consent of his parents.[11] No reason was given for this

7. Ward, *Marriage amongst the Yorubas*, p. 60
8. (1943) 17 N.L R. 59 at p. 62.
9. (1909) R.G.C.R. (Renner Gold Coast Report) 505
10. (1911) R.G.C.R. 605.
11. See also his earlier judgment in *Savage* v. *Macfoy* where he regarded the marriage contract as being between the girl and her family on one side, and the boy on the other side.

view and one fails to see why a distinction should be made between the man and the woman. Section 5 of the 1958 Adoptive Bye-Laws provides that:

> "When any parent or guardian of a bride refuses his or her consent to a marriage or refuses to accept his or her share of the dowry, the bride, if she is 18 years of age or above, and the groom jointly may institute legal proceedings in a competent court against the parent to show cause why he should refuse consent or to accept his or her share of the dowry . . . The court may therefore dispense with such consent"

(c) **Statutory Law**

Under the Statute, the consent of the parties to the marriage is also essential. Parental consent is required if the parties to the intended marriage (neither being a widower or widow) are under the age of twenty-one. Such consent must be given in writing. Thus, unlike customary law, no consent is needed after the age of 21 has been reached.[12] Furthermore, even if under twenty years, no consent is needed if the person involved is a widower or widow. A statutory marriage even though celebrated without parental consent is not void, but remains valid after celebration.[13] This is because section 33(3) of the Marriage Act as illustrated in *Agbo v. Udo*[14] provides that "no marriage shall after celebration be deemed invalid by reason that any provision of this Act other than the foregoing has not been compiled with".

The consent required for a Statutory Marriage is that of the father and if he is dead or absent from Nigeria, that of the mother.[15] For a customary marriage, it is generally said that the consent of the 'family' is necessary. 'Family' in this context would appear to mean the immediate parents of the parties involved.[16] It is however not clear whether it is the consent of one or both parents that should be obtained.

The question of parental consent in respect of Statutory marriage needs further clarification.

(a)   Assuming X and Y who are married under customary law after obtaining the consent of their respective parents now intend to convert this existing customary law marriage to a marriage under

---

12.   *Ugboma v. Morah* (1940) 15 N.L.R. 78; s. 11 Marriage Act.
13.   Contrast this with a customary law marriage which is void if any of the essential requirements is not satisfied. *Savage v. Macfoy* (1909) R.G.C.R. 505.
14.   (1947) 18 N.L.R. 152.
15.   S. 33(i) and (ii).
16.   *Savage v. Macfoy* R.G.C.R. at p. 505

the statute. Will it be necessary for them to get the consent of their parents again, assuming that they are still under twenty-one years? On a strict interpretation of section 11 of the Marriage Act, such consents must be obtained. This would mean that parental consent is only given for a particular form of marriage, and that a conversion of the existing marriage into another form could not be effected while the parties are still under twenty-one years without asking for further consent from their parents.[17]

(b) Under the Statute, a "widow" or a "widower" under 21 does not have to get the consent of his or her parents to marry under the Statute. It is submitted that the term "widow" or "widower"[18] should also apply to a person married under customary law. Thus if X marries Y under customary law, X should be able to marry under the Statute (after Y's death) without the consent of the parents even though he is under twenty-one years.

It is submitted that it is possible to integrate the law relating to consent in the two systems of marriages so long as the interest of the family is recognized, especially in customary marriage. By way of summary, the following guidelines are suggested for both systems of marriages:

1. The parties to the impending marriage must give their consent publicly. Lack of consent will render the marriage void.
2. (a) Where a party to an impending marriage is under 21 years, the consent (in writing) of at least one parent (of the person under 21) must be obtained by that person.
   (b) If there is no parent alive, or if the parent is outside Nigeria, the consent of the guardian or the court must be obtained.
   (c) The court can dispense with the consent of a parent or a guardian if this is unreasonably withheld.
3. Parental consent will not be required from a person to a marriage if that person is a widow, widower, divorcee, or already married. It is immaterial that he or she is under 21 years.[4]
4. (a) Notwithstanding section 3, the consent of at least one parent in writing must be obtained by a girl, if the intended marriage is under customary law. This provision applies even if the girl is over 21 years.
   (b) The court can dispense with parental consent if it is

17. This problem will not arise when the first marriage is a Statutory marriage. The current belief is that whereas a Statutory marriage with a woman abrogates an earlier customary marriage with the same woman, the reverse is not the case.
18. See *Coleman* v. *Shang* (1961) 2 All E.R. 406 where the term widow in the Ghana marriage Act was held to include the widow of a customary marriage. See also *Jirigho* v. *Anamal* (1958) W.N.L.R. 195.

unreasonably withheld. The court shall in this case order the dowry to be paid into Court.

(c) Except as provided for in this section, no parental consent will be required if the parties to the marriage are over 21 years.

5. Lack of parental consent will not affect the validity of a marriage after celebration.

In view of our submission later on that the payment of a dowry should not be regarded as an essential requirement for a valid customary marriage, section 4 of the above draft will apply only when dowry is payable. Otherwise the marriage of a girl over 21 years should not, like that of the boy, require parental consent.

Capacity

There are three separate issues to be discussed here: (a). The prescribed age when one could marry (b) Restrictions on marriage of people related by blood or marriage (c) who are those who could marry under customary law.

Age

Nearly all the wirters agree on the point that under customary law, there is no minimum age for marriage. The question of whether a person is old enough for marriage depends on that persons physical development and also on whether that person has attained the age of puberty or not.[19] Even though the agreement to marry might be entered into while the parties are very young, the celebration of the marriage and sometimes its consummation occur after the parties have attained the age of puberty. There is no definite legal authority on the effect of a marriage celebrated below the age of puberty. Doubt as to its legal effect is also exhibited by section 7 of the Marriage Divorce and Custody of Children Adoptive Bye Laws of 1958. Instead of declaring such a marriage void, the section provides that the fact that a marriage was celebrated when the parties were below the age of puberty should be taken into consideration when making an order for the dissolution of the marriage. This provision surely negatives a contention that such a marriage is void ab initio.

The Marriage Act is silent on the age one must attain before going through a statutory marriage. What then is the required age for a statutory marriage? There are two possible answers to this:

---

19. For various views as to when puberty is reached see Elias, *Groundwork of Nigerian Law*, p. 287 that it is 14 years of the girl, and 17 for the man. Johnson, *History of the Yorubas* (1919) pp. 100-3 that it is 25 years.

(a) That the age limit is 16 as it is in England under section 2 of the 1949 English Marriage Act. The application of this Act in Nigeria depends on the interpretation one gives to section 16 of the High Court of Lagos Act[20] which provides that:

"The jurisdiction of the High Court of a Region in relation to marriages, and the annulment and dissolutions of marriages and in relation to other matrimonial causes shall subject to the provisions of any laws of a region so far as practice and procedure are concerned, be exercised by the court in conformity with the law and practice for the time being in force in England"

This section would appear to give the Nigerian courts *jurisdiction* in Matrimonial causes similar to that of the English courts, but the Nigerian courts have interpreted the section as also importing the application of the current English law on marriage, annulment, dissolution and other matrimonial causes. If the interpretation adopted by the Nigerian High Courts is correct, then a marriage celebrated in Nigeria under the age of 16 will be void since such a marriage would be void in England.[21]

(b) A second view for which there is no judicial support is that the English common law rule (14 for males, 12 for females) should be the applicable law in Nigeria. If this second view prevails, a marriage celebrated under the prescribed age would be voidable and not void, since such marriages are only voidable at common law.

It should not prove difficult to establish a common minimum age for both customary and statutory marriages. For example, an attempt was made in 1956 under the Age of Marriage Law to fix the minimum age at 16 for both customary and statutory marriages. Whether the minimum age should be lower or higher than 16 is perhaps not as important as to what should be the effect of a marriage celebrated in breach of the age requirement. The rule whereby such a marriage is declared void would appear to be too harsh particularly after the spouses have voluntarily lived together after being aware of the defect. The danger that a lot of marriages will be celebrated below the required minimum age is greater in Nigeria where majority of births are not registered and one has to rely on memory or other traditional events to ascertain a person's age. It is therefore suggested that a marriage under the required minimum age should only be void if the parties deliberately set out to flout the law.

---

20. S. 8 High Court Law Western Nigeria Cap. 44. S. 16 High Court of Lagos Law. Cap. 80
21. See generally, Kasunmu and Salacuse, *Nigerian Family Law*, ch. 3

Prohibited degrees of relationship

Yoruba customary law prohibits certain marriages as incestuous. These arise either from affinity (i.e. relationship by marriage) or consanguinity (blood relationship). Even though it is impossible to draw a list of such prohibited marriages, it is quite clear that these are wider than those under English law, which applies to Statutory marriage. The Yorubas, being patrilineal, object especially strongly to marriages between those related by blood if they are related through the male side.

It has been suggested that relationships created through paternal links often operate as a bar to a marriage than those created through maternal links, and that in many Yoruba towns, maternal links for the purposes of marriage are rarely traced beyond four generations while paternal links are traced beyond the fourth generation.[22]

As regards prohibition due to affinity, it appears that there is no rigid rule prohibiting such marriages. Schwab[23] is of the opinion that between those who call each other 'ano' (in-law) there are no rules forbidding marriage since a union between a man and another member of his wife lineage, while not viewed with favour, is not prohibited. Despite this laxity, it is recognised that a man cannot marry his wife's mother.

The Marriage Act by section 33(i) provides that for those marrying under the Act, the degrees of consanguinity and affinity should be the same as under English law. Thus a man cannot marry his wife's sister (after the dissolution of the prior marriage) under the Statute. He can do this only if the wife is dead.[24] Similarly, he cannot marry his father's widow under the Statute. Needless to say that he can do this under customary law, so long as the widow is not his own mother.[25]

It is submitted that it is desirable to have uniform rules governing prohibited marriages and that such rules must take into account the social and cultural background of the persons involved. The wholesale importation of English law as is the case with section 33(1) of the Marriage Act has created anomalies and situations difficult to justify. For example, H will be regarded as lawfully married under customary law to W (an inherited wife after the death

---

22. Yoruba lineage by Lloyd, 25, Africa, 235. Contrast this with the view that among the Ife people, blood relationship ends at three (meta ni itantan)
23. Terminology of Kinship and Marriage among the Yorubas, 28 Africa 301.
24. 1949 Marriage Act (First schedule).
25. *The Estate of Agboruja* (1949) 19 N.L.R. 38, *Aileru* v. *Anibi* (1951) 20 N.L.R. 46.

of H's father) while under the Marriage Act, H. would not be allowed to convert the marriage with W to one under that Act.

Who could marry under Customary Law

Writing on the position under early customary law, Judge Folarin asserts that "marriage between a foreigner and a native is not prohibited or banned, if the husband pays all the necessary dowry and parents give their consent and the girl does desire it.[26] It has however been held in two cases[27] that only natives can marry under customary law. Customary law, it is argued, applies only to 'natives'.[28] In Western Nigeria, the term 'Nigerian' as opposed to 'native' is used. A Nigerian is a "person whose parents were of any tribe or tribes indigenous to Nigeria and the descendants of such persons and includes any person one of whose parents was a member of such a tribe."[29]

Thus, unlike the conflict of laws rule that capacity to marry is normally determined by one's domicile, a person cannot marry under customary law, even if domiciled in Nigeria or of Nigerian nationality, if he is not a native or a 'Nigerian'.

It is submitted that this restrictive view as to the application of customary law is wrong. Quite apart from violating the principle that capacity to marry is determined by the domicile of the person involved, it works injustice on the woman involved. For example, in *Fonseca's*[30] case the plaintiff, who had lived with the deceased, a Portuguese, for 30 years (after marrying him under customary law), failed in her action for letters of administration to his estate.

That a "non-native or "non-Nigerian" can sometimes be bound by transactions under customary law is apparent from section 12 of the High Court Law of Western Nigeria. This section, overlooked in *Fonseca's* case, provides that though customary law will not apply to transactions between a "Nigerian" and a "non-Nigerian", it will apply "where substantial injustice would be done to either party, by

---

26. Folarin, *Laws and Customs of Egbaland*, p. 23.
27. *Savage* v. *Macfoy* (1909) R.G.C.R. 505, *Fonesca* v. *Passman* (1958) W.N.L.R. 41.
28. 'Native' includes 'native foreigner'—a person one of whose parents belongs to an indigenous tribe in Nigeria or Africa. 1958 Interpretation Act Cap. 89, Laws of Nigeria (now the 1964 (Miscellaneous Provisions) Act.) This definition has been abolished in the 1964 Interpretation Act, though the term still appears in the Lagos High Court Act.
29. S. 2 Customary Courts Law, Western Nigeria.
30. *Fonseca* v. *Passman* (1958) W.N.L.R. 41.

strict adherence to any rules of law which would otherwise be applicable."[31]

Any person can marry under the statute so long as the statutory provisions are satisfied. It is therefore suggested that the same simple rule be adopted for customary marriage instead of restricting it only to "natives" or "Nigerians". This will, however, create two problems:

    (i) customary courts in Western Nigeria have jurisdictions only over Nigerians. This will have to be extended to cover non-Nigerians;

    (ii) how will the sections of the Customary Courts Law dealing with the choice of law rules operate in the case of a non-Nigerian?

Dowry

This term is preferred by the writer to other suggested names[32] since it is the term used by the courts.[33] It is the consideration given by the bridegroom or his parents to the brides' parents for the marriage. It comprises of money, presents or services. It is quite different from the presents given at a betrothal or engagement ceremony, though section 2 of the Adoptive Bye-Laws seems to group both types of presents as dowry.

The payment of dowry (unless waived by the parents) has always been regarded as being essential to the validity of a customary marriage. Although it is not necessary to pay a dowry for a Statutory marriage, people do invariably pay it before going through or after such a marriage. In fact one of the reasons why some parents are reluctant to allow their daughters marry under the Statute is because they get nothing from the husband since the payment of a dowry is not necessary. What is common now is for the parties to first fulfil all the requirements for a valid customary marriage and then add to this the statutory requirement, i.e., going to the church or court.

It is appropriate at this time to consider the effect of a combination of the two forms of marriage. Once a person is married under customary law, he or she cannot marry another person under the

---

31. See also s. 27 High Court Act of Lagos. On an identical section under the Ghana Courts Act, 1951 s. 87(1), a Non-African was made liable to maintain his illegitimate child under customary law. *Adjei & Dua* v. *Ripley* (1956) 1 W.A.L.R. 62.
32. Bride wealth, bride price, marriage consideration, marriage payment.
33. *Savage* v. *Macfoy; Re Sapara.* See also s. 2 of the 1958 Marriage Adoptive Bye-Laws.

Statute. He can however marry[34] the same person to whom he or she was married under customary law under the Staute. The position in Nigeria is that the earlier customary marriage is converted into a Statutory marriage if the statutory marriage takes place *in Nigeria*.[35] It appears that the husband on a dissolution of the Statutory marriage will forfeit the dowry he paid before the conversion. The law as it stands only allows for conversion from a customary marriage into a Statutory marriage, and not vice-versa.

In the view of the writer, the payment of dowry is an anachronism. One of the reasons given for paying it is that it gives the parents, or the family some control over the marriage. This might have been true at a time when parents paid the dowry for their sons, or received it on behalf of their daughters, or even had to pay it on a dissolution of the marriage. However, as indicated earlier, nowadays the sons are able to pay for their marriages, and dowry could be received on behalf of an unwilling parent. Again, the dowry on dissolution is repaid by the next husband and not the parents of the receiving wife. It is therefore suggested that the payment of dowry in a customary marriage should have the same effect as in a statutory marriage. It could still be paid, but its non-payment should not affect the validity of a marriage.

This simple solution will also avoid the almost impossible task of fixing a maximum sum for dowry. Even though this has been done in both Eastern and Western Nigeria, it is common knowledge that this law is not observed. It might well be that some parents will prefer men who will pay them dowry. If because of this they refuse to give their consent, this could be dispensed with as provided for under consent. It would therefore be not obligatory on any person to pay dowry if demanded. If he decides to pay, the amount payable, and what is recoverable on a dissolution of the marriage should depend on the agreement between him and the parents of the girl.

By way of summary, it is suggested that:

1. A marriage (customary or statutory) should be valid despite the fact that dowry was not paid.

2. When dowry is paid, the amount payable or recoverable on a dissolution of the marriage should depend on agreement between the person paying and the parents of the girl.

34. A remarriage has to be distinguished from a mere religious blessing in a church after a customary marriage. *Re Ammettefe*, (1889) Redwar 157.

35. s. 33(i) Marriage Act. Such a conversion could only occur if the second marriage is celebrated in Nigeria. See however *Ohochuku v. Ohochuku* (1960) 1 W.L.R. 183 where the second marriage celebrated in England was regarded as existing side by side with the earlier customary marriage.

3. Any parent refusing to give his or her consent to a marriage merely because dowry was not paid would be deemed to have unreasonably withheld that consent.

4. When a marriage has been celebrated with X under any of the two systems of marriages, a later marriage with X under another system will be regarded as dissolving the earlier marriage.

5. Nothing in the above section should be construed as restricting the right of a man married under customary law from taking more than one wife, provided the subsequent marriages are also under customary law. A person married under the statute can only have one wife.

Celebration of Marriage

On the issue of a certificate by the Registrar or a Licence[36] by the President the parties to a Statutory marriage will then proceed with the celebration of the marriage. This could either be in a licensed place of worship before a recognised minister of the licensed church or in the Registrar of marriages' office. Marriages in a licensed place of worship must take place between the hours of eight o'clock in the forenoon and six o'clock in the afternoon, in the presence of two or more witnesses. As regards a marriage taking place in the Registry, this must take place between the hours of ten o'clock in the forenoon and four o'clock in the afternoon. Marriage certificates must be submitted for registration to the Principal Registrar on the completion of every marriage ceremony. This if done will be admissible as evidence of the marriage to which it relates. A marriage celebrated in an unlicensed place or by unlicensed person or outside the authorised hours is void if both parties knowingly and wilfully acquiesce in its celebration under the vitiating circumstances.[37]

From the above short account, it is clear that the existence of a statutory marriage is easy to prove. Furthermore, a valid marriage comes into existence only after a celebration as discussed above. But these issues are not settled in the case of a customary marriage. When does the marriage come into existence? Is it after the betrothal, after the payment of a dowry, or only when the bride has actually been led to the residence of the bridegroom? This is a repetition of the question: What are the legal essentials of a

---

36. A licence differs from a certificate in that
    (i) it dispenses with the filing of notice and the 21-day period before a certificate is granted.
    (ii) it can authorise the celebration of marriage at a place other than a licensed place of worship.

37. s. 33(2) Marriage Act.

customary marriage? Ames, J. in *Abiodun* v. *Soluade & Beckley* [38] regarded the taking of the bride to the bridegroom as the culmination of the marriage ceremony. Without this, there is no marriage. But the writer is of the opinion that a valid customary marriage comes into existence once the dowry has been paid. The wedding feast and ceremony have a social and evidential significance, but not a legal one. This point was stressed by Ward, who said that "the payment of the dowry is usually a family affair, and as far as the public is concerned, may or may not have taken place, for one cannot always believe what one is told here. What the people do see is that a man has taken a girl to his home to all appearances in the way a common concubine is taken. If he wants to convince them otherwise, it should be a relatively easy thing for him to send the girl home and marry her in the accustomed way."[39]

Since customary marriage is solely a family affair, the existence of such a marriage is difficult to prove. It is therefore suggested that a system of registration be introduced similar to that for statutory marriages. This will have two effects. It will make it easier to prove the existence of a customary marriage. Furthermore, registration would be of more than evidentiary significance. Since we have suggested that the payment of a dowry should no longer be a legal requirement, the validity of a customary marriage will now depend on its being registered.

Thus, although the present provisions dealing with statutory marriage will be retained, customary marriage law might be brought closer to statutory marriage by providing that:

   (i) A customary marriage will be recognised as valid only from the date of registration.

   (ii) The existence of a customary marriage can be proved only by the production of a certificate of registration.

   (iii) On registration both parties must appear before the Registrar of Marriages.

   (iv) No marriage should be registered unless the Registrar is satisfied that the parties and parents (if necessary) have given their consents.

   (v) Where the parties are married to each other under any other system, the Registrar must be satisfied that the existing marriage has been dissolved.

---

38. (1943) 17 N.L.R. 59. See however Ajisafe who regarded the marriage as coming into existence once the betrothal has taken place: *Laws and Customs of the Yorubas*, p. 55; Contrast Folarin, that it is after dowry has been paid: *Laws and Customs of Egbaland*, p. 19.
39. *Marriage Among the Yorubas*, p. 15.

Dissolution of Marriage

This is another important way in which customary marriage differs considerably from marriage under the Statute. There are three main differences. The first is as to substance. While there are specific grounds on which a statutory marriage can be dissolved, there are none in respect of a customary marriage. There are only "reasons" for dissolving a customary marriage, and these reasons are important mainly in deciding whether the dowry should be returned by the wife or not. However, the 1958 Adoptive Bye-Laws, which was principally aimed at unifying customary law, has also effected integration with statutory marriage. Section 7 [40] provides specific grounds (similar to those for a statutory marriage) on which customary marriage can be dissolved. The remarks of a Lagos Chief in *Re Sapara* who took a hat and described the position of a woman married under customary law as follows: "a woman is like this hat, if one man drops it, another may pick it up"[41] should no longer be taken seriously. In fact, Osborne, C.J., in *Re Sapara* disagreed with the above views and observed that "native marriage is not a capital knot which is loosely tied and can be untied by the man at will."[41a]

This, however, does not mean that there is complete integration in the substance of the law. The death of the husband does not automatically terminate a marriage under customary law. Death (whether of the husband or wife) terminates a marriage under the statute. Under customary law, on the death of the husband, the widow is inherited by a member of the deceased's family. If she refuses to be inherited, she must formally dissolve the marriage by paying back the dowry. The Adoptive Bye-Laws have modified this by providing that no dowry should be repaid by the widow when seeking a divorce on the death of her husband.

The second main difference is procedural. A statutory marriage can only be dissolved by judicial process. However, a customary marriage can be dissolved extra-judicially by mutual consent or even unilaterally. It would appear that despite the fact that the Customary Courts have "unlimited jurisdiction in matrimonial causes and matters between persons married under customary law,"[42] extra-judicial divorce is still recognised.[43]

40. Some of the grounds are wider than those under the statute, e.g. (i) No divorce order would be granted to a wife nursing a child under three years or a wife who has three or more children for the husband. (ii) Neglect. (iii) Lunacy for more than three years. (iv) Desertion for a period of 2 years. (v) Leprosy.
41. (1911) R.G.C.R. 605 at p. 613.
41a. Ibid at p. 613.
42. S. 18(2) Customary Courts Law.
43. *Chaware v. Johnson* (1935) 12 N.L.R. 4; *Alayo v. Tunwase* (1946) 18 N.L.R. 88.

The third difference concerns the question of jurisdict on. The jurisdiction of the courts over customary marriage and divorce is governed by the Customary Courts Law. By section 17, the court has jurisdiction over all Nigerians. The effect of this is that irrespective of domicile, the customary court has jurisdiction to dissolve the customary marriage of any Nigerian.

However, domicile is the basis of jurisdiction for the dissolution of a statutory marriage. The reported cases are in conflict as to whether one has to establish a Regional or a Federal (Nigerian) domicile for purposes of jurisdiction.[44] Section 18 of the 1950 English Matrimonial Causes Act has also given the English courts jurisdiction to dissolve a marriage on a petition by the wife on the grounds of three years continuous residence in the United Kingdom. It has been held in a Nigerian case that Section 18 does not apply in Nigeria.[45]

Is it then possible to integrate the two systems of marriages in the field of divorce? Let us begin with the procedural problems. Section 18(2) of the Customary Courts Law gives customary courts unlimited jurisdiction in matrimonial causes and matters between persons married under customary law. The current belief is that despite the above provisions, extra-judicial divorce is still recognised, at least when the parties mutually agree to terminate the marriage. It is even assumed that the husband could unilaterally terminate the marriage without going to the court. A simple way to achieve integration is to provide that dissolution of a customary marriage otherwise than by a customary court will not be recognised.

This will only be partial integration since there will still be two different courts exercising jurisdiction over the two systems of marriages—High Courts in respect of a statutory marriage and customary courts in respect of a customary marriage. A special problem is created by the abolition of extra-judicial divorce. It has been suggested previously that a "non-native" or "non-Nigerian" should be able to contract a customary marriage. Since the customary courts in the West have jurisdiction only over Nigerians, it would follow that such courts will not have jurisdiction over a non-Nigerian who is married under customary law. It is therefore suggested that the jurisdiction of customary courts be extended to a

44. *Okonkwo* v. *Eze* (1960) N.N.L.R. 80. For other decided cases see *Nwokedi* v. *Nwokedi* (1958) L.L.R. 94 (Nigerian). *Ero* v. *Ero* (unreported) (Regional). *Machi* v. *Machi* (1960) L.L.R. 103 (Regional). *Odunjo* v. *Odunjo* (unreported) WD/42/62 (Nigerian).
45. *Adeoye* v. *Adeoye* (1961) All N.L.R. 792. Contrast with *Becker* v. *Becker* (unreported) Lagos High Court, Jan. 1964 where the court assumed jurisdiction based on residence (5 years) of the wife in Nigeria even though the husband was domiciled in Germany.

person who enters into a transaction which is governed by customary law.

The attempt made in the Adoptive Bye-Laws to provide for grounds of dissolution of customary marriages could also be used as the basis of substantive integration.

(a) Desertion is a ground for divorce both under the statute and under the Adoptive Bye-Laws. It must have lasted for two years before it is a ground under the Bye-Law, whereas under the statute, it must have lasted for at least three years. Despite these minor differences, it should be possible to work out a compromise rule.

(b) Cruelty, adultery and insanity are also grounds for divorce under the two systems.

(c) The death of either spouse should be regarded as terminating the marriage.

(d) One of the prime aims of marriage among the Yorubas is the procreation of children. Sterility on the part of either spouse should also be a ground for divorce.

(e) The main aim of the courts should be to reconcile the parties irrespective of whether a matrimonial offence has been committed. At present, this appears to be the object of the divorce courts under customary law, where the courts would often not grant a dissolution until genuine efforts at reconciliation by the family are of no avail. Statistics are not available to show how many marriages have been salvaged as a result of family intervention at reconciliation, but it is the view of the writer that such a provision in the law would help.

In suggesting grounds for dissolving a customary marriage, one hopes that this will not lead to a rigid application of the law as is now observed in courts applying the received English law. The desirability of the 'matrimonial offence' principle as the basis for divorce has been seriously questioned in English law,[46] and it might well be that there is some, virtue in not elevating the 'reasons' for divorce under customary law into rigid 'grounds' for divorce.

Incidents

This section deals with the incidents of marriages. Succession is however excluded since it is a separate topic at the present conference. It is our view that with the exception of the rule of monogamy that is, one man, one wife, applying to a statutory marriage, the incidents of both forms of marriages should and can be integrated.

In the field of parent and child, there are some differences of doubtful merit between the two forms of marriages. The Legitimacy

46.   See the Report of the Royal Commission on Divorce, 1965

Act, which applies only to statutory marriages, provides that as a general rule, only children born in wedlock are legitimate. Children born out of wedlock can be legitimatized by the subsequent marriage of their parents under the statute, and it would appear that legitimation is still possible even if the child is born as a result of adultery. Thus the basis of legitimacy or legitimation depends on the existence of a valid marriage. However, under customary law, one can have a legitimate child with no marriage at all, merely by acknowledging paternity.

The effective date of legitimation under the Legitimacy Act is the date of the subsequent marriage. It would appear that under customary law, the child on being acknowledged would be regarded as legitimate from birth. If a child is legitimate under the Act, he is deemed to be legitimate for all purposes. However, acknowledgment presumably confers on him only succession rights from his parents though in *Williams* v. *Williams*[47] an acknowledged child was given succession rights in a will made by a third party.

It would appear that acknowledgment is limited to instances where the father is a "native". If such a father is married to X under customary law, he can acknowledge children born to him by Y, either before, during or after the marriage with X. If however, he is married to X under the Statute, he could acknowledge children born to him by Y only if they are born before or after the marriage with X. If born during the marriage, they cannot be acknowledged, and can be legitimized only by a marriage with Y under the Statute.

Suggested integration

1. A child is legitimate only if born in lawful wedlock.

2. An illegitimate child may be legitimatized by (a) the subsequent marriage (whether customary or statutory) of its parents; (b) acknowledgment by the father.

3. (a) Acknowledgment could be a solemn declaration before the court or any other admission of paternity.

(b) The father acknowledging must have the capacity to acknowledge either by the law of his domicile, or by the law of the place where the acknowledgment takes place.

4. Legitimation either by acknowledgment or by subsequent marriage should be effective from the child's date of birth. This, however, should not affect accrued rights before the date of marriage or acknowledgment.

5. A child born in adultery may be legitimized only by the subsequent marriage of the parents.

47. (unreported) M/112/63) of the Lagos High Court.

6. A child who is legitimized by acknowledgment or the subsequent marriage of the parents will be recognised as legitimate for all purposes.

In the application of the general law, the need for integration is also necessary. The fiction of the unity of husband and wife in English law rests on the concept of monogamous marriage. This fiction therefore does not apply to a customary marriage. For example, under the Criminal Code, the unity of husband and wife is confined to statutory marriages. Husband and wife of a customary marriage can therefore be guilty of conspiracy, stealing each other's property and also there is liability for each other's crimes as accessories after the fact. The plea of coercion or compulsion by the husband is not available to the wife. Similarly, "husband and wife" as used in the Evidence Act refers only to statutory marriages. Husbands and wives of a customary marriage are therefore both competent and compellable witnesses for the prosecution as for the defence.[48]

Presumably, the fiction of the unity of husband and wife will also be restricted to statutory marriage in the sphere of tort. It has been suggested that the fiction should "not follow from a polygamous marriage for the rule that one man and one woman are one in law would be extended to the breaking point if it were held that one man and four women are one person"[49] While this might be true where there are more than one wife, there should be no difficulty in applying the doctrine of unity of husband and wife to customary marriage if there is only one wife. Though complete integration may be unattainable, it is still possible to achieve partial integration by providing that:

(a) Where the husband of a customary marriage has only one wife, the husband or the wife should be able to claim the advantage of the doctrine that the husband and wife are one in law.

(b) Where there is more than one wife, the wife or wives alone should be able to assert the doctrine.

We have clearly demonstrated that though complete integration is not possible, the customary law of husband and wife can still be substantially integrated with the statutory law. Where the customary law is vague or not known, and where it is known but contrary to equity, and good conscience, integration has been through the

48. See however s. 161 of the Evidence Act which provides that in the case of a Mohammedan marriage, the parties are competent and compellabe but there is a privilege not to disclose communications made during the existence of the marriage.
49. (1953) Harv. L.R. 961 at p. 1001.

discretion of judges trained in English law. This process is rather slow and it is suggested that legislation, be it in the form of a Code, Restatement or an Adoptive Bye-Law, would be preferable.

TOWARDS THE INTEGRATION OF THE LAWS RELATING TO HUSBAND AND WIFE IN GHANA

by

DR. W. C. EKOW DANIELS

UNIVERSITY OF GHANA

TOWARDS THE INTEGRATION OF THE LAWS RELATING TO HUSBAND AND WIFE IN GHANA

The seven million people inhabiting Ghana today consist of more than one ethnic group. Politically and constitutionally the country is governed without distinction as to race or religion. The social systems of the various ethnic groupings, however, differ from one another. Some of the groups are:

(a) The Akan[1]

The Akan are the largest single ethnic group, though made up of three main branches; namely the Ashanti, the Fante, and what has been described as "the Nta group" (e.g. Effutu, Asebu and the Ahanta peoples).[2] With the exception of a strip of land in the south, the whole of Southern and Middle Ghana is populated by the Akan. The social organisation of the Akan is mainly based on matrilineal descent. By that it is meant that they reckon their relationship with one another on the basis that they are all lineally descended from a common ancestress in the female line.[3] In a typical Akan family, the husband is not regarded as a member. He belongs to his mother's family and the wife and her children, on the other hand, are related to *her* mother. The mode of reckoning kinship also determines the pattern of succession. Hence the Akan practise the matrilineal principle of succession. On the death intestate of a husband, the wife and children are not in the strict sense entitled to share in the husband's estate.

(b) The Ewe[4]

The Ewe-speaking people who inhabit the extreme eastern coastal land of Ghana and extend to the Togo border, are predominantly patrilineal. Most of the town and village communities consist of a

1. For a more detailed account of the Akan, see, e.g. J. M. Sarbah: *Fante Customary Law* (1904); R. S. Rattray: *Ashanti* (1923)· *Religion and Art in Ashanti* (1927); *Ashanti Law and Constitution* (1929); E. B. Danquah: *Akan Laws and Customs* (1928).
2. J. B. Danquah, *Akan Society*, London 1951: Bureau of current Affairs (West African Affairs, 8) p. 4.
3. It must not be interpreted to mean that patrilineal relationship is unimportant in Akan society. See, e.g. J. B. Christensen: *Double Descent among the Fante* (New Haven, 1954).
4. Manoukian M., *The Ewe-Speaking People of Togoland and the Gold Coast* (1952).

number of localised patrilineages. As a rule succession to property and to political offices is governed by the patrilineal system of descent. In Ho, for example, individual property devolves according to the patrilineal system of inheritance. There a man's heir is his son. But in some areas, such as Anlo and Glidyi, owing to the Akan influence, property is transmitted matrilineally, i.e., a man's heir is his sister's son.

(c) The Ga-Adangme[5]

The Ga-Adangme also inhabit the Southern strip of Ghana, which includes Accra and its neighbourhood. Their kinship system is based on the patrilineal system. A number of writers hold the view that this group follows a patrilineal system of succession, whilst some court decisions have taken the view that the Ga people practise a matrilineal system of inheritance.[6] The whole matter is in an unsettled state. As a general rule, succession among the Ga-Adangme is patrilineal but there are other "Units", which as a result of Akan influence have adopted the matrilineal system of inheritance.

(d) Northern and Upper Ghana[7]

Northern Ghana is inhabited by about three million people. Although they share a basic culture, there are so many ethnic groups that they lack homogeneity. They are predominantly a patrilineal society and practise a patrilineal system of inheritance. The better known groups are the Tallensi, the Nankanse, the Kusase, the Konkomba, the Manprusi and the Dagamba. In most of these areas some Mohammedan influence can be detected, but that religion has not altered considerably their own laws relating to marriage and land tenure.

MARRIAGE LAW IN GHANA

In Ghana today three forms of marriage are recognised by law. They are:

(a) marriage according to the various types of customary law;

5. For a detailed account of this group, see M. J. Field: *The Social Organisation of the Ga People* (1940).
6. For the various theories see: Allott, "A note on the Ga Law of Succession" (1953) *B.S.O.A.* 165; Ollennu: The Law of *Succession in Ghana* (1960); A. B. Quatey-Papafio, "Law of Succession and the Akras or the Ga Tribes Proper of the Gold Coast" (1910) 10 *Journal of the African Society* 64-72.
7. See Rattray: *Tribes of Ashanti Hinterland* (1932) 2 Vols; D. Tait: *The Konkomba of Northern Ghana* (1961).

(b) marriage according to the rites of Mohammedan law; and
(c) marriage under the provisions of the Marriage Ordinance.

A. Customary Law Marriage

As has already been observed, the formalities and essentials of a valid marriage under this head differ slightly from one ethnic group to another.[8] Provision is however made by the Courts Act, 1960, section 66, for ascertainment by the court of the applicable customary law.[8a] A close study of the subject soon reveals that customary marriages have many features in common. Customary marriages are polygamous, or, to be more accurate, generally potentially polygamous. Hence, a man is entitled to marry more than one wife if he so wishes, whilst a woman is prohibited from marrying more than one husband at the same time.

A number of learned writers have expressed the view that not only does a customary marriage involve a social re-arrangement, but it is also regarded as an alliance between the families of either spouse. Indeed, in 1929, Rattray had this to say in one of his writings:

> "It is perhaps almost a platitude to state that marriage in Ashanti is not so much a contract between the individuals directly concerned, as one between the two groups of individuals whom they represent."[9]

In *Yaotey* v. *Quaye*, 1961,[10] the High Court described this feature of customary marriage as follows:

> "Now, one peculiar characteristic of our system of marriage which distinguishes it from the system of marriage in Europe and other places is that it is not just a union of 'this man' and 'this woman' ; it is a union of 'the family of this man' and 'the family of this woman,'"

Obviously there is a shift of emphasis in the latter description. Whereas Rattray in his time had defined marriage in Ashanti as principally a contract between the families of the spouses, the dictum in *Yaotey's Case* makes it clear that in modern times a marriage is not only a "union" between the families of the spouses,

---

8.   See J. M. Sarbah *Fanti Customary Laws*, 2nd edition London (1904) S. B. D. Danquah *Akan Laws & Customs* London, (1928) R. S. Rattray, *Ashanti*, London (1923); *Religion ;& Art in Ashanti* London (1927). *Ashanti Law and Constitution*, London, (1929 M. Fortes. "Kinship and Marriage among the Ashanti" in *African Systems* of *Kinship* and *Marriage*, O.U.P. 1956 (edited by A. Radcliffe Brown, A. R., and ed. D. Forde, M. Manoukian, the Ewe-speaking peoples of Togoland and the Gold Coast. Ethnographic Survey Part VI

8a.   Now see (The Courts Decree (1966) N.L.C. para. 84 section 64.

9.   R. S. Rattray *Ashanti Law and Constitution*, (1929) p. 26.

10.   (1961) G.L.R., p. 73 at p. 579; *Asumah* v. *Khair* (1959) G.L.R. 353.

but also a contract between the individuals concerned. For the sake of clarity, customary marriage in Ghana may be defined as principally the union of, or a contract between, a man and a woman to live as husband and wife, during which period there arises an alliance between the two family groups based on a common interest in the marriage and its continuance.

It ought also to be mentioned that section 109 of the Criminal Code,[11] which applies to all marriages, provides that "Whoever by duress causes any person to marry against his or her will, shall be guilty of a misdemeanour". Therefore, the view that marriage is primarily a contract between two families cannot now be sustained.

The payment of "marriage consideration" is also regarded as a distinguishing feature of customary marriages in Ghana. The Fante call it *tsir nsa* (head drink) and the Ashanti and the Akim describe it as *aseda* (thanking gift or thanks money). Usually it is in the form of cash, except in the North where cows or kola nuts may be given; and it is paid, either by the prospective husband or on his behalf, to the family of the prospective wife, not directly to her.[12] The acceptance of this amount implies that the family of the prospective wife have given their consent to the marriage. It need hardly be emphasised that the amount of the marriage consideration is nominal and does not represent the purchase price of the bride. In most cases, it is the payment of the marriage consideration on behalf of the future husband and its acceptance on behalf of the future wife which constitutes the validating element of the marriage.[13] *But a marriage is not necessarily rendered invalid because of the lack of payment of the marriage* consideration. Among the Fante, for example, where the consent of a woman's family is witheld a man and a woman can contract a valid marriage without any monetary payment, provided that such agreement to marry is made in the presence of "creditable and responsible witnesses, or in the presence of the Chief or headman of the place".[14] However, should the wife later commit adultery, the chances of such a husband recovering damages from his wife's paramour will be rather slim.[15]

The essential requirements of a valid customary marriage in Ghana generally may thus be recapitulated as follows:

11. Act 29.
12. The amount is distributed between the bride's father and other members of her family. See e.g. *Sackie* v. *Accosua Agawa* (1873) Sar. F.C.L. 126.
13. *Penin* v. *Ducan* (1869) Sar. F.C.L. 118
14. Sarbah: *Fanti Customary Laws*, op. cit p.48
15. He cannot be expected to have any right to claim damages for adultery nor can he be liable for his wife's debts or torts, see *Quassua* v. *Ward* (1845) Sar. F.C.L. 117; Danquah, op. cit. p. 176.

1. The consent of the bride and her family;
2. the giving of the marriage consideration by the husband or on his behalf and its acceptance by the bride's family, and/or
3. the agreement by the parties to live together as man and wife.[15a]

Registration

Marriages under customary law do not have to be registered, but certain Local Councils have made bye-laws to that effect. The Nsawam-Aburi Urban Council (Marriage and Divorces Registration) Bye-Laws, 1962 make provision for the registration of every marriage and divorce occurring in that area within a month of the event.[16] Customary marriages are not restricted to Ghanaians only. Indeed there are many instances of Englishmen and other Europeans contracting such a marriage in spite of the controversial decision in *In re Bethell*[17] that a person domiciled in England cannot validly contract a polygamous marriage. As far as Ghanaian law is concerned such marriages are valid and such a person domiciled in England or elsewhere cannot escape marital liability. In *Duncan v. Robertson*[18] it was held that

"Where a man enters into concubinal relations with a native woman his liabilities (and rights if any) should be determined by the same rules whether or not that man is a European or a Native. The position of the one should be no worse nor better than of the other."

B. Mohammedan Law Marriage

Mohammedan marriages in Ghana are also polygamous. Whereas customary marriages, to a large extent, have not been the concern of the legislature, from as far back as 1907, there has been in the Laws of Ghana an Ordinance which provides for the registration of marriages and divorces amongst Mohammedans.[19] The Marriage of Mohammedans Ordinance does not stipulate in detail how such marriages are to be celebrated but some of the essentials are incorporated. Thus, it provides that every Mohammedan marriage celebrated in Ghana must be registered within a week thereafter, at the office of the registering official. It is categorically stated by section 9 of the Ordinance, that

15a. For an exchaustive account see *Yaotey* v. *Quaye* supra p. 578.
16. Local Government Bulletin March 15, 1963.
17. (1887) 38 Ch.D. 220. Contra, *Risk* v. *Risk* (1957) p. 50; see also Chershire, *Private International Law*, 6th ed. p. 312.
18. (1891) Sar. F.C.L. 134, followed in *Adjei & Dua* v. *Ripley* (1956) 1 W.A.L.R. 62.
19. Marriage of Mohammedans Ordinance, Cap 129 (1951 Revision)

"No marriage contracted or divorce effected in Ghana after the commencement of this Ordinance by persons professing the Mohammedan faith shall be valid unless registered under this Ordinance".

The bridegroom, the bride's wali, two witnesses of the marriage and a licensed Mohammedan priest are required to be present. It is the duty of the Mohammedan priest to certify that the particular marriage is valid according to Mohammedan law. Again, it is clear that the payment of a dowry by the husband is an essential feature. The Ordinance is, however, silent as to the type of Mohammedan law which is practised in Ghana. However, this section, and indeed the whole Ordinance, has been honoured by its breach rather than by its observance.

It is further provided that whenever a Mohammedan marriage or divorce is in issue, it can only be proved by the production of the register in which the same is entered or of an extract therefrom. There must be very few cases where the appropriate court has insisted on compliance with this provision.

C. Marriage under the Marriage Ordinance, Cap. 127

The alternative to customary marriage and to Mohammedan marriage is marriage under the provisions of the Marriage Ordinance, Cap. 127.[20] The crucial difference between an Ordinance marriage and the other two types is that the former is monogamous in form whilst the latter two tolerate polygamy. The Marriage Ordinance, which was first enacted in 1884, is largely based on the English Marriage Acts prior to that date. Wherever possible, amendments to the English Act of 1884 have been incorporated. As will be pointed out below, there are other provisions in the Ordinance which take into account the interaction of customary marriage with Ordinance marriage. With the exception of one or two provisions, the Marriage Ordinance is available not only to Ghanaians, but also to foreigners resident in Ghana.

One of the provisions which is lacking in our Marriage Ordinance is section 2 of the English Marriage Act, 1949.[21] This renders void a marriage celebrated between persons either of whom is under the age of sixteen years. The Registrar of Marriage must be satisfied by affidavit that each of the parties to the intended marriage under the Ordinance is twenty-one years old, or that, if he or she is under that age, the written consent of his or her parents has been obtained.[22]

20. Laws of the Gold Coast 1951 Revion
21. 12 & 13 Geo. 6, c. 76.
22. Marriage Ordinance, cap. 127, ss. 14 and 28.

If, after the celebration of the marriage, it is found that consent was obtained under circumstances which make the consent void, or that a false declaration was made in the affidavit, the party to the marriage making that declaration will be guilty of perjury.[23] The validity of the marriage is, however, not affected. In the Nigerian case of *Agbo* v. *Udo*,[24] the old Supreme Court, interpreting a similar provision in the Marriage Ordinance of Nigeria, ruled that the absence of the consent of the father of a minor did not invalidate a marriage already celebrated under the Ordinance.

A marriage under the Ordinance may be celebrated under the authority of:

1. A Registrar's certificate;
2. A Marriage Officers certificate; or
3. A special licence from the President.[25]

After the issue of the certificate, a marriage may be celebrated either (a) by a recognised religious minister in a licensed place of worship in the presence of two or more witnesses besides the officiating minister, or (b) by any Registrar in the presence of two witnesses in his office with open doors. In exceptional cases, the President may authorise the celebration of marriage at a place other than a licensed place of worship or the office of a Registrar.[26] After due celebration of the marriage the parties become husband and wife in the same sense as is understood in English law.

SPHERES OF INTER-RELATION AND CONFLICT

Thus far, we have sketched the three types of marriage existing in Ghana. It would, however, be wrong to create the impression that the various types are entirely distinct and do not at any given time relate one to the other. Similarly, it would be incorrect to assume that there are no areas of conflict. The law governing a breach of promise to marry has its conflictual problems. If a person subject to customary law promises to marry a girl it will normally be assumed that he wishes the contract to be governed by customary law. If he breaks the promise (in the absence of evidence of seduction) by marrying another girl, his betrothed would be ill-advised to bring an action for damages, for the chances of success are very slender. But if the man broke his promise after having made the preliminary payments in respect of the forthcoming marri-

---

23. Criminal Code, Act 29, ss. 210-211.
24. (1947) 18 N.L.R. 152.
25. Cap. 127, s. 9
26. Cap. 127, s. 38

age, he would then forfeit his right to recover them.[27] If, however, he promises to marry a girl under the Marriage Ordinance and later incapacitates himself by marrying a second girl, e.g. under customary law, then the first girl can bring an action for damages for the breach; for while the Ordinance marriage subsists, the man cannot validly contract a marriage with the first girl as promised.[28]

It was pointed out earlier that although the three types are distinct in character, persons married under one type of marriage are not always and entirely outside the purview of the other types of marriage laws. For during the subsistence of a marriage in one form, the parties can switch over. It is possible for a man and a woman married according to customary law to convert their potentially polygamous marriage into a monogamous form either under the Ordinance in Ghana,[29] or under any legislation outside Ghana which relates to monogamous marriages.[30]

Commenting on the relevant provision in the Ghana Marriage Ordinance No. 14 of 1884, in *Re Isaac Annetifi*,[31] Hutchinson, C.J., expressed the view *"that persons already lawfully married could not be married over again."* The learned Chief Justice, however, admitted that the provisions of the Marriage Ordinance permitted "double marriage" and provided further that the second monogamous marriage should have certain important consequences on the devolution of the property of the parties. The problem that faced the learned Chief Justice is not likely to be repeated again in the

---

27. *Neizer v. Donton* (1874) Sar. F.C.L. 129
28. *Mensah* v. *Lomoh* (1935) Div. Ct. 1931-7 p. 119; *Newton* v. *Holm* (1913) D & F. 1911-1916. *Jones* v. *Mends* (1872) F.C.L. 128, is a difficult case. Here the defendant asked the plaintiff to marry him and his offer was accepted on the understanding that the customary marriage would be entered into as soon as possible but that it would be converted into an Ordinance marriage later. No time was fixed for the conversion marriage. Later the defendant contracted a second customary marriage with another woman. *Held,* that the defendant was not liable as he had not incapcited himself by marrying another person lawfully. But surely whilst the second customary marriage subsisted the defendant would be precluded in law from marrying the plaintiff under the ordinance: cap. 127, S. 14(4). For a recent decision see *Appiah* v. *Acheampong* (1968) C.C. 24.
29. Cap. 127 s. 14(4). Indeed as a rule Ghanaians contracting Ordinance marriages perform the marriage first according to customary law. The difference in time and space in this particular instance should not be construed to mean the existence of two separate marriage contracts.
30. See e.g. the Nigerian case of *Ohochuku* v. *O.hochuku* [1960] 1 All E.R. 253. This device may be described as statutory conversion. According to English law, a marriage may also be converted by change of domicile or change of religion: see *Sinna Peerage Claim* [1946] 1 All E.R. 348. See also *Cheni* v. *Cheni* [1963] 2 W.L.R. 17.
31. (1889) Red. 157.

same form. In that case, persons already married according to native law and custom, later had their marriage either "blessed" or converted in a Basel Mission Chapel, before the passing of the Marriage Ordinance, 1884. On the death intestate of the husband, the question arose as to whether the property of the deceased ought to devolve in accordance with the provisions of the Marriage Ordinance (i.e. according to English law) since religious ceremonies previous to 1884 had been validated by the Ordinance; or according to customary law. If the marriage ceremony in the Basel Mission Chapel was regarded as a "blessing" giving solemn recognition to an already existing customary marriage, then the property of the deceased had to devolve exclusively according to customary law. On the other hand, if the marriage in the Chapel could be treated as though it were a marriage between a native bachelor and a spinster, or if the marriage could be treated as one converted to a monogamous form of marriage, then the property of the deceased intestate devolved according to English law. The evidence before Hutchinson, C.J., was vague, hence he drew the conclusion that the second marriage in the Chapel did not convert the customary marriage into a monogamous one so as to justify the application of English law in respect of the devolution of the property of the deceased. On the other hand, four years later, in *Ackah* v. *Arinta*,[32] Francis Smith, Ag. C.J., ruled on similar facts that a second marriage in a Wesleyan Church altered the status of the parties already married according to customary law. (These two cases are not really in conflict. In the latter case, the evidence was clear that a "ceremony of marriage" took place in the Church, whereas in the former case the evidence was a little vague.)

One problem arising in connection with this type of statutory conversion is whether the subsequent Ordinance marriage merely monogamises an already existing marriage between the parties or whether it can be regarded as a fresh marriage. According to section 36 of the Ordinance, the standard question to be answered by the parties to the Ordinance marriage is the same for parties already married under the customary law as for unmarried parties. The person officiating:

"shall either directly or through an interpreter address the parties thus: 'Do I understand you AB and you CD that you are here for the purpose of becoming man and wife?' [33]

Thus, *prima facie*, it would appear that the second marriage is a fresh one. But the treatment of parties of a converted marriage as

32.   (1893) Sar. F.L.R. 79.
33.   Cap. 127, s. 36. The form of address used in Kenya is more realistic. See *post*.

husband and wife *de novo* gives rise to difficult questions. It will give the erroneous impression that a polygamous marriage does not create a status. Commenting on *Kassim* v. *Kassim*[34] one writer said,[34a] "Even though a polygamous marriage differs much from the concept of the monogamous or "christian" marriage, it is now beyond peradventure that the polygamous marriage not only alters the status of the parties but also creates a relationship between them which the English Courts do, for some purposes at any rate, recognise". Another difficult problem may be raised: Suppose that AB marries CD according to customary law and that three children are born during the subsistence of this marriage. Later AB and CD convert their customary marriage into a monogamous marriage under the Ordinance. Can the subsequent marriage be nullified if after the celebration AB wilfully refuses to consummate that marriage? If the marriage is a fresh one, then lack of consummation will render it voidable.[35]

Or suppose that a decree of divorce is granted by the High Court in respect of the Ordinance marriage. Will the decree affect the marriage celebrated according to customary law, even though the necessary formalities of customary law divorce have not been complied with? A dictum of Wrangham J. in the Nigerian case of *Ohochuku* v. *Ohochuku*[36] would seem to suggest that in such a situation two "decrees" of divorce are essential. With respect, as well be shown later, this view is erroneous.[36a]

The other alternative is to regard the second marriage in the case we are considering as a converted marriage in the sense that the parties are to be regarded as husband and wife not as from the date of the beginning of celebration of the Ordinance marriage, but rather from the beginning of the customary marriage.[37] The phrase "to convert" has many meanings.[38] "To convert" does not necessarily mean to make new. In the law of real property a covenant not to convert a dwelling-house into a shop is breached by the making of a structural conversion or by the exposing of goods for sale. In other words, it means that premises may be

34.   [1962] 3 W.L.R. 865 at p. 870; 26 M.L.R. p. 86
34a. P. R. H. Webb: "Mistake as to the nature of marriage created by the ceremony". (1963) 26 M.L.R. p. 86.
35.   According to our Matrimonial Causes laws, the person affected should within one year petition the High Court for a decree of nullity. This is perhaps an extreme case, but not impossible.
36.   [1960] 1 All E.R. 253.
36a. See p. 14
37.   Subject to this caveat: that at the time of the customary law marriage, the parties had the capacity to marry each other under the Ordinance.
38.   See Stroud, Judicial Dictionary, Vol. I

converted either by user, or by an alteration of structure.[39]

Similarly, when we speak of "conversion" of marriage in this context, it must be construed to mean that the parties to the customary marriage are to be regarded as husband and wife even for the purposes of "marriage" under the Ordinance. The only change that comes about as the result of the Ordinance marriage is a change of user, or a structural alteration of the original union. In this sense, the status of the customary marriage becomes merged in the wider status offered by the Ordinance marriage. The matrimonial incidents of the Ordinance marriage also supersede those of the customary marriage.

This view is supported by the Kenya African Christian Marriage and Divorce Ordinance.[40] According to its provisions, a licensed minister or a registrar shall address the parties as follows:

"Do I understand that you AB and you CD, have been heretofore married to each other by native law and custom, and that you come here for the purpose of binding yourselves to each other as man and wife so long as both of you shall live?"

The parties are then made to understand that once they have taken each other as man and wife under the Ordinance, that marriage cannot be dissolved during their joint lives except by a valid judgment of divorce. In the example under consideration, it follows that a divorce of the pre-existing customary marriage will have no effect on the Ordinance marriage. Contrarywise, a decree of divorce granted in respect of the subsequent Ordinance marriage is sufficient to dissolve both the customary and ordinance marriages. It is submitted that this interpretation holds good for Ghana. Unfortunately, this view of the matter was not suggested to the learned judge in *Ohochuku's* case. In that case, the parties were married according to the appropriate Nigerian customary law. Such a marriage was potentially polygamous in the sense that the husband could lawfully marry another woman during its subsistence. In 1950, the husband went to England, where in January 1953, he was joined by the wife. In July, 1953, the parties went through a monogamous ceremony of marriage at the register office at St. Pancras. They did this not because of any doubt about the validity of the Nigerian ceremony, but because the wife found it desirable to have a marriage certificate which she could produce when required for practical purposes in England. Thereafter the parties became unhappy and the wife petitioned the English court for

39. *Wilkinson* v. *Rogers* (1864) 12 W.R. 119.
40. Cap. S. 9 (1962) Rev.).

divorce on the ground of cruelty by the husband. In granting a decree of divorce to the wife, Wrangham, J., emphasised that the decree was in respect only of the marriage at St. Pancras register office, i.e. the monogamous marriage. He felt satisfied on the authorities that the courts in England could not assume jurisdiction to dissolve a polygamous marriage.[41] If the English case of *Thynne* v. *Thynne*[42] has been cited to the learned judge, he might have derived assistance from the ruling of the Court of Appeal. There it was held that a decree of divorce dissolves the marriage status and not the *marriage ceremony*. Thus where two marriage ceremonies had been celebrated between the same parties on different dates it was held that a decree of divorce granted in respect of the second marriage also dissolved the first marriage ceremony.

The Ghana Marriage Ordinance contemplates only the conversion of customary marriages into Ordinance marriages. By section 14(4), the registrar, before he issues a certificate, must be satisfied that neither of the parties to the intended marriage is married by *native law and custom* to any person other than the person with whom the Ordinance marriage is proposed to be contracted. Breach of this rule will render the marriage under the Ordinance void, for section 42 of the Ordinance declares that no marriage shall be valid.

"where either of the parties thereto at the time of the celebration of such marriage is married by native law and custom to any person other than the person with whom such marriage is had."[43]

Hence by the interpretation of these two provisions, a practising Muslim married to three wives according to Mohammedan law, can lawfully marry a fourth under the provisions of the Ordinance during the subsistence of the previous marriages. It cannot be the case that the legislature intended to permit such an anomalous situation. The section should be amended to read as follows:

"Provided that neither of the parties to the intended

41.   Bromley, in his *Family Law* (1962) p. 11 fn. (d) is of the opinion that the decision in *Ohochuku* is wrong but his reasoning suffers from a misunderstanding of conversion marriages. He posits the view that "as English courts will recognise the Nigerian (customary) marriage the second marriage was of no legal significance at all". If the English courts recognise polygamous or potentially polygamous marriages, it is also established that English courts have no jurisdiction to grant matrimonial relief to the parties to such marriage. *Sowa v. Sowa* [1961] 1 All E.R. 687

42.   [1955] P. 272

43.   If such second marriage was celebrated outside Ghana, the parties will have committed an offence under s. 265 of the Criminal Code, 1960 (Act 29).

marriage is married by customary law or in accordance with Mohammedan law to any person other than the person with whom such marriage is proposed to be contracted."[44]

Some Other Legal Incidents

The important incidents may be listed as follows:

1. A person who is already married by customary law cannot contract an Ordinance marriage with any other person while the customary marriage is still subsisting. If he goes through a "second marriage" he commits a criminal offence,[45] and the marriage is invalid.[46] Again, a person is guilty of an offence under section 264 of the Criminal Code[47] if, having contracted a monogamous marriage with any person, he purports to marry any other person under customary law. However, section 42 of the Marriage Ordinance, which deals with invalid marriage, is silent as to the validity of the second customary marriage. After listing the circumstances in which a marriage shall be deemed to be invalid, the section merely states that—

"no marriage shall after celebration be deemed invalid by reason that any provision of this Ordinance has not been complied with."

The second customary marriage is therefore valid according to section 42; section 44, however, clearly declares the customary marriage invalid.[48] It is submitted that it would be better to incorporate section 44 into section 42 so as to reconcile the conflict. The relevant part of section 42 should be amended to read as follows:

---

44. The Kenya Marriage Ordinance, Cap. 150 is drafted on similar lines See s. 11(1)(d). The reason for this omission may have been due to the fact that our Marriage of Mohammedans Ordinance is rarely used.
45. Criminal Code, 1960 (Act 29) s. 265. In re *Sapara* (1911) Ren. 605; *Quaye* v. *Kuevi* (1934) Div. Ct. 1931-7 p. 69. It is not bigamy as the headnote suggests in *R. v. Menans* F. Ct. (1922) p. 61. In *R. v. Sarwan Singh* [1962] 3 All E.R. 612, it was held in the U.K. that a polygamous or potentially polygamous marriage is not a valid first marriage for the purposes of founding a successful prosecution for bigamy under s. 57 of the Offences Against the Person Act. Perhaps the time has now come for U.K. to follow the example of Ghana in dealing with this problem in future.
46. Marriage Ordinance Cap. 127, s. 42.
47. Under the old Criminal Code, the sentence imposed by law differed; where a party to customary marriage purported to marry a third person under the Ordinance, he was liable to be sentenced to 5 years imprisonment; in the converse case, the offence was punishable only by 2 years imprisonment. Under our new Code, the punishment is uniform. In Kenya too, the punishment is uniform. See Kenya Marriage Ordinance, 1962 Revision, Cap. 150, ss. 49 and 50.
48. See, e.g. *Coleman* v. *Shang* [1959] G.L.R. 390 at p. 402.

"Any person who contracts a monogamous marriage, whether within or without Ghana, either under this Ordinance, or in accordance with the provisions of any other enactment relating to monogamous marriage, shall be incapable during the continuance of such marriage of contracting a valid marriage by customary law or in accordance with Mohammedan law.[49]

But save as aforesaid, no marriage shall after celebration be deemed invalid by reason that any provision of this Ordinance has not been complied with."[50]

This new provision would also emphasise the fact that once a person is married under the Ordinance, or his marriage is declared to be valid by the Ordinance, he cannot contract a valid polygamous marriage during the subsistence of the monogamous marriage. Thus, even if one of the parties is converted to the Mohammedan religion, he still cannot contract a valid Mohammedan law marriage with a third person during the subsistence of the Ordinance marriage.

2. When a person, otherwise subject to customary law contracts a marriage under the Ordinance, or in accordance with the provisions of any other enactment relating to monogamous marriage, he is deemed to accept the doctrine that his obligations, rights and duties *in respect of the marriage* shall be governed not by "native law or custom," but by (a) the received English law, and (b) local legislation on such matters. The courts in the early days interpreted the doctrine rather too narrowly. In *Cole* v. *Cole*,[51] for example, Brandord Griffith, J. went so far as to state that parties to this type of marriage and their offspring were clothed "with a status unknown to native law". In *Re Otoo*[52] (now overruled by *Coleman* v. *Shang*[53]), Michelin, J. declared that the only form of will which a party to such a marriage may legally make is one in accordance with the provisions of English law.[54] However, in *Smith* v. *Smith*,[55] Van Der Meulen, J., wondered whether it was right to suppose that just because the parties have married under the Ordinance, "their whole lives should be regulated in accordance with English Laws and standards".

49. Perhaps the phrase "polygamous marriage" should apply to both customary marriage and Mohammedan marriage.
50. The Kenya Marriage Ordinance, Cap. 150, s. 37 also suffers from this uncertainty. See also P. A. Adjetey: "Some Consequences of Polygamous Marriage", (1961) 4 *Universitas* 168.
51. (1898) 1 N.L.R. 15 at p. 23; a Nigerian case.
52. (1926) Div. Ct. 1926-29, 84 at p. 86
53. [1961] 2 All E.R. 406 (P.C.); [1959] G.L.R. 390 (C.A.).
54. As the Court of Appeal put it in that case, the making of a will is not a matter which arises out of the contract of marriage.
55. (1924) 5 N.L.R. 105; a Nigerian case.

The whole matter has now been put beyond doubt by the recent
Ghana case of *Coleman* v. *Shang*.[56] In that case, the Court of Appeal
(as it was then known) laid down the rule that the only limitation
which a marriage under the Marriage Ordinance can place upon a
person's right to have his or her case or matter determined in
accordance with customary law, is in matters relating to his marriage,
and as to them only during the subsistence of the marriage, save
as where otherwise provided by law. The law is clear that a person's
incapacity to contract a second customary marriage lasts only
during the subsistence of the Ordinance marriage.

3. When a Ghanaian ordinarily subject to customary law contracts
a monogamous form of marriage, he cannot, during the subsistence of the marriage, expect, in respect of that marriage, to
claim benefits that accrue to parties married under customary law.
As Aitken, J., put it in *Akwapim* v. *Budu*:[57]

"I am also clearly of opinion that a native of this country
cannot have it both ways, that is, he cannot by marrying,,
another native in accordance with the Marriage Ordinance,
give himself the choice of asserting or defending his
matrimonial rights either by suit in a native tribunal or
by petition in the Supreme Court as circumstances may
dictate or convenience may prescribe."

4. Similarly, a Ghanaian who is married to another person under
customary law can pursue his matrimonial rights only through a
customary law process.[58] This was the essence of Hyde's case,[59]
which was approved in *Baindail* v. *Baindail*.[60] In the latter case,
Lord Greene said:

"For the purpose of enforcing the rights of marriage or
for the purpose of dissolving a marriage, it has always
been accepted as the case, following Lord Penzance's
decision, that the courts of this country (Britain) exercising
jurisdiction in matrimonial affairs do not and cannot give
effect to, or dissolve marriages which are not monogamous ... rightly or wrongly the courts have refused
to regard a polygamous marriage as one which entitles the
parties to come for matrimonial relief to the courts of this
country."

This ruling applies to both polygamous and potentially

56.   *Supra* at p. 402.
57.   Div. Ct. 1931-37, 89 at p. 90.
58.   *Setse v. Setse* (1959) G.L.R. 155. Here the Ghana courts have tended
      to follow the line of reasoning adopted by the English courts.
59.   (1866) L.R. 1 P. & D. 130.
60.   [1946] P. 122 at pp. 125, 126.

polygamous marriages. Thus, in *Sowa* v. *Sowa*[61] a Ghanaian woman whose marriage to another Ghanaian was potentially polygamous unsuccessfully applied to an English Magistrate's Court for a maintenance order against her husband on the ground of his desertion. It would be interesting to know what attitude the English courts would have adopted had Mr. Sowa acquired an English domicile by the time of the proceedings. Would the wife in such circumstances be unable to sue in the court of her domicile?[62]

5. Section 48 of the Ghana Marriage Ordinance stipulates that where any Ghanaian contracts a monogamous marriage, whether within or without Ghana, and later dies intestate, leaving a widow or husband or any issue of such marriage, the devolution of his property shall be as laid down in the Ordinance. That is, two-thirds of his property (both movable and immovable) shall be distributed in accordance with the provisions of the law of England relating to the distribution of the personal estates of intestates [in 1884], and one-third in accordance with the provisions of the customary law which would have obtained if such person had not married monogamously. Briefly stated, two-thirds of the property goes to the widow and children and one-third to the extended family of the intestate. The circumstances in which section 48 applies must be carefully noted:

First, the intestate must have been a Ghanaian subject to customary law. The citizenship of the other partner to the marriage is irrelevant.

Second, the intestate must have been survived by a widow or husband or issue of such marriage. The expression "leaving a widow or husband or any issue of such marriage" in section 48 does nothing more than indicate the condition upon which English law will be applied to the estate of an intestate married under the Ordinance.[63] But the distribution of the property under the Statute of Distribution, 1670, is not confined to the widow or issue of the Ordinance marriage alone; it extends to all persons regarded as lawful widows and children[64]under Ghanaian law.

Consequently, it would appear that if the intestate is not survived by a widow or issue of the Ordinance marriage, customary law rather than English law will apply to the distribution of his estate.

---

61. [1960] 3 All E. R. 196
62. For an account of conversion of marriage by change of domicile, see *Cheni v. Cheni* (1963) 2 W.L.R. 17. The case has been extensively reviewed, see: P.R.H. Webb (1963) 12 I.C.L.Q. 672; Z. Cowen (1963) 12 I.C.L.Q. 1407; M. J. Higgins (1963) 26 M.L.R. 205.
63. *Coleman v. Shang* [1961] 2 All E.R. 406 at p. 411
64. *Bamgbose v. Daniel* [1955] A.C. 107

The same consequence will follow if he is survived by a widow of a subsequent customary marriage.[65]

Section 48 goes on to provide that where any person who is the issue of an Ordinance marriage dies intestate, his property shall be distributed in accordance with English law on the same lines as outlined above. In this case, it is irrelevant whether, on coming of age, the issue of such marriage himself contracted a polygamous or monogamous marriage. It is difficult to appreciate why the devolution on intestacy of the property of the issue of monogamous marriages should be governed by the previous marriage contract of their parents, irrespective of the nature of their own marriages. It is one thing to hope that the children of monogamous marriages will not relapse into polygamy; it is another thing for the law, as it does at present, to prevent them from making their own choice.

The wisdom of the enactment of section 48 has often been questioned. In some Commonwealth African countries, marriage by Africans under the marriage laws in their countries has no effect on the devolution of their property on death intestate.[66] In 1905, a Commission of Inquiry was set up to investigate whether, *inter alia*, a general law of succession to the movable or immovable property (or both) of an intestate was desirable. Perhaps the time has now come for action.

Apart from express limitations such as those discussed above, Ghanaians who contract monogamous forms of marriage are not otherwise precluded from conducting their affairs according to customary law.[67]

HUSBAND AND WIFE

Customary Law[68]

When the marriage contract is completed, whether by payment of the marriage consideration or by any act valid according to customary law, the husband and wife acquire certain rights and duties in their relations, *inter se* and as against third parties. Here, it is unnecessary to distinguish between matrilineal and patrilineal societies.[69]

In Ghana, "consortium" does not literally mean "the right to live together in one household." In Ga customary law, it is usual

65. Conclusions drawn from *Coleman* v. *Shang* supra.
66. e.g. Sierra Leone and Kenya.
67. See e.g. *Sackey* v. *Okanta*, D & F 1911-16, p. 88
68. See also Allott, *Essays in African Law;* T. O. Elias, *Ghana and Sierra Leone*, Chapter 9
69. It is equally unnecessary to distinguish between parties who have embraced the Mohammedan faith and married under that law.

for the wife and children to live apart from the husband; and among the Akan, since the wife does not belong to the husband's extended family, it was not unusual for the wife to stay with her mother after the celebration of the marriage, though in modern times, this practice is gradually dying out. Whether the wife lives away from the husband or not, the legal incidents of customary marriage are almost uniform as between different systems.

The husband, on marriage, acquires exlusive rights over his wife. The wife has no such exclusive claim to her husband. If someone commits adultery with the wife, the husband may either divorce the wife on that ground and reclaim what Sarbah describes as the "consawment" money,[70] together with all his expenses, from the woman's family,[71] or continue with the marriage after claiming what the Akan describe as *ayefar*,[72] from his wife's paramour and a "pacification fine" from the wife.

Since customary marriages tolerate polygamy, during the continuance of the marriage the husband may marry other wives in addition to the existing one. But

> "It is the practice for the elder wife to be consulted by the husband on taking a "second wife", if husband takes a second wife without doing so, it is not cause for discontinuance of the marriage, but it brings disputes and the husband must give the elder wife satisfaction."[73]

The husband is in duty-bound to maintain the wife during the subsistence of the marriage.[74] The term used in our Criminal Code is: "necessaries of health and life to his wife", which is defined to include proper food, clothing, shelter, warmth (!), medical or surgical treatment, and any other matters which are reasonably necessary for the preservation of health and life.[75] However, during the subsistence of the marriage, a wife should be wary of the receipt from her spouse of large presents not falling within the definition of necessaries of life, for after divorce she may well be called upon to return these gifts.[76]

Generally, the husband is expected to be responsible for the

70. i.e. marriage consideration: see Sarbah, *op. cit.* p. 48
71. The wife's family may demand that her paramour pay the money and marry her; see *Half Jack* v. *John* (1913) D. & F. (1911-16) p. 60.
72. *Yer* means wife and *fa* means take. Originally the Ahanti regarded it as a crime: it was not treated as a sexual offence but as a theft: Rattray, Ashanti Law and Constitution, pp. 307 and 317.
73. *De Graft* v. *Abba Mansah* (1871) Sar. F.C.L. 125.
74. *Okua* v. *Yankah* (1894) Ren. 109
75. Criminal Code, 1960, (Act 29) s. 79. This is similar to the English notion of maintenance. See, e.g. *Kallin* v. *Kallin* [1944] S.A.S.R. 73 at p. 75; *Ackworth* v. *Ackworth* [1943] P. 21, at p. 22
76. Danquah, *op. cit.* p. 153.

debts and torts of his wife during coverture, [77] but in the strict legal sense it is the family of the wife who are responsible[78] unless the husband admits liability. In Akim Abuakwa, the husband is liable to pay half the debts incurred by the wife "in connexion with her marriage."[79] Normally, before any husband pays his wife's debts or damages assessed against her in tort, he would notify the wife's family so as not to prejudice his right of recovering the amount or part thereof in the event of divorce. It was held in *Dolphyne* v. *Ansah*,[80] that a husband is liable for expenses reasonably incurred in connection with his wife's funeral, but it should be noted that the husband in that case admitted liability from the outset. It cannot, therefore, be treated as a general statement of the law. Among the Ewe, for example, on the death of a wife, the husband is required to return her body to be buried by the house that gave her birth.[81]

A wife, on her part, is expected to submit to the husband and to bear and look after the children of the marriage during the early stages.[82] She is also required to perform normal house-duties. She has no obligation to pay any part of her husband's debts,[83] although there are cases of affluent women gladly doing so.

Under the old Criminal Procedure Code, a distinction was made between the competence and compellability of witnesses according to whether they were married monogamously or by customary law. No such distinction is now made. Section 123 of our new Criminal Procedure Code[84] provides, *inter alia*, that in any

"enquiry or trial the wife or husband (whether married by customary law or otherwise) of the person charged shall be . . . a competent and compellable witness for the defence."

In Ghana, the fact that the parties are Moslems does not as a general rule make their married life relationship any different from those married under customary law.

The venue of courts through which husband and wife can enforce their legal rights is usually through the local courts which have jurisdiction in suits for divorce and other matrimonial cases, where

---

77.   Among the Ashanti, the husband is liable for his wife's debts and torts—Rattray: *Ashanti Law and Constitution*, p. 26.
78.   This is definitely so where the husband paid no marriage consideration
79.   Danquah, *op cit* p. 153
80.   (1885) Ren. 60
81.   Address given by Madam Justice Jiagge to a meeting of the International Missionary Counci in 1958 at Accra.   Needless to say, most husbands would agree to pay such expenses.
82.   Prolific child-bearing is honoured: Fortes *op. cit.* p. 262
83.   *Ashon v. Snyper* (1869) Sar F.C.L. 136.
84.   1960, Act 30, See now the Courts Decree N.L.C.D. 84 para. 49

the law applicable is exclusively customary law.[85] Owing to the fact that our courts system is integrated, cases and other matters involving customary law can be heard and determined by the general courts by way of appeal. It is also specially provided that the High Court shall have original jurisdiction in all matters.[86]

As a general rule of customary law, marriage has no effect on the property of the spouses.[87] Rattray states categorically that an Ashanti wife's private property remains her own, which is true in most of the matrilineal groups. The basis for the rule is that even during coverture, the wife does not in the strict sense regard herself as belonging to the *ebusua* (extended family) of the husband. The converse is also true for the husband. An exception to this general rule is found in Danquah[88] writing on the Akim Abuakwa. There, if the wife cultivates cocoyams on her own family lands, or trades, the husband is entitled to half the property in the event of divorce. The wife has reciprocal rights to the husband's profits. Further, Danquah writes that if a wife finds a treasure trove, the husband is entitled to half of such treasure. The Ga also regard the property of each spouse as private property. It was held in *Swapim* v. *Ackuwa*,[89] a Fante case, that if husband and wife contribute to the building of a house on the husband's family land, the interest of the wife lasts only during the life-time of the husband.

As has already been observed, exchange of gifts between the spouses during marriage is hard to classify, for in the event of divorce some of them are recoverable.

In order to avoid doubt, the legislature enacted the Married Women's Property Act, 1890.[90] It is described as an Ordinance to confer power on married women to make contracts and hold and deal with property. Details of that provision will be given later. Some writers have expressed the view that this Ordinance only applies to women married under the Marriage Ordinance.[91] It is difficult to see why this should be so since the Ordinance confers this power on *any married woman*. If the legislation was intended only for women married under the Ordinance, it would clearly have so defined the expression "married woman".

85. Courts Act, 1960, s. 98 (1) (b) and by Act 130. Now governed by the Courts Decree.
86. Courts Act, s. 29. See e.g., *Adjei & Dua v. Ripley* (1956) 1 W.A.L.R. 62
87. See Sarbah, *op. cit.* p. 56
88. Akan Laws and Custom p. 154
89. (1888) Sar. F.C.L. 191
90. Cap. 131 (1951 Revision) which apparently applies only in Southern Ghana.
91. Redwar, *Comments on some Ordinances of the Gold Coast Colony*, p. 39

Ordinance Marriage

The law governing the enforcement of rights and duties between the husband and wife of a monogamous marriage is English law: the common law, the doctrines of equity and the statutes of general application in force in England on the 24th day of July, 1874. Thus the modern legislation relating to the right of spouses to sue each other in tort has no application in Ghana. In dismissing a wife's claim under the old Courts Ordinance for maintenance (without a petition for divorce) against her husband, Acolatse, J., (as he then was) said: "I find that at common law, a wife had no right to sue her husband in contract; all that she had power to do was to pledge his credit".[92]   No legislation has been passed to bring the law on this point up to date. It can be argued that, since the Courts Act, 1960, provides that the High Court has jurisdiction in all matters, claims for maintenance by wives during coverture can now be entertained, but legislation is nevertheless called for.[92a]

Another way of avoiding the application of archaic common law rules in Ghana lies in the approach that statutory modifications of the common law should be in force in Ghana subject to local conditions. As a judge said in an Indian case: "When one finds a (common law) rule has been abrogated by legislation, that rule becomes an unsafe guide".[93]

Mention has already been made of the Married Women's Property Ordinance, which is based on, though not identical with, the English statute. By section 2,

"The wages and earnings of any married woman acquired or gained by her in any employment, occupation, or trade, in which she is engaged or which she carried on separately from her husband, and all investments of such wages, earnings, or property shall be deemed and taken to be property held and settled to her separate use, independent of any husband to whom she may be married, and her receipts alone shall be a good discharge for such wages, earnings, money and property."

A married woman can maintain an action in respect of such property as if she were an unmarried woman.

---

92. *Davy-Hayford* v. *Davy-Hayford*. Unreported; Divisional Court at Sekondi, Suit No. 52/1957. A wife has also authority in equity to borrow money for necessaries suitable to her situation in life. *Wilson v. Glossop* (1888) 20 Q.B.D. 354.

92a. The Court of Appeal has now ruled that an application for maintenance can be made to the Court by a wife during coverture *Ashong* v. *Ashong* (1968) C.C. 26. This overrules *Gall* v. *Gall* (1965) C.C. 195.

93. *Secretary of State* v. *Rukhminibai* A.I.R. [1937] Nag. 354 at p. 268, at p. 268, per Stone, C.J.

It has been held in *Abbapesiwa* v. *Krakue*[94] that a husband and wife are legally capable of being partners; thus if a woman trades as a partner with her husband for her own benefit, she will in that sense, be trading separately from her husband. The court further held that section 3 of the Ordinance, enabling a married woman to be sued for any debt incurred by her, does not exclude suits by her husband.

Apart from the duty of the husband under the civil law, our criminal law also imposes on the husband a duty to supply the necessaries of health and life to his wife.[95]

PARENT AND CHILD

Owing to the variety of laws existing in Ghana, earlier judicial dicta had encouraged the view that if a Ghanaian marries under the Marriage Ordinance, then his rights and duties should be governed by English law.[95a] On the other hand, if the parents contract a customary marriage then the applicable law should be customary law. Hence, our local courts are given jurisdiction in suits for the paternity and custody of children, where the law applicable is exclusively customary law.[96] There is no real difference between the rights and duties of parents married under the Marriage Ordinance and parents who practise a patrilineal system of kinship. In the latter case, the son is deemed to be a member of the father's extended family. Among the matrilineal Akan, some writers have expressed the view that as the children belong to the mother's extended family, the father has but little claim over them.[97] On the face of it, this argument is plausible, for by the law of inheritance in Ashanti, a child may not generally succeed to his father's estate and *vice versa*. In the olden days, a father could not pawn his child without the authority of the child's maternal uncle. The children

---

94. (1943) 9 W.A.C.A. 161
95. See p. 22 above.
95a. *Re Otoo* (1927) D. Ct. 26-29, 84. This line of thinking seems to have stemmed from a dictum in the Nigerian case of *Cole v. Cole* 1 N.L.R. 15 at p. 22 where Brandford *Griffith* J. said, "In fact a christian marriage clothes the parties to such marriage and their offspring with a status unknown to native law."
96. Courts Act, s. 98 (1) (b). See now the Courts Decree N.L.C.D. 84 para. 49.
97. A. B. Ellis: *Tschi* [Twi]—*Speaking Peoples of the Gold Coast*, p. 10 Rattray is of opinion that even if a father exercises, for example, his rights to chastise the children, he was these rights by virtue of natural law and equity rather than by any legal process. He argues that the position of the father is a weak one: *Ashanti Law and Constitution* p. 8 Fortes, *op. cit.*, states that an Ashanti father has no legal authority over his children.

were not obliged to contribute to the father's family's funds or levies in the event of his family incurring a debt. But as Rattray observes,[98] these were social laws which were modified by actual practice. It need not be emphasised that for a considerable period of time, an Akan father has been able to exercise legal rights over his children. Admittedly, among the Akan, the blood tie is transmitted through the females; yet when an Akan child is born, the father is believed to transmit his *kra* or *sunsum* to the child. The child therefore inherits the totemic spirit of the father only (which the Ashanti call *ntro*) and not that of his mother. In spite of the fact that the Akan are predominantly matrilineal, succession to political offices is generally patrilineal.[99] The right of naming the child vests in the father. On the death of a Fante-Akan father, the surviving children, and quite often the widow, are allowed by the customary successor to the deceased father's estate to reside in any house built by deceased *quamdiu se bene gesserint*,[100] unless when the interest of the deceased's family is at stake.[101]

When the children are young, they normally remain under the influence, custody and protection of the mother. The woman does her share in providing food and clothing and seeing to it that the child goes to school regularly. This actually makes for a solid bond between mother and child even after majority. One of the ambitions of a son is to be able to build a house for his mother when he is successful in business.

It has been held that no person has the right to detain a child away from his father or mother.[102] Presumably, this right can be enforced by an application for a writ of habeas corpus in the High Court.[103]

When they are old enough, the children are under the *potestas* of the father in respect of discipline and the like. Whilst they are under his subjugation, any property they acquire by Fante-Akan customary law belongs to the father.[104] However, in Akim Abuakwa (we

98. Rattray; *Ashanti*, p. 45
99. For the importance of the patrilineal aspect of Akan society, see Christensen: *Double Descent among the Fante* (1951)
100. *Halmond* v. *Daniel* [1871] Sar. F.C.L. 182; *Barnes* v. *Mayan* [1871] Sar. F.C.L. 180; *Boham* v. *Marshall* [1892] Sar. F.C.L. 193; *Mensah* v. *Krakue* [1894] Sar. F.L.R. 87.
101. *Swapim* v. *Ackuwa* [1888] Sar. F.C.L. 191
102. *Chiba* v. *Agoowah* [1873] Sar. F.C.L. 128
103. Surprisingly in the Western Nigerian case of *Omodion* v. *Fasoro* [1960] W.R.N.L.R. 27, an application to the High Court for the issue of a writ of *habeas corpus* to secure the custody of a child, was refused on the ground that questions relating to the control of children governed by customary law were not justiciable before the High Court.
104. See Sarbah, *op. cit.* p. 63; for the Ewe-speaking people, see Manoukian, *op. cit.* p. 28

are told by Danquah[105]) a father has no right to his child's private property, except insofar as his halfshare in a treasure trove or gold-nugget discovered by the child is concerned. Among the Ashanti, a child may own property over which the father has no control.[106] Some fathers still regard it as their duty to find wives or husbands for their children, and to set them up in business.

The children on their part, whether in matrilineal or patrilineal society, are expected to obey and respect their parents. It is considered sacrilege for the children to break off relations with their natural parents. They take pride in the fact that they are required by customary law to provide a coffin for the burial of the father in the event of his death.

From this account, it will be seen that in actual practice, it is misleading to consider the rights and duties of parents in respect of their children differently according to whether they belong to a matrilineal or a patrilineal society. For a very long time, our criminal laws have contained provisions concerning parental duties, and no distinction has been made between the parents of a customary and of an Ordinance marriage. One case which illustrates this principle is *Commissioner of Police* v. *Ewiah*.[107] By section 72 of the courts Ordinance, 1951,[108] any police officer, having reasonable ground for belief that the parent or guardian of a juvenile does not exercise proper guardianship, was empowered to bring such juvenile before any court. The court, if satisfied that the juvenile needed care and protection, could, *inter alia*, commit him to the custody of any fit person willing to undertake his care. In 1955, two children of Alex Ewiah (an Akan) were brought before the juvenile court at Sekondi on the statutory ground. Before the proceedings in the juvenile court, the children's aunt had removed them from their father's house on the ground that the father had failed to observe his parental responsibilities. The juvenile court later made a fit person order in favour of the aunt, and further ordered the father to pay £G2 per month in respect of each child. The father appealed aganst this payment order. It was argued on his behalf that according to customary law, the custody of the children of a marriage belongs to the mother and not to the father; if the mother chose to remove them from the father his responsibility towards them thereupon ceased. The Supreme Court, affirming the payment order, held that a parent could not relieve himself of his parental responsibilities

105. *op. cit.* p. 209
106. Rattray: *Ashanti Law and Constitution*, p. 15
107. (1956) 1 W.A.L.R. 69
108. Now repealed, but re-enacted in similar form in the present Criminal Procedure Code.

merely because a relative is good-natured enough to shoulder them. In other words, the obligation placed upon a parent or guardian is absolute.

Detailed provisions relating to the parent—child relationship are now contained in Part IX of the Criminal Procedure Code.[109] The Criminal Code[110] also imposes a duty on every man to supply the necessaries of health and life to his legitimate or illegitimate children. Parents who have no means of providing their child with food or medical attendance are required to seek assistance from an appropriate public officer.

The right of parents to correct their legitimate or illegitimate children under sixteen years of age is recognised, but such correction is justified under the Criminal Code only if it is reasonable having regard to the physical and mental condition of the child.[111]

Finally, the Maintenance of Children Act,[112] provides *inter alia* that where a father neglects to provide reasonable maintenance for his infant child, the mother of the child may apply to the Minister of Social Welfare to persuade the father to make reasonable provision for the maintenance of that child or to make such other award as the Minister may consider appropriate.

TERMINATION OF MARRIAGE

Death

The death of a spouse married under the Marriage Ordinance necessarily terminates the marriage,[113] whilst under customary law it does not automatically do so. If the wife predeceases the husband and her family have a good opinion of the widower, they may ask the wife's next unmarried sister to marry him.[114] The union of the deceased wife's sister with the widower is not considered a fresh marriage, for the husband is not required to pay new marriage consideration. He is required only to give a thanks-giving drink to the young sister's family. It is reported that this practice is almost dying out, and that in Ashanti it is confined to chiefs. If such an offer is not forthcoming, the marriage is formally brought to an end. In such a case the marriage consideration will not be returned, but

---

109. Act 30
110. Act 29, s. 79
111. Criminal Code, (Act 29) s. 41
112. 1965 Act 297.
113. To avoid relapse into polygamy, S. 13 of the Kenya Christian Marriage and Divorce Ordinance, Cap. 151, provides that an African widow shall not be bound to co-habit with the brother or any relative of her deceased husband, or any relative of any other person.
114. The Akan call it *ayete*.

certain valuable gifts such as "trinkets," might be claimed by the husband.[115]

If the husband dies first, the wife has the option of "marrying" the husband's successor.[116] It is a criminal offence to force the widow to enter such a relationship against her will.[117] If the widow opts for this re-arrangement, her children have the advantage of remaining in her ex-husband's house and being maintained by his successor.[118] The successor does not go through a new ceremony of marriage. If the widow refuses marriage with her husband's successor, the marriage is formally brought to an end. She may or may not be asked to return the valuable gifts given to her by her former husband. It is becoming unusual to ask for these. In 1943, the Old Asanteman Council recomended that

> "Where a widow has faithfully served her deceased husband prior to his death, his successor should not call upon her to refund any expenses made by her deceased husband towards her."[119]

DIVORCE AND MATRIMONIAL CAUSES

(a) English Law

Persons who enter into a monogamous form of marriage may have their marriage terminated by a decree of dissolution or divorce pronounced by a court of competent jurisdiction. The jurisdiction conferred upon the High Court in probate, divorce and matrimonial causes and proceedings may, subject to Rule of Courts, be exercised by it in conformity with the law and practice for the time being in force in England.[120] As we have our own Matrimonial Causes Rules,[121] it would appear that the English Practice Rules may be applied only when the local Rules are silent. As far as the substantive law relating to matrimonial causes is concerned, it is permissive, not compulsory, for the High Court to exercise its jurisdiction in conformity with the law for the time being in force in England.[122] However, since our Matrimonial Causes Rules were framed on the basis of the English Supreme Court of Judicature

---

115. See Allott: (1956) I.C.L.Q. at p. 529.
116. The Akan word for it is *Kunawar*.
117. Criminal Code, Act 29, s. 100.
118. *Swapim v. Ackuwa* (1888) Sar. F.C.L. 191
119. Matson: *A Digest of the Minutes of the Ashanti Confederacy Council*, p. 24. This recommendation is without legislative effect.
120. Courts Ordinance, Cap. 4 (1951 Rev.), repealed, but section 17 is saved by s. 154 of the Courts Act, 1960, now para. 93 (2) of the Courts Decree 1966 N.L.C.D. 84
121. order 55 of the High Court (Civil Procedure) Rules, 1954 Revision
122. Redwar: *Comments*, p. 19.

(Consolidation) Act, 1925, as subsequently amended, and the Matrimonial Causes Act, 1937, it could be argued that the High Court should always exercise its jurisdiction in conformity with the Ghana Rules of Court which were based on the 1925 and 1937 English Acts.

The enabling Act clearly speaks of the application of "the law for the time being in force in England." It could be assumed that by interpretation the High Court could apply such recent English legislation as the Matrimonial Causes Act, 1950 and the Matrimonial Causes Act, 1965, which, *inter alia*, makes collusion a discretionary bar and abolish the revival of condoned adultery.[123]

If this view is accepted, it could be argued that this could be repugnant to section 4 of the Statute of Westminster, 1931, which reads as follows:

"No Act of the Parliament of the United Kingdom passed after the commencement of this Act shall extend, or be deemed to extend, to a Dominion as part of the law of that Dominion, unless it is expressly declared *in that Act* that that Dominion has requested, and consented to, the enactment thereof."[124]

The only way whereby this conflict can be resolved is by taking the view that the laws in Ghana before independence permitted the application of the current English law on probate, divorce and matrimonial causes. Hence, it will fall within the definition of "existing laws" in Ghana before independence which will apply until repealed.[125]

It is not desirable that our divorce and matrimonial causes laws should be patterned on English law without modification, for the two societies are culturally different. When Members of the British

---

123. "The phrase 'for the time being' may according to the context mean the present or denote a single period of time: but its general sense is that of time indefinite, and refers to an indefinite state of facts which may arise in the future and which may (and probably will) vary from time to time." Stroud's Judicial Dictionary (1933 ed.) Vol. 4 p.3030.

But see the Sierraleonean case of *Godwin v. Growther* (1934) 2 W.A.C.A. 109, which interprets the phrase to mean the application of English law in force in England at the time when the local ordinance was passed. In Ghana the Court of Appeal on *Ashong v. Ashong* 1968 C.C. 26, has ruled that "the argument that the (English) Act of 1950 (and by implication the English Matrimonial Causes Act of 1965) does not apply to Ghana, cannot be accepted".

124. The section was incorporated into the Ghana Independence Act, 1957. 5 & 6 Eliz. 2 Ch. 6 First Schedule s. 2.

125. For the definition of "existing laws", see Daniels: *Common Law in West Africa*, (1964) p. 143.

Parliament are debating such bills, they think of social conditions in the United Kingdom, not in Ghana.[126]

In practice, our judges apply such English law with caution, and bear in mind local conditions. The time is, however, ripe to introduce fresh legislation to remove a number of doubts. For example, section 17(2) of the Matriominial Causes Act, 1937, empowers a married woman to apply to a court of summary jurisdiction under the Summary Jurisdiction (Married Women) Act, 1895, for certain orders.[127] Since that Act was passed in 1895, it would not normally be applicable in Ghana. It is doubtful whether an order under the 1895 Act has ever been made by our District Court, which, although a court of summary jurisdiction, has no such jurisdiction under the Courts Decree, 1966. However, since paragraph 27 of the Courts Decree gives the High Court original jurisdiction in all matters, can it not be argued that High Court in Ghana can apply the provisions of the 1895 Act? Normally, in the absence of a statutory definition, "summary jurisdiction" connotes proceedings before magistrates.[128] It was on the basis of this understanding that in the Nigerian case of *Okpaku* v. *Okpaku*[129] a superior court refused to make an order for the maintenance of a married woman on the ground, *inter alia*, that the procedure laid down in the Summary Jurisdiction (Married Women) Act, 1895, provides for a hearing before a court of summary jurisdiction with appeal to the High Court. With the greatest respect, it is submitted that "superior court" should be construed to mean a court having inherent jurisdiction to administer justice according to law and not one (an "inferior court") limited as to its jurisdiction and powers.[130] Superior courts in Ghana are therefore entitled to apply the provisions of the 1895 Act. After all, it is provided by the Courts Decree, 1966,[131] that English Acts declared to extend or apply in Ghana "shall be in force so far only as the limits of the local jurisdiction and local circumstances permit and for the purpose of

---

126. In *Dolling* v. *Dolling*, The Times, May 22, 1958, it was held that change of sex does not amount to cruelty so as to entitle the court to grant a decree of divorce to the petitioner. African notions will be entirely different.

127. This Act enables a court in of summary jurisdiction to make, in certain cases, orders for the seperation of husband and wife, for the maintenance of the wife, and for the maintenance of the children. Express statutory rules have been made by Sierra Leone's married women's Maintenance Ordinance, No. 7 of 1888, and Gambia's Maintenance of Deserted Wives Ordinance, Cap. 11 (1955 Rev.).

128. *Lamb* v. *Threshie*, 29 Sc. L. R. 727 at p. 728.

129. (1947) 12 W.A.C.A. 137

130. Stroud's *Judicial Dictionary*, (1935) Vol. 4, p. 2934.

131. para 93 (2) which saves ss. 17 and 85 of the Courts Ordinance, Cap. 4 (1951 Rev.).

facilitating the application of the said imperial laws, it shall be lawful for the said courts to construe the same with such verbal alterations, not affecting the substance, as may be necessary to render the same applicable to the matters before the court. . . . . . ''

(b) Customary Law

Where the parties are married under customary law, their marriage can be dissolved only by customary law process. This can be achieved either judicially, through the machinery of the District courts,[132] or extra-judicially, by the act of the parties. In practice, resort is had to the District courts after an extra-judicial divorce to enforce ancillary rights and orders accruing therefrom. The procedure for obtaining divorce is almost uniform everywhere. "Sentence" of divorce is not pronounced *in limine*.[133] When the parties have major disagreements or one of them has been guilty of misconduct, he or she can be summoned either before representatives of their family, or before some of the elders in the locality, to have the matter settled amicably. If this process of reconciliation fails, the matter is taken before arbitrators including members of the families of both spouses. The arbitrators may again try to effect a reconciliation; if they fail, they will then pronounce the "sentence" of divorce.

Grounds for divorce: Unlike the English legal system, the grounds[134] for divorce in the case of customary marriages are not limited, but a careful examination will reveal that by and large they are similar to the English grounds for nullity and dissolution of marriages.

(i) By the Husband

1. *Adultery*: one act of sexual intercourse of the wife with her paramour is enough. Actual penetration is not essential. The mere handling of the wife's waistbeads will be a sufficient ground.[135] Confession on oath of the adultery by the married woman is more than *prima facie* proof. If the husband does not wish to divorce the wife, he can chastise the wife, ask her or her family for "pacification money", and claim *ayefar* money[136]

---

132. C.A. 9, s. 98 (1) (b). N.L.C.D. 1966, No. 84 para. 49.
133. According to the evidence of one Assessor, which was accepted, a husband cannot validly divorce his wife by mere word of mouth: certain ceremonies must be performed: *Penin v. Duncan* [1869] Sar. F.C.L. 118.
134. The grounds may vary in different communities. Westmann says that a Glidyi man may divorce his wife on the grounds of disobedience, rebelliousness, laziness and adultery: cited in Manoukian, *op. cit.* p. 27.
135. Danquah, *op. cit.* p. 166.
136. A fine imposed for having "stolen another's wife".

from her paramour.[137] According to Danquah,[138] if the same man again commits adultery with *the wife*, the amount will be doubled. The husband may not recover more than three adultery fees in respect of the same wife, for she will by then be regarded as good for nothing. If the husband is desirous of divorcing his wife on the ground of adultery, he is technically entitled to recover the whole, or a part of, the marriage consideration, in addition to other claims for expenses. The amount may be reduced, for example if the woman has been married before.

2. *Barrenness:* procreation is an essential aim of marriage,[139] and failure to conceive may be a ground for divorce. As Fortes puts it, prolific child-bearing is honoured.[140] A man's social or political standing is enhanced if he is the father of many children. Most husbands, however, will take a second wife rather than divorce a barren woman solely on that ground.

3. *Desertion:* according to some authorities, it appears that there is no prescribed period of desertion. The matrimonial offence is committed once the wife refuses to return to her husband after she has been asked to do so. In the Fante-Akan case of *De Graft* v. *Mansah*,[141] where judgment was given to the plaintiff, the husband asked the wife to show cause why she,

"having refused to live with the "Plaintiff" as his customary wife, and having left his home, should not, be ordered by this Court to pay him the sum of £40: 12: 7½d, the same being the amount incurred by the Plaintiff on your account according to the custom of the country."

On divorce, the wife's family will be liable to return the marriage consideration and "all the property which the wife possessed when she left her husband, if supplied by the husband.[142]

4. *Witchcraft:* proof that the wife has practised or is practising witchcraft constitutes a ground on which a husband may divorce his wife.

---

137. In *Akwapim* v. *Badu* (1935) Div. Ct. 1931-39, p. 89, a native tribunal imposed £25 or in default, 3 months imprisonment on an adulterer. The conviction was quashed on appeal on grounds not connected with the imposition of the sentence.
138. *Op. cit.*, p. 169.
139. *Contra* the English case of *Baxter* v. Baxter [1949] A.C. 277 at p. 286 *per* Viscount Jewitt. L.C.
140. Article in *African Systems of Kinship and Marriage*, p. 262.
141. [1871] Sar. F.C.L. 125.
142. *Sackie* v. *Acosua Agawa* (1873) Sar. F.C.L. 126.

(ii)   By the Wife

1.   *Cruelty:* if the husband ill-treats the wife, she is justified in leaving him and returning to her own family. In one case the husband was made to forfeit the marriage consideration.[143]
2.   *Neglect:* neglect of the wife, or wilful refusal by the husband to maintain her and the children, once proved to the satisfaction of the arbitrators or the court, gives a wife ground to divorce her husband.[144]
3.   *Impotence of the husband.*
4.   *Desertion:* if the husband deserts the wife, or if he does not cohabit with her for a reasonably long period of time, the wife's family may be left with no alternative but to return the marriage consideration to the husband's family and bring the marriage to an end.[145]
5.   *Extra-marital associations:* if the husband is found to be having too many affairs with other women the wife may be entitled to divorce him. It must be noted that extra-marital intercourse with an unmarried woman does not constitute adultery by the husband.[146] Section 4(2) of the Marriage Ordinance provides that "adultery shall not be held to include intercourse of a man married by native customary law with an unmarried woman".[147] As the husband is allowed greater freedom of action,[148] it is unusual for the wife to divorce her husband on the ground of adultery, unless the adultery is persistent.

(iii)   The Final Act:

The pronouncement of the divorce is followed by the submission of bills of expenses incurred by either party during the subsistence of the marriage. The husband's bill may include the following: the marriage consideration;[149] an account of debts, etc., paid by him for and on behalf of the wife; gifts of *valuable "trinkets"* and the like. It may not include housekeeping money, certain classes of gifts made to the wife's family, or the cost or return of clothes

143. *Aggryba v. Aban* (1845) Sar. F.C.L. 118.
144. *Penin v. Duncan* (1869), supra.
145. Danquah, *op. cit.*, p. 159.
146. He may be liable to pay a fine to the girls father. The Fante call it *domufar.*
147. Surely this section ought to be amended to include persons married according to Mohammedan law?
148. Phillips (ed.) *Survey of African Marriage and Family Life,* (1953) p. 279.
149. *Sackie v. Accosua Agawa* [1873] Sar. F.C.L. 126. The amount may be forfeited or reduced by order of the court if the husband is the guilty party.

bought for the wife during the marriage.[150] The bill presented by the wife and her family will include monies advanced to the husband and gifts of valuable articles. As soon as the exact amount owed by each side is agreed upon, the smaller amount is set off against the larger and the remainder paid or ordered to be paid by the party concerned.

The custody of the children is usually given to the wife when they are young, because, as their mother, she is regarded as the better person to look after them at that stage. The father will at all times have access to the children. If the wife and her family are unable to pay back the marriage consideration, difficult questions may arise as to the custody of the children, especially if the father is not in favour of the children remaining with the wife. Ellis[151] records that, in the old days, the children would be "pawned" to their father for the amount outstanding and required to "serve" him until the whole sum with fifty per cent interest was paid. In modern times, there is little doubt that the interest of the children will be the paramount consideration.

When these complicated transactions have been completed, the ex-husband is obliged to "send the wife off". Among the Fante-Akan, this means that the ex-husband pays an amount called send-off money (*akwangyadze*).

Among the Akan the divorce becomes absolute when the husband performs the ceremonial act of "chalking the wife".[152] Some days later the ex-wife dresses in white clothes and, accompanied by a few friends, makes her debut, showing herself in public as a person free to marry again.[153]

(c) Mohammedan Law

The Marriage of Mohammedans Ordinance[154] says nothing about the grounds for divorce. It lays down certain rules as to registration, and provides that every Mohammedan divorce effected in Ghana must be registered in the manner prescribed by the Ordinance. Within one month of the divorce, the man, the woman's wali, two witnesses to the divorce and a licensed Mohammedan priest must go and register the divorce. All that is required of the priest is a certification that the divorce is valid according to Mohammedan law.

---

150. See Matson, *op. cit.*, p. 24 for the Ashanti custom.
151. *Tschi Speaking Peoples of the Gold Coast of West Africa*, p. 284.
152. i.e., the sprinkling of white clay on her, which may be symbolic or actual according to the nature of each case.
153. This ceremony varies according to the ethnic group of the parties.
154. Cp 129, (1951 Rev.).

LEGITIMACY

In Ghana, like many other African countries, it is almost fruitless to quibble about legitimacy. In this connection, the dictum of Osborne, C.J., in the Nigerian case of *In Re Sapara*[155] is apposite:

"... again in English law, marriage is necessary to legitimatize offspring of two persons, such offspring if illegitimate having no right of inheritance; but under native law a child's right of succession to his father's property can be legalised by his mere acknowledgment of paternity, without the necessity of any form of marriage between the parents. Consequently, the legal importance of the marriage ceremony is not nearly so great under native law as it is under the law of England."

There is also the Privy Council decision of *Khoo Houi Leong* v. *Khoo Hean Kwee*[156] where Lord Phillimore, in delivering the judgment, said:

"In deciding upon a case where the customs and the laws are so different from British ideas a court may do well to recollect that it is a possible jural conception that a child may be legitimate, though its parents were not and could not be legitimately married.

This case, which was on appeal from Straits Settlements, was relied upon in the Nigerian case of *Bamgbose* v. *Daniel*,[157] which was in turn followed in the Ghana case of *Coleman* v. *Shang*[158] by the former Court of Appeal.

The ease with which the question of legitimacy is solved is further illustrated by the provisions of section 49(1) of the Marriage Ordinance:

"Any child born before the intermarriage of his parents under this Ordinance and not procreated in adultery shall on such intermarriage be deemed the lawful issue of a marriage under the Ordinance and shall be entitled to the same rights and privileges and his property shall in the case of his intestacy be subject to the same incidents as though his parents had been at the date of this birth

---

155. Ren. 605 at p. 606.
156. [1926] A.C. 529 at p. 543
157. [1955] A.C. 107.
158. [1959] G.L.R. 390. The Court of Appeal observed at p. 409 that a child born of extra-marital intercourse between the father and another woman may be illegitimate as far as the Marriage Ordinance is concerned. But this observation must be construed to mean that once such a father acknowledges paternity, the children will be legitimate for all other purposes.

married under the Ordinance."[159]

In Ghana it may be said that legitimacy follows from the acknowledgment of paternity by the father. Any child whose father has not acknowledged him is nonetheless regarded as the legitimate child of his mother and will enjoy normal rights and privileges among the mother's extended family. Thus "illegitimate child" must be interpreted to mean a child whose father has refused to acknowledge paternity.[160]

The rights and duties of a father towards a child he has acknowledged are the same as towards his children born in wedlock. In this sense there is no difference between marriage under customary law and under the Ordinance.

ADOPTION

Until 1962, adoption of children could be effected only by customary law. According to Akan law, a stranger, *i.e.* a member of a different clan, could be adopted into the clan and thereby made a full member. In the old days, "slave women" and their dependants were adopted into various families to improve their status. Sarbah[161] recounts that the following conditions must be satisfied in order to effect a valid adoption in Fanteland:

(a)   it must be done publicly;

(b)   the adopter must obtain the consent both of the extended family and the parents of the child to be adopted; and

(c)   he must state before witnesses his desire and intention.

Rattray says that in Ashanti, adoption into a clan was achieved by the slow and almost imperceptible process of time rather than by any public ceremony.[162]

Adoption of children is now governed by the Adoption Act, 1962.[163] On the application of a man and his wife, an adoption order may be made authorising them jointly to adopt a juvenile.[164] In special circumstances the order may be made in favour of a sole applicant. The order is made only after the following conditions have been complied with:

(a)   the adopter or adopters at the time of the application must

---

159. Even those born "in adultery" but acknowledged by the father are in no worse a position, except as indicated in footnote 158.
160. See *Lintott Bros. v. Solomon* (1888) Sar. F.C.L. 122 at p. 123. "Father in relation to an illegitimate child means the natural father-Adoption Act, 1962 (Act 104) s. 21.
161. Sarbah, *op. cit.*, 34.
162. Rattray, *Ashanti Law and Constitution*, p. 70.
163. Act 104.
164. "juvenile in this connection means a person who is under the age of seventeen years": Act 104, s. 21.

have attained the age of 25 years and must be at least 21 years older than the juvenile, or

(b) must have attained the age of 21 years and be a relative of the juvenile, or

(c) is the mother of the child;

(d) the applicant and the infant reside in Ghana;

(e) the juvenile has been continuously in the care and possession of the applicant for at least 3 months immediately preceding the date of the order, and

(f) the applicant has, at least 3 months before the date of the order, notified the Director of Social Welfare of his intention to apply for an adoption order in respect of the juvenile;

(g) the consent of every person who is a parent of the juvenile has been obtained (unless it is dispensed with by the court). The consent of the extended family under customary law may have to be obtained where necessary.

By section 2 of the Act, it is provided that when an adoption order has been made by the High Court

"all rights, duties, obligations and liabilities, including any arising under customary law, of the parents of the juvenile, or of any other person, in relation to the future custody, maintenance and education of the juvenile ... shall be extinguished,"

and shall vest in, be exercisable by, and be enforceable against the adopter.

The adopted child, in turn, acquires rights and duties which accrue to him on the death intestate of his parents as if they were married under the Ordinance. If the adopter makes a will, any reference to the child or children of the adopter shall be construed as including a reference to the adopted child.

The Ghana Adoption Act can be described as one of the experiments in legislation which is drafted to apply to all Ghanaians irrespective of whether they were married under the Marriage Ordinance or under customary law.

PREVIOUS APPROACHES TO FAMILY LAW

The Colonial Administration of the Gold Coast at first took the view that the marriage laws and family life of Ghana should not be disturbed or brought into line with modern developments. Thus in 1865 a Select Committee of the British House of Commons recommended, *inter alia*, that nothing should be done in the Gold Coast to encourage the inhabitants to lean on British help.[165]   Our

165. Select Committee Report, 1865, Vol. 5, pp. 15-16.

principal Supreme Court Ordinance, passed in 1876,[166] provided in part that customary law must be deemed applicable to causes and matters where the parties were "natives", to causes and matters relating to marriage and tenure and transfer of real and personal property; and to inheritance and testamentary dispositions.[167] Even where the parties, after embracing Christianity, had their marriage celebrated in a church by a minister of religion, the courts took the view that the marriage was customary and polygamous, irrespective of the wishes of the parties. It was not until the famous case of *Des Bordes* v. *Des Bordes*[168] that the Colonial Administration was forced to revise its views.

In that case, the court had to consider whether to grant a decree of divorce to the petitioner, who had been married to the respondent since 1878, on the ground of adultery and cruelty. MacLeod, J., first ruled that the English Marriage Acts, 1823 and 1836, were not "statutes of general application", and therefore did not apply. Second, even if they were applied in the Gold Coast, the judge was not sure he had jurisdiction to grant the relief prayed for, since the marriage was solemnised in a Wesleyan Chapel by a Wesleyan minister rather than a clergyman of the Church of England as provided for by the Act. Was he then to decline jurisdiction and let the matter be determined by the customary courts despite the parties' clear intention to contract a Christian monogamous marriage? He refused to take such a narrow view in the absence of local marriage legislation, and assumed jurisdiction to grant the relief sought on the ground that the parties had clearly intended to contract a monogamous marriage.

The year of this decision (1884) saw the passing of our first Marriage Ordinance, which has been subsequently amended. As we have seen, the main purpose of the Marriage Ordinance was to provide an alternative method of contracting marriages in Ghana. The Ordinance, however, did more than that. It also affected the devolution of the property of the parties in the event of either party dying intestate. With very few exceptions, the incidents of marriage under the Ordinance are quite different from those of marriage under customary law. That such a state of affairs is unfortunate need not be emphasised.

In recent times the recommendations of conferences on African law have tended to favour the idea of the discrete development of systems of family law. One of the resolutions of the Conference on the Future of Customary Law in Africa, held in Amsterdam in

166. No. 4 of 1876.
167. *ibid.* s. 19.
168. (1884) Sar. F.C.L. 267.

1955,[169] stated that:

> "the proper field of customary law should normally be regarded as restricted to family relations, succession ... "

Another resolution on Islamic law was framed in this form:

> "It is of particular importance, in view of the triple system of law which at present prevails in many African territories, that the application of Islamic law should be confined, wherever and as soon as possible, to matters such as family law, succession and (where these exist) *awqaf*."

The next important conference, from the point of view of the topic under discussion, was that on the Future of Law in Africa, held in London in December 1959. Members attending the conference concluded that:[170]

> "Questions of family relations, marriage, divorce, wills and succession are so essentially personal that they must in large part continue to be governed by the customary law of the community to which the person belongs."

Hence no positive steps were recommended for the integration of the various systems of laws.

Finally, in 1963 many African states had become independent, and it would appear that this encouraged the members of the Conference on Local Courts and Customary Law in Africa to re-examine the question of integration more positively. Their recommendation on marriage, which deserves to be quoted at length, read as follows:[170a]

> "In the present state of African Society it was difficult, if not impossible to devise a single system of marriage law replacing these different kinds of marriage, but the conference strongly recommended that a general regulatory enactment in regard to specific aspects of marriage should be passed in each country. This legislation should:-
>
> (a) Unify, so far as possible, the procedural requirements for different forms of marriage and state minimum requirements (e.g. in regard to age, consents, registration) for all marriages.
>
> (b) Ensure that the different types of marriages enjoy social and legal parity of status.
>
> (c) Eliminate, so far as possible, the variable consequences at present attaching to different kinds of marriages (e.g. in

---

169. Proceedings of the conference were published in 1956 under the same title. Universitaire pers Leiden 1956 pp. 268-69.
170. Allott (ed.) The Future of Law in Africa (Record of Proceedings of the London Conference) (1960) p. 45.
170a Record of Proceedings of the Conference held in Dar-es-Salaam Tanganyika pp. 26-27.

regard to the evidence of wives married by different forms), more particularly in regard to those who are not themselves parties to the marriage (e.g. children of the marriage). It is recognised that some of the essential features of different kinds of marriage (e.g. monogamy or polygamy) are at present incapable of being integrated into a single system, but other aspects e.g. maintenance of wife and children, matrimonial property rights, may be capable of being unified.

(d) Bring the law of marriage more closely into line with people's requirements. Certain parts of the existing statute law (e.g. concerning bigamy) are presently rarely enforced. The law, once it has been revised, should be more strictly enforced but arrangements should be made (e.g. at the marriage ceremony or during registration) to ensure that the parties clearly understand the legal consequences attaching to the particular form of marriage they have chosen."

Some of these recommendations will no doubt be re-examined at this Conference. In this connection, it is pertinent to give examples of Ghanaian experimental legislation aimed at integrating the systems of law.

EXPERIMENTS IN INTEGRATION

One experiment in this field has been to pass legislation designed to cater both for persons subject to English—based law and for those subject to customary law. Thus, for the purposes of the Workmen's Compensation Act,[171] the word "dependents" is defined in such a way as to avoid any inquiry into the type of marriage contracted by the worker. It includes all members of the family of a workman who were wholly or in part dependant upon his earnings at the time of his death or of the accident which incapacitated him. The second schedule to the Act then classifies the claimants according to whether the worker belongs to a patrilineal or matrilineal Family.

The Administration of Estates Act[172] is another legislative experiment designed to be adaptable to the administration of estates of persons subject to customary law as well as those subject to English-based law. Section 1(2), for example, is framed in the following manner:

"In the absence of an executor the estate shall, until a personal representative is appointed, vest as follows—
(a) if the entire estate devolves under customary law—in

---

171. 1963, Act 174.
172. 1961, Act 63. For a more detailed review of the Act, see Daniels (1962) 6 J.A.L. 30-34.

the successor (according to customary law)
(b) in any other case—in the Chief Justice."
The Maintenance of Children Act [173] can also be described as an enactment which seeks to unify our laws on maintenance.

By the Ghana Adoption Act, 1962,[174] adoption of children requires not only the consent of the parents, but also, by section 4(1),

"Where it appears to the Court that any person who is not the parent of the juvenile, has, under any order of a Court or agreement, or under customary law, or otherwise, any rights or obligations in respect of the juvenile the Court may, if they think fit, require that that person's consent shall be obtained before the adoption order is made."

It has also been noted that provisions in our Criminal Code and Criminal Procedure Code imposing duties on the parents, do not distinguish between those married under cusomary law and those married under the Marriage Ordinance.

The boldest experiment so far was the Bill on Marriage, Divorce and Inheritance,[175] which was drafted to streamline the laws of marriage and divorce. This Bill incorporated a number of suggestions made to the Government by Chiefs, religious bodies, and interested members of the Republic. The Memorandum to the Bill, a part of which is quoted below, epitomises its main objects:

"This Bill proposes that a man can only register one marriage . . . , thus according public recognition to the wife whose name appears in the Register. Any other woman with whom a man has children will not be entitled to any inheritance under the law; but her children will be entitled in the same way as the children of the registered marriage. A woman married under the existing Marriage Ordinance will be regarded, for the purposes of this new law, as the wife under a registered marriage. In the case of [other] marriages contracted before, and subsisting at the commencement of this Act . . . the person concerned may register all the marriages within a reasonable time after the coming into operation of the new law . . . If a wife dies or is divorced her husband may register a second marriage. This Bill preserves the concept of arbitration and attempted reconciliation in divorce matters. It is also considered desirable to keep the question of dissolution of marriage away from the Courts, but provision is made for the order of dissolution to be made in open Court with rights of

173. Published March 19, 1963. 1965 Act 297.
174. Act 104.
175. The latest draft was published on June 13, 1963.

appeal in relation to such incidental matters as restoration
of property, maintenance of the divorced wife and children,
etc. This appeal would take the form of a petition to the
Chief Justice . . .
It is considered that Ghana should set an example by
approaching marriage in a constructive way. The proposed
legislation would accentuate the aim of reconciliation and
the sanctity of marriage. Divorce would be treated as a
last resort."

Although this Bill has been withdrawn for further consideration,
the intention of the Government is clear. As soon as practicable,
polygamy should be discouraged and, further, a future law on
marriage should ensure that the different types of marriage enjoy
social and legal parity of status.

SUGGESTION FOR REFORM

Since the integration of marriage laws is the ultimate objective
and since the trend of enlightened thinking is in favour of encouraging monogamy it may be useful to consider some of the measures
which may be necessary for achieving it.

Polygamy

The idealist would argue that as marriage is very much a personal
affair, the State should not abolish polygamy by legislation. He
would contend that the best way to get rid of polygamy is to educate
the public. It is submitted that this approach is not by itself enough.
We have stated that the first marriage law in Ghana was passed in
1884 with the gradual abolition of polygamy as one of its main aims.
One cannot say with any conviction that the presence of the Marriage
Ordinance in our Statute Book for a period of 80 years has done
much to discourage polygamy. It has rather tended to preserve
the co-existence of monogamy and polygamy.

Another argument used to discourage legislation is that economic
circumstances will in due course force men to abandon the practice
of polygamy. But there is no statistical data to prove that polygamy
thrives best in a country which has a sound economy. It has also
been argued that polygamy in Africa has been necessitated by the
fact that there are more African women than men. Certainly the
last census figures published in Ghana disprove this argument.[176]

Undoubtedly some of the points mentioned above can help to
discourage polygamy. It is, however, submitted that something
more can be done by way of legislation. Although the law to abolish

176. See London Times Jan. 3, 1963.

polygamy must not be retroactive in character, for such a procedure would cause great social upheaval, it should stipulate that as from a particular date polygamous marriages will be illegal. It should also preserve the validity of existing polygamous marriages. Article 90 of the Yugoslavia law on marriage is instructive. It is there provided that:-

"A marriage contracted before the entry into force of this law is valid if it was contracted with the laws existing at that time."[177]

One major drawback to this approach is that it cannot be completely successful unless there is an effective system of registration of existing marriages. Nevertheless, it is submitted that an Act of Parliament expressly abolishing the practice of polygamy, followed by intensive educational campaigns in the rural areas, can be more effective than the alternative method of hoping vaguely for an unconscious disappearance of the practice.

Uniform Legislation

In view of the disparity in status engendered by the existence of three different types of marriage, there cannot be any genuine opposition to the passing of a law to standardise the legal incidents and remove unnecessary conflicts. How to tackle this question has been a major problem. There is no dearth of legislative precedent. The English Marriage Act,[178] 1949, deals in one enactment with the solemnisation of more than one "type" of marriage, namely:

(a) marriage according to the rites of the Church of England;

(b) marriage in the office of the Superintendent Registrars;

(c) Quaker marriages, which allow members of the Society of Friends to be married according to the usages of the Society;[179]

(d) Jewish marriages.

This precedent could be followed. Thus in addition to the existing types contained in the Marriage Ordinance, provision could be made for the celebration of marriage either according to the rites of the Mohammedan faith or according to customary law. As has already been observed, there are variations within customary law regarding the celebration, etc., of customary marriages. In this connection, a recording and restating of the laws of marriage, such

177. See *Collection of Yugoslav Laws*, Vol. 4, p. 32.
178. 12 & 13 Geo. 6 c. 76.
179. *ibid*. s. 47.

as that being done at the School of Oriental and African Studies under Professor Allott's direction, would help the work of the draftsman. The Ministry of Justice has now a large collection on the various customary law marriages sent in by various sections of the country since the publication of the Government White Paper on this subject in 1961.

The next task of the legislator will be to ensure that the essentials of a valid marriage are made uniform. It is obviously desirable that a minimum age should be laid down for all types of marriage. All marriages, moreover, should be subject to the same rules as to registration. (it is not suggested that a marriage proposed to be celebrated in the rural areas must take place before a registrar in a capital city or nearest town. District Administrative Officers, and District magistrates and certain classes of chiefs could be entrusted with this job. They could send monthly returns to the Registrars of marriages in the nearest town.)

The rules of consanguinity should also be made uniform. Section 42 of our Marriage Ordinance provides that no marriage in Ghana "shall be valid, which if celebrated in England, would be null and void on the ground of kindred or affinity . . ." Does this provision mean that where two Ghanaians are already married according to customary law, and are desirous of converting their marriage into an Ordinance Marriage, they will be unable to do so if their customary rules of consanguinity differ from those of the English? Few preople are likely to know the English rules as to consangunity and affinity, especially as these rules are not to be found in our Marriage Ordinance.

Another defect of the present Marriage Ordinance is the exclusion from it of penalties connected with marital offences.[180] It would be a good idea to include all the essential ones in the Marriage Act. The grounds for divorce, etc., should also be made uniform. In view of the points raised in this paper, new matrimonial causes rules may have to be made. Finally, it will be necessary to confer limited jurisdiction in divorce, matrimonial causes, maintenance and other matters on courts of inferior jurisdiction. These suggestions are by no means exhaustive, nor is it being contended that the problems that have to be dealt with in order to choose a means of unifying the legislation on family law are slight.

---

180. They are now contained in the Criminal Colde, Act 29.
   S.100 deals with the effect of avoidance of marriage with respect to Consent; s. 262 deals with bigamy and similar offences; s. 268—unlawfully performing a marriage ceremony; s. 269—making a false declaration, etc., for marriage; s. 270—false pretence of impediment to marriage; s. 271—wilful neglect of duty to fill up or transmit certificate of marriage; s. 272—mode of proving marriage or divorce.

THE LAW OF HUSBAND AND WIFE
IN EAST AFRICA

by

JAMES S. READ

READER IN AFRICAN LAW, UNIVERSITY OF LONDON
FORMERLY SENIOR LECTURER IN LAW,
UNIVERSITY COLLEGE, DAR-ES-SALAAM

THE LAW OF HUSBAND AND WIFE
IN EAST AFRICA

Often, when questions of law reform are under discussion in Europe, it is found useful to distinguish between fields of "lawyers' law" and "politicians' law". However, the problems of legal change in modern Africa are such that this distinction cannot often be made. In the realm of the law relating to husband and wife it would be particularly irrelevant and, indeed, impossible. African governments rightly see law as one of the important instruments by which the social, political and economic development of their countries can be promoted. Nation-building and social progress are the spurs to the reform of family law and therefore political questions are immediately raised in this connection. But, in addition, one legacy of colonial rule in many parts of Africa, and especially in East Africa, has been the presentation to independent governments of an incoherent assortment of conflicting laws relating to the family: it is a task for *lawyers* to investigate and discover the areas of this law in which reform is vital merely for legal reasons, to promote order and consistency. Those who undertake such a task require to be persons of unusual determination. In short, in the integration of family laws in East Africa, politician and lawyer are called upon to co-operate to the full; and the result of their labours will be the more successful in accordance with the degree to which each can enter into the sympathetic understanding of the other's problems.

I. A general outline of the present position

The general features of the present position must be stated before the problems raised can be seriously considered; but it is clear that the position is similar in other parts of Africa.

The fundamental characteristic of the present situation is the recognition of several differing systems of law which apply to relations between husbands and wives. Customary law, Islamic law, Hindu law and statute law of English type are all applicable. Each of these operates in East African countries to regulate the formation, termination, and legal consequences of marriages. The Hindu and Islamic laws in part rest upon statutory foundations.[1]

---

1. For example, the Hindu Marriage and Divorce Act of Kenya (Cap. 157) or Uganda (Cap. 214) or the Marriage, Divorce and Succession (Non-Christian Asiatics) Ordinance of Tanzania, Cap. 112 (the laws of Tanzania cited in this paper are those applicable in the mainland—Tanganyika—only.)

The statutes make some provision relating to the interaction of these different forms: for example, marriage under the Marriage Acts[2] is of monogamous type and therefore cannot be entered by a person already married to another partner under some other form, nor can it be validly followed by such a marriage during the life of the first wife. Similarly, the law relating to matrimonial causes is differentiated: remedies under the Matrimonial Causes Acts (of Tanzania and Kenya[3]) or the Divorce Act (of Uganda[4]) are available only in the case of monogamous marriages within the famous definition laid down by Lord Penzance in the old English case of the Mormon Marriage[5].:

"'marriage' means the voluntary union of one man and one woman for life to the exclusion of all others".[6]

But the separation of forms of marriage is by no means complete, and in fact considerable confusion and conflict arise. To some extent, with regard to formation and judicial remedies, the different forms of marriage may be regarded as represented by the metaphor of parallel railway tracks; but in practice there are numerous "points" at which particular spouses may move from one track to another—often unconsciously—and very often it may be difficult to determine upon which track a particular marriage has in fact commenced its journey.

Thus, for example, an African couple may marry under the Marriage Act of their country, whether in a Christian form in church or merely by a civil ceremony before a registrar. Their marriage is monogamous and dissoluble only by a court decree under the appropriate statute. But by choosing this form of marriage, the persons concerned cannot opt out of their customary law so far as it governs other obligations, even those which arise directly in the course of the marriage. It is probable that property rights between the spouses of such a marriage are governed by customary law; yet in terms of the statutory remedies, which are available to them, certain rights—with regard, for example, to maintenance, or damages for adultery—become subject to the rules of the statute.

In the more complex, but quite typical, situation, a couple may marry under the Marriage Act but also complete the requirements for a valid marriage at customary law, by the usual sequence of negotiations, visits, agreements, ceremonies and payment of "bride-price". By what law are they then bound? The problems of the "double-decker marriage" are considered later.

2. Kenya: Cap. 150; Tanzania: Cap. 109; Uganda: Cap. 221.
3. Caps. 364, 152 respectively. 4. Cap. 215.
5. *Hyde* v. *Hyde* (1866) L.R. I.P. & D. 130.
6. Tanzania; Cap. 364, s. 2; Kenya: Cap. 152, s. 2.

But undoubtedly the principal defects in the existing law, which an integration of the laws would redress, are those relating to the unequal treatment of persons who marry according to different laws. It is quite clear that all the forms of marriage listed above are fully recognised as valid by the laws of the East African countries. But nevertheless, when specific rules in the general law which impinge upon the marriage relationship, or derive from it, are raised, the recognition given is certainly not equal in fact. The question may well be asked, "when is a wife not a wife?" If the lady in question was married according to customary law, then the answer might be: "when she is called as a witness at her husband's trial[7]," or, possibly, "when she is charged with stealing from her husband."[8] But she may be regarded by the court as a wife if her husband alleges that he was provoked, by finding her in the act of adultery, to kill the adulterer[9]; or if the adulterer is charged with an offence.[10] And of course in a leading case the Privy Council, on an appeal from Tanganyika, has held that a Muslim wife comes within the common law rule that a wife cannot be convicted of conspiring with her husband[11].

It might be objected that these examples of discrimination are in accordance with the English law, which has only gradually and of recent years weaned itself from the position of refusing recognition to polygamous marriages, or marriages entered into under a system of law which would permit polygamy, and which even today appears to maintain the distinction in unexpected situations—so that a potentially polygamous marriage, for example, is not a valid first marriage upon which to found a charge of bigamy following a second marriage in England.[12] But there are two answers to this

---

7. This is the position in Uganda and Zanzibar: Evidence Act, Uganda, Cap. 43, s. 119, reversing the decision in *R. v. Oumu* (1915) 2 U.L.R. 152; *Abdulrahman bin Mohamed and Anor.* v. *R.* (1963) E.A. 188. Formerly also this distinction was applied in other countries: see *R. v. Amkeyo* (1917) 7 E.A.L.R. 14 (Kenya), followed in *R. v. Robin* (1929) 12 K.L.R. 134 (Nyasaland) and *Mwakio Asani s/o Mwanguku* v. *R.* (1930) 1 T.L.R. (R.) 662 (Tanganyika). But now the law in Kenya and Tanganyika has been changed so that wives of customary law marriages are treated equally, as witnesses, with wives of statutory forms of marriage: Evidence Act, Kenya, Cap. 80, s. 127; Evidence Act, Tanganyika, No. 6 of 1967, s. 3. For an examination of the case-law concerning the unequal treatment of different kinds of wives in East Africa see Read, "When is a wife not a wife?", *Journal of the Denning Law Society*, Dar es Salaam, Vol. 1, No. 2, December 1964.
8. See *Mphumeya* v. *R.* 1956 R. & N. 240, *Neva* v. *R.* 1961 R. & N. 538 (Nyasaland).
9. *R. v. Obongo* (1920) 3 U.L.R. 31 (Uganda).
10. *R. v. Daudi Odongo* (1926) 10 K.L.R. 49 (Kenya).
11. *Mawji and Anor* v. *R.* (1957) A.C. 126; 23 E.A.C.A. 609.
12. *R. v. Sarwan Singh* (1962) 3 All E.R. 612.

comment: firstly, these other forms of marriage are in fact given recognition in the laws of African countries, and this basic position should not be qualified by inappropriate distinctions drawn from English law; and, secondly, it appears more clearly from recent cases in East Africa that the distinction in question is not really based upon the difference between polygamy and monogamy but upon something more delicate. It is relevant to cite the express statutory provision in Tanganyika:

> "The marriage in (Tanganyika) of non-Christian spouses either of whom is an Asiatic, . . . shall, if the marriage is contracted in the manner customary in (Tanganyika) among persons professing the religion of either party to the marriage, be deemed *for all purposes* to be a valid marriage."[13]

It is clear that the words underlined here have not in fact been given their apparent effect.

Yet it appears that discrimination between different kinds of wives does not rest upon the differences between potentially polygamous and monogamous marriages. In holding, in a recent appeal from Zanzibar, that the wife of a customary law marriage was a competent witness against her husband at his trial for murder, following the older cases, the Court of Appeal for Eastern Africa indicated that the law of Zanzibar, a Muslim state, did not distinguish between monogamous and polygamous marriages; the reason why the wife in question was not subject to the normal rule of the incompetency of wives as witnesses in such cases was based upon the nature of marriage at customary law.

> "To sum up, this court has held in two cases, *R. v. Mwakio Asani*[14] and *R. v. Toya s/o Mamure*[15] that in Kenya, where the common law of England is in force and where the Criminal Procedure Code contains a section which is in identical terms with the Zanzibar section 147, a wife married according to the native custom is a competent witness for the prosecution. As in Zanzibar, the criminal law of Kenya does not distinguish between monogamous and other marriages. Those two decisions have stood for many years and so far as we are aware have never been differed from. In criminal cases this court is bound by its own decisions unless the court is of opinion that to follow the earlier decision which is considered to be erroneous would involve supporting an

---

13. Marriage, Divorce and Succession (non-Christian Asiatics) Ordinance, Cap. 112, s. 2 (1).
14. Above, footnote 7.
15. (1930) 14 K.L.R. 145.

improper conviction: *Joseph Kabui* v. *R.*[16] The first appellant
was not represented at the hearing of the appeal and we have not
had the advantage of any argument on his behalf but, having
given the matter full consideration, we are not prepared to differ
from those earlier decisions. In our view they should be followed
in determining whether one party to a marriage contracted
according to native law or custom is a competent witness for the
prosecution.

African customary marriages in East Africa are usually polygamous or potentially polygamous. Does the fact that the
marriage in this present case was monogamous take it out of the
class of customary marriages which were in the contemplation of
the court in *R.* v. *Mwakio Asani* and *R.* v. *Toya s/o Mamure*?
We do not think so. The marriage appears to have all the elements
of 'wife-purchase' the description given to an African customary
marriage in *Amkeyo's* case. There was no religious ceremony or,
indeed, any ceremony at all. The first appellant merely paid
Shs. 200 for her, which money was paid through her father to
her former husband to release her. Either party could buy his or
her release at any time. It may well be a valid marriage in Zanzibar but, bearing in mind *Amkeyo's* case and the decisions of this
court in which that case was followed, we do not think the wife
of such a marriage is within the purview of the general rule that
husband or wife of the person charged is not a competent witness
for the prosecution."[17]

With this indication of the nature of the legal problems to be
encountered in this field, it is convenient to turn to a consideration
of the problems faced in integrating the laws.

II. Main problems in the integration of the laws

The problems are of various kinds, and it is not easy to indicate
them in order of priority: they are so closely interrelated that they
should, if possible, be dealt with in one operation.

The first category of problems are those which raise questions of
policy which are properly referable in the last resort to politicians.
Should different legal forms of marriage be allowed to continue or
should one common basic legal form be imposed—which would
amount only to a system of registration—while permitting religious
and other special forms of marriage to continue without legal effect?
To what extent can full integration, with the introduction of one
system marriage, be attained? Inadequate attention has perhaps

16. (1954) 21 E.A.C.A. 260.
17. *Abdulrahman Bin Mohamed* v. *R.* (1963) E.A. 188.

been given to the possibility of a solution of this kind to the vexed problems of conflicting laws in East Africa, but that is not to suggest that such a solution would be simple. It would entail determination of the key question of whether the common form of marriage accepted would permit polygamy or not, and if so, to what extent and under what conditions. It is unlikely that the abolition of polygamous forms of marriage would be widely acceptable, yet there are many elements in East African society which would desire, and indeed insist upon, the retention of the option of a binding mono-gamous form of marriage. The fact that these are two alternatives which offer no compromise position, no happy medium between one wife or many, is the source of many lesser difficulties.

But other questions of policy are also pressing. The treatment of the present offences of bigamy or crimes akin thereto, consisting of marriages under the Ordinance and under customary law irrespective of the chronological order of such marriages, would be determined, presumably, according to the treatment of the first question raised in the preceding paragraph. But the place of customary "bride-price" in the future law of marriage is a question for politician and sociologists. Various alternatives may be presented to them by the lawyers: bride-price could be retained as an essential factor in the formation of marriage, as it is in many present day customary law systems, and it could be limited within certain maximum amounts; it could be abolished, and the disparaging comments made by the Court of Appeal for Eastern Africa in *Abdulrahman's* Case, quoted above, suggest that there would be support from the judiciary at least for such a solution: this would not, however, be likely to be the view of the majority of citizens. A further alternative, and one in fact adopted by the Government of Tanganyika,[18] is to provide that bride-price may be paid but is no longer an essential feature of customary marriage: in such a case it is, of course, necessary to provide some alternative formality (in Tanganyika, registration) which is essential and which provides the test of the validity of the marriage.

Policy decisions would also be required with regard to the form of the divorce law to be provided upon integration: in this connection the merits and disadvantages respectively of the present statute law in East Africa (embodying many rules of English divorce law including, in particular, the notion of the matrimonial offence as the basis and justification for divorce) and of the customary law proceedings and rules (which consider rather the whole relationship between the spouses and make provision for powerful attempts at

18. By the Declaration of local customary law, G.N. No. 279 of 1963

reconciling them) would demand consideration. If alternative forms of marriage are provided, and clearly distinguished, there is of course no reason why different systems of divorce law should not also apply. In any case, it would be difficult to integrate fully the Islamic law relating to divorce, with the unilateral repudiation by *talak*, with another system based primarily upon customary or English law.

In the second group of obstacles to integration of the laws are found those which result from an existing lack of knowledge of the law. This operates in a number of ways. There is, for example, a general ignorance among jurists and draftsmen of the content of customary law. East Africa in the past has had few serious investigators of customary law as such, although there is a considerable documentation of different customary laws in various types of record, including anthropologists' field work reports, investigations of specific topics by committees and an occasional study of a particular system of customary law by an expert. Most notable in earlier years was the work of Dr. Hans Cory in Tanganyika. E. S. Haydon produced an account of "Law and Justice in Buganda". One of the best studies was Gutmann's "Das recht der Dschagga" (1926). But there was no comprehensive study of customary law until that undertaken in Kenya by the Restatement of African Law Project of the University of London and completed by E. Cotran, but not yet published.

It is not merely that customary law happened not to be studied in detail; there was a widespread attitude among the judiciary and government lawyers that such study was not to be encouraged. To some extent this view may have been based upon considered arguments: that customary law was changing and should not be crystallised, and even that it would disappear in the melting pot of social and economic changes. But the result was the sort of unenlightened comments that were made by judges in, for example the cases quoted above concerning the recognition of wives of customary law marriages with regard to privileges applied to wives in general in the law of evidence or criminal law.

This general ignorance of the detailed rules of customary law is a pressing problem when questions of law reform are discussed. But almost as pressing is the uncertainty as to the precise rules concerning the inter-action of the different systems of law which apply. There are many aspects of the law of husband and wife on which it is difficult to ascertain what the present law is, because of the confusion between these systems, and because the terms of the statute laws which apply are themselves not always clear, and in any case appear to take little account of the context within which they operate.

There is therefore ignorance, even in informed legal quarters, as to the effect of the totality of laws which apply. One simple problem in this respect is the question as to the effect of the "double-decker marriage" mentioned earlier. If a couple marry according to customary law formalities and then again in church, which is in fact a very common procedure in modern East Africa, what is the legal effect of these proceedings? Does the first form of marriage prevail, making the church marriage a meaningless charade, on the ground that a couple who are married cannot marry again even in a different form? Some authorities support this view, and the Acts of Kenya and Uganda make special provision for the "conversion" by special ceremonies of a customary law marriage into a monogamous marriage. Or could it be successfully argued that the binding monogamous marriage is a superior form which prevails over the earlier customary marriage? Modern African governments are unlikely to accept this view.

There are various other grounds of uncertainty as to the operation of the modern laws. Many of these turn upon the unsatisfactory nature of the statutes themselves: drafted in an earlier age, when the problems of modern African society and the persistence of customary law were hardly understood, and when the forms of English law, upon which the Acts were largely based, were themselves not in a settled pattern, many provisions of these Acts today like a voice from another world. One difficulty raised in Uganda and Tanganyika is that concerning the age of marriage under the legislation in the absence of any special provision in the statute law, it seems that the age of marriage may be tested by personal law—which would in many cases indicate a system of customary law—or by the old English common law (which would enable boys to marry at 14 years, girls at 12—and marriages at earlier ages might be valid).

Finally there is great uncertainty, and usually misunderstanding, among people in general in East Africa as to the actual purport of the laws even where these are definite in their terms. Thus, in Kenya and Uganda at least, it is clear that a person who marries under the Ordinance, being already married under customary law, or vice versa, commits a serious criminal offence.[19] In practice, of course, the provisions are virtually unenforceable because the social pattern is such that in some areas this is a very common practice indeed.

In short, it would be misleading to limit the idea that the law is at present uncertain to the content of customary law only. But much of the uncertainty about the statute and common law, and

19. See Marriage Acts, Kenya, ss. 49 and 50; and Uganda, ss. 51 and 52.

about the conflicts between these systems of law, can be resolved not by research alone but by Government policy decision.

Such questions of policy at once raise the vital issue: how far can African states cater in the future for diversity of social practice among their citizens? Unifying the customary law has been regarded by the Government of Tanganyika as an important aspect of nation-building. But in fact this process will be hard to pursue further: social conditions are very different in different parts of the countries, and even in a specific area, the modes of life of different citizens may be very diverse in pattern. This is, of course, a factor heightened by differences of religion. Is there a limit to the number of options for social behaviour with regard to such matters as marriage and divorce which a modern state can afford to offer? At what time in the future will it become practicable to impose by law a common standard, or a common form, of marriage and divorce? Should that stage be reached by steps over a period or by a major and wholesale reform of the law (perhaps the adoption of a code) which might be costly by standards of law enforcement and the common under-standing of the reform, but might hasten the day when possibly more costly problems of conflicts of law, discrimination and social division could be eliminated?

Indeed, a key question in the integration of marriage laws will be seen to be the question whether or not it is possible to provide a common framework for such laws, even if within such framework diversity of choice were to be allowed for citizens. Could a basic system of registration of marriage, with certain minimum require-ments for consent, publicity, fundamental husband-wife obligations (such as maintenance) and the like, be reconciled with a range of options for marriage in church, or in civil form, or according to Islamic law, or by customary formalities?

III.   Objectives of integration

This raises the deeper questions which must govern the legal techniques of integration. What are the objectives of any reform of the law? It is submitted that, while precise definition of such objectives is a matter for each country in the light of its social and religious conditions and aspirations, some general aims can be regarded as generally accepted.

In the first place, integration will not be achieved or even wished at the cost of throwing overboard the elements of African customary law and traditional social practices in favour of some general, detached scheme of law derived from alien sources. The reception of some system of law, whether directly derived from some other country or based upon a form of distilled jurisprudence of diverse genealogy, will not be satisfactory for two reasons. One is a negative reason: such law will merely exist on paper, for the social content which will make it appropriate will be lacking; husband and wife relationships will not in fact be changed by legislation alone, whatever sanctions are proposed. The second reason is a positive one, although it is the reverse of the same coin.

Much is heard these days of the African personality. One of the most important elements of this-however elusive-concept is that it does not refer only to the personality of the individual. *The personality of the African family* is perhaps even more significant, even more resilient and even more influential. Any reform of the law in Africa which sets out to ignore this factor is surely doomed to a purely theoretical existence.

Integration of the laws can only be achieved, therefore, by careful and serious investigation of the law that is, of the customs and behaviour of the present society of the country concerned. These things may need reform and pruning: but integration which ignores the content of the present law will produce a situation no better than the present.

Secondly, clearly a principal aim of integration must be to end the present uncertainty, confusion and conflict in the law. And the solution adopted for this conflict should be one which will cater if possible not only for the society of the present but for that of the future, at least so far as estimates can be made of the extent to which present and impending social changes can be calculated to have their effect. And lawyers must consider the extent to which the impending integration of courts systems in many African countries, with the ending of the former division between "African" or "local" courts, and the magistrates' and High Courts (which division has often cloaked problems of conflict in the law and consequent problems of social tension) will in fact intensify and multiply these conflict problems.

Thirdly, present discrimination and selectivity of treatment of different forms of marriage must be brought to an end as far as possible. This aim was, indeed, one of the agreed recommendations of the African Conference on Local Courts and Local Customary Law at Dar-es-Salaam in 1963. If various forms of marriage are to be permitted in the future, it must be because those forms of marriage are accepted by the State concerned as good, valid and proper forms of marriage, and no kind of moral scale of different forms of marriage can be countenanced by such a State. Therefore, if a wife is married according to customary law, Islamic law or Christian ceremonies, she is at least a wife and as such entitled to whatever legal privileges flow directly from her status. This would not necessarily exclude special provisions for divorce or some specifically marital obligations consequent upon the form of each particular marriage.

IV. Present methods of Law reform in East Africa

It is perhaps a little premature to speak of present methods of integration of laws in East Africa, for although the Governments have shown themselves to be aware of the problems raised by the present law, they have yet to take any specific steps towards integration of the laws as such. But certain preliminary stages of the process involved have been initiated.

In Uganda, where the problems of conflict and confusion between the laws are perhaps the most pressing, a Commission of Inquiry was set up by the President of Uganda on 14th January, 1964, with the following terms of reference:

"To consider the laws and customs regulating marriage, divorce and the status of women in Uganda, bearing in mind to ensure that those laws and customs while preserving existing traditions and practices, as far as possible, should be consistent with justice and to morality and appropriate to the position of Uganda as an independent nation and to make recommendations."

The Commission (which included one woman) finally reported in 1965. It recommended unifying legislation to provide for the registration of all marriages: except for existing marriages, a man should be allowed to register one wife only. Sixteen years should be the minimum age of marriage, with parental consent necessary below eighteen years. Divorce should be possible only by judicial proceeding, but a judge would preside over a divorce committee which would first endeavour to reconcile the spouses before granting a dissolution of the marriage. A surviving spouse should be given a substantial interest in the property of a deceased person: it was found by the Commission to be a serious problem that the widow in a customary law marriage was inadequately provided for at present; her lot was described as "deplorable". An unusual recommendation was that where a man and woman had lived together as man and wife for at least a year, neither of them could deny the subsistence of a marriage between them. The Report of the Commission, as a whole, is a disappointing document which does not demonstrate a full appreciation of the many issues involved: and the laws of Uganda regarding marriage and divorce have yet to be amended in the way proposed, or at all.[20]

20. For a discussion of the Report, see Morris, "Uganda: Report of the Commission on Marriage, Divorce and the Status of Women", *Journal of African Law*, Vol. 10, No. 1, 1966, p. 3-7.

In Kenya, the customary laws of marriage, divorce and succession have been thoroughly studied and recorded for publication by the Restatement of African Law Project of the University of London. The next stage in reform of the law commenced in 1967 when the Government of Kenya appointed two strong commissions of enquiry into, respectively, the laws of marriage and divorce and the laws of succession. The secretary of each commission is the lawyer who conducted the investigations of customary law (Mr E. Cotran). The reports of these enquiries, expected in 1968, will undoubtedly be given close attention as well as informed and thoughtful examinations of the basic problems, and possible solutions, in these areas of law.

In Tanganyika, the Declarations of Local Customary Law made and enforced under statutory authority have since 1963 changed the basis of customary law in most parts of the country. These Declarations, the result of lengthy and diligent enquiry and, in so far as the operation was directed in its early stages by the late Dr. Hans Cory, the result of his lifetime of study in Tanganyika, have introduced a new measure of uniformity between the different customary law systems. The Declaration, however, unlike Cotran's Restatements in Kenya, does not stop short at recording the customary law but proceeds to modify or amend it when considered necessary. Thus, with regard to the formation of marriage, the requirement of registration has been introduced as an essential for the validity of customary marriages; and "bride-price", while not prohibited, is no longer an essential feature.

"5. The payment of bridewealth is not essential for the validity of a marriage.

10. A. All rules restricting the amount of bridewealth must be revoked.

B. The amount of bridewealth demanded should take into account the ability of the bridegroom to pay."

In fact, the Declaration anticipates the continuance of the custom of bridewealth in general, and makes numerous provision regarding its payment, refund and so on.

"86. A. Whether the marriage is the result of an arrangement between father-in-law and son-in-law, or of an arrangement between the two persons immediately concerned, it must be legalized by the issue of a marriage certificate. The traditional ceremonies which formerly legalized the marriage may continue but they have no legal force.

B. Particulars of all marriages shall be reported to the (primary) court near to the bride's home or, in case the

bride is not living with her parents, near to the bridegroom's home.

C. The following persons together with the bride and
bridegroom shall be required to appear before the court as
witnesses to the marriage:

    (a) the father of the bride or his deputy if the bride has
        not attained the age of 21 years—

    (b) one independent witness for each party.

D. All relevant particulars shall be recorded in a register
kept by the court and entered also on certificates issued by
the court to the two parties.

E. (a) Such particulars shall include full details of the
total bridewealth agreed upon by the two parties and shall
show the amount paid and that outstanding in this respect.

    Subsequent payments shall be reported to the court, so
that they are entered both in the court register and on the
certificates."

    (b) Even if no bridewealth is to be paid, the certificate
must be issued and this information entered in the court
register."[21]

This clarification and unification of the customary laws in
Tanganyika is also likely to be of the greatest importance when
further measures are planned to integrate the laws.

V. Conclusion

From this summary of the present law, the problems it raises and
the objectives proposed for any integration of the laws, some
concluding observations may tentatively be offered.

Firstly, any serious attempt at integration must presuppose a
study of the existing law at all levels: in Kenya and Tanganyika this
process has advanced to the stage where the customary law is well
documented or even superseded by enactment; in Uganda the
process has yet to begin. Throughout East Africa, serious study of
the inter-action of the different legal systems has only been undertaken in recent years, mainly in connection with university teaching
or research.

Secondly, integration will mean change in all the existing laws,
unless some of them are to be merely superseded or absorbed by
another system of law. Changes may be substantial but they should

---

21. The quotations are given in the official translation from the Swahili of
     the original Declaration, G.N. No. 279 of 1963. For an informed
     criticism of the methods and results of the Tanganyika project see
     Tanner, "The codification of customary law in Tanzania," *East
     African Law Journal*, Vol. 2, No. 2, 1966, pp. 105-116.

be in accordance with the possible measures of adaptation in actual social life, and they should be fully acceptable to those who control political decisions, preferably after investigation of the state of public opinion through various channels, such as the churches, women's organisations and the like.

Thirdly, some changes which will ameliorate the discriminations drawn by the present law can be effected without amendments to the law of the family as such: for example, statutes concerning evidence could be reformed to bestow equal competence on all married women.

Forthly, in the integration of the laws about marriage and divorce as such, certain basic and controversial issues must be faced, such as the problem of providing alternative forms of marriage. If full integration of the law proves unacceptable, at least it would be possible to reduce the area of conflict between different systems. It is also desirable, for the maintenance of law in general, that unenforceable provisions, which reduce the law to being merely exhortatory, should be eliminated.

Finally, it may be suggested that the problems raised by this subject in East Africa are not unique and are in fact shared in other parts of the continent. The opportunity for international discussion and exchange of experience on this matter is therefore particularly marked, and the tasks of investigation and of producing possible draft legislation might well be accepted by some international agency: the Commission of African Jurists would seem to be the best fitted to undertake this work.

INTEGRATION OF THE LAWS OF MARRIAGE AND DIVORCE IN KENYA

by

EUGENE COTRAN

LL.B.; LL.M.; LECTURER IN AFRICAN LAW, SCHOOL OF
ORIENTAL AND AFRICAN STUDIES,
UNIVERSITY OF LONDON

Note:

This paper was prepared in August, 1964, and represents the author's views at that date. In April, 1967, the Government of Kenya appointed a Commission, of which the author is a Member and the Secretary, whose terms of reference include the recommendation of a new marriage and divorce law for Kenya to replace the existing statutory, customary. Islamic and Hindu laws. The Commission expects to submit its report by August, 1968. The author wishes to emphasise strongly that the views expressed in this paper are his individual views *held in August* 1964, and in no way represent the views of the Kenya Commission.

INTEGRATION OF THE LAWS OF
MARRIAGE AND DIVORCE IN KENYA

Although many writers and Conferences in the last 10 years have urged the unification of the statutory and customary laws in Africa, it has always been recognized that this presents special difficulties in the fields of personal law, especially in the law relating to marriage and divorce. Thus in the recent Conference on Local Courts and Customary Law held in Dar-es-Salaam, it was generally agreed that:

"In the present state of African society it was difficult if not impossible, to devise a single system of marriage law replacing these different (statutory, customary and Islamic) kinds of marriage."

While I agree that full-scale unification of the laws of marriage in Africa is unrealistic at this stage of development, I believe that much can be achieved by way of integration. "Integration", as used here, means the bringing together under one enactment of the different marriage and divorce laws—customary and non-customary—with a view to laying down rules governing all marriages and divorces, where this is feasible, and leaving the matters where unification cannot at present be achieved to the personal law of the parties.

This paper is concerned with possible ways of achieving the integration of the customary and statutory marriage laws of Kenya. No attempt is made to deal with the integration of the Mohammedan and Hindu systems of marriage. These are outside the scope of the present Conference, which will be dealing with the integration of the customary and Western systems of law. However, it must be pointed out that any final attempt at integration of the Kenya marriage laws will have to take account of Mohammedan and Hindu marriages, which govern a substantial minority of Kenya's population.[1]

Although this paper deals specifically with Kenya, the problems are very similar in other Commonwealth African countries, and my remarks probably apply with equal force in these other African states.

---

1. Mohammedan marriages are governed by the Mohammedan Marriage, Divorce and Succession Act (cap. 156), and their registration by the Mohammedan Marriage and Divorce Registration Act (cap. 155). Hindu marriages are governed by the Hindu Marriage and Divorce Act (cap. 157).

It is impossible to discuss the integration of the laws of marriage in any territory without first dealing with the existing marriage systems in that territory. By way of introduction, therefore, Part I of this paper will state briefly the elements of the statutory and customary marriage laws in Kenya. In Part II, I shall attempt to set out some of the problems that have arisen or are likely to arise due to the existence of the dual system. Part III contains my proposals for integration, which I hope will provide a useful basis for discussion. I must make it clear that any proposals for the integration of two completely divergent marriage systems are bound to contain various proposals for reform. It will be seen that the proposals contained in Part III, in many cases involve, not merely the integration of two rules, but the introduction of a new one. I make no apology for adopting this course, as I believe that in many instances neither the existing statutory law nor the customary law is adequate to meet the requirements of a developing African society, and hence a new rule is necessary.

EXISTING LAWS OF MARRIAGE AND DIVORCE

A. MARRIAGE
1. Marriage Under The Marriage Act[2]
This Act contains provisions regulating marriage and is basically a codification of English law principles. Marriage under this Act is open to all persons irrespective of race or religion.[3]

Preliminaries to marriage
Sections 8 to 18 of the Act prescribe certain preliminary formalities. These are that notice of the intended marriage shall be given to and published by a Registrar, who shall, after he has been satisfied by an affidavit that certain essential conditions are fulfilled,[4] issue a certificate authorizing the celebration of the marriage.

---

2. Cap. 150, Laws of Kenya (1962 Revised Edition).
3. In *Fanuel Lemama*, 19 K.L.R. (1941) 48, it was held that there was nothing in the Act to prohibit a marriage between a Muslim and a Christian.
4. The conditions are:
    (a) That one of the parties has been resident in the district for at least 15 days.
    (b) That both parties are over 21 or if under that age that the consent of the person having custody has been obtained.
    (c) That there is no impediment on grounds of kindred or affinity.
    (d) That neither of the parties to the intended marriage is married by native law or custom or by Mohammedan law to any other person.

Celebration of marriage

After the issue of the Registrar's certificate a marriage may be celebrated either in the Registrar's Office by means of a brief ceremony in the presence of two witnesses, or in any licensed place of worship, by any recognized Minister of the church, denomination, or body to which such place of worship belongs and according to the rites and usages of marriage observed in such church, denomination or body.

Registry and Evidence of Marriage

Whether celebrated in the Registrar's Office or in church, a Marriage Certificate, signed by the Registrar or Minister (as the case may be), the parties to the marriage and two witnesses, is issued to the parties and a duplicate filed in the Registrar's Office. The Registrar must also register the certificate in a book called the marriage register book. Under Section 34, provision is made for the reception in evidence as proof of the marriage, Marriage Certificates, entries in the marriage register book and certified copies thereof.

Age of marriage

Section 35(2) now provides that a marriage shall be null and void if either party thereto is under the age of 16 years at the time of celebration.

Consent to the marriage of Minors

Even after attaining the age of 16 a person's capacity to marry, is subject, until the attainment of the age of 21, to the written consent of the person having the lawful custody of him or her.[5] If such consent is refused, the Supreme Court may, on the application of the party, consent to the marriage.

Prohibited Degrees of Relationship

The prohibited degrees for marriages under this Act are those recognized under English Law. Section 35(1) provides that "no marriage in Kenya shall be valid which, if celebrated in England, would be null and void on the ground of kindred or affinity."

---

5. It appears, however, that the failure to obtain consent does not render the marriage invalid since it is not one of the grounds specifically included in Section 35 relating to the invalidity of marriages. Section 35(4) provides "but no marriage shall, after celebration, be deemed invalid by reason that any provision of this Act other than the foregoing has not been complied with."

Monogamy

The most important characteristic of a marriage under the Act (as opposed to a customary law marriage) is that it is monogamous. Legal effect is given to this in two ways:

(a) By providing that no marriage in Kenya shall be valid where either of the parties thereto at the time of celebration is married by native law or custom to any person other than the person with whom such marriage is had (Section 35(1)). In addition, a marriage contracted in breach of this condition constitutes a criminal offence punishable by five years imprisonment. (Section 49); and

(b) By providing that any person married under the Act shall be incapable during the continuance of such marriage of contracting a valid marriage under native law and custom (section 37). Here again a person contracting such a marriage is guilty of an offence punishable by five year's imprisonment (Section 50).

Offences

Apart from the two offences mentioned above, the Marriage Act creates other offences relating to marriage in Sections 42 to 48 e.g. a marriage with a person previously married; making false declarations for marriage; unlawfully performing the marriage ceremony; impersonation in marriage etc.

2. Marriage under the African Christian Marriage and Divorce Act[6]

This Act only applies to the marriage of Africans "one or both of whom profess the Christian religion". The Act has a twofold purpose:

(a) It provides for a simplified procedure for the marriage of African Christians by licensed church Ministers. Under Section 7, "The formalities preliminary to marriage, established, usual or customary for African Christians in the denomination to which one or both of the parties belong, shall apply to marriages under this Act, and sections 8 to 18 inclusive of the Marraige Act shall not apply, but no minister shall celebrate any marriage under this Act unless he considers that adequate notice has been given of the intended marriage;" and

(b) It enables a person already married by native law and custom to convert that marriage into a monogamous statutory marriage. The conversion is effected by a ceremony before a licensed Minister or before a Registrar in his office. A special form of address which takes into account the existing customary relationship is used.

6. Cap. 151

Section 13 of the Act contains two interesting provisions which affect the customary law relating to guardianship of widows and minors. It provides:

"13(1). Any African woman married in accordance with the provisions of this Act or of the Marriage Act or of the Native Christian Marriage Act (now repealed), whether before or after the commencement of this Act, shall be deemed to have attained her majority on widowhood, and shall not be bound to cohabit with the brother or any other relative of her deceased husband or any other person or to be at the disposal of such brother or their relative or other person, but she shall have the same right to support for herself and her children of such marriage from such brother or other relative as she would have had if she had not been married as aforesaid.

(2)   Any such woman shall upon the death of her husband become the guardian of any children of the marriage, and shall, so long as she remains a Christian, continue to be the guardian of such children until such children, if males, attain the age of sixteen years, or if females, attain the age of sixteen years or marry, and shall be competent to dispose of such children in marriage, but in such event the customary bride price shall on demand be paid to such person as is entitled thereto by native law and custom."

Finally, Section 14 gives to Subordinate courts of the first class jurisdiction to dissolve or annul marriages entered into under this Act.

3.   Marriage under Customary Law

The first thing to remember under this head is that there is no single system of customary marriage law in Kenya. There are some 40 different tribes, and although they happen to be in one country, they differ extensively in their ethnic origin,[7] language, mode of life, and traditional political and social systems.

It is, therefore, natural to find that the customary laws of marriage

---

7.   Anthropologists divide the tribes of Kenya into 4 ethnic or linguistic groups:
        (i) Central Bantu e.g. Kikuyu, Kamba, Meru, Embu
        (ii) Kavirondo Bantu e.g. the Luhyia group, Kisii, Kuria
        (iii) Coastal Bantu e.g. the Nyika or Mizichenda group, Taita, Taveta, Pokomo
  (b)   *Nilotic*, i.e. the Luo.
  (c)   *Nilo-Hamitic*, e.g. Turkana, Masai, Nandi, Kipsigis, Pokot, Elegeyo, Marakwet and Tugen.
  (d)   Hamitic, e.g. the Somali, Galla, Merille.

of these tribes are in certain ways different. But, in my opinion, these differences have been exaggerated in the past, and more often relate to matters of detail than to principle. There are certain broad principles common to the marriage laws of all the Kenya tribes, and I shall state them here briefly.

Polygamy

Without exception, all tribes in Kenya permit a man to have as many wives as he pleases (there is no restriction in number to four as in Islamic law). A woman however, may not have a plurality of husbands, and in some cases, may not even re-marry after her husband's death.[8]

Formalities and Ceremonial

These are characterised by the active participation of the parties' family groups at all stages from the commencement of negotiations until the marriage is finally concluded. The ceremonies often extend over many months and may involve beer-drinking, the slaughter of livestock, feasting and dancing. With a few tribes, there is one particular ceremony[9] which legalises the union, but more often, the ceremonies are simply social occasions, and it is very difficult to ascertain at what exact point of time the parties become legally married.

Age of Marriage

Under none of the Kenya customary laws is there a fixed age at which a person becomes legally capable of entering into a marriage. Generally speaking, however, a girl cannot marry before she has reached the age of puberty. Amongst tribes that practice circumcision (the majority of Kenya tribes), no girl or boy may marry before he or she has been circumcised.

Consents to Marriage

Although the consent of the spouses was relatively unimportant in the past, all Kenya customary laws would now hold that no marriage can take place unless the spouses consent. More important than the spouses consent, however, is that of the spouses' parents or families. It is as much true in Kenya as in other parts of Africa that customary marriage is not merely a union between two individuals, but rather an alliance between two family groups. Although this

8. This is exemplified by the institution of "levirate unions" or "widow inheritance", where a widow is required after her husband's death to cohabit with a brother or other relative of her deceased husband.
9. E.g. the *Ratet* amongst the Nandi and Kipsigis.

aspect of customary marriage is gradually breaking down, it is still true to say today that the consent of the parties' parents is an essential requirement of a customary marriage.

Prohibited Degrees

The detailed rules prohibiting persons from intermarrying on the ground of kindred or affinity vary between the different customary laws. The striking feature amongst all tribes, however, is that the prohibited degrees are far more extensive than those recognized under English law, and normally extend to persons from the same clan or kindred group, i.e. a group tracing descent from a common ancestor several generations distant. With certain tribes,[10] the rule is so broad that a man will often find it necessary to marry a girl from a different geographical location. Furthermore, the breach of the rule may result in the commission of a very serious offence with penal sanctions.

Payment of Bride Price[11]

With the exception of three tribes,[12] customary marriage in Kenya is preceded, accompanied or followed by a payment or payments by the bridegroom or his family to the bride's family. Bride price is normally in the form of cattle or other livestock, though nowadays money is often given instead. Its amount is not normally fixed[13] but is subject to negotiations between the parties' families. Bride price is normally returned in part or in full in the event of dissolution of the marriage.

Various theories[14] have been put forward by writers on customary law explaining the significance of the payment of bride price on

10. For example amongst the Luo, persons belonging to the same *dhoot* (a group of people tracing descent from a common ancestor twelve generations distant) may not intermarry. Persons who contravene this rule commit the offence of "incest", and in the past were banished from the tribe. Nowadays, the matter is treated as a criminal offence. (See my *Report on Customary Criminal Offences in Kenya*, Govt. Printer Nairobi, 1963)
11. I have used this term because it is the one employed in Kenya legislation, e.g. in section 13 of the African Christian Marriage and Divorce Act cited above. Its use does not imply acceptance of the implicaions (e.g. that it is a form of wife purchase). A more suitable term would be "marriage consideration".
12. The Elgeyo, Marakwet and Tugen.
13. Amongst the Meru and the Masai, the amount is fixed.
14. E.g. that bride price is a compensation to the woman's family for the loss of one of its members; that it is a security for the good treatment of a wife; that it is a security for the maintenance of the marriage by the respective families; that it is merely a symbol to seal the marriage contract; that it is no more than "child price", i.e. compensation for the transfer of a woman's reproductive capacity and her issue to the husband's family.

marriage. It is unnecessary to go into these in this paper. Suffice it to say that as a general principle the payment or agreement to pay bride price remains up to the present day an essential legal requirement of Kenya customary marriages.

B. DIVORCE
1. Divorce under the Matrimonial Causes Act[15]

The substantive law of divorce and matrimonial causes as contained in this Act closely follows the present English law on the subject.

Jurisdiction under the Act is confined to the Supreme Court and is based on the domicil of the petitioner.

The Act contains provisions relating to Divorce and Nullity of marriage (Part II), which are given on the same grounds that obtain in England. The grounds for divorce by either husband or wife are adultery, desertion for three years, cruelty, and incurable unsoundness of mind. In addition, rape, sodomy or bestiality by a husband are grounds for divorce by a wife.

Part III of the Act deals with Judicial Separation, Part IV with Restitution of Conjugal Rights, and Part V with dissolution of a marriage on the ground of presumption of death.

Part VI, entitled "Ancillary Relief", deals with damages and costs against a co-respondent in adultery cases; alimony and maintenance of a wife; settlement of the wife's property; and custody and maintenance of children.[16]

2. Divorce under the Christian Marriage and Divorce Act

Although, as shown above, this Act provides for a special procedure for the marriage of African Christians, the Act does not affect the substantive law of divorce. Thus Section 14 provides:

"Subordinate courts of the first class shall have the same jurisdiction, in the case of marriages solemnized or contracted under this Act... as is vested in the Supreme Court by virtue of the Matrimonial Causes Act."

Thus Africans who contract a statutory marriage, whether under the Marriage Act or the African Christian Marriage and Divorce Act are bound by the same law of divorce as non-Africans and may not resort to customary law for the purpose of dissolving the marriage.

15. cap. 152.
16. It is unnecessary to go into the details of these matters, since, as pointed out earlier, they follow the general principles of English law on the subject.

3. Divorce under the Customary law

The first matter to notice in regard to divorce under Kenya customary laws is that it was traditionally very rare. It is certainly not correct to say, so far as the Kenya tribes are concerned, that divorce may be obtained at the will of the parties. Indeed, among certain tribes divorce was almost unknown, especially when there were children of the union. Unfortunately, divorces under customary law have increased considerably in the last 20 years,[17] but it is still true to say that generally the dissolution of a marriage is resorted to only in extreme cases and when all else fails.

The second important feature relating to customary divorces is its provision for conciliatory or arbitration machinery by the family groups of the quarrelling parties. Indeed, amongst all tribes in Kenya, the first step is for the parties' family elders to meet and attempt a reconciliation. Only if this fails, does the family group with the assistance of independent traditional elders become a "judicial body" to determine whether or not a divorce should be granted.

What factors do the elders take into account in coming to their decision? Are there any grounds for divorce in customary law? My investigations in Kenya have shown that there are grounds for divorce under customary law in this sense: that should the elders find that the grounds or reasons for seeking dissolution are frivolous, they may refuse to grant the divorce. It is true that they would not normally compel the parties to remain living together, but that is very different from being divorced. For example, unless the dissolution of the marriage has been effected through the elders according to the customary processes, the man and woman will still be regarded as husband and wife, and the husband will always be able to claim the children that the wife may have by another man, and also may sue that other man for adultery under customary law.

To the extent, then, that the elders might refuse to grant a divorce because the parties' reasons therefore are insufficient or unacceptable, it may be said that there are grounds for divorce under customary law just as there are under English law. However, there are at least three marked differences relating to grounds under English law and in customary law, viz.:

(a) The grounds under the two systems may be very different. For example, though beating of a wife will constitute cruelty, and hence a ground for divorce under English law, it may be held to be justifiable under most customary laws. Again, whilst incurable

---

17.   Most Africans would argue, with considerable justification, that this is due to Western influence.

unsoundness of mind is a ground for divorce under the statutory law, most customary laws do not recognize insanity as a ground for divorce.

(b) Whereas there are certain fixed grounds for divorce in English law, no exhaustive list of grounds can be given for any tribe in Kenya. Although certain offences, e.g. witchcraft or incest, will obviously constitute grounds for divorce under certain customary laws, there are other borderline matters to which remedies other than divorce may apply. In other words, unlike an English court which is bound by a certain list of fixed grounds, the elders have a wide discretion to accept new grounds or to refuse to be bound by matters previously held to be grounds, as the circumstances of each case dictate.

(c) Whereas under English law the establishment of grounds is the only factor taken into account, under customary law it is but one of many factors, which include, *inter alia*, the existence and number of children, the ability of the wife's father to return the bride price, and the existence of other possible remedies.[18]

Just as payment of bride price is an essential element in customary marriage, so is its return, or partial return, a feature of customary divorces. The rules for the return of the bride price amongst the tribes of Kenya rarely depend on fault, i.e. on which party was instrumental in bringing about the dissolution, but on the existence or otherwise of children, and in some cases, upon their number and sex. In certain cases, the rules of return of the bride price are linked with the question of custody of the children.

Unlike the statutory law, customary law does not impose any obligation on the part of a husband to maintain his wife after a divorce.

Although African Courts[18a] in Kenya have jurisdiction to dissolve marriages entered into under customary law, cases of divorce proper rarely reach the African Courts. More frequently, litigated cases involve matters subsequent to the divorce, e.g. the return of the bride price or the custody of children. Cases in connection with marriage under the statutory law are expressly excluded from the

---

18. Professor Allott in his *Essays in African Law* argues (at p. 221) that "In most customary laws throughout Africa divorce . . . proceedings did not turn on establishing grounds for divorce, the so-called 'grounds' being motives which led a party to seek dissolution, reasons which justified a party's acting to bring a marriage to an end, or factors to be taken into account in adjusting the financial liabilities of both sides".

18.a African Courts have now been abolished. Under the new Magistrate's Courts Act (No. 17 of 1967), their jurisdiction is now exercised by District Magistrates.

jurisdiction of African Courts "except where the claim is one for bride price or adultery only, and is founded on native law"[19]

II. Problems arising due to the Existence of the Dual Marriage System

The problems that arise due to the existence of a dual marriage system may involve:

(a) Legal difficulties, i.e. problems that face the lawyer, whether an academic, practitioner or Judge, and essentially related to questions of internal conflicts of laws. Because Africans, who are normally subject to customary law, are given the option of contracting a statutory marriage, questions arise as to the extent to which this statutory marriage exempts them from the operation of customary law in matrimonial and other matters;

(b) Questions of policy, e.g. whether it is right and proper that the nationals of one country should be subjected within that country to different marriage laws with varying legal and social consequences;

(c) Social considerations, e.g. how far the law of marriage should be in line with the people's requirements.

I shall not attempt to deal with all these problems in detail here, but I feel that it may be helpful, in stressing the urgency of unification and reform, to particularise some of these problems.

1. "Inferiority" of Customary Marriage

Although customary marriages are expressly recognized under the statute law of Kenya,[20] both Kenya legislative provisions and case-law (at least in the past) have emphasised the distinction between statutory marriage and customary marriage with implications as to the inferiority of the latter.

Thus the African Christian Marriage and Divorce Act, which provides for the conversion of a customary marriage into a statutory marriage, states that the form of address to be used by the Registrar at the prescribed ceremony shall be as follows:

"Whereas you, A.B., and you, C.D., profess that you have been heretofore married to each other by native law and custom, and whereas that marriage does not bind you by law to each other as man and wife so long as both of you shall live, and whereas you desire to bind yourselves legally each to the other as man and wife so long as both of you shall live . . . "[20a]

19. African Courts Acts, section 13 (cap. 11).
20. e.g. Section 37 of the Marriage Act provides that " . . . nothing in this Act contained shall affect the validity of any marriage contracted under or in accordance with any native law or custom, or in any manner apply to marriages so contracted."
20a s. 9 (3)

The previous attitude of the Judges to customary marriage can best be illustrated by the dictum of Sir Robert Hamilton, C.J., in *Rex* v *Amkeyo*,[21] where he said:

"In my opinion the use of the word "marriage" to describe the relationship entered into by an African native with a woman of his tribe according to tribal custom is a misnomer which has led in the past to a considerable confusion of ideas .. The elements of a so-called marriage by native custom differ so materially from the ordinarily accepted idea of what constitutes a civilized form of marriage that it is difficult to compare the two."

It was then held that a marriage under customary law was not a marriage within the meaning of section 122 of the Indian Evidence Act, which relates to the privilege attaching to communications between husband and wife during a marriage.

Happily, this case has now been overruled by the new Evidence Act of Kenya,[22] which, dealing with communications during a marriage, defines it as "a marriage, whether or not monogamous, which is by law binding during the lifetime of the parties thereto unless dissolved according to law." Furthermore, the attitude of judges, as exemplified in *Mawji* v. *Regina*.[23] appears now to take a more liberal attitude towards customary marriages, and treat them on an equal footing with statutory marriages. In that case it was held that the rule that a husband and wife cannot alone form a conspiracy applies to any marriage, whether monogamous or polygamous, which is valid by Tanganyika law, and that the words "husband" and "wife", where unqualified, are not in Tanganyika restricted to monogamous marriages.

But perhaps the most unfortunate aspect of the status of customary marriage, is that there are many Africans (especially amongst the educated class) who treat it as an inferior form of marriage. It is unnecessary to go into the reasons which may have contributed to this attitude here, but there is no doubt that it is a matter which requires the early attention of African governments.

2. Exclusion of the Customary Law of Marriage and Divorce where Africans marry under the Act

In Kenya, as in other parts of Africa, the option given to Africans to marry under the Act does not merely involve the obligation of

21. 7 E.A.L.R. (1917) 14.
22. It is surprising, however, that just before this Act came into force, the dictum of Hamilton C.J. was cited with approval and the case was followed by the Court of Appeal for East Africa in *Abdul Rahman Bin Mohamed & An.* v. *R.* (1963) E.A. 188
23. [1957] A.C. 126

monogamy, but also acceptance of all other aspects of English marriage relating to age, prohibited degrees, formalities, and the like. Thus in *Riogi Omari* v. *Mochama Akama*,[24] a case decided by the Kenya Court of Review (the highest appeal tribunal from African Courts) it was held that a marriage under the African Christian Marriage and Divorce Act is valid even if no bride price has been paid.

Similarly, Africans who contract a statutory marriage are bound by the same law of divorce as non-Africans. The parties may not resort to customary law for the purpose of dissolving the marriage under the Act.

The question of principle that arises here is whether it is right that Africans should be subjected in all respects to the English-based law of marriage and divorce simply because they have opted for monogamy. In the words of a learned writer.[25]

"The principle of making available to Africans the option of statutory marriage is, as has been seen, accepted in the majority of territories, and there are strong reasons in favour of it. But it may be doubted whether there is equal justification for imposing on Africans as a matter of course—or virtually so—all the changes which may from time to time be dictated (especially in regard to divorce) by the public opinion of European communities. In other words, while the opportunity of contracting legal monogamous marriage (Christian or civil) may rightly be given to Africans, it does not seem to be a necessary corollary that the law which makes such provision should continue to reflect all the contemporary vissitudes of European law."

3. Customary Marriage during the continuance of a Statutory Marriage

It has been shown earlier that any person who contracts a customary marriage during the continuance of a statutory marriage commits an offence punishable by imprisonment for five years.[26] It is no secret that such subsequent customary marriages are often the rule rather than the exception in African countries, and yet the penal sanctions are invariably disregarded.[27] The question here is whether any useful purpose is served by having in the statute book an offence which is never enforced.

Furthermore, these subsequent customary marriages are invalid,

---

24. Court of Review Law Reports, Volume 1, 1953, p. 4
25. Phillips, *Survey of African Marriage and Family Life*, p. 295
26. See text preceding note 6, supra
27. Phillips, *Report on Native Tribunals*, p. 301, paragraph 907.

and it follows that the children of such marriages are illegitimate.[28] Surely, this is a most undesirable consequence which an integrated marriage law must seek to avoid.

4. Effect of Statutory Marriage on the personal relationship of the spouses

Kenya statutory provisions do not indicate what law governs Africans in relation to their personal rights and duties *inter se* when they contract a statutory marriage, e.g. what law governs questions of choice of matrimonial home, the right to chastise a wife, or the wife's right to be maintained during the marriage. Although some cases from West Africa may offer some guidance on this question (even these are conflicting), there is virtually no case-law in East Africa on the subject. It is probable, however, that the real answer to the problem is the one suggested by Professor Allott[29] who says:

"It is reasonable that any rights or duties that a spouse may have under customary law that are clearly incompatible with the marriage state as known to English law should be overridden by the English rules; but it is also reasonable to remember that the spouses are Africans, though married by forms imported from England, and that they will tend to conform, as far as possible, to standards of behaviour usual in Ghana."

In regard to rights as against strangers, e.g. the husband's right to recover customary damages against an adulterer, it was shown earlier that African Courts in Kenya have no jurisdiction to deal with cases concerning statutory marriage unless the claim is one for bride price or adultery founded on native law. It seems, therefore, that a husband, even though married under the Act, may recover damages for adultery under customary law in an African Court.

5. Effect of Statutory Marriage on Rights of Property and Succession

Here again, there is no express legislative provision as to how far a statutory marriage entered into by Africans affects the law of property and succession. The older view in West Africa, as exemplified by the case of *Cole v. Cole*,[30] was that a marriage under the

---

28. See *Onwudinjoh* v. *Onwudinjoh*, (1957) II E.R.L.R. 1; and *Coleman* v. *Shang*, 1959, G.L.R. 390, upheld by the Privy Council in [1961] A.C. 481.

29. Allott, *Essays in African Law*, p. 219

30. (1898) I.N.L.R. 15. The decision was followed in *Haastrup* v. *Coker* (1927) 8 N.L.R. 68, and in *Coker* v. *Coker* (1943) 17 N.L.R. 55. Cf., however, *Smith* v. *Smith* (1924) 5 N.L.R. 102.

statutory law negatived the application of the customary law, and
that the deceased's estate must devolve according to English law.
This view no longer prevails, especially in view of the decision in
Coleman v. Shang,[31] where it was held that marriage under the
Ghana Marriage Ordinance did not remove a person from the
application of customary law except for matters specifically excluded
by stature. As far as East Africa is concerned, this view seems to
have been accepted as long ago as 1912 in the case of *Benjawa
Jembe v. Priscilla Nyondo*,[32] where it was held that the fact that a
deceased African had contracted a Christian marriage did not affect
the question of succession.

6. Effect of Statutory Marriage on Widows and Children

As far as I know, Kenya is the only Commonwealth African
country where express provision is made for the custody of widows
and minors when the widow was married under the Act. These
provisions have already been cited, but it is extremely doubtful
whether they work in practice. It runs contrary to most customary
laws, for example, to allow the mother to be the guardian of her
children, and unless the matter reaches the courts, a family meeting
will invariably appoint a male relative of the deceased husband
(usually a brother) to be the legal guardian of the children.

III. PROPOSALS FOR INTEGRATION

There are some who would argue that a statute regulating all
types of marriages at present recognized in Kenya would not be the
best way to achieve integration. They suggest that it would be
better to let the two systems evolve side by side, since they will naturally converge with the passage of time and a common Kenya
marriage law through judicial pronouncements will emerge. I do not
share this view, nor do I think it desirable to give the judges the
task of integrating the law of marriage through case-law. As pointed
out in Part II, there are matters of deep principle involved, and I
submit that African Governments will be failing in their duty if
they omit to take action, through legislative provision, on such an
important part of the law, which touches the lives of their people so
closely.

The integration of the marriage laws in Kenya by means of a
statute has now been facilitated because the customary law in Kenya

31. [1961] A.C. 481
32. (1912) 4 E.A.L.R. 160.

has been fully recorded.[33] The criticism that it would not be possible to integrate the statutory and customary laws of marriage because the latter are not easily ascertainable, does not, therefore, apply in Kenya. The legislator, in his task of integration, is fully equipped with a thorough knowledge of all customary laws as well as statutory law; in producing the new law he is thus fully aware of what is being integrated, what is being abolished, and what is being modified or reformed. Furthermore, it will be seen from what follows that the suggested new law is an attempt at integration, not unification, and will thus leave many matters to be decided by the personal law of the parties. The existence of an authoritative statement of the customary laws (i.e. the personal law of Africans) will therefore facilitate tremendously the operation of the new integrated law

A. MARRIAGE

What should the new integrated marriage law attempt to achieve? Generally speaking, I can do no better than to cite the following recommendation of the recent Dar es Salaam Conference on Local Courts and Customary Law:

". . . the Conference strongly recommended that a general regulatory enactment in regard to specific aspects of marriage should be passed in each country. This legislation should:

(a) Unify, so far as possible, the procedural requirements for different forms of marriage and state minimum requirements (e.g. in regard to age, consents, registration) for all marriages.

(b) Ensure that the different types of marriages enjoy social and legal parity of status.

(c) Eliminate, so far as possible, the variable consequences at present attaching to different kinds of marriages (e.g. in regard to the evidence of wives married by

33. In 1960, the Kenya Government set up an organisation to ascertain and restate the various tribes in Kenya. This was done in collaboration with the Restatement of African Law Project of the School of Oriental and African Studies, University of London. I was seconded by the School to the Kenya Government, and spent two years carrying out field research in Kenya. The recording was done with the assistance of Law Panels set up for the purpose, and consisted of experts on customary law, including African Court judges, Chiefs, local elders, etc. The following aspects of customary law were recorded: Criminal Offences (see my *Report on Customary Criminal Offences in Kenya*, Nairobi, 1963); Marriage and Divorce; Succession; certain aspects of Family Law. These will shortly be published and used as guides to the customary law. The investigation covered all the Kenya tribes.

different forms), more particularly in regard to those
who are not themselves parties to the marriage (e.g.
children of the marriage).
(d) Bring the law of marriage more closely into line with
the people's requirements . . ."[33a]

To pass from the general to the specific, I would suggest that the
new enactment should include specific provision regarding the
following matters:

1. **Monogamy** *v.* **Polygamy**

Undoubtedly, the most fundamental difference between the
statutory and customary laws of marriage is that the former is
monogamous and the latter potentially polygamous. To talk of
unification of this aspect of the marriage law is futile: unification
must inevitably involve the abolition of one or other of the systems.

To suggest the abolition of polygamy at this stage of development
in Kenya, or any other part of Commonwealth Africa, would be
senseless. Polygamy is so essentially part of the African way of life
that it cannot be wiped out by a stroke of the pen. The result of the
abolition of polygamy would simply be that the new law compelling
monogamy would not be observed, just as the present law prohibiting a customary marriage after a statutory marriage is ignored.[34]
No one is prepared to support the imposition of a law that would
simply result in the multiplication of illegitimate children. It is
perfectly true that there are many Christian Africans who marry
monogamously, but it would be no exaggeration to say that probably
over 70% of them subsequently take other wives under customary
law.

To talk of the abolition of monogamy at this stage in Africa is
equally absurd. Quite apart from the religious uproar that it is
likely to cause, there is no doubt that an influential minority of
Africans are moving towards monogamy[35] and would violently
oppose the abolition of the institution for those who want it.

The conclusion, therefore, is that both monogamy and polygamy

---

33a. African Conference in local Courts & Customary Law, Record of the
Proceedings of the Conference held in Dar es Salam, Tanganyika,
8th Sept, 1963—18th Sept, 1963. p. 26.
34. Professor Arthur Phillips in his Introductory Essay to *Survey of
African Marriage and Family Life*, says at p. xxxv: "there seems to
be little doubt what is the typical attitude of Africans towards statutory,
marriage, as disclosed by a survey of the whole field: it is one of resistance to any attempt to impose this form of marriage upon them as an
obligatory requirement."
35. For example, in Buganda, statutory marriage has been accepted by a
large majority of the population, to the almost total exclusion of
customary marriage.

must remain for the present, and that the integrated marriage law must recognize both institutions.

This is not to say that the new law should not attempt to remove any ill-effects that may result from polygamy. Africa is moving away from tribal life and Africa's women are being emancipated. In certain African countries, there is a problem of over-population. In such cases, the State must see to it that a man taking subsequent wives, must do so conscious of his obligations towards these other wives in a modern State. Where Government considers it necessary, it might well enact a new marriage law designed to minimize poly-gamous unions, by providing, for example, that before a man marries a second or third time, he must be in a position to fulfill his matri-monial obligations of providing for these subsequent wives and any children resulting from the unions.

The new law should also regulate the relationship between a monogamous and polygamous marriage, and remove the anomalies of the present law with respect to the variable consequences of the different marriages. This can be done in the following ways:

(a) Before entering into the marriage, which will be subject to the same formalities, whether monogamous or polygamous (see below), the parties must make it clear whether their intention is that their marriage be monogamous or potentially polygamous.

(b) If they state that their intention is to have a monogamous union, the law will provide that they will be incapable during the subsistence of the marriage to enter into any other union, and if they do so, will commit an offence . It has been shown earlier that this in fact is the present law in Kenya and most other Commonwealth African countries It is submitted, however, that this provision could work under the proposed law, where it cannot under present law, for this reason: under the new law, a subsequent marriage can be entered into only through a prescribed procedure before a Marriage Officer (see below). Hence a man will not be able to evade the law, as he can now, by taking a subsequent wife under "native law and custom"; the new marriage law will not recognize a marriage by "native law and custom", but, instead, will recognize a polygamous marriage only if entered into under the new enactment in accordance with the procedure there set forth.[36]

(c) The new Act should state that monogamous and polygamous marriages contracted under the provisions of the Act shall rank equally in all respects. It should also be made clear that whenever

---

36. But cf. my suggestion, *infra*, that the new law should come into force only after a period of time, dating from its enactment, sufficient to ensure that the people gain familiarity with, and understanding of. its provisions.

the terms "marriage", "husband" and "wife" are used in any Kenya legislation (unless otherwise indicated), the terms will include all marriages recognized under the Act, whether monogamous or polygamous It was shown earlier[37] that the new Evidence Act of Kenya has in fact done this, but it is submitted that this must be extended to cover the meaning of marriage wherever it occurs.

(d) The new enactment must make it clear that a marriage entered into under the Act, whether monogamous or polygamous, affects neither the rights and duties of the parties *inter se,* nor the law relating to property or succession applicable to the parties. These matters will continue to be governed by the personal law (defined below) of the parties, unless other legislative provision is made therefor.

2. Procedure and Formalities

It has been shown in part I that the customary marriage procedure is such that it is often difficult to determine at what point of time a man and a woman legally become husband and wife. When evidence of a marriage under customary law is required, the normal test used is whether bride price has been paid or not.

It is submitted that any serious attempt to reform the law of marriage must be accompanied by the establishment of a uniform procedure for the solemnization of all marriages. It is not enough to provide for the registration of customary marriages. This has been tried in many African countries, including some Districts of Kenya, but the registration requirements, whether compulsory or voluntary, and whether by central or local legislation, have been largely ignored.

The new procedure for the solemnization of all marriages could well be based upon the procedure now contained in the Marriage Act law, but should be as simple as possible, so as not to subject the parties to difficulties and unnecessary expense.

The procedure could thus provide that parties intending to marry must give notice of the intended marriage to a Marriage Officer. (Many new Marriage Officers will have to be appointed depending on the size of population in the district or location. Naturally the task will have to be entrusted to persons carrying out other administrative duties.) The parties will have to indicate clearly whether they intend to enter into a monogamous or potentially polygamous marriage. The Marriage Officer, on being satisfied that certain essential requirements have been fulfilled (these are spelled out below), will issue a certificate authorising the solemnization of the

---

37.   See text at note 22, supra.

marriage. The marriage will then be solemnized in the presence of witnesses either by the Marriage Officer in his office, or—if the parties so desire and if they have indicated their intention of contracting a monogamous marriage—by a minister of the church. Where the parties indicate their intention of contracting a monogamous marriage, the Marriage Officer or church minister, as the case may be, will warn them in suitable language that they cannot marry again during the subsistence of their marriage, and that if they do so they will commit an offence.

It might be argued, with some justification, that it would be extremely difficult to transform the existing customary marriage procedure, with all its ceremonies, feasting, and so forth, into the procedure outlined above. The answer is that the above procedure is not necessarily a supersession of the customary methods, but simply an additional state requirement for all marriages. In other words, there is nothing to prevent the performance of the usual customary ceremonies (as they are in fact performed now even when Africans marry under the Act), but the law will impose an additional obligation which must be fulfilled by all.

Of course the new procedure will create difficulties, and might well be ignored to start with. To cover this, it will be necessary to make some provision for saving customary marriages that are entered into without the procedure provided under the new Act, for a period of (say) two years. During this time, all possible measures must be taken by Government to publicize the new law so that all persons may know what the new procedure involves. Similarly, the provision suggested earlier—that a marriage entered into after a monogamous marriage should be invalid and bigamous—should not come into operation until a similar period has elapsed.

The Act should also provide for a simple procedure for the conversion of an existing polygamous marriage into a monogamous marriage; and also of an existing monogamous marriage into a polygamous marriage. In both cases, both parties to the existing marriage must naturally agree to the conversion.

3. Conditions Applicable to All Marriages

The new law should provide that no marriage can be contracted unless certain conditions are satisfied, viz.:

(a) Age

The minimum age for marriage under the statutory law is 16 for both males and females. Under customary law, there is no fixed age, but males rarely marry before the age of 16. It is true that in the past girls were often married before the age of 16, and that the institution of infant betrothal was common amongst certain tribes. However, this is now very rare, and in any case would hardly be encouraged by progressive African opinion. I would, therefore, suggest that under the law, no male or female should be able to marry before attaining the age of 16.

(b) **Parental consent**

The difference between the present statutory law and customary law on this subject is that, in the former, parental consent is required only if the party is under 21, whereas in the latter it is always required irrespective of age, especially in the case of females. However, since the majority of African girls marry under the age of 21, the difference is only academic. Here again, the growth of individualism supports the adoption of the statutory rule, and I would suggest that this should become the rule governing all marriages under the new Act.

(c) **Consent of the Parties**

As pointed out earlier, most customary laws would now hold that the consent of both parties must be present before a marriage is entered into. However, to cover the isolated cases of "forced marriages", which still occur amongst some of the less advanced tribes, the new marriage law should provide that the consent of both parties is essential to the validity of any marriage.

(d) **Prohibited degrees**

The relationships within which intermarriage is prohibited vary greatly, not only as between the present statutory and customary laws, but also as between the different customary laws. It is therefore impossible to unify this branch of the law, and the new Act will have to contain a provision to the effect that two persons are incapable of intermarrying if they are prohibited from doing so according to the personal law to which they are subject.[38]

(e) **Payment of bride Price**

The older view that the payment of bride price is no more than wife-purchase has now been generally discarded, and it is generally accepted that there is nothing intrinsically evil about the custom. It is submitted that any attempt to abolish the payment of bride price through legislation is bound to fail[39] Even attempts at limiting the

38.   See text at note 41, *infra.*
39.   The Local Customary Law (Declaration) Order, 1963 of Tanganyika provides in section 5 that "the payment of bridewealth is not essential for the validation of a marriage."

amount of bride price have failed.[40] It has been shown that the payment of bride price under most of the Kenya customary laws is the means by which a marriage becomes legally valid. In the eyes of most Africans, it is the all-important factor in marriage, and, though not required under the present statutory law, it is in fact invariably paid even if Africans opt to marry under the Act. It is, therefore submitted that the new Act should provide that a marriage, whether monogamous or polygamous, may be accompanied by the payment of bride price, if such bride price is payable according to the personal law of the parties. However, to cater for those tribes where the payment of bride price is becoming less important, and for those people who agree to contract the marriage without payment of bride price, the suggested provision should be prefaced by the phrase "unless otherwise agreed by the parties." The law should also provide that the Marriage Officer should record, on the marriage certificate or elsewhere, the amount of bride price paid or agreed upon. This will greatly facilitate the determination of the numerous disputes that arise in connection with the payment, return, etc., of bride price.

4. Definition of Personal of Law

It is clear that the suggested Marriage Act is not a complete unification of the customary and statutory laws of marriage, but only a unification of certain aspects to the extent set out above. All other matters, therefore (prohibited degrees, payment of bride price, etc.), are left to the personal law of the parties. It is thus necessary that the Act should contain a definition of personal law, and also rules for determining choice of law where the parties are ordinarily subject to different personal laws. I would suggest something on the following lines:

> Subject to the rules set out below, any reference in this Act to the personal law of a person is a reference to the customary law to which he is subject, if he is an African,[41] or if he is not an African, is a reference to the common law of England.
> *Rule* 1. Where the parties to the marriage are both Africans subject to the same customary law, the personal law shall be the customary law to which they are subject.
> *Rule* 2. Where the parties to the marriage are both Africans subject to different customary laws, their personal law shall be the customary law which they intended to apply, or which, from the nature of the transaction, they may be taken to have agreed to apply.

40. E.g. in the Kisii District of Kenya; and in Eastern Nigeria.
41. As defined in the Interpretation and General Provisions Act, cap 2.

Rule 3.   Where one party to the marriage is an African and the other party a non-African, the personal law of the parties shall be either the common law of England or the customary law to which the African party is ordinarily subject, depending on which of the two laws the parties intended to apply, or, from the nature of the transaction, they may be taken to have agreed to apply.

B. DIVORCE

The most unsatisfactory aspect of the present law of divorce is that statutory marriage for Africans automatically subjects them to the rigid statutory law of divorce, which was designed to meet conditions in England and not in Africa. The new law should avoid this by providing that whether a marriage is monogamous or polygamous, the same law of divorce should apply to all persons.

The question is whether the unified law of divorce should be based on the statutory law or the customary laws. This is a field where much can be done in bringing together those aspects of the statutory and customary laws that are good and suitable for application in modern African society, and rejecting those aspects from the two systems that are bad. For example, there is no doubt that the rigid statutory grounds for divorce are unsuitable. On the other hand, the conciliatory machinery afforded by customary law, through family and other arbitration bodies, is of considerable value, and might well be adopted as the required first step in all actions for divorce.

The proposed divorce legislation of Ghana[42] goes a long way towards achieving this objective. It provides that a husband or wife may petition a High Court Judge for a divorce. On receipt of the petition, the Judge shall appoint a Divorce Committee of which he shall be Chairman to arbitrate the matter and attempt a reconciliation. The hearing shall take place *in camera* and no legal practitioner may appear before the Committee. If the arbitration fails, the Committee has power to grant a dissolution of the marriage, which shall be pronounced in open court by the Judge. The Bill does not enumerate any grounds for divorce.

I believe that this type of legislation should provide the basis for the new divorce law, subject to the objection that the proposed legislation gives too wide a discretion to the Divorce Committee in ultimately granting or refusing the dissolution of the marriage. Whilst I do not suggest that there should be rigid grounds for divorce in the English sense, it would, in my view, be preferable to

42. Marriage, Divorce and Inheritance Bill, 1963.

lay down a general provision that the Divorce Committee, in their
final decision, should be "guided" but not bound by the "grounds"
or reasons of divorce recognized under the personal law of the
parties.

Further, I believe that the Divorce Committee should be given
powers to adjust the financial liabilities of the parties (e.g., to settle
the return of bride price where the parties' personal law is customary
law); to make orders for maintenance; and to provide for the
custody of the children to the marriage. The new law should make
provision for these last two matters with special attention to the
welfare of the divorced wives and the children.

BIRTH, DEATH, AND THE MARRIAGE ACT: SOME PROBLEMS IN CONFLICT OF LAWS

by

JESWALD W. SALACUSE

ASSOCIATE DIRECTOR, AFRICAN LAW CENTER, COLUMBIA
UNIVERSITY, NEW YORK. FORMERLY LECTURER IN LAW,
AHMADU BELLO UNIVERSITY, ZARIA

BIRTH, DEATH, AND THE MARRIAGE ACT: SOME PROBLEMS IN CONFLICT OF LAWS

Introduction

The co-existence in Nigeria of English and customary law naturally gives rise to conflict of laws problems. As a guide in resolving such problems, the High Court Laws of the Regions and of Lagos provide that no person normally subject to customary law shall be deprived of its benefits unless there is an agreement, express or implied, that English law is to govern or unless the transaction involved is unknown to customary law.[1] With regard to particular, discrete transactions having limited consequences, these rules have been relatively easy to apply and have provided just solutions. For example, English law has been held to govern where a person subject to customary law made a will in English form[2] and where a covenant to convey land was involved and the parties evidently wanted English law to apply.[3]

In the area of family law, however, conflict of laws problems of this sort are not so easily resolved. Marriage, whether under the Marriage Act[4] or under customary law, works a transformation of status and creates extensive legal consequences fundamentally affecting not only the spouses, but their children and relatives as well. In this respect, marriage as a "transaction" is totally unlike the normal commercial contract or land conveyance, the legal consequences of which affect only the parties immediately involved for a very short time, in an area which is a minute part of their total lives and scope of activity.

The purpose of this paper is to investigate some of the conflict of laws problems which arise as a result of statutory marriage in Nigeria. The basic questions are: When a man and woman who are ordinarily subject to customary law contract a marriage under the Marriage Act, do they, their future children, and their relatives thereby become completely subject to the entire body of received statutes and judicial doctrine known as English family law? And

---

1. Northern Region High Court Law, no, 8 of 1955, s. 34; Estern Region High Court Law, no. 27 of 1955, s. 22; Western Region High Court Law, 1959 Laws of Western Nigeria, Cap. 44, s. 12; High Court of Lagos Act, 1958 Laws of the Federation of Nigeria and Lagos, Cap. 80 s. 29. See generally Park, *The Sources of Nigerian Law* (1963) 98-115.,
2. *Apatira v. Akanke* (1944) 17 N.L.R. 149
3. *Griffin v. Talabi* (1948) 12 W.A.C.A. 371.
4. 1958 Laws of the Federation of Nigeria and Lagos, Cap. 115.

if not, *which* of the multitude of acts and transactions pertaining to the family remain controlled by customary law?

The Marriage Act iself sets forth extremely few of the incidents of a marriage contracted thereunder. For example, it does not state the law which is to govern divorce, status of children, or the rights and duties of spouses. However, it is clear that native law and custom ought not to govern such basic matters as those relating to the creation and dissolution of such a marriage, for statutory marriage is a transaction unknown to customary law and the Regional Courts (Federal Jurisdiction) Act, Cap. 177, s.4, specifically directs that the jurisdiction of the High Court of a Region in relation to non-customary marriages, and the annulment and dissolution of such marriages be exercised in conformity with the law for the time being in force in England. But it is less clear that English law should control more remote matters such as intestate succession, the extent of a husband's rights in his wife's property, the ability of spouses to sue each other in contract or tort, and the nature of parental rights in the services and income of children. The English law on these subjects was developed in response to social and economic conditions peculiar to England. One wonders, therefore, how rational and just it is to apply only English law to a Christian or statutory marriage where, except for the monogamous nature of the union, the spouses and their children are living a customary and traditionally African way of life.

Unfortunately, the courts have considered this conflict of laws problem—the effect of a Christian or statutory marriage upon the applicability of customary law—mainly in only two respects: its effect on intestate succession and on family status. An examination of these cases will perhaps bring to light the appropriate principles to be applied in resolving other problems caused by the conflict between English and customary family law.

Intestate Succession

The courts have given no consistent, uniform answer to the question of whether English or customary law will govern intestate succession to the estate of a person who has contracted a Christian marriage. Some cases have held that a Christian marriage auto-matically makes English law applicable; others have held that whether English or customary law is to govern depends upon the intentions and manner of life of the parties.[5] It is submitted that

5. At present, this type of conflict of laws problem cannot arise in Lagos and Western Nigeria. By virtue of the Marriage Act, 1958 Laws of the Federation of Nigeria and Lagos, Cap. 115, s. 36, and the Adminis-tration of Estates Law, 1959 Laws of Western Nigeria, Cap. I, s. 49(5), the customary law of intestate succession is made inapplicable to the estates of all persons who have married under Marriage Act.

the reason for this inconsistency is that the courts, in trying to resolve this problem, have proceeded upon two fundamentally different theories as to the essential nature and incidents of a Christian or statutory marriage.

The first group of cases is based upon what one might call the "inherent incident" theory, according to which intestate succession is so closely tied to the essential nature of a Christian marriage that the law which governs the marriage must also govern intestate succession. The very act of undergoing a Christian marriage, in and of itself, ousts the customary law and brings English law into play regardless of the intention and manner of life of the deceased. The second group of cases proceeds upon the assumption, never specifically stated, that intestacy rights are not an inherent part of Christian marriage and that the courts, in deciding whether to apply English or customary law, should therefore be guided by other factors and circumstances rather than solely by the fact that the deceased had contracted a Christian marriage.

1.   The Inherent Incident Theory—

The theory that intestacy rights are an inherent part of a Christian marriage and therefore must be governed by the law which created the marriage was the basis for the judgment in *Cole v. Cole*.[6] There the deceased, John William Cole, had contracted a Christian marriage in Sierra Leone in 1874. He died intestate in Lagos and was survived by his wife, a brother, and a lunatic son. The brother sought a declaration that he was the customary heir of the deceased and as such should succeed to the property and be declared trustee for the son. The widow, however, claimed that since the deceased had contracted a Christian marriage, the English law of intestate succession, not the customary law, should govern, and that the son was therefore the lawful heir. The lower court gave judgment for the brother, but on appeal the Full Court reversed, holding that English law should govern succession to the deceased's estate. In arriving at this conclusion, Brandford Griffith, J., examined the differing natures of Christian and customary marriage and compared the positions of the spouses in each, stating that:

> "In fact, a Christian marriage clothes the parties to such marriage and their offspring with a status unknown to native law."[7]

Because of the Christian marriage and the new status which it created, the court held that customary law could not be applied to

6.   (1898) 1 N.L.R. 15
7.   (1898) 1 N.L.R. 15 at p. 22

govern the deceased's estate. Thus it would seem that the court, by stressing the change in status, by ignoring such factors as the deceased's intentions and manner of life, and then by proceeding to apply English law, demonstrated a belief that intestate rights were an inherent part of that marital status.

During the course of his opinion, Brandford Griffith, J., considered the example of a doctor or barrister who marries an educated woman according to Christian rites. He argued that to apply customary law to such a marriage, thereby requiring the wife to enter a levirate marriage with the deceased's brother to obtain support, would be a "monstrous" result. The inclusion of this illustration in the judgment might lead one to believe that the court in *Cole* intended English law to apply only in circumstances similar to those in the illustration. Indeed, it would appear that at least one of the later cases has so concluded.[8] But it is difficult to agree with such an interpretation if one views the case as a whole and examines the court's general approach to the problem. The court in *Cole* made no reference at all to the intentions, manner of life, or education of John W. Cole or his wife. A close reading of the judgment does not indicate whether the Coles were illiterate or highly educated. It therefore seems that the court considered such matters to be irrelevant in deciding which law to apply. This, coupled with the statement that Christian marriage creates a complete change of status unknown to customary law, indicates that the court felt that a Christian marriage, in and of itself, will automatically invoke the English law governing intestate succession, and that the hypothetical example was included in the judgment merely to show in concrete terms the justice of the rule enunciated.

Some years later, in 1921, *Adegbola* v. *Folaranmi*[9] not only followed but extended *Cole* v. *Cole*. In that case, the deceased, a native of Oyo, had contracted a customary marriage in his youth, the plaintiff being the only child of this union. Thereafter, the deceased was taken as a slave to the West Indies, where during a stay of forty years, he converted to Christianity and married a woman in the Roman Catholic Church. Returning with his second wife to Nigeria, he purchased land, built a house, and took up residence in Lagos. In 1900, he died intestate. His wife by the Christian marriage continued to occupy the house and property until her own death in 1918, when she left a will devising the Lagos property to the defendant. The plaintiff sought recovery of the house, claiming that since she was the deceased's only child

8. *Smith* v. *Smith* (1924), 5 N.L.R. 105.
9. (1921) 3 N.L.R. 89.

she was entitled to the property according to native law and custom. The defendant, however, contended that since the deceased had contracted a Christian marriage, the English law of intestate succession should govern; therefore, since the plaintiff was not the issue of a Christian marriage, she had no right to share in the estate.

The court gave judgment for the defendant. To surmount the obstacle created by the deceased's prior customary marriage, the court presumed, on the facts presented as well as on the theory that the deceased could easily have terminated the union, that the deceased considered the customary marriage dissolved at the time he married according to Christian rites. Having thus decided that the Christian marriage was valid, the court, relying on *Cole v. Cole* and without making any investigation as to the basic nature and incidents of a Christian marriage, applied English law and held that the plaintiff, since she was not a legitimate child of a Christian marriage, had no claim to the deceased's estate. It should be noted that *Adegbola* went even further than *Cole*, for not only did it decide that English law should govern as to the *order* of succession to the deceased's estate but also that it should govern as to the status of persons entitled to come within that order. If the court had followed *Cole* and had held that English law was to govern the order of succession, but had then applied customary law to determine the plaintiff's status as a legitimate child of the deceased, the plaintiff would have been entitled to the property. In failing to distinguish the two questions involved, and in mechanically applying English law, the court bastardized (for the purposes of inheritance) a legitimate child of a valid customary marriage.

With the passage of time, *Cole v. Cole* was accepted in several cases as holding that "the intestate estate of a native who contracts a Christian or civil marriage is removed from the operation of native law and custom and brought under the common law."[10] No reappraisal was made of its basic assumption. A good example of the unquestioning application of *Cole* as well as of the failure to distinguish the issue of order of succession from the issue of status is found in *Gooding v. Martins*,[11] a case decided by the West African Court of Appeal. In that case the deceased had first contracted a Christian marriage, during which the plaintiff was born. After the death of his first wife, he married under native law and custom; the defendants were children of this marriage. In a case stated, the court was asked to decide whether the defendants were

---

10. *Coker v. Coker* (1943) 17 N.L.R. 55 at p. 57: See also *Fowler v. Martins* (1924) 5 N.L.R. 45, *affirmed sub nom. Martins v. Fowler* [1926] A.C. 746 (P.C.)
11. (1942) 8 W.A.C.A. 108.

to have any share in the deceased's estate. Here then was a true conflict of laws problem. Both marriages were valid. The defendants were the legitimate issue of a customary marriage. The plaintiff was the legitimate issue of a Christian marriage. The court, however, did not involve itself in these considerations. In an extremely terse opinion, it simply cited *Cole* v. *Cole* as controlling and held that the defendants had no claim to their father's estate.

Thus *Adegbola* and *Gooding* expanded the holding of *Cole* v. *Cole* to the point where, once a person who is normally subject to customary law contracts a Christian marriage, whether before or after a valid customary marriage, his estate is thereby automatically and irrevocably subject to English law both as to order of succession and as to the status of persons entitled to share in his property. Fortunately, as will be seen below, this stand was to be somewhat modified in later years.

2. The "Intention" or "Manner of Life" Theory—

Some cases have rejected *Cole*'s mechanical application of English law and have applied customary law to govern estates of persons who have contracted Christian marriages. The first of these was *Asiata* v. *Goncallo*[12] decided just two years after *Cole*. There the deceased, a Yoruba, had been seized as a slave in his youth and taken to Brazil, where he married a woman first according to Islamic rites and then according to Christian rites. During his stay in Brazil, two daughters were born. When he returned to Nigeria with his wife, he married a second woman under Islamic law. Upon the deceased's death intestate, the plaintiff, the only child of the second marriage, brought an action claiming a share of the estate. The Divisional Court applied English law and rejected the claim on the ground that the plaintiff was illegitimate. The full Court, however, reversed, holding that the second marriage was valid and applied Islamic law, thereby giving the plaintiff a share of the estate.

In arriving at its decision, the court was faced squarely with the obstacle of *Cole* v. *Cole*, a case which would seem to compel the application of English law because of the deceased's Christian marriage. *Cole* appeared to worry the court, for each of the three judges wrote a separate opinion attempting to distinguish it. The chief result of their efforts was not to show that *Cole* did not apply, but rather to obscure the *ratio decidendi* of the case they were trying to decide. For example, in his concurring opinion, Speed, A.C.J., wrote:

"I do not admit that the parties in this case contracted a

12. (1900) 1 N.L.R. 41.

Christian marriage at all. They were Mohammedans and they merely for local reasons, went through the marriage ceremony in Christian form."[13]

Assuming that Speed, A.C.J., was correct concerning the non-existence of a Christian marriage, then the case would have been quite simple to decide; *Cole v. Cole* would have had no relevance at all, and there certainly would have been no need for three separate opinions. If there was no Christian marriage, then there was no reason why English law should have been considered at all: in none of the cases on this subject has it been decided that anything but a Christian marriage could make the English law of intestate succession applicable to the estate of persons normally subject to customary law. In fact, in *Bolajoko v. Layeni*[14], Rhodes, J., abruptly rejected any such claim and said that it revealed a "gross ignorance of the law."

The other judges in *Asiata* did not accept the Acting Chief Justice's view. Indeed, Griffith, J., specifically stated that "there can be no doubt that the Christian marriage was legal."[15] He tried to distinguish *Cole*, however, on the ground that whereas *Cole* dealt with the application of intestacy law, the issue in *Asiata* was the validity of the second marriage. Such a distinction, it is submitted, cannot effectively avoid the thrust of *Cole*. For once the court had decided upon the validity of the second marriage, it then had to proceed to determine whether English or Islamic law should be applied to the deceased's estate.

On what basis, then, was Islamic law applied? The court was much concerned with the facts that the deceased had been a "*bona fide* follower of the Prophet" and that both he and his wife "lived and died as Mohammedans." The court was looking toward the deceased's manner of life. It seemed to feel that it would be unjust to apply a law which was totally unrelated to his manner of life and expectations. As Griffith, J., stated:

"But it may fairly be argued that assuming the marriage to be legal, still it would be contrary to justice that, Selia (the first wife) having impliedly contracted by her Christian marriage for monogamy, her offspring should suffer by breach of that contract by their father. But the contract which a Christian marriage would ordinarily imply was clearly not implied in the present case as Selia not only went through a Mohammedan ceremony of marriage but

13. (1900) 1 N.L.R. 41 at p. 44.
14. (1949) 19 N.L.R. 99
15. (1900) 1 N.L.R. 41 at p. 43.

she does not appear to have raised the slightest objection to her husband's subsequent marriages and wives."[16]

Thus it seems that the court did not view intestacy rights as an inherent and unalterable incident of Christian marriage.

The "manner of life" approach was more fully developed several years later in *Smith* v. *Smith*,[17] a case much like *Cole* v. *Cole* in that it involved a single Christian marriage. There, the deceased contracted a Christian marriage in Sierra Leone in 1876; he later purchased property and took up residence in Lagos. After his death intestate, his widow and children continued to occupy the deceased's property. Later, the daughters, basing their claim on customary law, brought an action for partition. The defendant, the deceased's eldest male child, opposed the action on the ground that he was the deceased's heir at law and was therefore solely entitled to the property. He relied upon *Cole* v. *Cole* and argued that since his parents had contracted a Christian marriage, English law must govern intestate succession.

Judgment was given for the plaintiffs. Van Der Meulen, J., in rejecting the defendant's argument, clearly demonstrated that he did not consider intestate rights to be an inherent part of Christian marriage, for he refused to apply English law simply because the deceased had been married according to Christian tenets.

"Any such general proposition would in my opinion be no less unjust in operation and effect than the converse proposition,—with which I think the court must have been concerned in the case of *Cole* v. *Cole*—that because a man is a native the devolution of his property must be regulated in accordance with native law and custom, irrespective of his education and general position in life."[18]

To decide which law to apply, he said that it is necessary to look at all the circumstances in each case. English law would be applied where the deceased was educated and not living a strictly customary and traditionally African way of life. Customary law would be applied in the converse situation. As in *Asiata*, the court in *Smith* sought to apply the law which was most in keeping with the deceased's expectations and living habits.

In arriving at its conclusion, the court in *Smith* v. *Smith* interpreted *Cole* v. *Cole* in such a way as to avoid a conflict. A few years later in *Haastrup* v. *Coker*[19] the conflict between the *Cole* and *Asiata* lines of cases was more strongly felt. *Haastrup* v. *Coker*

16. *Id.* at p. 43.
17. (1924) 5 N.L.R. 102
18. *Id.* at p. 104.
19. (1927) 8 N.L.R. 68

involved the estate of a man who had first married according to Christian rites and thereafter took some fifty wives according to native law and custom. The plaintiffs, children of the customary marriages, claimed that their father was a Pagan living a customary way of life and that therefore, according to *Asiata* v. *Goncallo*, Customary Law should govern his Estate. The court, however, applied English law, but it is difficult to discover which theory as to the nature and incidents of a Christian marriage was followed. On the one hand, the court seemed to accept *Cole* and the rule that a Christian marriage in and of itself brought English law into play, for as Petrides, J., wrote:

"The *ratio decidendi* of the judgment in that case (*Cole* v. *Cole*) was that the Coles were married according to Christian rites, and that a marriage according to such rites clothed the children of the marriage and their children with a status unknown to native law and that in such circumstances the question of inheritance to the deceased person cannot be decided by native law and custom.[20]"

In answer to the argument that the deceased in *Haastrup* was not a Christian but that Cole was, he said:

"Such a distinction was in my opinion unnecessary as the decision of *Cole* v. *Cole* was based not on the fact that the parties were Christian, *but on the fact that they had gone through a marriage by Christian rites*"[21]

On the other hand, he attempted to reconcile *Asiata* v. *Goncallo:*

". . . . I have no hesitation in deciding that it is not in fact necessary to prove that the deceased was a professing Christian when he married, *as the law will presume that the parties, by going through a marriage according to Christian rites, intended to be bound by its consequences unless there was evidence to the contrary,* of which there was none." [22]

It is difficult to reconcile these statements and determine the theory upon which the court based its decision. For in the first two passages, intestacy rights were analyzed in terms of the status of Christian marriage, whereas the final passage, which stressed the importance of the parties' intentions, analyzed intestacy rights in terms of contract. If intestacy rights are a part of the marital status, as for example is the obligation of monogamy, then the intentions of the parties should be of no effect.

In *Ajayi* v. *White*,[23] the manner of life theory was followed

20.   At p. 70
21.   At p. 70 (emphasis supplied).
22.   At p. 71 (emphasis supplied).
23.   (1946) 18 N.L.R. 41.

without apology. The deceased had been the widow of Reverend James White, whom she had married according to the provisions of the Marriage Ordinance. She had had several children, of whom one was the defendant in the case. Her other children married under native law and custom, the plaintiffs being her grandchildren by these marriages. Upon the widow's death intestate, the plaintiffs brought an action for partition of the property in their grandmother's estate, basing their claim upon customary law and relying upon *Smith* v. *Smith* as authority for its application. Rejecting the defendant's contention that because of the Christian marriage English law must be applied to the estate, the court held that, while a Christian marriage is strong evidence that succession should be regulated by English law, it is not conclusive. It merely creates a presumption which can be rebutted. Among the relevant factors to be considered are parties' education, manner of life, social position, and conduct with reference to the property in dispute. With regard to the case before the court, Baker, A.C.J., said:

> "The original owner was no doubt the wife of an educated
> man but it is very doubtful whether she was literate or
> knew anything about the English law of succession; if she
> had done so it is more than likely that she would have left a
> will."[24]

Aside from its implication as to the standard to be employed in assessing a person's manner of life, this statement is of interest: it suggests that where the husband is educated and the wife is illiterate, English intestate succession law will govern the husband's estate while customary law will govern the wife's. One wonders to what extent this double standard could be applied to other aspects of family law.

3. The Two Theories: An Evaluation—

The virtue of the inherent incident theory as a basis for resolving this conflict of laws problem is its certainty and ease of application. There is no need to engage in speculation as to the parties' intent—speculation which often proves fruitless, for when, as often happens, the deceased and his wife never stated and probably never had any specific intention at all. And, in a country such as Nigeria, where a person's way of life very often includes European and traditionally African elements in varying proportions, one can easily imagine the almost insoluble evidentiary problems which could confront a judge required to decide whether a decedent's manner of life was such as to warrant the application of customary law. Faced with

24. *Id*. at p. 44.

such problems, a judge would obtain little assistance from the judgments in *Ajayi* v. *White* and *Smith* v. *Smith*, for the tests which they set down are at best vague and indefinite.

The great objection to the inherent incident approach is that it imposes a system of law which was not developed in response to local conditions and which may not be in accord with local habits and expectations. The manner of life theory acknowledges this fact and therefore premises the application of English law on a showing that the parties are living a type of life more or less similar to that for which the English law of intestate succession was developed. For example, in his book on family law in England, P. M. Bromley introduces his subject by saying:

> "For our purpose, we may regard the family as a basic social unit which normally consists of a husband and wife and their children."[25]

It was upon this basis that Bromley wrote his book, and it was upon this assumption that English family law developed. Although the assumption is perfectly valid for England, it is certainly questionable when applied in the context of African extended family systems. That a person contracts a Christian marriage does not mean that he will thereafter lead a typically English family life or that his notions about "family" and his responsibilities to those who make up his "family" will undergo a revolutionary change. S. N. Chinwuba Obi, stating that the spirit of African law recoils at the notion of a woman's personal law controlling the property rights of her family,[26] has indicated some of the inequites resulting from the mechanical application of English law; as for example where a widow inherits the bulk of the deceased's estate and then returns to her own family, refusing to contribute to the maintenance and education of the deceased's children.[27] Indeed, in many systems of Nigerian customary law, daughters and widows inherit hardly anything because it is felt that when they marry they will take the property with them—away from the family to which it rightfully belongs.

But aside from the harsh effects of applying English law indiscriminately to an African family, the very assumption which led to this application and upon which *Cole* v. *Cole* was based is open to question. One must agree that the act of marriage confers status upon the parties involved. The rights and duties which are a part of this status are imposed by law, not by contract, and are, for the most part, not subject to alteration at the will of the parties. Thus

25. *Family Law* 1.
26. Obi, *The Ibo Law of Property* 212. (1963)
27. Id. at pp. 218-219.

to accept the assumption that intestacy rights are an inherent incident of Christian marriage is to agree that the law which governs the marriage and created the status must also govern intestate succession. But at the time *Cole* v. *Cole* was decided it was quite possible for a husband, by making a declaration in bar of dower under the Dower Act, 1833 and then leaving his entire estate to a third party, to cut off his wife and children without a penny.[28] It is difficult therefore to classify intestacy "rights" as an inherent part of Christian marriage when, by the unilateral act of one of the spouses, these "rights" could be destroyed.

Moreover, at the time of *Cole*, the statutory provisions which authorized a departure from customary law provided not only that customary law should not be applied where the transaction was unknown to customary law and where the parties had agreed that customary was not to apply, but in addition that "in cases where no express rule is applicable to any matter in controversy the court shall be governed by the principles of justice, equity and good conscience." It was upon this last provision that *Cole* v. *Cole* was based, for the court believed it to express the general rule, the preceding provisions relating to agreements and to transactions unknown at customary law being merely particular instances of this general rule. Assuming then that *Cole* v. *Cole* presented a case where no express rule was applicable, it would seem that the court was not bound to apply English law rigidly and completely, but could, on the basis of the latitude allowed by the statute, have fashioned a ruling from general principles of justice, equity and good conscience so as to achieve its main purpose of protecting Cole's widow and child. Had Cole adopted this approach, it might have been possible for later courts, in the absence of specific legislation, to develop a body of law which was in accord with the basic notions of Christian marriage and at the same time not too disruptive of traditional African expectations and family life.

It should be noted that the statutory provision which was the basis for *Cole's* holding exists today only in the Northern Region High Court Law.[29] Does this mean that the rule of *Cole* v. *Cole* is applicable only in Northern Nigeria? A. E. W. Park[30] has argued that since succession cannot be called a "transaction", and since the present statutory provisions, except in the Northern Region, refer only to "transactions", then in strict theory English law should not be applied to matters of succession where a person subject to

28. See Bromley, *Family Law* 473.
29. S. 34.
30. *Op. cit. supra* note 1, at p. 111.

customary law has contracted a Christian marriage. He points out however, that this technicality has been overlooked by the courts. With respect, it is submitted that even though the statutory provision on which *Cole* v. *Cole* was based has been repealed, there is ample provision in the present statute to allow the application of English law. If one accepts the underlying theory of *Cole* v. *Cole* that intestacy rights are an inherent part of Christian marriage, the "transaction", for purposes of the statutory provision making English law applicable, is not succession but *Christian marriage*. This same result would follow if one accepts the intention or manner of life theory, for the cases upon this theory indicate that intestate rights are normally a consequence of the transaction of marriage, except when the parties' manner of life or intentions indicate otherwise.

Family Status

It will be recalled that in such cases as *Gooding* v. *Martins* and *Adegbola* v. *Folaranmi* English law was applied both as to the order of succession and as to the status of persons coming within that order, thereby bastardizing otherwise legitimate children of a valid customary marriage. The failure to distinguish the two issues could also have inequitable results in connection with section 36 of the Marriage Act[31] which makes mandatory the application of English law to the estates both of persons married under the Act and of the issue of such marriages, whether or not such issues have themselves married under the Act.[32] If, for example, the son of an Act marriage contracted a marriage under customary law and died leaving a widow and children, by applying English law both as to order of succession and as to status, neither the widow or the children would be entitled to share in the deceased's estate. The wife would be considered as never having married the deceased; the children would be considered as having been born out of wedlock.

In 1941, the West African Court of Appeal faced a situation similar to the above example in *Re Adline Subulade Williams*,[33] where it held that the only persons entitled to the deceased's property were his brothers, not his wife and children by a customary union. The Administrator-General had argued that the words "wife" and "children" in the English Statute of Distributions—made applicable to Lagos by section 36 of the Marriage Act—should include the widow and children of a lawful customary marriage. The court rejected this argument, pointing out that the Statute of Distributions

---

31.   1958 Laws of the Federation of Nigeria and Lagos, Cap. 115.
32.   It should be noted that section 36 applies only to Lagos.
33.   (1941) 7 W.A.C.A. 156.

and the Marriage Ordinance of 1884 were enacted at a time when the courts of England did not profess to decide upon the rights of succession which it might be proper to grant to the wives and issue of a polygamous marriage.

The holding in *Williams* did not stand. Ten years later, in *Re Sarah Adadevoh*[34] it was overruled. In *Adadevoh*, the deceased had been the issue of an Ordinance marriage and had himself married under the Ordinance. This marriage was terminated after a year by the death of his wife. There were no children of this marriage; however, before and after it, he had contracted customary marriages, as a result of which the defendants were born. After the deceased's death intestate, the defendants claimed a share of the estate. The lower court, apparently considering them to be illegitimate under English law, ruled that they were not entitled to the deceased's property unless it could be shown that in the absence of next of kin the estate would escheat to the Crown. The West African Court of Appeal reversed, holding that under English law questions of status were to be determined by the law of the domicil of origin; if by the law of the defendants' domicil of origin they were legitimate children of the deceased, then they were legitimate for the purpose of the Statute of Distributions. The *Williams case*, said the court, was not binding because in that case the court had not considered how English law would view the status of the issue of a polygamous marriage. Since English law would have referred the *Williams* court back to the law of the domicil of origin and since this reference was not made, the court in *Williams* had acted *per incuriam*. In *Adadevoh*, the West African Court of Appeal found that under native law and custom the defendants were legitimate and therefore were entitled to share in the deceased's estate.

A few years later, in *Bamgbose* v. *Daniel*, the question was raised again before the West African Court of Appeal[35] and ultimately before the Privy Council.[36] There, the deceased, issue of an Ordinance marriage, had married under customary law. The respondents were the children of these polygamous marriages. The appellant, the only son of the deceased's brother, claimed that he alone was entitled to the deceased's estate and that respondents should be excluded because "children" under the Statute of Distributions meant children who could claim kinship with the deceased through a monogamous marriage. The court held that under English law legitimacy was to be determined by the law of the

34. (1951) 13 W.A.C.A. 304.
35. (1952) 14 W.A.C.A. 111.
36. [1955] A.C. 107. (1954) 14 W.A.C.A. 116.

domicil of origin. Once this status had been determined, the Statute of Distributions was to be used merely to determine the order of succession.

Both the above cases dealt with children born of valid customary marriages. In *Alake* v. *Pratt*,[37] however, the deceased had married under the Ordinance but during the course of the marriage had fathered several children out of wedlock. These children claimed to be entitled to share in the deceased's estate along with the respondents, the legitimate children of the Ordinance marriage. The lower court found that if a man acknowledges the paternity of children born out of wedlock, those children are legitimate under native law and custom; however, it felt that it would be against public policy to place children born out of wedlock on equal footing with children born during the course of a lawful marriage. It therefore rejected the appellant's claim. The West African Court of Appeal reversed. Referring to the *Bamgbose* and *Adadevoh* cases, the court held that legitimacy was to be determined by the law of the domicil of origin and that since the appellants were legitimate under Yoruba law they were legitimate for purposes of the Statute of Distributions.

With respect, it is submitted that the West African Court of Appeal in *Alake* v. *Pratt* failed to make a complete analysis of the problem confronting it, accordingly its holding is questionable. The court quite properly referred to English law, which in turn referred the court back to Nigeria to determine the appellants' status as legimate children. But it then automatically assumed that Yoruba law was the appropriate law of the domicil of origin. The domicil of origin, of course, was Nigeria. Thus the law of the domicil of origin was not simply Yoruba law, but rather Nigerian law—which includes both customary and received English law. Under the received English law, the appellants would have been considered illegimate; under Yoruba law, they would be legitimate. The court was therefore faced with another conflict of laws problem—whether received English law or Yoruba customary law should be applied to determine the appellants' status.

In *Bamgbose* and *Adadevoh*, this type of analysis of the problem was not made. But in those cases, there was no real conflict of laws since the children in *Bamgbose* and *Adadevoh* were children of valid customary marriages. In *Alake*, however, English law was brought into the picture by the deceased's Ordinance marriage. The precise question was whether, by virtue of the Ordinance marriage, English law will govern the status of children born out of wedlock during

37. (1955) 15 W.A.C.A. 20.

its existence. This is, in effect, a particularized version of the general question with which this paper began: What is the effect of a Christian marriage upon the application of customary law?

In 1960, the Federal Supreme Court faced the same problem as in *Alake*, but saw somewhat more clearly the conflict presented. In *Cole* v. *Akinyele*,[38] the deceased had contracted a marriage under the Marriage Ordinance, the first respondent being a child of this marriage. After the death of his wife, the deceased married the second respondent, also under the Marriage Ordinance. During the course of both of these marriages, the deceased maintained an irregular association with another woman who bore him two children, the appellants. The first appellant was born out of wedlock during the first Ordinance marriage. The second appellant, although conceived out of wedlock during the first Ordinance marriage, was born some six weeks after the death of the first wife and before the second marriage. The appellants claimed that they were entitled to share in their father's estate since he had acknowledged their paternity, an act which under Yoruba law made them legitimate. The High Court of Lagos gave judgment against the appellants, distinguishing *Alake* v. *Pratt* on the ground that in *Alake* the deceased's wife had died at the time of the appellants' birth. On appeal, the Federal Supreme Court found that there was nothing in the *Alake* judgment to warrant such a distinction; however, it held that the first appellant was illegitimate while the second was legitimate. The court felt that to apply Yoruba law to the first appellant would be contrary to public policy. Brett, F.J., stated:

"I am not prepared to treat *Alake* v. *Pratt* as authority for the proposition that while a man is married under the Marriage Ordinance he can make a child born to him during the continuance of that marriage by a woman other than his wife, legitimate by the mere acknowledgement of paternity, and I should regard such a rule as contrary to public policy."[39]

As to the second appellant, the court held that he was legitimate, because he had been born at a time when the Ordinance marriage had been dissolved. At that time, the deceased was free to marry according to customary law. English law was no longer applicable to him. And since under English law the relevant time for determining legitimacy is the time of the child's birth, rather than conception, public policy was not contravened by allowing Yoruba law to govern the appellants' status.

38. ·(1960) 5 F.S.C. 84.
39. *Id.* at p. 87.

Although the Federal Supreme Court saw the conflict of laws problem, it is submitted with respect that its articulation of that problem and its method of solution leaves something to be desired. There is little doubt that Brett, F.J., based his decision on public policy grounds:

> "I would prefer, however, to base my judgment not on the failure to prove any applicable rule of Yoruba native law and custom, but on the ground that such a rule would be contrary to public policy."[40]

But public policy as a *ratio decidendi* is too often a vague and treacherous concept which gives little guidance for the future. It is sometimes employed to settle a case when in fact there are already existing legal principles upon which a judgment could be founded. *Cole* v. *Akinyele* indeed, demonstrates the difficulty which public policy can cause. The public policy which Brett F.J., sought to protect seems to be the policy against promiscuity and extra-marital relations; the court therefore held that the first appellant could not have the benefit of legitimation by Yoruba customary law. But if this is the case and the policy against extra-marital relations is being enforced, is not public policy equally violated by allowing the second appellant to be legitimized by customary law when he too was born as a result of the deceased's promiscuity and extra-marital relations? Brett, F.J., acknowledged this situation as an anomaly, but said that at the time of the second appellant's birth the deceased was not bound by English law. Here, he came closest to putting the problem in proper perspective. The problem was one of conflict of laws, the same general kind of problem which faced the courts in *Cole* v. *Cole* and subsequent cases. The use of public policy as a ground of decision merely obscured the issue. For example, if a man who has married under the Ordinance attempts to divorce his wife according to the customary law, the divorce, of course, is invalid. But what is the reason for its invalidity? One might quite simply say that such a divorce is contrary to public policy. The real reason for its invalidity, however, is to be found in the High Court statutes which set down the choice of law rules governing the application of English law to transactions by persons normally subject to customary law. A Christian marriage, whether it is considered a "transaction unknown to customary law" or an agreement to be bound by English law, ousts customary law as to its basic elements: certainly divorce is a basic element of any marriage transaction.

The court in *Cole* v. *Akinyele* should have employed this same type of choice of law approach. The only reason that English

40. 1*d., loc. cit.*

law might apply is that the deceased had married under the Ordinance. The question then becomes whether matters of legitimacy are such an integral part of Christian marriage that they ought to be governed by English law. There seems little doubt that legitimacy of children is an inherent part of Christian marriage. Thus when a person marries under the Ordinance, customary law as to legitimacy is ousted. In *Cole v. Akinyele*, the deceased had, before his Christian marriage, the right to legitimize any of his children born out of wedlock by simply acknowledging paternity. By contracting a Christian marriage, he gave up that right, and any such acknowledgement would be without legal effect. When the Ordinance marriage was dissolved by his wife's death, the English law was no longer applicable to the deceased. He reacquired the right to legitimize children born thereafter by mere acknowledgement, just as he reaquired the right to marry under customary law. Therefore the second child, who was born at a time when the deceased was not governed by English law, was legitimate while the first appellant, born during the Christian marriage, was illegitimate.

The cases just discussed have all involved questions of status of children. Thus far no Nigerian case had decided that a widow of a customary marriage is a widow for the purpose of the Statute of Distributions.[41] In *Coleman v. Shang*, a case decided by the Ghana Court of Appeal[42] and affirmed by the Privy Council[43], it was held that the law of domicile also governs the status of widows. In this case the deceased had first married under customary law. There were three children of this marriage, of whom the respondent was one. On the death of his wife, he married under the Ghana Marriage Ordinance; when the second wife died, he married the appellant under customary law. Relying on the cases dealing with legitimacy of children, the Ghana Court of Appeal and the Privy Council held that whether a woman was a widow for the purpose of intestate succession was to be determined by the domiciliary law and the appellant was entitled to share in the estate as a widow.

In *Coleman v. Shang*, the problem of distribution of the deceased's estate was fairly simple because there was only one widow. Under the Statute of Distributions a widow is entitled to a one-third share. But what share does each widow of a customary marriage receive, however, when two, three or four widows claim under the Statute? If, for example, the deceased, the issue of an Ordinance

41. But see Lawal v. Younan (1961) 1 All N.L.R. 245.
42. 1959 G.L.R. 390
43. [1961] A.C. 481.

marriage, was a Moslem and married four wives, it would be impossible to apply the Statute strictly. Is each wife to receive one-fourth of the estate with no residue for the issue? Such a situation is completely opposed to traditional African notions. Or is the one-third share to go to the wives as a class to be divided up among them? This is perhaps the better solution, but it does violence to the language of the Statute. The reason for the difficulty, of course, is that the Statute of Distributions was simply not drafted with Nigerian social conditions in mind.

Conclusion

This paper began by asking to what extent English law will govern the family life of persons, normally subject to customary law, who contract a Christian or statutory marriage. The investigation of this problem in terms of conflict of laws has been confined to matters of intestate succession and family status, for it is in these areas that the courts have been most active. Occasionally, related questions have been answered. For example, it has been held that even when the customary law which governs a man and woman does not recognize an action for breach of promise, the woman may sue the man for breach of promise if the agreement was to marry under the Marriage Ordinance.[44] But there are a host of other problems yet to be solved. What law will govern a wife's ability to sue her husband in contract or tort? If the applicable customary law provides that a widow has a right to support from her deceased husband's family, will she be entitled to it if she has contracted a Christian or statutory marriage? And, as is often the case, where a bride-price payment is made even though the parties are contracting a statutory marriage, what law will govern the right to reclaim it if the marriage fails?

It is submitted that, because the family law of England was developed for the conditions of England, it ought not to be applied indiscriminately and across the board to African families simply because there has been a Christian marriage. In deciding what law to apply, the courts should approach the problem with this point in mind and should heed the words of Van Lare, J. A. in *Coleman v. Shang*:

We are of the opinion that a person subject to customary law who marries under the Marriage Ordinance does not thereby cease to be a native subject to customary law by reason only of his contracting that marriage. The law will be applied to him in all matters, save and except

44.   *Ugboma* v. *Morah* (1940) 15 N.L.R. 78.

those specifically excluded by statute, and any other
matters which are necessary consequences of marriage
under the Ordinance.[45]

What are the "necessary consequences" of a Christian or statutory
marriage? There are, of course, certain basic matters, such as the
validity of marriage, its dissolution, and the legitimacy of children,
which are an inherent part of Christian marriage, no matter who the
parties are, and therefore ought to be governed by English law. But
beyond this, it is extremely difficult to decide what is and what is
not a "necessary consequence." For what may seem a necessary
and inherent part of Christian marriage when viewed in the context
the family life of an educated, successful Lagos lawyer may not
seem so when viewed in the context of the family life of an illiterate
farmer living in much the same manner as his forefathers. Applying
the whole of English family law to the Lagos lawyer and his family
will accord with their expectations and bring about just results;
imposing the whole of English family law on the illiterate farmer
will probably frustrate normal expectations and disrupt his family
life.

It would seem, therefore, that the manner of life theory as
expressed in *Smith v. Smith* and *Ajayi v. White* would be helpful
in deciding when to apply English law in a particular case to the
more remote matters of family life. But applying English law in the
one case and not in another must not be based upon the notion of
granting a complete exemption from customary law to those persons
who have achieved a high level of education. The purpose is not to
create a special class of individuals, but rather to give effect to the
justified expectations of the parties.

Certainly a man and woman do not draw up, on the eve of their
marriage, a list of those aspects of their marriage which are to be
governed by English law; nevertheless, they do have general
expectations as to the manner in which they will lead their marital
lives. Their manner of life will indicate which law is to be applied
to a particular family law matter. It is true that the manner of life
theory is crude; it is certainly difficult to apply. But it does achieve
what is probably one of the main goals of any system of conflict of
laws rules—it gives effect to the justified expectations of the parties.
This goal is of particular importance in the field of family law,
where there must never be too great a divergence between what the
law is and the way in which people live.

45. *Supra* note 42 at p. 401.

LIST OF PARTICIPANTS

1. Dr. F. A. Ajayi,
   Solicitor-General and Permanent Secretary, Ministry of Justice,
   Western Nigeria, Ibadan.

2. Prof. Michel Alliot,
   Professeur de Droit et des Sciences Economiques de Paris,
   23, quai de Boulogne, Boulogne (Seine), France.

3. Prof. A. N. Allott,
   Professor of African Law, School of Oriental and African
   Studies, University of London, London, W.C.1.

4. Mr. James K. Baker,
   Director of African Programmes, The American Society of
   African Culture, P.M.B. 2814, Lagos, Nigeria.

5. K. Bentsi-Enchill, Esq.,
   Center for Internal Affairs, 6, Divinity Avenue, Cambridge 38,
   Massachusetts.

6. Dr. S. O. Biobaku,
   Chairman, Conference Working Committee
   Director, Institute of African Studies, and Pro-Vice-Chancellor,
   University of Ife, Ibadan Branch.

7. Prof. Xavier Blanc-Jouvan,
   Faculté de Droit et des Sciences Economiques,
   Aix-en-Provence, France.

8. Mr. Justice G. B. A. Coker,
   The Supreme Court, Lagos, Nigeria.

9. Dr. P. Contini,
   c/o United Nations, Mogadiscio, Somali Republic.

10. Eugene Cotran, Esq.,
    School of Oriental and African Studies, University of London,
    London, W.C.1.

11. E. B. Craig, Esq.,
    Nigerian Bar Association, Mokola,
    Ibadan, Nigeria.

12. Dr. W. C. Ekow Daniels,

Faculty of Law, University of Ghana,
Legon, Ghana.

13. Prof. Réné David,
Professeur de Droit Comparé à la Faculté de Droit et des
Sciences Economiques de Paris,
2, rue Leon Vaudoyer, Paris VII, France.

14. Dr. Mario Guttieres,
International Juridical Organization,
3, Via Barberini, Rome, Italy.

15. T. Hassan-Metzger, Esq.,
Dean, Faculty of Law, Fourah Bay College,
University College of Sierra Leone, Sierra Leone.

16. Prof. William B. Harvey,
Faculty of Law, University of Michigan,
Ann Arbor, Michigan, U.S.A.

17. J. O. Ibik, Esq.,
Customary Law Commissioner,
Blantyre, Malawi.

18. A. B. Kasunmu, Esq.,
Faculty of Law, University of Ife,
Ibadan Branch.

19. Professor J. Keuning,
Juridisch Studiecentrum "Gravensteen",
Rijksuniversiteit te Leiden,
The Netherlands.

20. R. L. Marshall, Esq.,
Institute of Administration, University of Ife,
Ibadan Branch.

21. Prof. Richard Maxwell,
University of California, Los Angeles,
California 90024, U.S.A.

22. Dr. H. F. Morris,
School of Oriental and African Studies, University of London,
London, W.C.1.

23. Dr. B. O. Nwabueze,
Lecturer in Law, Universty of Lagos,
Lagos.

24. Dr. S. N. C. Obi,
    Debelaku Chamber,
    2, Bernard Carr Street, Port Harcourt, Nigeria.

25. M. Odje, Esq.,
    School of Oriental and African Studies, University of London,
    London, W.C.I.

26. Dr. Nwakamma Okoro,
    10, Zik Avenue, P. O. Box 618,
    Enugu, Nigeria.

27. Mr. Justice N. A. Ollennu,
    Supreme Court of Ghana,
    P. O. Box 119, Accra ,Ghana.

28. S. A. Omabegho, Esq.,
    Federal Ministry of Justice,
    Lagos, Nigeria.

29. J. S. Read, Esq.,
    Faculty of Law, University College,
    Dar es Salaam, Tanzania.

30. J. W. Salacuse, Esq.,
    Faculty of Law, Institute of Administration,
    Ahmadu Bello University,
    Zaria, Nigeria.

31. Prof. A. Arthur Schiller,
    School of Law, Columbia University,
    New York 27,

32. Chief F. R. A. Williams,
    Rotimi Williams Avenue,
    P. O. Box 1499, Ibadan, Nigeria.